MEDICINES FOR THE SOVIET MASSES DURING WORLD WAR II

Mary Schaeffer Conroy

AF722009

University Press of America,® Inc.
Lanham · Boulder · New York · Toronto · Plymouth, UK

Copyright © 2008 by
University Press of America®, Inc.
4501 Forbes Boulevard
Suite 200
Lanham, Maryland 20706
UPA Acquisitions Department (301) 459-3366

Estover Road
Plymouth PL6 7PY
United Kingdom

Front Cover Photos: Akrikhin Pharmaceutical Factory near Moscow
1—The Main Building
2—The Warehouse
3—The New Italian Equipment

All rights reserved
Printed in the United States of America
British Library Cataloging in Publication Information Available

Library of Congress Control Number: 2007943309
ISBN-13: 978-0-7618-4009-1 (paperback : alk. paper)
ISBN-10: 0-7618-4009-5 (paperback : alk. paper)

The paper used in this publication meets the minimum requirements of American National Standard for Information Sciences—Permanence of Paper for Printed Library Materials, ANSI Z39.48—1984

To Tom and Alexandra Conroy; Margaret, Mike, Tommy, Fiona and Sean Doyle; and to the memory of my father Edward M. Schaeffer and especially my mother Blanche Pelikanova Schellenbauer Schaeffer, who lived through World War I in Austria-Hungary

Table of Contents

Figures and Tables vii

Preface ix

Acknowledgements xiii

Introduction 1

Part I On the Eve: 1938

Chapter 1 Sickness in Soviet Health Care 17

Part II The First Phase of World War II: 1939 to June 22, 1941

Chapter 2 War! Medical Hardware 39

Chapter 3 Vaccines and Pharmaceuticals during The First Two Years of World War II 45

Chapter 4 At the Apteka during the First Two Years Of World War II 75

Chapter 5 Pharmacologists Investigate *Narodnaia Meditsina* and Phages during the First Two Years of World War II 89

Part III The Great Patriotic War: June 22, 1941-1945

Chapter 6 Production of Pharmaceuticals during the First Two Years of the Great Patriotic War, 1941-1943 109

Chapter 7 Points of Light? Production and Foreign Assistance, 1943-1945 147

Chapter 8 At the *Apteka* during the Great Patriotic War 175

Chapter 9 *Narodnaia Meditsina* during the Great Patriotic War 199

Chapter 10 Reforming the Pharmacy Sector: Ideas from Below and Their Fate 213

Bibliography 223

Index 235

List of Figures and Tables

Figure 1.1 Raw Materials, Needed and Supplied, in tons: 1938 23

Figure 1.2 Raw Materials, Needed and Supplied, in tons, 1938 34

Table 6.1 Production in Thousands of Units (*Shtuk*) and Tons, 1942.
Information from the Central Archive of the Ministry of Defense 125

Table 6.2 Production, Percent of Plan Fulfilled
Industry Report, 1942 125

Table 7.1 Medical, Surgical Production, Second Half of 1941 and
First Half 1942, Central Archive of the Ministry of Defense 156

Table 7.2 Medical/Surgical Instruments' Production, 1940-1942
from Reports of the Medical/Surgical Instruments' Industry 156

Table 7.3 Materials From Abroad, 1943 158

Table 7.4 Amounts of Materials (in Tons, Except Ampules) from Abroad
in 1943, Report of the Chief Pharmacy Administration 159

Table 7.5 Production in 1944 in Terms of Percentage,
Pharmaceutical Industry Reports 162

Table 7.6 Production in 1944 in Terms of Percentage,
Pharmaceutical Industry Reports 162

Table 8.1 Rebuilding Pharmacies 192

Preface

This book is the third of a trilogy started in the 1980s to examine pharmacy and the availability of pharmaceuticals in Imperial Russia and then in the Soviet Union. My decision to focus on pharmacy, the pharmaceutical industry and pharmaceuticals stems partly from my own experiences. Pharmaceuticals helped my medical problems. Conversely, lack of pharmaceuticals made my life very unpleasant. Physicians could do nothing to assuage the severe bouts of asthma I suffered, from early childhood until the age of thirty when the disease summarily vanished, because there were no cures for asthma. The therapies physicians applied to supposedly mitigate my asthmatic attacks were completely ineffective and unpleasant to boot. Similarly, when traveling in the Soviet Union in 1963, a skin cut resulted in serious infection because there were no antibiotics available; I finally got relief at the American Embassy to which I returned at the end of my tour. On the other hand, penicillin saved my life when I came down with pneumonia as a child. The black tarry ointment I got from a local pharmacy helped the boils that plagued my teenage years. The DDT that eliminated mosquitoes in my Indiana hometown made summer evenings bearable. The very portable aspirins that I always carried with me eliminated headaches, fevers and simple aches and pains. They were greatly sought after by librarians and archivists in the Soviet Union in the late 1980s and early 1990s.

Of course I also was prompted to study the pharmaceutical sector in Imperial Russia and then in the Soviet Union because of the subject's scholarly implications. Since pharmaceuticals are a sine qua non for surgery and for preventing and treating diseases and medical problems, investigating pharmacy and the pharmaceutical industry in Imperial Russia and in the Soviet Union provided indicators of the quality of health care in the pre-Soviet and Soviet eras, revealing continuities but also differences in the two systems. Probing the pharmaceutical sector also illustrated the differences between the economy and government policies in Imperial Russia and the Soviet Union. Although the Imperial Russian government was domineering and intrusive, the economic system and the pharmaceutical sector served the people reasonably well. The Soviet government, on the other hand, in attempting to establish the most rational economy in the world, curtailed market forces and entrepreneurship in the pharmaceutical sector as elsewhere. As a result, pharmaceutical production and the dispensing of pharmaceuticals was problematical. In fact, the Soviet pharmaceutical sector documents how the Soviet economic experiment went awry.

The present work continues the story of Russian/Soviet pharmaceuticals and pharmacy into World War II. It reviews how a less than robust pharmaceutical sector, and hamstrung institutes that produced vaccines, serums, antitoxins, and bacteriophages affected morbidity and mortality in the Soviet Union during the late 1930s. It then suggests that a lack of pharmaceuticals may have contributed to the deaths of Soviet citizens during World War II, although that is not proven conclusively. However, the book does show that lack of pharmaceuticals, including soap, made the lives of Soviet citizens more difficult during the war. Credit, though, is given where credit is due. This study acknowledges that pharmaceutical specialists on the ground—managers of pharmaceutical enterprises and pharmacists—tried to surmount difficulties and fulfill their mandate to provide pharmaceuticals and medical items to the Red Army and civilians. Meanwhile, a lack of factory-prepared pharmaceuticals steered Soviet citizens and pharmacologists into using traditional, home-made remedies (*narodnaia meditisna*). As a result, at the end of the war, Soviet medical care was qualitatively different from American medical care. The Soviet system had negatives but also a few pluses—a more holistic approach to patients on the part of physicians and the use of bacteriophages, now regarded as an antidote for antibiotic-resistant bacteria.

The archival sources used in this work include materials from the Russian Archive of the Economy in Moscow; materials from the Pharmacy Files in the State Archive of the Russian Federation, Moscow (with a sincere thank you to Liudmila Gennad'evna Kiselova, archivist at GARF); materials from the State Archives of the Bashkir Republic, in Ufa; and the National Archives of the United States, Bureau of Foreign and Domestic Trade. A note about Soviet statistics in these materials is in order. Soviet statistics are sometimes vague. Some historians doubt their veracity. This book relies on statistics from the pharmaceutical industry in newly accessible archival records. Since they present a negative as well as a positive picture of the industry, I believe they are authentic. Additionally, the book tries to correlate figures on production with what was being reported in publications of the period and with reminiscences of Soviet citizens who lived through the war.

A note about transliteration also is in order. I have used Western spelling for pharmaceuticals that correspond to Western items. For items specific to or cloned by Soviet pharmaceutical factories, I have used indigenous terms, for example Liuminal instead of Luminal. On the other hand I have used "Gorky" instead of the more correct "Gorkii" because that spelling is more familiar to Western readers. And I have used the anglicized plural of *raion* and *oblast'*, terms used a great deal in this book, to avoid annoying non-Russian-speaking readers. The names of respondents to the *anketa* or questionnaire are spelled as they were written even if they violate the transliteration format selected for this book.

Mary Elizabeth Schaeffer Conroy
Professor Emerita
University of Colorado in Denver
Cherry Hills Village, Colorado
September 2, 2007

Acknowledgments

My deepest thanks to Dr. David Genis, who enabled me to better understand the medical needs of the Soviet Union during World War II and who helped me devise a questionnaire used to elicit information from individuals who were teenagers or adults in the Soviet Union during the war. The respondents include émigrés from the former Soviet Union now living in Denver; individuals living in Russia; and individuals living in Belarus. I am especially grateful to Samson Geltser, Peter Geyman, Tamara Nikolaevna Khazieva, and Mariia Sergeevna Kuznetsova, who responded with lengthy stories of their wartime experiences. I am grateful to Mikhail Gershteyn, Red Army veteran, and Vladimir German, President of the Denver Association of World War II Emigrants from the Former USSR, who served as conduits to most of the wartime survivors in Denver. I also am grateful to Dr. Rustem Khaziev, State University of Bashkortostan, who helped me gain access to archival materials in Ufa, as well as access to wartime survivors there, and to Tat'iana Petrishche, historian and lecturer at the Medical Institute of Vitebsk, who assisted me with her own research on the pharmaceutical industry in Belarus well as interviews with individuals there about their wartime experiences. I appreciate Bella Evseevna Kaganovich's gracious interview in Chicago about her work as a doctor with evacuated soldiers in Siberia and at the front and the nursing activities of Iraida Shishkina at the front, sent me by her son-in-law Viktor Melik-Shakhnazarov, although they were not used since this book concentrates on civilians.

I appreciate the help extended by American colleagues: Dan Goldberg, of the U. S. State Department, who sent me many e-mails about bacteriophages; Professor Laurie Cohen, University of Innsbruck, conduit of information from German colleagues; and Professor Paula Michaels, University of Iowa, whose realization that pharmaceuticals are integral to health care and her fine work on this subject fortified my conviction that a study of the pharmaceutical sector in the Soviet Union, in general, and in World War II, in particular, was important.

Above I extend heartfelt thanks to my husband Thomas F. Conroy, who took time from his own international businesses to assist me in preparing this manuscript, in giving me insights into the subject and correcting infelicitous phrases, and for his unflagging support of this and other projects.

Introduction

The Great Patriotic War, that portion of World War II fought on Soviet soil—June 22, 1941 to the end of 1944/ early 1945—was a defining moment for Soviet citizens. The war still grips historians and ordinary readers in the former Soviet Union, the United States and other countries. A myriad of books and articles have been devoted to dramatic aspects of the war—diplomacy before and during the war, the level of the Soviet Union's military preparation, major battles of the war, and the travails of the citizenry. Less attention has been paid to medical care during the war and scarcely any to whether the pharmaceuticals available were sufficient for health needs and surgical procedures. Thanks to the opening of the archives, the hagiographic accounts of Soviet medical care provided by wartime observers and by an official post-war Soviet work that, despite its thirty-five volumes provided only discrete pieces of information,[1] have been superseded by more informative studies based on research in newly accessible archival records. Nevertheless, there are contradictions among the new works and gaps remain.[2] One relates to the production and distribution of pharmaceuticals.

Information about the availability of pharmaceuticals is important since demographers estimate that approximately 25 million Soviet citizens died during the Great Patriotic War. Michael Haynes, for example, asserts that "excess" deaths amounted to 26.6 million[3] while Mark Harrison cites the lesser figure of 25 million "real" deaths.[4] The vast majority of those who died were civilians. Historians have stressed the importance of food to survival during the war. But medical care was crucial too. And in addition to statistics on physicians, surgeons, nurses or sisters of mercy, and hospital beds typically cited in Soviet publications as proof of excellent medical care, in addition to hygiene education and preventive health measures, such as immunization and good sanitation, pharmaceuticals were sine qua non for adequate health care. Vaccines and antitoxins depended upon reagents and other pharmaceuticals. Medical personnel could not cure or even treat without pharmaceuticals. Surgical procedures required pharmaceuticals. Pharmaceuticals could not help those blown up by bombs or hit with gunfire. Otherwise, pharmaceuticals—disinfectants, febrifuges, antiseptics, anesthetics, hemostatics, antidiarrhea products, antimalarials, vitamins, infant formula, articles of hygiene and soap—were necessary for the prevention and treatment of infection and disease.

The first line of inquiry in this book—based on that hypothesis and the author's previous study that showed the Soviet pharmaceutical industry less than robust in the 1920s and 1930s[5]—was whether shortages of pharmaceuticals impacted mortality and morbidity during the Great Patriotic War. The correlation between certain infectious diseases and decreased life span, on the one hand, and inadequate amounts of vaccines, antitoxins, and pharmaceuticals, on the other, in 1938 and the first phase of World War II—1939 to June 1941—is established in Chapters 1 and 3 of this work. Establishing the same correlation *during* the Great Patriotic War, namely, linkage between infectious diseases, morbidity and mortality and inadequate amounts of pharmaceuticals and soap proved more difficult.

That is because the jury is still out on how much pharmaceuticals contribute to health and long life. Gerald Grob's *The Deadly Truth* (Harvard University Press, 2002), an historical survey of infectious diseases, appeared to contradict the notion that pharmaceuticals were integral to health and longevity, for it related that strong constitutions could withstand epidemics and some infectious diseases waxed and waned without pharmaceuticals. Nevertheless, Grob did detail how vaccines prevented certain infectious diseases and how soap and disinfectants—that is, products of the pharmaceutical industry—also prevented their spread. On the other side of the ledger, Bryan G. Reuben and Harold A. Wittcoff, co-authors of *Pharmaceutical Chemicals in Perspective* (John Wiley and Sons, 1989), deliver statistical tables illustrating how pharmaceuticals have prolonged life. They emphasize that first sulfa drugs and then penicillin—the miracle drugs of the 1930s and 1940s—caused a precipitous decline in mortality, especially for children between the ages of one and fourteen.[6] John E. Lesch is even more adamant about the importance of sulfa drugs in modern medical practice as the title of his recent study, *The First Miracle Drugs: How the Sulfa Drugs Transformed Medicine* (Oxford University Press, 2007) indicates.

It is true, however, that some constitutions are so strong as to withstand meager food and medicines. My own mother survived a childhood in Austria-Hungary during World War I in which she had little more than mushrooms, rabbits and an occasional egg to eat and no milk. She lived until the age of eighty-five, a beautiful, vibrant, healthy woman who rarely visited a doctor. Admittedly, she did have dental troubles. It also must be conceded that the arsenal of pharmaceuticals was still fairly limited in the 1940s. There were no therapies for asthma and polio, for example. Soviet pharmaceutical factories did produce the new wonder drugs of the 1930s, the sulfa drugs, although they were not able to effectively mass-produce penicillin until 1945 or possibly later. Nevertheless, sulfa drugs did not attack all infectious diseases. Further, some sulfa drugs had unpleasant side effects. This also was the case with the synthetic antimalarials, used against malaria, both the three debilitating varieties and the lethal variety, *Plasmodium falciparum*, both of which were endemic and sometimes epidemic in Imperial Russia and the Soviet Union, becoming a scourge during the Great Patriotic War.

From his practice in the Soviet Union, Dr. David Genis, a highly published parasitologist,[7] now living in Denver, Colorado, agrees that medicines were not foolproof in the 1930s, 1940s. Further, in his own medical practice, conducted in the Soviet Union in the 1960s and 1970s, Genis met patients who survived life-threatening illnesses without any medical treatment. These individuals developed antibodies which henceforth protected them. He further cautions that one Soviet sulfa drug in particular—Red Streptotsid—was highly toxic. So taking this remedy might have been worse than taking nothing.[8]

Nevertheless, in line with Ruben and Wittcoff and John Lesch, Dr. Genis avers that "with serious illnesses, especially against a background of famine in wartime, the absence of good medicines caused severe consequences or death."[9] In other words, in his opinion, lack of pharmaceuticals did affect Soviet mortality during the Great Patriotic War.

Along with pharmaceuticals for treatment, we must reiterate that some pharmaceuticals—disinfectants, insecticides, vitamins, and food supplements—served to prevent disease. So did vaccines, serums, antitoxins, and bacteriophages, which were produced by special institutes rather than in pharmaceutical factories. So too did soap, production of which had been removed from the purview of the pharmaceutical industry. Also important were medical apparatus, such as x-ray equipment and ambulances; surgical instruments, such as pincers, needles and syringes, surgical knives, and so forth; and simple items like hot-water bottles, ice-bags and sterile gloves. *Medicines for the Soviet Masses* surveys the production and distribution of these items as well as pharmaceuticals, per se.

To conclude the argument about the degree to which pharmaceuticals and these other items were important during the Great Patriotic War we can state the following: if not always crucial for life, pharmaceuticals improved the quality of life. Anesthetics made surgery bearable; antiseptics prevented the loss of limbs, hearing and eyesight; febrifuges allowed workers to be more productive and their lives to be more pleasant. The strong and healthy did not require pharmaceuticals. But, since pharmaceuticals help repair the maimed, restore the sick and revive the weakened, we can theorize that they impacted Soviet mortality and morbidity during the Great Patriotic War. However we cannot quantify the extent to which they did so.

So, while the answer to the first line of inquiry remains inconclusive, nevertheless, this study yielded four other valuable findings. The first pertained to the quality of Soviet medical care before the war as well as during it. The second was how an industry not directly connected with the war performed during the conflict. The third was how the shortages of pharmaceuticals before the war and during it pushed Soviet pharmacology and Soviet medical practice into different trajectories from American. Finally, the study displayed suggestions from pharmacists and pharmaceutical specialists at the grass-roots level on how to improve the Soviet pharmacy sector, suggestions that unfortunately were not implemented until the past decade.

Since it is logical to assume that there would be a shortage of pharmaceuticals during World War II, *Medicines for the Soviet Masses* begins the story in 1938, the last peacetime year. Chapter 1 emphasizes that the while Soviet pharmacological research was pretty much on a par with that in Western Europe and the United States, the pharmaceutical industry had trouble bringing products downstream and adequately distributing them. The Soviet Union trumpeted its health care system in the 1930s and later as the best in the world, offering excellent medical care to the populace at a low cost. This claim was widely believed. But if Soviet medical care was stellar then the Soviet pharmaceutical industry must have been stellar also.

In his 1967 publication, *Ocherk razvitiia khimiko-farmatsevticheskoi promyshlennosti SSSR* (Moscow, 1967), A. G. Natradze asserted that under Soviet rule, in the 1920s and 1930s, pharmacies had proliferated and the Soviet pharmaceutical industry had made important discoveries and advanced scientifically.[10]

Complaints from pharmacists in the late 1930s and early 1940s, however, contradicted this rosy view. Scientific discoveries in the laboratory did not necessarily translate into ample products that were readily available to Soviet citizens. Indeed, in 1945, Natradze himself, then Assistant Commissar for Health and chastened by the vicissitudes of the war, admitted that there were serious shortages of basic pharmaceuticals and medical/surgical equipment on the eve of the Great Patriotic War.[11]

New publications, based on archival materials, document the problems in the Soviet pharmaceutical industry and in Soviet health care before the Great Patriotic War commenced. M. Ia. Siatinia's tome on the Ukrainian pharmaceutical industry, *Istoriia farmatsii* (L'viv, 2002) describes a sector that was floundering well before the war. In 1934, for example, there were drastic shortages of disinfecting substances, reagents and medicines in the Ukraine.[12] This situation might appear the result of a vendetta by Moscow, which was the hub of the All-Union core pharmaceutical industry, but accounts in Russian pharmacy and industry journals of the time indicate that there were deficits of pharmaceuticals all over the Soviet Union. Shortages of pharmaceuticals, in turn, were a major contributor to the very low average life spans in the Soviet Union in 1938 and 1939 that Anotoli Vishnevskii cites in *Demograficheskaia modernizatsiia Rossii, 1900-2000* (Novoe izdatel'stvo, 2006).[13] Certainly deaths related to the famines of the early 1930s influenced these statistics. But another cause of short life expectancy was the prevalence of serious infectious diseases. While the incidence of typhoid, smallpox, whooping cough, and diphtheria declined spectacularly during Soviet times, Vishnevskii documents that the incidence of malaria (which fluctuated from year to year) was just slightly lower than in 1913 and the incidence of typhus, measles, scarlatina, and dysentery was higher at the end of the 1930s than in 1913.[14] This indicates lack of vaccines, serums, antitoxins and lack of pharmaceuticals—soap, disinfectants, pesticides as well as sulfa drugs.

Thus many factors retarding the Soviet pharmaceutical industry were not due to the Great Patriotic War but antedated it. In his *Shaping the Industrial Century: The Remarkable Story of the Evolution of the Modern Chemical and Pharmaceutical Industries* (Harvard University Press, 2005), Alfred D. Chandler, now unfortunately deceased, analyzed six large and some small American pharmaceutical companies, from their beginnings in the nineteenth and early twentieth centuries to determine how the American pharmaceutical industry had emerged from being in tutelage to German and Swiss houses early in the twentieth century to being a dominant world player by the 1930s and 1940s. Many of the companies had started as chemical or petrochemical companies. Their paths to success varied but there were some common elements: sufficient investment; the development of niche products through good R&D, serendipitous acquisitions of German patents as a result of World War I, mergers with other companies, spin-offs of unsuccessful ventures, and aggressive marketing. My earlier study, *The Soviet Pharmaceutical Business During Its First Two Decades, 1917-1937* (Peter Lang, 2006), emphasizes that the Soviet pharmaceutical industry, in contrast to Chandler's illustrations, was a textbook case of how not to run a pharmaceutical industry.[15] Chapter 1 of *Medicines for the Soviet Masses* details the reasons the Soviet pharmaceutical industry still lagged behind, despite efforts of factory managers to bolster it, on the eve of World War II.

The book then moves into World War II proper. Chapters flow chronologically. However, they also are thematic and interactive. Therefore some look at what diseases and medical problems obtained during different phases of World War II and what sorts and amounts of pharmaceuticals were produced to counter them. These chapters rely heavily on the reports of the special institutes that produced vaccines and antitoxins and the Soviet pharmaceutical industry's reports reposing in Russian archives. Other chapters look at the distribution end. These chapters attempt to ascertain what pharmaceuticals were available to the citizenry and what pharmaceuticals Soviet citizens, particularly civilians, actually used. These chapters are based largely on interviews with Soviet citizens who were teenagers or young adults during the war. Both the chapters on production and the chapters on distribution are buttressed by foreign and Soviet publications from the period. Next, the book utilizes Soviet pharmacological journals to determine what pharmacologists, pharmacists and physicians recommended for the prevention and treatment of disease and medical problems. All the chapters dip into some recent studies on the German and American pharmaceutical industry to provide perspective.

By 1939 the Soviet Union was at war, albeit offensively. Wars usually stimulate production of materials crucial for the conflict. This certainly was true in the production of biological weapons, as Anthony Rimmington has demonstrated.[16] Chapter 2 of *Medicines for the Soviet Masses* investigates production of medical/surgical instruments and apparatus during the first phase of World War II, 1939 to June 22, 1941, while the Soviet Union was engaged in offensive conflicts but before war came to Soviet soil, to see how military clashes stimulated output of ambulances and other items. Chapter 3 looks at the production of vaccines, serums and antitoxins and pharmaceuticals during the first two years of World War II. These chapters acknowledge that there were improvements in output. However, Chapter 3 determines that the flare up of dysentery, typhoid, diphtheria, scarlatina, pneumonia, and other infectious diseases in the period 1938 through 1940 was related to inadequate amounts of vaccines, antitoxins, and bacteriophages produced by special institutes and to inadequate amounts of disinfectants and sulfa drugs produced by pharmaceutical factories.

Chapters 6 and 7 look at pharmaceutical production during the Great Patriotic War, June 22, 1941 to 1945, that is, when the Soviet Union was on the defensive. These chapters emphasize that while the wartime environment was dire is was not so dire as might be expected. The Germans encircled Leningrad and swiftly took over western parts of the Soviet Union, Belorussia and the newly acquired Baltic States. Pharmaceutical factories in Moscow and the Ukraine also were threatened. However, a major pharmaceutical factory in Kazakhstan was not in harm's way. Some of the problems confronting the industry were due to the war. But others were due to poor decisions on the part of the government and to systemic factors that had retarded the industry for the past decades. For example, core factories in Moscow and the Ukraine were evacuated to Siberia. However, evacuation was very disruptive and the Moscow factories continued to supply the bulk of pharmaceuticals, bereft of equipment and workers.

A number of recent publications, both in English and in Russian, discussed in the text of *Medicines for the Soviet Masses*, now give fuller information and more data on the availability of pharmaceuticals and medical/surgical instruments during the Great Patriotic War. But there are still ambiguities. Some medical historians stress that there were ample stores of pharmaceuticals available for the military but admit shortages of medical supplies and surgical instruments at the outset of the war. They insist, however, that the medical and pharmaceutical industries greatly increased output during the war.[17] Other historians aver that there were ample amounts of sulfa drugs even in remote areas.[18] Still others, however, emphasize the prevalence of infectious diseases, implying a lack of sulfa drugs as well as soap, disinfectants, insecticides, and basic pharmaceuticals.[19] There also is the hypothesis that some epidemics, particularly of tularemia, were caused by microbes that accidentally escaped from biological weapons' laboratories or were deliberately unleashed to foil the enemy, but infected Soviet citizens in the bargain.

Medicines for the Soviet Masses attempts to sort out these claims and counterclaims. Chapter 6 surveys diseases and medical problems prevalent during the war, whatever their etiology, and then the production of pharmaceuticals during the first two years, 1941-1943. Output of both state-of-the-art medicines and also basic items like disinfectants, insecticides, soap, vitamins, and food supplements are examined. Chapter 7 briefly notes the availability of pharmaceuticals and medical/surgical supplies at the front, for the military; production of medical surgical items during the war; production of pharmaceuticals during the last two years of the war (1943-1945); and assistance from allies of the Soviet Union during this period. These chapters acknowledge the achievements of managers and workers in pharmaceutical factories but emphasize that shortfalls remained, some due to wartime exigencies and others due to the poor organization of the Soviet economy and the pharmaceutical sector. Chapter 7 explores how help from the United States aided Soviet citizens.

Chapters 4 and 8 are mirror images of the preceding chapters. Chapter 4 examines what pharmaceuticals were available for citizens trekking to the pharmacy during the first two years of World War II. Chapter 8 looks at what pharmaceuticals were available for three main cohorts of Soviet civilians—those under enemy occupation, those evacuated to safer regions, and those continuing to live in remote parts of the Soviet Union—during the Great Patriotic War.

These chapters document that there were serious shortages of medicines available in pharmacies and drug stores not only during the war but before it. Soap, detergents, disinfectants, and insecticides were important means of combating infectious diseases. Soap making-making no longer was the purview of the pharmaceutical industry but under a separate Soap Trust in the 1930s. The pharmaceutical industry did produce the other preventive agents, however. All, especially soap, were deficit.

The information in these chapters is based on responses from approximately twenty-five war survivors to an *anketa* (questionnaire) drafted by author and former Soviet physician Dr. David Genis. The sample is relatively small. Nevertheless, it is representative and catholic. It includes reminiscences of Jewish émigrés from Belarus and Moscow, now living in Denver; reminiscences of war survivors, mainly Orthodox, still living in Belarus; and reminiscences of Russians still living in Russia. Most of the Jewish émigrés were evacuated to various parts of the Soviet Union. Most of the respondents still living in Belarus, on the other hand, were trapped there and lived under German occupation during the first three years of the war. The Russians living in the hinterlands were shielded from the war, although some of this cohort moved to Moscow for training and other reasons between 1943 and 1945. Some individuals in each of these cohorts were affiliated with the military, an important consideration because military medicine and pharmacy was better than that for civilians.

The respondents comprise a variety of religious-ethnic backgrounds, professional backgrounds and current residence status. The Jewish émigrés came to the United States in the 1980s and 1990s. Some left because they suffered from anti-Semitism. In addition, some of the Jewish émigrés admit that they and their parents were hostile to the Soviet government. Some still are. However, others among the émigrés were career Red Army men, proud of Soviet military achievements. The responses from the second set of respondents, those still living in Belarus, are subject to other caveats. Cautious about divulging information via e-mail, because of the political situation in Belarus, these respondents have requested anonymity. Further, their attitude toward the Germans and the Soviet government is ambivalent. Some fought the Germans as partisans while others provide a revisionist picture of the occupiers. Some have bitter memories of the Soviet government. For example, the parents of one were negatively affected by collectivization and the father of another was put into a "*shtrafbat*" [penal battalion] for "not succeeding to get to the front" when the Germans invaded. "He was killed at Konigsberg in 1945." Most confirm a paucity of pharmaceuticals in Belarus not only during the war but before it. Nevertheless, they have made peace with the situation in Belarus. The third group of respondents, Russians still residing in Russia, serve as a corrective to the other two groups because they were not endangered by the war, have remained loyal post-Soviet Russian citizens, and apparently feel fairly free to speak their minds.

The recollections of war survivors bring a dose of reality to the study of medical care during the war. From the accounts of the evacuees from Belarus and Ukraine, to provide one example, we learn that the availability or lack of soap and medicines was only one component of their confrontation with disease. As Peter Abramovich Geyman, Samson Geltser and Dr. David Genis recount, being crammed for weeks into train cars that were dirty, with no chance for change of underwear and clothes, with no access to water in which to bathe and wash garments spawned typhus.[20]

The accounts of war survivors also add chiaroscuro to wartime experiences. For example, the war survivors trapped in Belarus remarked that some Germans gave medicines to them (supposedly sub-human Slavs). The Germans may have had pharmaceuticals because the German pharmaceutical industry worked well,[21] because the Germans pilfered Soviet factories, or because the Swiss Red Cross gave the Germans medicines. As for their motives, the German high-command feared epidemics. However, common soldiers may have been motivated by decency and humanitarianism.

The personal accounts further raise questions about non-medical issues, specifically, who were able to evacuate or chose to evacuate and why they did so and conversely why those who stayed put did so. Many Soviet citizens, of course, had no choice in the matter. But it is interesting to note that those still living in Belarus, who lived there during the war, are Orthodox. The only ones of this cohort who were able to evacuate were the wife and daughter of a Red Army officer. The respondents living in the United States are Jewish. At the time of the war some also lived in Belarus, as well as in Ukraine and in Moscow. All but one left on their own or were evacuated. These data may result from the fact that the sample is small or that happenstance—proximity to a railroad station or other fortuitous conditions—was a factor in evacuation but was not noted in the response. On the other hand, one wonders whether there were other reasons. For example, perhaps knowledge of Hitler's ill treatment of the Jews in Germany, even though the "Final Solution" was not implemented until after the German invasion of Russia, propelled Jews in the Soviet Union to flee from the invader. We know that Ukrainians, on the other hand, because of their hatred of Moscow and the Soviet government, greeted the Germans with bread and salt at the outset of the war. Additionally, one Jewish Muscovite, Samson Gel'tser's father, "did not believe in the brutality of the Germans and in general did not believe in Soviet propaganda." Not being drafted into the Red Army because of severe nearsightedness, he remained in Moscow during the war to protect the family's room and possessions in their communal apartment.[22]

The medical experiences of the war survivors vary as to whether the respondents lived in towns or the countryside before the war, whether they spent the war years in cities or the countryside, and whether or not they were affiliated with the military. There are some commonalities in their stories. Almost all the respondents, whether émigrés or still living in countries of the former Soviet Union were proud of the fact that Soviet medical care was free (though some noted high prices of medicines). Many expressed pride in Soviet medical training, surgical achievements and the caliber and caring of Soviet medical personnel, particularly at the front. On the other hand, almost all confirm shortages of medicines and soap before the war, as well as during it. And all report use of *narodnaia meditsina* (popular, traditional remedies) not only during the war, but before the war.

Because factory-produced soap and medicines were deficit, although ironically cosmetics were prevalent, citizens and pharmacologists relied a great deal on *narodnaia meditsina* to fill the gaps.

This brings us to the third and very significant theme of *Medicines for the Soviet Masses*—the importance of what we today call "alternative medicine" in the Soviet Union. In her path-breaking work, *Curative Powers* (University of Pittsburgh Press, 2003), Paula Michaels documents that although Russian physicians and medics brought modern medicine, which she terms "biomedicine," to Kazakhstan in the 1920s, 1930s and 1940s, the Kazakh people often preferred their own medicine, which Michaels labels "ethnomedicine." Chapters 4 and 8 of *Medicines* examine what therapies ordinary people actually used during the first two years of World War II and during the Great Patriotic War, respectively.

These chapters emphasize that in the 1930s and 1940s not only semi-nomadic Turkic peoples of the Soviet Union but Jews and Slavic peoples living in Belorussia, the Ukraine and Russia, in other words the European peoples of the Soviet Union, relied heavily or even exclusively on traditional, popular medical practices which they called *narodnaia meditsina* because they lacked factory-prepared medicines. Some citizens even made their own soap before the war; many did so during the war.

Further, not only did ordinary people use *narodnaia meditsina* but pharmacologists investigated and advocated medicinal botanicals and other traditional, popular medical practices, both those of Slavic and non-Slavic peoples, because of insufficiencies of factory-produced medicines, especially chemically-synthesized ones. Chapters 5 and 9 focus on this research.

Some "alternative" remedies touted by Soviet pharmacologists and medics were dubious. However, some were meritorious and had futuristic aspects. Bacteriophages—viruses developed to kill bacteria—particularly fall into this category. Studied by Americans in the 1940s, bacteriophages nevertheless were not incorporated into American medical practice. Rather, American medical practice pushed sulfa drugs from the late 1930s and penicillin and antibiotics during and after World War II. In Russia, on the other hand, during the war "alternative medicines" were integrated into mainstream medical practice.

Ironically, according to John E. Lesch, during the 1930s Hitler and his National Socialist party tried to increase the use of "natural products" or folk medicine in Germany, considered the leader of scientific medicine. However, the German pharmaceutical industry, particularly the management of I. G. Farben, resisted and continued to produce sulfa drugs and other state-of-the-art medicines during World War II.[23] Meanwhile, the Soviet government touted Soviet medical practice as the most scientific in the world. But, in fact, there were shortages of vaccines and pharmaceuticals that propelled citizens, pharmacologists and physicians to use folk medicine. The shortages never disappeared. Lack of state-of-the-art apparatus and synthesized pharmaceuticals, antibiotics as well as other medicaments, caused Soviet medical practice to lag behind Western despite brilliant scientists' theoretical work.[24]

Dr. Genis emphasizes that although herbal products helped some medical conditions, other illnesses could only be treated by sulfa drugs, factory-prepared penicillin, other chemotherapy, and factory-prepared quinine or its synthetic versions. And these were difficult to come by in the 1950s and 1960s.[25]

Visitors to Russia the 1960s, 1970s and 1980s could see for themselves that pharmaceuticals and medical/surgical items were inadequate.[26] Post-Soviet Russian accounts now admit the defects.

> Emergency medical care, as well as health care in general, had been one of the great prides of the Soviet system and was often mentioned as an example of socialist achievement. Emergency medical care was free to all and readily accessible for any level of care. Doctors brought services to patient's homes and hospital beds were in abundance. Nevertheless, this system suffered from lapses in quality of care. Most physicians were poorly trained. There was frequently a shortage of medications and supplies. Medical technology in most places was 20-100 years behind that in the West. [27]

As for the pharmaceutical industry specifically, an article in *Kommersant* as recently as March 2007, lamented that "2/3 of Russia's Pharmaceutical Enterprises Not in Line With Global Demands."[28]

Lack of factory-prepared medicines perpetuated the reliance on botanicals and traditional remedies. Reliance on *narodnaia meditsina* continued to influence not only ordinary individuals in Russia and émigrés from Russia and Belarus but Soviet medical care and the training of medical personal. It has steered

Soviet medicine into a different direction from Western medicine to some extent. *Narodnaia meditsina* continued to be accepted and promoted by Soviet scientists and medical personnel as well as ordinary people. Soviet citizens and medical personnel have enshrined "natural remedies" and castigate putting "chemicals into one's body" or "over-reliance on medical apparatus." From this point of view, war clouds had a silver lining. Dr. Genis has emphasized that, making a virtue of necessity, Soviet physicians relied less on readings from state-of-the-art apparatus and more on tell-tale signs and accounts from patients to diagnose disease. Soviet physicians took a more holistic approach to their patients than American physicians did.[29]

Interestingly, although the United States became the world-wide pharmaceutical leader after World War II, Americans in the twenty-first century also have become more skeptical of chemically synthesized medicines and their preservatives and more respectful of "natural remedies."

Moreover, although some Soviet and post-Soviet remedies are dismissed as charlatanism, bacteriophages are now considered a breakthrough remedy. The use of phages is now being resurrected to combat bacteria that have become resistant to antibiotics, putting Soviet pharmacology in the avant-garde in this respect.[30]

The final chapter of *Medicines for the Soviet Masses*, Chapter 10, analyzes the suggestions proffered by pharmacists and pharmaceutical specialists on how production and distribution of pharmaceuticals could be improved. Although these suggestions were not implemented, they prefigured economic changes that were put into place during Nikita Khrushchev's administration in the 1950s. Shedding light on the health and well-being of the populace during the war is a major aim of this study. Nevertheless, investigation into the performance of the pharmaceutical and medical/surgical instruments industries themselves, what internal and exogenous factors influenced their operations, and what insiders thought about the situation are also interesting and important topics

For perspective, *Medicines for the Soviet Masses* compares pharmaceutical developments in Germany and in the United States before and during the war. Dennis Worthen's *Pharmacy in World War II* (Haworth Press, 2004) helps us to appreciate the Soviet pharmaceutical industry's difficulties and achievements and Soviet citizens' trials and tribulations for it documents that the American pharmaceutical industry suffered some shortages at the outset of the war, although American citizens generally did not.

On the other hand, the failures of the Soviet pharmaceutical industry—and the shortcomings of the Soviet economic system—are highlighted by the successes of the German pharmaceutical industry as described by Christopher Kobrak in *National Cultures and International Competition: The Experience of Schering AG, 1851-1950* (Cambridge University Press, 2002) and by John E. Lesch, who concentrates on I. G. Farben in *The First Miracle Drugs: How the Sulfa DrugsTransformed Medicine.*[31] Some Germans suffered shortages of sulfa drugs and other pharmaceuticals, as Ernestine Bradley relates in her moving memoir *The Way Home* (New York: Pantheon Books, 2005). But we cannot reiterate too strongly that Soviet citizens suffered shortages of pharmaceuticals *before* the war. *Medicines for the Soviet Masses* builds on the premise that a Soviet pharmaceutical sector more robust before the Great Patriotic War might have saved some lives during the war and made life more pleasant for Soviet citizens who managed to survive. The changes suggested by some pharmaceutical specialists at the war's end—greater decentralization and autonomy—discussed in the final chapter, might have made the industry healthier and more receptive to Soviet citizens in the post-war period.

Medicines for the Soviet Masses does not definitively account for the losses of Soviet lives during the Great Patriotic War. But it does elaborate on the sufferings and ingenuity of those who survived. It fleshes out our picture of how Soviet health care and the Soviet economy functioned in peacetime as well as in wartime and how the macro economy and Soviet government decisions influenced health care and the welfare of the citizenry.

Medicine for the Soviet Masses demonstrates the courage and determination of Soviet citizens before the war, during it and in the present day. Their lives give testimony to the triumph of good and decency. This book is dedicated to those who helped me formulate and disseminate my questionnaires and those who responded to them. I am deeply grateful for their generosity and kindness in helping me develop this project.

Notes

1. The thirty-five volume work on medical care during the Great Patriotic War, published under the general editorship of E. I. Smirnov in the 1950s, was the main work on wartime surgery and medical care until recently. Although it gave only discrete statistics, the constituent tomes did enumerate pharmaceuticals not only used in World War II but in World War I and nineteenth-century Russian wars E. I. Smirnov, ed. *Opyt sovetskoi meditsiny v Velikoi Otechestvennoi Voine, 1941-1945 gg.* (Moscow: Medgiz, 1950-1955). [Hereafter cited *Opyt sovetskoi meditsiny.*]

2. David Glantz, *Colossus Reborn: The Red Army at War, 1941-1943* (University Press of Kansas, 2005), for example makes two short references to abysmal medical treatment of the soldiers and shortages of both medical/surgical instruments and pharmaceuticals. P. F. Gladkikh and A. E. Loktev in *Sluzhba zdorov'ia v Velikoi Otechestvennoi Voine, 1941-1945 gg.* (St. Petersburg: Dmitrii Bulanin, 2005) acknowledge shortages of medical/surgical instruments in military warehouses at the outset of the war but aver ample stocks of pharmaceuticals for the military and praise output both of medical instruments and pharmaceuticals during the war. They mention infectious diseases among civilians but focus mainly on medical care. Chapter 1 by Nadezhna Cherepenina and chapter 3 by Mikhail Frolov in John Barber and Andrei Dzeniskevich, eds. *Life and Death in Besieged Leningrad, 1941-44* (Palgrave Macmillan, 2005), an English translation of a 1991 Russian-language work, note shortages of medical supplies, pharmaceuti-

cals and soap for civilians in Leningrad and other *oblasts* before the Great Patriotic War, as well as during it but do not investigate the reasons for the shortages.

3. Michael Haynes, "Counting Soviet War Deaths in the Great Patriotic War: A Note," *Europe-Asia Studies*, vol. 55, no. 2 (2003): 308.

4. Mark Harrison, "Counting Soviet Deaths in the Great Patriotic War: Comment," *Europe-Asia Studies*, vol. 55, no. 6 (2003): 943.

5. Mary Schaeffer Conroy, *The Soviet Pharmaceutical Business During Its First Two Decades, 1917-1937* (New York: Peter Lang, 2006).

6. Bryan G. Reuben and Harold A, Wittcoff, *Pharmaceutical Chemicals in Perspective* (New York: John Wiley and Sons, 1989): 7-17. The text on page 11 and chart on page12 compares the decline in childhood mortality as a result of improved hygiene and chemotherapy. Public health measures lowered childhood mortality greatly. However, chemotherapy lowered childhood death rates more dramatically than public health measures. In the words of the authors, "there are about 300,000 people alive in England and Wales today who would have died in childhood but for the new drugs." (11)

7. D. E. Genis, *Meditsinskaia parazitologiia*, edition 2, rewritten and enlarged, (Moscow: Meditsina, 1979), 343 pp, illustrations. The book was awarded a prize.

8. David Genis, Responses to anketa (August 20, 2006).

8. Genis, loc. cit.

9. A. G. Natradze, *Ocherk razvitiia khimiko-farmatsevticheskoi promyshlennosti SSSR* (Moscow: Izdatel'stvo "Meditsina," 1967)

10. A. G. Natradze, *Zadachi khimiko-farmatsevticheskoi promyshlennosti v 1945 g.*," *Farmatsiia*, vol. 8, no. 1 (1945): 12-13.

11. M. Ia. Siatinia, *Istoriia farmatsii* (L'viv, 2002): 309, 362-367.

12. Anatoli Vishnevskii, *Demograficheskaia modernizatsiia Rossii, 1900-2000* (Novoe Izdatel'stvo, 2006): 264.

13. Vishnevskii, ibid.: 262.

14. Nationalization dealt the first blow to the industry. Skilled and dedicated managers were cast aside; partly loyalists, most without credentials, took over pharmaceutical companies. The entire pharmaceutical sector became bureaucratized. In due time the new managers rose to the occasion. However the structure of the economy and inhospitable political decisions impeded pharmaceutical R&D and production and distribution until the end of the 1930s. The Soviet economy was strictly compartmentalized from 1921. The new Soviet government put companies deemed to be purely producers of chemicals into one commissariat. Those deemed to be producers of chemicals and pharmaceuticals were put into another. Entities producing ancillary items like glass and packaging were put into yet another commissariat and so too at many times was the production of medicinal botanicals which were the basis of many pharmaceuticals until the end of the 1930s. The walls between the pharmaceutical industry and industries with which it had natural affinities made sourcing, research and distribution difficult. By the 1930s the prewar factories worked with outdated plant and equipment. The core pharmaceutical industry, a joint-stock conglomerate although government entities subscribed to all the shares, complained that chronic under-investment and inadequate loans from the State Bank prevented modernization. Although there were able Soviet scientists, Soviet R&D was somewhat stunted; the pharmaceutical industry relied heavily on cloning European pharmaceuticals. Limits on imports of raw materials by Foreign Trade officials hampered the pharmaceutical industry throughout the 1920s and 1930s. In the 1930s, excessive imports of botanicals and chemicals shorted the industry. Careless workers spoiled resources and

ruined pharmaceuticals. Corrupt workers stole pharmaceuticals and sold them on the black market. To show profits on their balance sheets demanded by officials and the State Bank, at times pharmaceutical factories in the core industry avoided producing complex and costly items that were needed by the populace and instead put out large amounts of cheap items that were not needed, dumping them on *aptekoupravleniia*, which in turn dumped them on the citizenry. Abrupt price hikes in 1935 thwarted purchases. Officials' demands that old stock be sold before new pharmaceuticals were distributed shorted consumers.

15. See Anthony Rimmington, "The Soviet Union's Offensive Program," in Susan Wright, ed. *Biological Warfare and Disarmament* (Lanham: Rowman & Littlefield, 2002): 105-108, 116, 121-123.

16. Gladkikh and Loktev, *Sluzhba zdorov'ia v Velikoi Otechestvennoi Voine, 1941-1945 gg.*: 78-79.

17. V. A. Isupov, "Demograficheskoe 'chudo': sokrashchenie detskoi smertnosti v Sibiri v 1943-1945 gg.," Elektronnyi zhurnal Sibirskaia zaimka, no. 7 (2002) www. zaimka.ru_2002/isupov_mortality. Accessed 6/15/2006, through an e-mail attachment sent by Rustem Khaziev, Ufa , Russia.

18. Mikhail Frolov, "Evacuation from Leningrad to Kostroma in 1941-42," in Barber and Dzeniskevich, eds. *Life and Death in Besieged Leningrad, 1941-44* : 76.

19. Peter Abramovich Geyman, phone conversation (Denver, CO, September 16, 2006); Samson Geltser, e-mail communiqué (Denver, CO, September 20, 2006); David Genis, e-mail communiqués (Denver, CO, September 21 and September 27, 2006).

20. Tat'iana Petrishche, e-mail communiqué (Belarus, September 29, 2006).

21.Samson Geltser, e-mail communiqués (Denver CO, September 20, 2006 and September 28, 2006).

22. John E. Lesch, *The First Miracle Drugs: How the Sulfa Drugs Transformed Medicine* (Oxford University Press, 2007): 74, 120.

23. Susan Gross Solomon, ed., *Doing Medicine Together: Germany and Russia between the Wars* (Toronto: University of Toronto Press, 2006), passim.

24. David Genis, Interview (Denver, August 2006).

25. Michael Kaser, *Health Care in the Soviet Union* (London: Croom Helm, 1976): 21, 35, 36-92.

26. "Medicine—Emergency Medicine in Russia": Article by Slava V. Gaufberg, MD, FACEP, http:// www. emedicine.com/emerg/topic725.html. Accessed 5/15/2007.

27. *Kommersant*, March 23, 2007, on line at www.kommersant.com, 3/25/2007. Accessed 3/25/2007.

28. David Genis, Interview (Denver, CO, August 2006).

29. For example, "New approach could lower antibiotic requirements by 50 times": Antibiotic doses could be reduced by up to 50 times using a new approach based on bacteriophages," according to Steven Hagen, formerly of the University of Vienna, SCI Press Office, Chemistry and Industry, http://www.chemind.org. Accessed 2/14/ 2007, via an e-mail (in addition to similar e-articles) from Dan Goldberg, U. S. Department of Defense Analyst, with thanks to him.

30. Lesch, *The First Miracle Drugs*: 104-105, 121.

Part I

On the Eve: 1938

Chapter 1
Sickness in Soviet Health Care

For some Soviet citizens, 1938 was the last pleasant peacetime year for six years.[1] For others, foreign threats and internal turmoil converged in nightmarish fashion. The Great Purge, which began in 1937, was still going strong. In March of 1938, at the same time Hitler invaded Austria,[2] a sensational public trial, the third since 1936, revealed that Nikolai Bukharin and twenty other erstwhile high Soviet leaders had planned and worked to enable Germany to take portions of the western USSR and to give Japan territory from the eastern Soviet Union.[3]

During 1937 and 1938 approximately 1,600,000 Soviet citizens were arrested on charges ranging from economic crimes—failure to complete quotas, release of inferior goods or ineptly fulfilling administrative duties—to political crimes, such as criticism of the Soviet Union or outright espionage and treason. The purges also revealed that the anti-Semitism of Imperial Russia still resonated in the Soviet Union. Soviet courts threw out some cases because the documentation was too flimsy. Some accused were exonerated. But others were given eighteen-year sentences in labor camps and nearly half of those arrested were executed.[4]

Soviet pharmacy administrators, executives of major pharmaceutical factories, and pharmacists were not spared and their arrests reflect the economic reasons, foreign policy considerations, and anti-Semitic biases for the Great Purge. Semen Isaakovich Pel'ts, Head of the Pharmacy Administration of the Ukraine, was arrested in 1938. Some of his crimes involved ineffectual administration of the pharmaceutical sector. He was attacked for closing the main Pharmacy Institute in the Ukraine and establishing "Factory Pharmacies" in five cities, where prescriptions were produced by assembly-line methods. The chief pharmacy journal, *Sovetskaia farmatsiia* (Soviet Pharmacy) had touted the factory pharmacies in the early 1930s as a panacea for insufficient numbers of pharmacies. Two, in fact, had been established in Moscow. Now they were repudiated for concentrating resources in large cities, too far from consumers. A more sinister charge against Pel'ts was that he was a member of a Trotskyite-Rightist, counter-revolutionary center and, additionally, that he had adopted fascist German methods.[5] In 1938 Ivan Grigorevich Shuvalov, Director of the Akrikhin Factory, established near Moscow to produce the new Soviet synthetic antimalarial Akrikhin, narcotic ether and salicylic preparations and which, in 1939, took over production of the new Soviet sulfa drug, White Streptotsid, was shot. He was accused of "aiding a 'parallel center'" and spying.[6] Engineers and other workers at the Dorogomilovskii Chemical-Pharmaceutical Factory in Moscow were repressed. The old Bolshevik (and Jew), Izrail Ionasovich Levinshtein, who had worked to reform pharmacy education, was accused of being a Trotskyite but was subsequently pardoned.[7]

Meanwhile, wars with Japan and with Germany or Poland loomed larger. By the summer of 1938 friction between Japanese troops, ensconced in Manchuria from 1932, and the Far Eastern Red Army, estimated to be between 300,000 and 400,000 strong and with "2,000 planes at its disposal," led to over 500 border clashes.[8] In the fall of 1938 Hitler sliced off the Sudeten German provinces from Czechoslovakia.

Soviet factories geared up for war, Soviet chemical-pharmaceutical factories among them. In 1938, Oleg Kononenko, a newly minted Ph. D. in Pharmaceutical Chemistry from Khar'kov was dispatched to Moscow to produce biological weapons in a top-secret basement facility in the Dorogomilovskii Chemical Factory, located on the Moscow River embankment opposite the Novodevichii Convent. Kononenko was convinced that this production was partly intended for offensive purposes—for a preemptive strike against Germany.[9] Scholars are still debating whether the Soviet government planned to attack Germany in the late 1930s. But Anthony Rimmington has verified that biological weapons were being produced in Russia "partially concealed within ostensible civil organizations such as the Commissariats of Health and Education"[10] So it is very possible that Kononenko was involved in making bio-chemical weapons at Dorogomilovskii.

Pharmacists and pharmacologists were made aware of their responsibilities, particularly should war come to Soviet soil. In an article published early in 1938 in *Farmatsiia i farmakologiia* (Pharmacy and Pharmacology), one G. Popov emphasized that " [P]opulation points . . . in the zone on the side of advances of the enemy (up to 100 kilometers from the border) must be prepared for air raids, defense of the population, and liquidation of the results of attacks. . . ." Popov discussed "local anti-air defense," "immediate struggle with . . . artillery," and "observation of the sky for the purpose of timely awareness of the enemy's appearance." He underscored the need for self-defense (anti-gas costumes) and collective defense (hermetically sealed rooms), contending that "in future wars there would be trauma from bombs of 50 to 100 kilograms and more in weight." He advocated the creation of "*sanpozitsii*" which could offer first aid; stationary institutions delivering more serious medical-pharmaceutical treatment; and the preparation of medical and pharmacy personnel and pharmaceutical enterprises.[11]

Would the Soviet pharmaceutical sector be able to supply sufficient amounts of medicines, anesthesia, antiseptics, and other crucial items if the Soviet Union became embroiled in war, particularly war on Soviet soil? For war would bring chemical weapons, trauma, wounds, and a flare up in infectious diseases due to troop movements and dislocation of civilians.

Special institutes produced vaccines, serums and antitoxins needed to prevent outbreaks of serious contagious diseases. For example, the Bacteriological Institute in Ufa produced antidysentery serum or dysentery antitoxin; divaccine against typhoid and paratyphoid B, which was analogous to Salmonella; diphtheria and scarlatina antitoxins; typhus, cholera, and smallpox vaccines; and bacteriophages—viruses bred to attack bacteria.[12] The Red Army had some special pharmaceutical factories, as had been the case with the Imperial Russian army. The Soviet pharmaceutical industry, though, produced most of the disinfectants, antiseptics and reagents needed for preventive medicine and the anesthesia, febrifuges, analgesics, drugs, vitamins, and food supplements needed for surgery and treatment both of the Red Army and Navy troops and civilians.

During the preceding decade, the pharmaceutical industry had made strides. However, output of key products periodically was thwarted by excessive exports of chemicals and botanicals needed by the industry; irregular deliveries of raw materials; obsolete equipment; poor treatment of equipment and materials and spoilage of finished products by careless workers; and disruption due to the central government's frequent reorganization of the industry.[13] Distribution was problematical, moreover, because the network of pharmacies was inadequate, because pharmaceutical factories sometimes dumped products on *aptekoupravleniia,* the intermediary pharmacy administrations that purchased for pharmacies; and because of periodically counterproductive government policies, such as abrupt price rises.[14]

At the beginning of 1938, the core pharmaceutical industry, Vokhimfarm (All-Union Chemical-Pharmaceutical), in the jurisdiction of the USSR Commissariat of Health, was rechristened the Administration of the Chemical-Pharmaceutical Industry—Khimfarmprom by resolution of the government, Sovnarkom, and by a *prikaz* (order) of Narkomzdrav, the USSR Commissariat of Health. The core pharmaceutical industry consisted of fourteen factories. Eleven dated from pre-revolutionary times, most, in fact, from the late nineteenth century. A few had been built during the First World War. The Schering Factory (subsequently Factory No. 3, No. 4, then shed from the core system) had been nationalized during that war. The rest of the factories that constituted the core industry had been nationalized by the Soviet government in 1918/1919.[15] Six pre-Soviet enterprises were located in or around Moscow: Salicylate, Karpov (the former Ferrein Factory), Semashko (the former Keler Factory), the Alkaloid Factory, and the Endocrine Factory, now with "Vitamin" added to its name. The Akrikhin Factory had been built in 1936 on the site of a mid-nineteenth century chemical factory to produce the new antimalarial Akrikhin, as well as other products, in the little village of Staraia Kupavna in Moscow *oblast'* (province). The Farmakon Factory, established in 1908, was located in Leningrad. The Dzerzhinskii factory in Chimkent, Kazakhstan, had been built in 1885 by two Russian merchants to produce Santonin, a vermifuge or expellant for roundworms in humans and the best treatment for ascarid diseases in livestock—a product crucial to the American hog industry. Other enterprises in the core industry included the Red Star Factory in Khar'kov, the Lomonosov Factory in Kiev, and the Factory of Artificial Teeth in Leningrad. The production of iodine, derived from seaweed and crucial as a water purifier, antiseptic and to prevent goiter, was difficult in Imperial Russia because, although the empire had vast amounts of ocean and Black Sea coastline, the alkaloid content in the seaweed was not high enough to satisfy the pharmacopoeia. Experimental stations produced small amounts of iodine during World War I. The Soviet pharmaceutical industry built three iodine factories—Nefte-Chalinskii, Surakhanskii, and Ramaninskii—in Azerbaijan to acquire more of this important product. The industry also included the All-Union Scientific Research Chemical-Pharmaceutical Institute in Moscow (VNIKhFI), now named in honor of Ordzhonikidze, Stalin's erstwhile comrade, who had perished shortly before, by his own hand, because of disagreements with the Boss. Khimfarmprom was charged with producing mainly "complex synthesized chemical-pharmaceutical preparations." Nevertheless, during 1938 the All-Union Institute of Medicinal and Aromatic Botanicals (VILAR) was added to the Trust.[16]

Regional factories supplemented the factories in the core pharmaceutical industry. For example, from the mid 1920s, Farmzavod in Minsk, the capital of the Belorussian SSR, prepared medicines and Belmedtorg, the trading agency in Belorussia, cultivated medicinal botanicals for local use and export.[17] Approximately eighteen pharmaceutical enterprises operated in the Russian Republic (RSFSR) in addition to those in the core industry. Fifteen pharmaceutical factories operated in the Ukrainian SSR, seven enterprises operated in the Georgian SSR, and there were other enterprises in other constituent republics.[18]

Local pharmacy organizations (*aptekoupravleniia*) and other local organizations had managed these regional enterprises, most small and medium-sized that put out galenicals and supplied packaging for the local market, since the enterprises had been nationalized in 1919. At the beginning of 1938, following resolutions of USSR Sovnarkom and the Russian Republic Council of People's Commissars, the eighteen manufactories in the Russian Republic were grouped into a special trust called Rosfarmtrest and put under the jurisdiction of the Russian Republic Commissariat of Health (RSFSR Narkomzdrav). The stated purpose of this centralization was to utilize "laboratories and workshops, which did not require large capitalization," in light of "the insufficiency of mechanized factories and manufactories . . . to fulfill the requests of regions (*oblast'* and *krai*)."[19]

The pharmaceutical enterprises in the Ukrainian and Georgian republics, mentioned above, were consolidated under the Commissariats of Health in those republics. They were ordered to focus on simpler medicines and products like salves, medicinal gypsum, and the like.[20]

This arrangement made some sense—at least on paper. It was intended to result in more cohesive production. Thinking, as always in a subjective mode, commentators waxed enthusiastic about the synergies that would result. These small-scale entities now would be guaranteed funds for raw materials and ancillary materials. Glass and ceramic production would improve. Non-viable entities would be closed down, and so forth.[21]

But whether this new system would allow the pharmaceutical industry to function more smoothly remained to be seen. In terms of quantity, the enterprises in the regional industries were more numerous than in the core industry. The number of employees was about the same—8,344 in the core industry as compared with about 6,000 in the regional industries.[22] However, due to contracts with local *aptekoupravleniia,* made in the second half of the 1920s, which obligated these suppliers to pharmacies to purchase from core industry factories,[23] the core industry, Khimfarmprom, supplied the great percentage of pharmaceuticals—and certainly sophisticated therapies like the new synthetic antimalarials and the new sulfa drugs—used throughout the Soviet Union. Would the realigned Soviet pharmaceutical industry and particularly the core enterprises be able to supply adequate amounts of high-quality items needed for military and civilian health care and surgery in the event of war?

Old Soviet histories portrayed the pharmaceutical industry, like other Soviet industries, moving in a steadily ascending trajectory of improvement.[24]

Indeed, Soviet R & D appeared to be impressive. In 1938, the industry promoted nine new products. Two were anesthetics, Narkolan made in the Salicylate Factory and Tiokain in the Alkaloid Factory. The Red Star Factory in Khar'kov produced antibacterial Pantotsid tablets to purify water. The Alkaloid Factory put out a new vermifuge named Geksil, to counter intestinal worms, and also produced a new expectorant Apomorfin. The Karpov Factory produced a new digestive preparation, Magnesia Pergidrop. Vitamin "C" was made in the Endocrine Factory and benzoic soda in the Farmakon Factory in Leningrad.[25]

However, health problems related to a dearth of disinfectants, antiseptics, insecticides, sulfa drugs and vitamins—all products of the pharmaceutical industry—were very visible. In 1938 the American Embassy in Moscow reported that although there were "70 medical schools . . . with an enrollment of 100,000 students, 90,682 doctors and 10,500 dentists in the Soviet Union (the last graduating from 8 dental schools), diseases arising from malnutrition and lack of sanitation" were "prevalent in the country . . . dysentery, typhoid fever and typhus" were "quite common and trachoma" was "widespread in the Asiatic portions of the U.S.S.R., smallpox" existed "and malaria" was "frequent."[26] Soviet propaganda trumpeted that its health care system had reduced mortality in general and particularly infant mortality. But new records from the archives tell another story. Typhoid, smallpox, scarlatina, and whooping cough had been greatly reduced by 1936. But the incidence of typhus in that year was just slightly less than in 1913; the incidence of scarlatina was higher; the incidence of measles and dysentery were far higher; and the incidence of malaria, which fluctuated from year to year, was only slightly lower. Statistics on life expectancy were shocking: in 1938-1939, according to Anatoli Vishnevskii, "life expectancy for Soviet men was 44 years and for women—49.7 years . . . lower than in some countries in 1900. And life expectancy for Russians was lower than for the general population of the USSR."[27]

Admittedly, these statistics had been affected by famine in 1932-1933 and by infant mortality. Further, the Soviet Union was an empire rather than a country, with remote regions populated by indigenous and sometimes primitive populations. Nevertheless, high rates of typhus, spread by lice, typhoid, and dysentery testified to poor hygiene and sanitation, as well as inadequate inoculation measures, for there were preventative vaccines or serums against all three diseases. The prevalence of malaria, spread by the anopheles mosquito and endemic and sometimes epidemic in the Soviet Union, as in Imperial Russia,[28] pointed to lack of insecticides and insect control.

These problems, in turn, raise a red flag about the robustness of the pharmaceutical sector. For vaccines require reagents and other pharmaceuticals. Disinfectants and insecticides are products of the pharmaceutical industry. Therefore lack of these items, meant either that pharmaceutical production or distribution systems were wanting or that both were. This hypothesis would appear to be confirmed by statistics provided by Christopher Kobrak, specialist on the German pharmaceutical house Schering. Data he presents show Russia in seventh place in terms of production and consumption of pharmaceuticals by the late 1920s but below Brazil, Spain, Argentina, and Mexico in per capita use of pharmaceuticals. Additionally, the American pharmaceutical industry, the leader at this time with a population similar to the USSR, outperformed the Soviet Union twenty-two times. The next four pharmaceutical leaders, England, Germany, France, and Japan outpaced the Soviet Union two to four times.[29]

In fact, at the time, Soviet officials and pharmaceutical specialists acknowledged their concerns about both the production and the distribution of pharmaceuticals. In 1936, the Central Committee of the Ukrainian Communist Party (Bolshevik) lambasted shortages of pharmacies, need for their repair and remodeling, and "*absence . . . in a significant part. . . of pharmacies of the most necessary medicines and sanitary and hygiene articles.*"[underlined in the original] In June 1937 delegates to the First All-Union Congress of Pharmacologists and Toxicologists heard a "State of the Industry Address" decrying serious inadequacies in the Soviet pharmaceutical sector. The industry was "severely backward, together with other physiological sciences" and "insufficiently answered to the needs of Soviet health care," delegates were told. Obsolescence, low investment and the severe compartmentalization of the Soviet economy, resulting in economic sectors being segregated from others with which they had affinity, were blamed for this situation. Soviet pharmacology had been hampered, Congress delegates were informed, by an "insufficient amount of workers," as well as by "insufficient connection with the chemical-pharmaceutical industry and with institutions managing the study and production of medicinal plants, not to mention . . . insufficiency of equipment. . . ."[30]

Why did this situation exist in an empire blessed with rich natural resources, brilliant pharmacologists and physicians, and a scientifically planned health system? Inadequate distribution was partly connected with the vastness of the Soviet Union, of course. But why was production still lagging in 1938, twenty years after the October Revolution and on the eve of a Second World War? More to the point what was being done to correct the situation?

The purges might well have been disruptive and torpedoed morale. Factory directors' complaints, in their annual reports for 1938, however, reveal that more bur-

Fig. 1.1 Raw Materials, Needed and Supplied, in tons: 1938

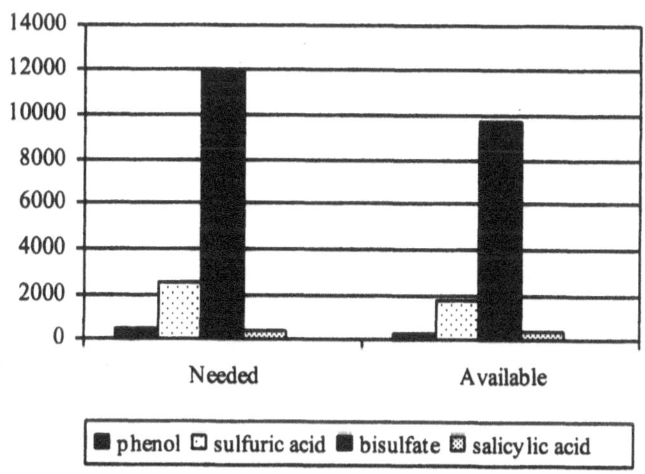

densome were the macroeconomic inefficiencies, worker carelessness, and political factors that had cramped the industry since its nationalization in 1918/1919.

Source: RGAE, f. 8009, op. 2, d. 3, ll. 5, 35-38, 40-43, 89.

A major frustration, as during the previous decades, was irregular delivery of raw materials. In 1938 salicylic preparations—aspirin and salol—did not meet their production targets because of "interruptions" in supplies of phenol, caustic soda, and fuel during November and December 1938. Although supplies of phenol had doubled since the previous year, the industry received only about three-fourths of the phenol it required. Almost all the salicylic acid required arrived, but only about half of the bisulfate and only about three-fourths of the sulfuric acid required.

Ancillary problems exacerbated shortages and uneven deliveries. Poor repair of the machinery and accidents at the Salicylate Factory contributed further to "underfulfillment" of Plan targets. Output of bromine, bismuth preparations, and iodine—a water purifier and antiseptic—were lower than projected. Production of two out of eleven preparations needed for culture media—pepton and pepsin—were held up because the sugar plan was not fulfilled. In the case of pepton, new methods also complicated production and in the case of pepsin, "interruptions" of fuel and electrical energy prevented planned output. Targets for technical morphine were not fulfilled during 1938. The plan for narcotic ether was "underfulfilled" because the shop making it was not finished. Lobelin was not produced in the Alkaloid Factory because the Scientific-Research Institute did not work out all the production methods. Raw materials for the anesthetic Tiokain were lacking. Production of Novocain was lower than projected because of "absence of a market." Production of Salipyrine was lower than projected because of lack of methods and equipment. The Red Star Factory had not been able to fulfill the target for Chloramine and Hydrokhinon, because transfer to the factory of the responsibility for making these items came too late to allow shops to come up to speed.[31] Chloramine, as well as iodine, was crucial to prevent outbreaks of typhoid and dysentery.[32]

Admittedly, output of some significant pharmaceuticals did greatly increase during 1938. Streptotsid production leapt from 4 tons to 13 tons, glucose from 48 to 55 tons. Phenacetin, pepton, Anestezin, Sergozin, and some other products all increased.[33] However, they did not meet Plan targets, which presumably were based on need. Further, although norms for some products were overfulfilled in specific factories during 1938—sometimes due to extraordinary Stakhanovite efforts—the industry as a whole did not meet total production targets for these items.[34]

A less than stellar work ethic caused additional problems. Sloppy workmanship cost the industry and consumers dearly, for spoilage cut the availability of items that had been put out in sufficiency. For example, in 1938, the Karpov Factory overfulfilled preparations of iodine, bismuth (though these products were underfulfilled for the industry as a whole), narcotic ether, Urotropin (clone of a Schering product), and terpinhydrate—and did so more cheaply than estimates had predicted.[35] Unfortunately, this achievement was offset by *brak*—the need to reject products that were spoiled, particularly by dirt from machinery. Losses from *brak* were higher for the pharmaceutical industry in 1938 than in 1937. They amounted to 1,567 thousand rubles—although that amount was only 0.6 percent of the cost (*sebestoimost'*) of all production. The Karpov Factory had the unpleasant distinction of having "the greatest loss from *brak*—777 thousand rubles," basically from the production of the antivenereal Novarsenol. In the Lomonosov Factory *brak* for narcotic ether amounted to 87 thousand rubles or 19 percent of cost.[36]

Khimfarmprom management and many managers in individual factories tried to eliminate spoilage and upgrade workers' skills. Classes in Russian and mathematics were conducted for poorly educated workers as well as special training for "the best Stakhanovites." Training was available for chauffeurs and machinists. Classes were held in foreign languages—English and German (undoubtedly to keep abreast of pharmaceutical developments in these countries); organic, analytical, and physical chemistry, technical safety, corrosion of metals, and so forth. Several hundred people studied various courses, some of which were taught in the Moscow Chemical-Technological Institute. Two factories in Moscow—Karpov and Akrikhin—and the Red Star Factory in Khar'kov, also had their own schools. On January 1, 1939, sixty-five people were studying in the Moscow factory schools. Seventeen "Masters'" candidates (*aspiranty*) and seventeen Ph. D. candidates were studying at the Scientific-Research Chemical-Pharmaceutical Institute. Unfortunately, the special courses to prepare specialists for the chemical-pharmaceutical industry, instituted in the Moscow Pharmacy School in 1937, "were liquidated by resolution of the USSR Commissariat of Health, because there were no qualified entrants."[37] The Red Star Factory attempted to increase the number of qualified workers by offering courses, taught by a professor, three docents, twelve engineers, and others in the factory and also by encouraging workers to take courses at the technicum. Only about one half of the 308 studying in 1939 and 1940 finished, however, either because they lacked textbooks, had no place to study, were fired or left factory employment, or because of sickness.[38]

Rising costs also caused a headache for enterprise managers. Costs for the entire industry shot up in 1938. Raw materials were more expensive. Packaging costs increased for the industry as a whole because "part of the ampules and cartons" were made "in collective farms according to prices set by the plan, but without sufficient funds" to actually pay for the contract work. Fuel prices went up in 1938.[39]

Production of lucrative perfumes, cosmetics, toilet soaps and toothpaste might have offset these expenditures. Unfortunately, output of these items had been removed from the pharmaceutical industry a decade earlier and, in the late 1930s, was in the jurisdiction of a separate body, "Glavparfiumer" (Chief Administration of the Perfumery, Cosmetics, Synthetic and Soap Industries). This was a pity for on the one hand, the perfume *glavk* did not seem to suffer from the same financial constraints as the pharmaceutical industry. On the other hand, TEZhE, the Soap and Toiletries Trust, a subsection of the *glavk*, did not produce enough soap of various kinds to satisfy the needs of the Soviet Union. Soap was a major means of preventing the spread of many infectious diseases. Soap production did increase in the 1930s as compared with Imperial times and Soviet output in the 1920s. However, soap still was deficit in the Soviet Union in 1938.

Soviet propaganda attributed the deficit to historical factors. In 1937, Soviet publicists reported to *The American Perfumer and Essential Oil Review* that in 1913 only one factory in Russia, Ralle and Broker, produced soap—to the amount of 160,000 tons.[40] This information was false. A 1913 publication on the Russian Chemical Industry listed 141 soap works in just about every province of the Empire. The sales of some enterprises were modest but the sales of others were very large. They produced toilet soaps, washing powders and soaps, and medical soaps and some produced eau de cologne, perfume and cosmetics as well. Some enterprises were localized. Others distributed their wares throughout the empire. One factory in the city of Saratov exported all of its production to the United States.[41] Another source from later times asserted that before the First World War "there were in Russia some 780 soap works, with total annual output of about 180,000 tons."[42] This source probably included small-scale soap makers. It is true that, although soap works existed in remote areas of Central Asia and the Far East, probably most peasants—and certainly nomadic peoples—who together comprised some 80 percent of Imperial Russia's population used small amounts of factory-made soaps or did not use factory-made soaps at all. But city people, no matter where they lived, seem to have had a sufficiency of soaps of various kinds for there was no hand-wringing about lack of soap in Imperial Russia.

In fact, lack of soap in the Soviet Union resulted more from the Soviet government's policies than historical factors. The Keler factory was one of the factories that produced soap in Imperial Russia and sold it throughout the length and breadth of the Empire. In the 1920s the Keler Factory, now called the Semashko Factory and part of the core pharmaceutical industry, continued to produce and sell soap. However, in 1927, officials removed soap production from the factory. This did allow the factory to concentrate on some other products. On the other hand, it hurt the finances of the pharmaceutical industry and did not increase soap production.[43]

In 1927 the eleven factories in TEZhE reported "underfulfillment" of the Plan mandated for the industry. The Plan called for 11,000 thousand dozen units of toilet soap. But only 8,104 thousand dozen units or 73.7 percent of Plan quotas were produced. The Plan had called for 18,000 tons of household soap. Only 78.4 percent of that was produced—14,112 tons. Liquid soaps fared better. Ninety percent of their Plan targets were fulfilled—1,213 tons. And tooth powder was "overfulfilled" coming in at 137.2 percent of Plan targets. It is hard to estimate tonnage amounts of "thousands of dozens" of units of toilet soap. However, the absolute amount of soap that was produced, according to the Soap Trust report, added up to less than 34,000 tons. This was far less than the amount produced in Imperial times and it is difficult to see how the units of toilet soap would fill the gap.[44]

The main cause of underfulfillment was "insufficient fats." Additionally, although the cost of production had been reduced by a quarter to almost a half in comparison with the production year 1925/1926, the cost of materials—chiefly fats—for one ton of soap had risen 18 percent in comparison with the previous year and 7.6 percent in comparison with the costs estimated in the Plan. Obsolescent buildings and equipment undoubtedly retarded production as well. The five factories in the Soap Trust that specifically produced soap had been built in the 1870s, 1880s and 1890s. Whereas 870,000 rubles had been allocated for building new soap factories less than half of that amount had been spent. Some new foreign equipment did arrive for four factories. However, the trust overspent "on re-equipping and capital repair" of existing factories. Despite producing less than the amount called for, prices for toilet soap were cut in 1927, perhaps compounding problems at the retail end.[45]

Soviet soap production plummeted in 1929 and 1930. During those years, peasants protesting collectivization slaughtered their animals. This resulted not only in a shortage of food and draught animals but in a shortage of soap. In its annual report TEZhE stated that production of household soaps was 30 percent less than mandated by the Plan and production of toilet soap, 40 percent less. The reasons cited in the soap factory reports were lack of fats and their greater expense.[46] Despite this, Soviet statistics for foreign consumption broadcast soap production in 1929-1930 at 234,000 tons.[47] This was not only a significant increase over Imperial times but a significant increase over the statistics cited in internal reports for 1927. Nevertheless, there appeared to be an insufficiency of soap for the Soviet people. It was estimated that 60 percent of schoolchildren did not use soap and that the amount of soap used per capita in the Soviet Union in 1930 was about a tenth of that used in the United States.[48] Soviet industry journals reported that desperate Soviet soap makers were experimenting with various kinds of additives to stretch the supply—which earned them not approval but censure from the government for expensive experiments with soap making.[49]

Meanwhile, cosmetics and perfumes were given as high a priority as soap. The government did cut imports of cocoa and ether oils in 1927. However, "in the slaughterhouse a department was organized for making zinc" to be used "chiefly for face powder" and "cosmetics" in place of imported bleach. Additionally, the Soap Trust "laboratory worked out methods of producing synthetic aromatic substances" to save on imports. Ether oils were increased 70 percent. A better recipe for "the fat mixture of toilet soap" was developed but so was "improvement in the distillation process" for perfumes. And TEZhE worked to improve the quality of cosmetics.[50]

In 1928/1929 the amount allocated for imports of ether oils was cut from over one million rubles to seven hundred thousand rubles, much to the consternation of the Soap Trust officials. However, to make a profit, the trust sent cheaper perfume and cosmetics out to the countryside. The trust's increasing turnover revenues in the fourth quarter resulted from perfume sales.[51]

By 1934, the Soap Trust, newly moved into the Commissariat of Food, was ordered to increase the output of soap two and a half times on the basis of existing equipment. However, industry reports protested that seven of the eleven factories were old and unsatisfactory. There also was "systematic lack of wagons." Meanwhile, the perfume factories had "large shop composition, laboratories in various shops, large carton and powder shops."[52]

Soviet publicists asserted that due to Stakhanovite policies and Joseph Stalin's wise leadership, output of toilet goods in general, in 1936, exceeded that of 1935 by 31.4 percent.[53] As for soap specifically, it was claimed that in 1936 Soviet factories produced 355,000 tons of ordinary soap along with large amounts of cakes of soap.[54] If accurate, output of soap had definitely superseded output in Imperial Russia and output in Soviet Russia in the late 1920s and early 1930s. Nevertheless, we shall see in the following chapters that shortages of soap persisted in the late 1930s and early 1940s.

Distribution, as well as production, was a problem. Most toilet soap, face powder, tooth powder and toothpaste, as well as eau de cologne and perfume, were made in Leningrad and Moscow, which involved "many long freight hauls" and "packing plants for local distribution."[55] Soap production, in particular, was slated to become more decentralized. In 1938 it was asserted that 36 metric tons of toilet soap were sold and, to keep up with demand new soap factories expected to produce 20,000 tons of soap per year and a perfume factory were to be erected in Novosibirsk, in Siberia. Additionally, the "Troitskii soap factory near Cheliabinsk" was to be brought to "full capacity of 7,000 tons of household soap per year." Moscow factories also were slated to begin to "put on the market . . . soap chips for washing silk and rayon fabrics and in 1940 the "Kaluga perfume 'combine'" was to "start operations, manufacturing synthetic aromatic products, most of which" had "hitherto been imported."[56] Further, a factory was operating in Kiev and factories were to come on line in Tashkent and Petropavlovsk in Kazakhstan.[57] If these plans were to be fulfilled it would be a boon to health care—but the big question was *if*.

Cosmetics, though, still retained the same importance as soap and, as far as investment was concerned, were on a higher plane than medicines and other pharmaceuticals. In the mid-1930s, cosmetics were deemed degenerate in Nazi Germany although German women used them anyway. In the Soviet Union, not only were cosmetics not disparaged, but production of them continued to be given great attention. In February 1934, according to *The American Perfumer and Essential Oil Review*, Paulina Zemchuzhina (Madam Molotova) was awarded the order of Lenin for "her work in supervising cosmetics manufacture of superior rouge, lipstick, powder, eyebrow pencil, and other cosmetics." Eight others received awards of the order of the Red Banner.[58] In 1936, *The American Perfumer and Essential Oil Review* recounted that a commission from the trust spent "5 months abroad, in Europe and America" to boost the quality of these wares, production of which was claimed to be 515 million rubles in that year, in terms of 1926-1927 prices.[59] The American trade journal noted in 1936 that while former Russian aristocrat Grand Duchess Marie was touted as a representative for the American perfume and cosmetics industry,[60] "Mrs. Ludmilla Chapochnikova [sic] and Mrs. Olga Karpovisskaia [sic], who head the official Soviet perfume business in Russia" had arrived in the United States "for a tour of inspection and period of study of American cosmetic and toilet preparation business." The two visited the Allied Products Plant in New York, the A. E. Mullen American Perfume Laboratories, and traveled to California. They were provided with interpreters from Amtorg (the Soviet Communist International front organization). Back in the USSR they were promised a new facility which would cost 75 million rubles[61] that was ostensibly approved by Joseph Stalin himself.[62]

Meanwhile, the Statutory Fund of the core Pharmaceutical industry, still called Vokhimfarm, was 49 and a half million rubles in March 1936, in terms of

1926/1927 prices and production for the first quarter of 1936 was valued at 11 and a half million rubles. Projected production for the entire year was somewhere around 46 million rubles.[63] Obviously, medicines were lower status than cosmetics and perfumes.

Out in the hinterlands, in 1938, there were shortages of pharmaceuticals. "Growth of turnover" at the pharmacy, one article noted, "to a large extent proceeds from non-medical wares (perfume) and less from medical wares." "Requests for medicinal wares" by the "population, especially rural" were not being met. "The materials of inspectors support the fact," the article continued, "that in many *apteki* (pharmacies) the public are refused (*otkazuvaiut*) the more important wares. The population is refused not because these wares are lacking but exclusively because of bad planning and regulation of distribution of wares so that managers of pharmacies cannot clearly make representation about what they must sell and for how much."[64] Another article called for better accounting, asserting that "Not infrequently complaints about refusals in pharmacies, refusals [to sell] non-deficit medicaments often appear in our press. But only part of these [problems] are addressed. The village is different from the city in regard to requests. . . .Absence of an assortment does not give the possibility to analyze the profitability of the work of apteki. . . . "[65]

These articles blamed poor accounting, poor planning and poor management for inadequate stocks and assortment in Soviet pharmacies. Yet readers could infer that another reason rural dwellers were bereft of good quality pharmaceuticals was because crucial pharmaceuticals were not being produced in sufficient amounts. Rural dwellers, who formed the overwhelming majority of the population of the Soviet Union, were faced with minimal choices of medicaments and disinfectants at the *apteka*. This supposition was substantiated by a table which, in the manner of Gogol's *Dead Souls*, documented that in 1937 rural dwellers (basically peasants living on collective and state farms) received 854 grams of valerian drops per 1,000 souls (*dush*) whereas city dwellers received 5,180 grams. Similarly rural dwellers received 571 grams of iodine solutions per 1,000 souls whereas city dwellers received 4,560 grams per 1,000 souls. Peasants received 345 grams of zinc salve per 1,000 souls in comparison with the 2,536 grams per 1,000 souls received by city dwellers. And they received only 787 grams of castor oil in comparison to the 5,604 grams per 1,000 souls received by city dwellers."[66]

High officials responded to both production and distribution problems in typically bureaucratic fashion. They reorganized. Throughout the 1930s, this had been their chief solution to industry travails. And so, in the fall of 1938, the Soviet pharmaceutical industry was reshuffled again. In the Russian Republic (RSFSR), the eighteen pharmaceutical factories not included in the core industry, which had been under the jurisdiction of local pharmacy administrations and then, in the beginning of the year, had been grouped in the Russian Pharmaceutical Trust (Rosfarmtrest), were now transferred to the Medical-Pharmaceutical Industry (Medfarmprom). Medfarmprom managed second-tier pharmaceutical factories in the Soviet Union.

Local pharmacy administrations continued, as before, to control some small production entities, which mainly produced galenicals (simple medicaments). Industry specialists claimed that, in the conditions then prevailing in pharmaceutical factories—"conditions of outmoded technique, which required significant hidden reserves, and unsatisfied demand of the sales network"—reorganization streamlined and strengthened the pharmaceutical industry.[67] The second-tier enterprises, which supplied about a quarter to a third of drugs and supplies, did contribute to pharmaceutical R&D and the output of pharmaceuticals. But their production could not entirely compensate for systemic problems in the pharmaceutical industry.

This did not quell bureaucrats' faith in reorganization, however. At the end of 1938, to the fourteen factories in the core pharmaceutical industry were added a Packaging Factory in Torzhok (a town in the former Tver' Province north of Moscow) and three entities in Moscow: a "Caffeine Factory"; the Marketing office "Khimfarmtorg"; and the Office of Supplies, "Khimfarmsnab". As before, the core pharmaceutical industry included the All-Union Scientific Research Chemical-Pharmaceutical Institute (VNIKhFI) and the All-Union Office of Medicinal and Aromatic Botanicals (VILAR). Now added on was a scientific research laboratory, LVEN. Further attached were a project office; a *montazh* office, that dealt with production methods and factory installation; and a construction trust.[68] Thus, by the end of 1938, Khimfarmtorg comprised twenty-four entities. The core industry had proliferated past the point of efficiency.

The *Upravlenie* (Administrative Board) of Khimfarmprom also was bloated. Twenty-three members—twenty-two men and one woman—comprised it. One Terent'ev served as chair. Directors of factories like T. T. Fillopos'iants, R. I. Kogan, and I. A. Maiorov of the Endocrine and the Karpov (former Ferrein) factories sat on the board. Only one name, that of Rabinovich, was even vaguely familiar. The rest were new, the names of some reflecting the rise of non-Russians in the industry. Bekdamirov, Agaev and Tagiev, for example, sat amongst the seven directors and assistant directors of the three iodine factories. Along with a representative from the Iodine-Bromine Bureau they participated at meetings concerning production in this area.[69]

The Soviet pharmaceutical industry was now intensely concentrated. For example, seventy-four entities all over the Soviet Union—cities; *oblasts*; ASSR's (Autonomous Republics) that were component parts of the Soviet Socialist Republics (SSRs), the "states" of the Soviet Union; the Chemical-Pharmaceutical Trading industry; the Chief Chemical Trading industry; and individual factories—all bought products from the Salicylate Factory, one of the enterprises of the core pharmaceutical industry in Moscow.[70]

If the Soviet postal service and transportation network had worked properly such extreme centralization would not have been a detriment. But the distribution infrastructure did not work efficiently. And, in the event of war, particularly war on Soviet soil, over-concentration could be problematical and even deleterious to the health of citizens and the Red Army.

On the surface pharmaceutical industry executives supported the existing economic and political system. In May 1938, *Farmatsiia* (Pharmacy) carried Stalin's speech to workers of higher schools. Later in the year, a photo of a Lenin-Stalin bas-relief introduced an article praising Stalin for continuing Lenin's work of propelling the Soviet Union forward, leading the struggle against capitalist countries and against "enemies of the people" within the Soviet Union. [71] Praise was even more effusive in 1939. But war definitely was on the horizon. Early in 1939 *Farmakologiia i toksikologiia* published a synopsis of the Eighteenth Party Congress, which averred that war with "Fascist aggressors" was imminent and that "pharmacologists and toxicologists" must be ready to play an important role in country's defense.[72]

And it appeared that the pharmaceutical sector was not ready. The political and economic system that Stalin had helped create and now managed thrust up many hurdles for the Soviet pharmaceutical industry. The pharmaceutical industry might have performed better with more freedom to source, control its product line, determine prices for its wares, make acquisitions and enter mergers. As things stood, both the pharmaceutical industry and the soap industry had difficulties providing for the needs of the Red Army and Soviet citizens in a world becoming more turbulent and dangerous.

Notes

1. Discussion with Maya Pankratova, Moscow, summer 1993.

2. "Death for 19 Asked at Russian Trial," *The New York Times* (Saturday, March 12, 1938) and "65,000 Reich Troops Move Into Austria" (Sunday, March 13, 1938): 1.

3. Robert C. Tucker and Stephen F. Cohen, eds., *The Great Purge Trial* (New York: Grosset and Dunlap, 1965): 6, 10, 360-371, and passim.

4. For statistics on court cases, convictions and executions see Peter H. Solomon, Jr., *Soviet Criminal Justice Under Stalin* (Cambridge University Press, 1996): 232. There is voluminous literature on the purges and more is published every day. A few historians have portrayed the purges as a sincere effort by the Soviet government to improve economic performance. See, for example, Roberta T. Manning, "The Soviet Economic Crisis of 1936-1940 and the Great Purges," in J. Arch Getty and Roberta T. Manning, eds., *Stalinist Terror: New Perspectives* (Cambridge: Cambridge University Press, 1993): 116-141. Because of the growth of forced labor camps, Oleg V. Khlevniuk and Galina Ivanovna have stressed that a major purpose of the purges was the acquisition of cheap labor for Soviet extractive industries in inhospitable climes. See Galina Mikhailovna Ivanova, *Labor Camp Socialism* , ed. Donald J. Raleigh, trans. Carol Flath, (Armonk, NY: M. E. Sharpe, 2000) and Oleg V. Khlevniuk, *The History of the Gulag: From Collectivization to the Great Terror* (New Haven: Yale University Press, 2004) .

The fact that German nationals were amongst those rounded up and some were accused and executed for alleged treasonous activity with Japan or with Germany and Poland prompted Khlevniuk and a number of other historians to emphasize that the purges also were an attempt by the Soviet government to eliminate internal threats as foreign invasion loomed. (Klevniuk, *The History of the Gulag*: 145.) During the thaws that took place in the administration of Nikita Sergeevich Khrushchev, some camp inmates were allowed to leave and individuals could write prosecutors' offices to find out the fate of their relatives. Professor El'vira Yershova of Moscow State Administrative University did so. Some of her relatives who perished in 1938 were said to be Chinese and Japanese spies. Copies of court documents are in my possession. See also her published account, "Sem'ia v vospominaniiakh rodnykh," from "XX vek v sud'bakh rossiiskoi provin-tsial'noi sem'i," in *INFOR "Veter vremeni": Materialy k pokolennym rospisiam rossiiskikh rodov Ural*, No. 1(June 2005): 17, 23. Information on the exile to the camps for those who had served in the Spanish Civil War from Vladimir Binevich, Lectures and interviews (Denver, 2004/ 2005). It ought to be noted that these slave labor camps were hotbeds of typhus and other diseases. (Ibid.: 172, 176)

5. Document No. 13: "Postanova zagal'nikh zboriv oseredku KP(b)U Aptekoupravlinnia ukraini u spravi zaareshtovanogo NKVS URSR direktora APTU S. I. Pel'tsa, 26 lipnia 1937 r.," in M. L. Siatinia, *Istoriia farmatsii*: 395-399; Document No. 16, "Protokol dopitu v NKVS URSR kolishn'ogo nachal'nika aptekoupravlinnia ukraini S. I. Pel'tsa, 11 kvitnia 1938 r.," ibid.: 401-403; and Document No. 17, "Visnovki komisii shchodo materialiv viluchenikh shd chas areshtu u kolishn'ogo nachal'nika aptekoupravlinnia ukraini S. I. Pel'tsa, 4 lipnia 1938 r.," ibid.: 404-407. For information on the Factory Pharmacies see Mary Schaeffer Conroy, *The Soviet Pharmaceutical Business During Its First Two Decades, 1917-1937*: 180-181.

6. V. K. Afanas'ev et al, *Zhivi, "Akrikhin"!* (Staraia Kupavna, 1996): 32.

7. For details see Conroy, *The Soviet Pharmaceutical Business During Its First Two Decades*: 239-242.

8. For details on this first phase of the Japanese-Soviet conflict, see David J. Dallin, *Soviet Russia and the Far East* (First published, New Haven: Yale University Press, 1948; reprint, Archon Books, 1971): 16- 39. Dallin assesses the August 1939 battles with the Japanese in Khalkin-gol as "bloody." The Japanese lost 18,000 men; Dallin believes the Russians lost fewer. Newer sources ascribe more losses to the Russians. On the conflict between Japan and Russia see also David R. Stone, *Hammer and Rifle: The Militarization of the Soviet Union 1926-1933.* (Lawrence: University Press of Kansas, 2000): 43-49 and Tsuyoshi Hasegawa, *Racing the Enemy: Stalin, Truman, and the Surrender of Japan* (Cambridge: Harvard University Press, 2005): 14.

9. Telephone interview with Oleg Kononenko (October 12, 1998).

10. Rimmington, "The Soviet Union's Offensive Program," in Wright, ed. *Biological Warfare and Disarmament: New Problems/New Perspectives*: 105-108, 121-122.

Secret bioweapons work later afforded post-Soviet researchers a contract with an American company. "American Biogenic Sciences Negotiates L. Anthrax and Smallpox Vaccine Agreement." November 26, 2001, 09:02:00 AM ET, US: MABA Recent Stock News: Investing-MSN Money. Accessed 2002. The American company has since folded.

11. G. Popov, "Osnovnye printsipy organizatsii mediko-sanitarnoi sluzhby naselennykh punktov i zadachi aptek i aptechnykh predpriiatii," *Farmatsiia i farmakologiia*, no. 1 (1938): 30-35.

12. Conroy, *The Soviet Pharmaceutical Business During Its First Two Decades*: 163-172.

13. For details see Conroy, ibid.: 187-254.

14. For details see ibid.: 173-186.

15. Conroy, ibid.: 11-73.

16. Conroy, ibid.: 215-252. On the Chimkent Santonin Factory see ibid.: 20-21, 60-61, 101-102, 124-125. On the difficulties of both the pre-Soviet and Soviet pharmaceutical industries in producing iodine see Mary Schaeffer Conroy, *In Health and In Sickness: Pharmacy, Pharmacists and the Pharmaceutical Industry in Late Imperial, Early Soviet Russia* (East European Monographs, 1994): 341-342 and Conroy, *The Soviet Pharmaceutical Business During Its First Two Decades*: 36-37 and passim. On clarification of the core industry's focus, see A. G. Natradze, *Ocherk razvitiia khimiko-farmatsevticheskoi promyshlennosti SSSR*: 139.

17. T. L. Petrishche, "Belmedtorg i lekarstvennoe obespechenie naseleniia BSSR v 1920-e gody," Vitebsk gosudarstvennyi meditsinskii universitet. Sent by the author via e-mail to this author (October 13, 2006).

18. Natradze, *Ocherk*: 141.

19. I. G. Stolkin, "O rabote mestnoi farmatsevticheskoi promyshlennosti," *Farmatsiia*, no. 3 (1938): 34.

20. Natradze, *Ocherk*: 139-141.

21. Stolkin, "O rabote," *Farmatsiia*, no. 3 (1938): 35-36.

22. Natradze, *Ocherk*: 141.

23. Conroy, *The Soviet Pharmaceutical Business*: 116-121.

24. Natradze, *Ocherk*: 139.

25. Russian State Archive of the Economy (hereafter cited RGAE), fond 8009, opis 2, delo 3, listy 7-8 (hereafter cited "f.," "op.," "d.," "l.," or "ll.,"). Pantotsid tablets would be used to purify water during the Great Patriotic War. Cited in F. G. Krotkov, "Vodosnabzhenie voisk Sovetskoi Armii," in Smirnov, gen. ed., *Opyt sovetskoi meditsiny v Velikoi Otechestvennoi Voine, 1941-45 gg.*, (Moscow: Medgiz, vol. 33, 1955): 95-96.

26. Moscow, February 21, 1938, "The Market in the Soviet Union for Dental, Surgical, Medical, and Hospital Equipment, Apparatus, and Supplies," in National Archives United States of America [hereafter cited NAUSA] RG 489, Box 82, 11,100, Bureau of Foreign and Domestic Commerce [hereafter cited BFDC], U. S. Dept. of Commerce.

27. Information first cited by Andreev, Darskii (Khar'kov, 1998): 164-165 as quoted and graphed in "Mifi i real'nosti sovetskogo zdravookhraneniia," Chapter 15, "Epidemiologicheskii perekhod" in Anatoli Vishnevskii, ed., *Demograficheskaia modernizatsiia Rossii, 1900-2000*: 264-265. Full discussion of issue, ibid.: 259-265.

28. See Mary Schaeffer Conroy, "Malaria in Late Tsarist Russia," *Bulletin of the History of Medicine*, vol. 56, no. 1 (1982): 41-55.

29. Christopher Kobrak, *National Cultures and International Competition: The Experience of Schering AG, 1851-1950* (Cambridge University Press, 2002): 157, 259.

30. "Pervaia vsesoiuznaia konferentsiia farmakologov i toksikologov, 1-5 iunia 1937 g.," *Farmakologiia*, vol. 1, no. 1 (1938): 84-85.

31. RGAE, f. 8009, op. 2, d. 3, ll. 5, 34, 35, 37, 38, 40, 41, 43, 89. The shortfalls of raw materials, in absolute amounts, were 430 tons of phenol required and 308 tons received; 2,600 tons of bisulfate required and 1,843 tons received; 12,000 tons of sulfuric acid called for and only 9,680 received; 340 tons of salicylic acid expected and, mercifully, only slightly less—330 tons—received. The term "absence of a market" is ambiguous. This may have meant that pharmacy organizations which ordered for pharmacies were unable to pay for the product.

32. The importance of chloramine to prevent typhoid and dysentery during the Great

Patriotic War, that portion of World War II fought on Soviet soil, is discussed by Krotkov, "Vodosnabzhenie voisk Sovetskoi Armii," in Smirnov, gen. ed., *Opyt sovetskoi meditsiny v Velikoi Otchestvennoi Voine, 1941-1945 gg.*, vol. 33: 40.

33. See Chart below:

Raw Materials, Needed and Supplied, in tons, 1938

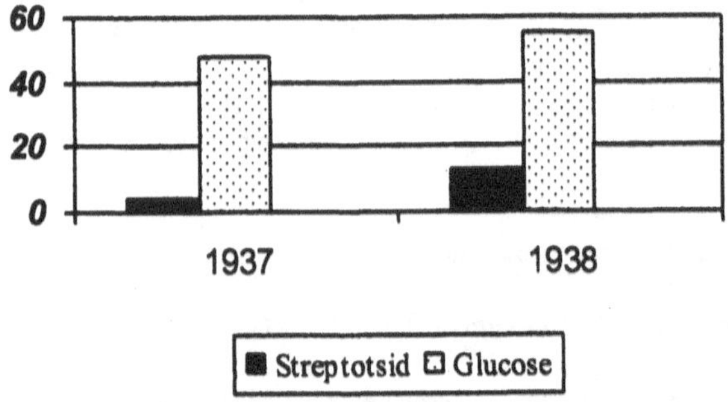

Source: RGAE. F. 8009, op. 2, d. 3, ll. 4, 39, 40.

34. RGAE, f. 8009, op. 2, d. 3, l. 5. The Stakhanovite Movement was one of the measures, employed by the Soviet Government in the 1930s, to increase worker productivity. It was named for a miner in the Donbass, Aleksei Stakhanov, who in 1935 mined an extraordinary amount of coal during his shift. He not only was held up as a model for other workers but campaigns were inaugurated to implement his achievement in other industries. Prizes were given to Stakhanovite workers and teams of workers. However, although the practice generated enthusiasm, Stakhanovite methods, as well as "storming" in the fourth quarter to fulfill the production plan, were very hard on machinery. One concise description of Stakhanov and the movement is provided by Martin McCauley, *The Soviet Union Since 1917* (London/New York: Longman, 1983): 81-82.

35. RGAE, f. 8009, op. 2, d. 3, l. 40.

36. RGAE, f. 8009, op. 2, d. 3, ll.49, 54, 55.

37. RGAE, f. 8009, op. 2, d. 3, ll. 77- 78.

38. RGAE, f. 8009, op. 2, d. 25, ll. 36-38.

39. RGAE, f. 8009, op. 2, d. 3, l. 53.

40. USSR Toilet Goods," *The American Perfumer and Essential Oil Review*, vol. 34, no. 2, (February 1937): 72.

41. *Khimicheskoe Delo v Rossii* (Odessa: Tipografiia "Poriadok," 1913), cols. 179-202. The firm was the Anan'iny and Arno Torgovii Dom, with branches in many Russian provinces. Col. 197.

42. Conroy, *The Soviet Pharmaceutical Business*: 39.

43. Conroy, ibid.:190-191.

44. "Ob"iasnitel'naia zapiska k balansu na 1 Oktiabria 1927 Gostrest TEZhE," RGAE, f. 8551, op. 1, d. 5, l. 4.

45. "Ob"iasnitel'naia zapiska k balansu na 1 Oktiabria 1927 Gostrest TEZhE," RGAE, f. 8551, op. 1, d. 5, ll. 1-4, 5, 6 ob., 15. See also Conroy, *The Soviet Pharmaceutical Business*: 191.

46. "Ob"iasnital'naia zapiska k promfinplan po trestu TEZhE za 1928/1929 gg.," RGAE, f. 8551, op. 1, d. 4, p. 2

47. Conroy, *The Soviet Pharmaceutical Business*: 192.

48. Conroy, ibid.: 193.

49. The additives involved clay and other materials. For details see Conroy, *The Soviet Pharmaceutical Business*: 193-194. Reprimand noted in a United Press Dispatch of 1932, according to "Trade Notes," *The American Perfumer and Essential Oil Review*, vol. 28, no. 12 (February 1934): 642.

50. "Ob"ianitel'naia zapiska . . . 1927 . . . ." RGAE, f. 8551, op. 1, d. 5, ll. 1, 4, 5 ob., 6, 13.

51. "Ob"iasnitel'naia zapiska . . . za 1928/1929 gg.," RGAE , f. 8551, op. 1, d. 4, pp. 2, 5.

52. Narkompishchprom Trest TEZhE. "Perechen' predstavliaemykh form godogo otcheta po osnovnoi deiatel'nosti za 1934," RGAE, 8551, op. 1, d. 11, pp. 1, 2, 4, 4 ob., 5, 6, 14 ob..

53. "U.S.S.R. Cosmetics," *Foreign Commerce Weekly:* Source: *Izvestiia* (November 28, 1940) NAUSA, RG 489, Box 82, 10,700, BFDC, U.S. Dept. of Commerce.

54. "USSR Toilet Goods," *The American Perfumer*, vol. 34, no. 2 (February 1937): 72.

55. "U.S.S.R. Cosmetics," *Foreign Commerce Weekly:* Source: *Izvestiia* (November 28, 1940) NAUSA, RG 489, Box 82, 10,700, BFDC, U. S. Dept. of Commerce.

56. "The Soviet Perfume Industry," *Izvestiia* (April 2, 1939) NAUSA, RG 489, Box 82, 10,700, BFDC, U. S. Dept. of Commerce.

57. "U.S.S.R. Cosmetics," *Izvestiia* (November 28, 1940) NAUSA, RG 489, Box 82, 10,700, BFDC, U. S. Dept. of Commerce.

58. "Trade Notes: Soviet Cosmetic Head Honored," *American Perfumer and Essential Oil Review*, vol. 28, no. 12 (February 1934): 642.

59. "Cosmetics and Perfumery in the U.S.S.R.," *Pravda* (November 24, 1936) NAUSA, RG 489, Box 82, 10,700, BFDC, U. S. Dept. of Commerce.

60. "News and Events," *The American Perfumer and Essential Oil Review*, vol. 32, no. 2 (February 1936): 67.

61. "News and Events," *The American Perfumer and Essential Oil Review*, vol. 32, no. 3 (March 1936): 75.

62. "USSR Toilet Goods," *The American Perfumer and Essential Oil Review*, vol. 34, no. 2 (February 1937): 74.

63. Conroy, *The Soviet Pharmaceutical Business*: 216.

64. G. S., "Ulushchit' nizovoi uchet i planirovanie," *Farmatsiia*, vol. 1, no. 4 (1938): 30-32.

65. "Aptechnoe delo: Uchet i planirovanie tovarooborota v aptekakh," ibid.: 33-35, 37-38.

66 Loc. Cit.: 6.

67. A. N. Sorokin, "Puty razvitiia farmatsevticheskoi promyshlennosti," *Farmatsiia*, vol. 3, no. 7-8 (1940): 9-10.

68. All information, since the last note, from RGAE, f. 8009, op. 2, d. 3, l. 2.

69. In a meeting on January 25, 1939, the *Upravlenie* of Khimfarmprom included

twenty-two men: Terent'ev, who served as chair, Kogan, Rabinovich, Kuvshinskii, Dmitriev, Makarenko, Prokushev, Berger, Maiorov, Petrov, Chaikovskii, Vinogradov, Cherkasov, Al'perovich, Fintiktikov, Forer, Mashbits, Vidrovich, Fil'kin, Sokolinskii, Avstreikh, Pinkhasik, and one woman—Turkovskaia. The representatives from the Sukharanskii Factory were Robert and Sarumov; from the Ramaninskii factory, Bekdamirov and Agaev; from the Iodo-Brom Biuro, Filippos'iants; from the Neftechalinsksii Factory, Tagiev and Panov. RGAE, f. 8009, op. 2, d. 3, l. 228.

70. RGAE, f. 8009, op. 2, d. 17, ll. 24-26 (1940).

71. "Rech' tov. Stalina na prieme v kremle rabotnikov vyshei shkoly 17 maia 1938 g.," *Farmatsiia*, vol. 1, no. 1-2 (1938): 1-2 and "K XXI godovshchine velikoi oktiabrskoi sotsialisticheskoi revoliutsii," ibid., no. 5: 1-3.

72. "Deistvitel'nost' sektsii farmakologii i toksikologii moskovskogo obshchestva fiziologov, farmakologov i biokhimikov po 21 dek. 1936 g. po 28 sent. 1938 g.," *Farmakologiia*, vol. 1, no. 2-3 (1938): 159-160. Defense work was part of the agenda for the society for 1938 and 1939. See also "Itogi XVIII s"ezda VKP (b) i nashi zadachi," *Farmakologiia i toksikologiia,* vol. 2, no. 2 (1939): 3-5.

The frequent discussions on the dangers of toxic industrial poisons in the pages of the journal reflected the new science of industrial hygiene. But ongoing references to the toxicity of paranitrochlorbenzol also appeared to have military implications. L. Z. Ponomareva-Astrakhantseva, "Deistviia paranitrokhlorbenzola na mocheotdelenie," *Farmakologiia,* vol. 1, no. 2-3 (1938): 84. The author was connected with the Institute of Hygiene of Labor and Professional Diseases in Leningrad. See also the section on General and Industrial Toxicology, in the Conference of Pharmacologists and Toxicologists, held in June 1937. "Vsesoiuznaia konferentsiia farmakologov i toksikologov, 1-5 iunia 1937 g.: Voprosy obshchei i promyshlennoi toksikologii," *Farmakologiia*, vol. 1, no. 2-3 (1938): 167-169.

Part II

The First Phase of World War II: 1939 to June 22, 1941

Chapter 2
War! Medical Hardware

By 1939 the Soviet Union was at war, albeit offensively—a phase that would last nearly two years. The first major battles occurred in the Far East. The Soviet Union and Japan were not official belligerents until August 1945. Nevertheless, the Red Army and Japanese forces were engaged in a major battle at Khalkin-gol, on the Mongolian-Manchurian border, in August 1939. According to David Dallin, Japanese losses "were stated in Tokyo to have exceeded 18,000." He estimated undisclosed Russian losses as "probably less" but "still significant."[1] Equally significant, future All-Union Minister of Health E. I. Smirnov recalled that the bloody Khalkhin-gol and Khasan Lake skirmishes served as a training ground for medical-surgical battlefield procedures that would be applied during the phase of World War II that racked Russia.[2]

On the heels of Khalkin-gol the Red Army became engaged in the west. The Ribbentrop-Molotov Pact, signed in late August 1939—nearly coincidentally with the fighting in the Far East—allowed the Soviet Union to recover territories on its western borders that it had lost after the First World War. On September 17, 1939, two weeks after Germany seized western Poland, the Soviet Union invaded eastern Poland. This military action restored Belorussian and Ukrainian territory that Poland had taken in1921, but required pacification of insubordinate and "hostile populations."[3] Next came the Winter War between Finland and the Soviet Union, lasting from November 1939 through March 1940. This trumped up conflict netted the Soviet Union Karelia and territory in the Far North but cost perhaps 25,000 men.[4] The so-called White-Finn War, as had Khalkin-gol, served as a training ground for battlefield medicine.[5]

The Finnish War in the west and Khalkhin-gol battles in the east, against Japan, highlighted defects in Soviet military medicine. E. I. Smirnov and other high-ranking physicians hurriedly tried to eliminate them, sensing that a larger conflagration was on the horizon. Both conflicts documented that the number of medical personnel and their training was woefully insufficient. Medical schools were producing only 49 percent of surgeons needed and, in turn, they had little knowledge if any of field surgery. More specialists in infectious diseases—epidemiologists, biologists—were required to determine what diseases were present and to assay supplies of food and water. Lower-level "disinfectors" were needed. An additional complication was that the majority of doctors, fel'dshers, and dentists were women, percentages being 63.5 percent, 84.5 percent, and 80 percent, respectively. The Soviet government intended to replace them as much as possible with men for battlefield medicine.[6] Women did serve as doctors and other medical personnel at the front during the Great Patriotic War, however.[7]

The method of giving blood transfusions had been perfected in 1937. However both the western and eastern theaters of war emphasized insufficiencies of many medical supplies and problems of distribution due to transportation lags and supply snags.[8]

Insufficiencies of medical personnel and medical/surgical supplies generated a myriad of plans in 1940/1941. Funding for the medical sector—apparently mainly for medical training and the medical instruments and equipment industries—was to be amplified from 421 million rubles in 1940 to 600 million rubles in 1941.[9] The medical curriculum was to increase the hours devoted to surgery and sanitation. Military academies existed in Leningrad and Moscow. Another was to be established in Kuibyshev[10] (and others subsequently were located in Kalinin—the former Tver'—and Samarkand, in the Uzbek SSR.)[11]

But obviously time was too short to train all the medics needed even though "quickie courses" were instituted. Thus, on the eve of the Great Patriotic War shortages of doctors in the Red Army amounted to 34.9 percent; dentists, 35.1 percent; fel'dshers, 36.3 percent; and pharmacists, 41.1 percent.[12] On the positive side, however, the medical command system in the Red Army was reorganized, the system of storage facilities and distribution were reorganized,[13] and the system of acquiring blood for transfusions and storing it was improved.

How did production of medical equipment and surgical instruments fare?

There was concerted effort to beef up output of ambulances from1939. At the Gorky Auto Plant "a modernized variant of the GAZ-AA with a motor GAZ-M" was produced. Called the GAZ-55, it "could carry 4 prone and 2 seated patients or 2 prone and 5 seated or 10 seated."

Its equipment was basic—"an air stove, operating on exhaust gases, and a ventilation system." The factory put out "more than 9 thousand . . . unfortunately not one of which remains." The BA-22, built "on the chassis of a truck "GAZ-AAA," was built to transport the wounded from the field of battle. Recommendations that the ambulance ride be smoother led to "placing layers of sand up to a thickness of some centimeters at the bottom of the body of the GAZ-AA and ZIS-5 and, above, straw or other soft material." "Special plank beds sometimes were fitted into the body" of this vehicle. "Medical autobuses" were "transformed" from regular city buses. Such was the ZIS-8, produced by the Moscow auto factory Aremkuz, and belonging in 1938 to the Moscow film studio, Mosfil'm. Existing city buses, model ZIS-16, were built on the chassis of the ZIS-5. In 1939 they were modified into the "medical autobus" called the ZIS-16S. These vehicles "could transport 10 prone and 10 seated patients" excluding places for the driver and the medic (*sanitar*). Other types of ambulances were produced, preserving the interior of those described above, but with more horsepower and amenities of a heater and ventilation windows.

Still, not enough ambulances were produced in the three-year prelude to the Great Patriotic War. As a result, during the war, most available ambulances were used at the front and civilian patients were transported to hospitals in ordinary trams, which also carried workers "to the factories."[14]

Nor were medical equipment and surgical instruments produced in sufficiency.

Eighteen factories located in Leningrad, Moscow *oblast'*, Gorky, Stalingrad, Kazan', Penza, Kiev, Mariupol, Odessa, and Molotov, in the Urals, produced medical-surgical instruments and pharmaceutical equipment for the Soviet Union. These entities were under the jurisdiction of a Glavk called Medinstrumentprom which was separate from Glavkhimfarmprom. In 1938 the American Embassy report had opined that the medical instruments' sector could benefit from more decentralized policy making and less autarky. Although the Soviet Union needed to import medical/surgical equipment, the embassy averred, "no individual medical institution or school in the U.S.S.R." was "authorized to purchase equipment abroad. . . .The official organization engaged in the sale and distribution of such equipment" was "SOYUZOBORUDOVANIE . . . subordinated to the People's Commissariat of Health" and it could block sales from American pharmaceutical companies.[15] But autonomy was out of the question.

Ominously, given what lay ahead, output of many key items like sterilizers and dryers, syringes, autoclaves, disinfecting chambers, and various surgical instruments and lamps "was lower in 1940 than in 1939." Additionally, many physical-therapy items were produced in lesser amounts than planned. Some were not produced at all. The reasons for the poor showing of factories in Medinstrumentprom were "insufficient materials and electrical energy, losses from *brak* or high rates of spoilage." The majority of factories defaulted on their contracts— "badly fulfilled contracts" was the terminology used in the report. Although this was partly due to lack of railway wagons rather than absolute production deficiencies, the factories were fined.[16]

In 1940, the medical instruments' industry developed some new processes.[17] This did not entirely offset the existing problems in Glavmedinstrumentprom factories, however.

Two modern historians of Soviet military medicine during World War II, using newly accessible Communist Party and government archival materials, praise the "growth of the chemical, chemical-pharmaceutical and medical-instruments industry [sic]."[18] In reality, these were three discrete industries, not one unified one. And in any case the historians admit that in 1940/1941 of ninety-six important medical items about thirty were available in amounts that were less than half of the established norms.[19] The items in short supply appeared to have been mainly x-ray equipment, operating equipment and bandages.[20] Bandages were produced by a factory in the pharmaceutical industry. The other items were put out by the medical/surgical industry.

The government stored pharmaceuticals for the military in a central warehouse and five district warehouses. In early 1941 there were 5,520 kilograms of glucose in the central warehouse and 2,553 kilograms of glucose in the five district warehouses. Additional amounts of glucose in ampules also were in storage. There were 4,000 kilograms of iodine in the central warehouse and 3,427 kilograms in the five district warehouses. The amount of ampules of morphia hydrochloride in the central warehouse amounted to 1,276.6 thousand; 1,032 thousand ampules were distributed in the five district warehouses. The central warehouse held 707 kilograms of Novocain with 124.4 kilograms in the five district warehouses. There were 4,019 kilograms of Streptotsid in the central warehouse and 3,201 kilograms in the district warehouses. It was not specified as to whether this was White Streptotsid or Red Streptotsid, which was highly toxic. The amounts of the Soviet Union's second major sulfa drug, Sul'fidin, were less at 316 kilograms and 145 kilograms, respectively. The ampules of chlorethyl in the central warehouse totaled 82.6 thousand; 121.3 thousand ampules of chlorethyl were in the district warehouses. There were 6.7 tons of narcotic ether in the central warehouse and 5.95 tons in the district warehouses. [21]

There also were some 12 million units (*shtuk*) of bandages and gauze in the central and district warehouses. But there were less than 40 million units of bandaging packets and less than 20 thousand syringes of various kinds.[22]

The medical and surgical instruments on hand were not sufficient for the military. And they were not sufficient for civilians. In 1941 a survey on "the condition of pharmacy matters" reported that "pharmacy vessels and items of care for the sick were insufficient or completely absent in the departments of the Chief Pharmaceutical Administration and also in the institutes of epidemiology and microbiology, depriving them of the possibility of normal work."[23]

In sum, the medical equipment and surgical instruments industry was not ready for war on Soviet Soil. What was the situation for the production of pharmaceuticals and vaccines and serums?

Notes

1. David J. Dallin, *Soviet Russia and the Far East* (Archon Books, 1971): 39. The Soviet Union and Japan signed a neutrality pact April 25, 1941, thus ending the problem of war in the Far East until the end of the war in Europe, in 1945. See Tsuyoshi Hasegawa, *Racing the Enemy: Stalin, Truman, and the Surrender of Japan* (Cambridge: Harvard University Press, 2005): 15 and passim.

2. For details see E. I. Smirnov, chief editor, *Opyt sovetskoi meditsiny v Velikoi Otechestvennoi Voine, 1941-1945* (Moscow: Medgiz, vol. 6, 1951): 19-21.

3. David E. Murphy, *What Stalin Knew: The Enigma of Barbarossa* (New Haven: Yale University Press, 2005): 29. Murphy notes that the locals "aided German intelligence in espionage operations before June 1941 and served as saboteur in the early hours and days of the [Great Patriotic] war, destroying Red Army communications and facilities."

4. Murphy, *What Stalin Knew*: 47-54.

5. Smirnov, *Opyt sovetskoi meditsiny v Velikoi Otechestvennoi Voine*, vol. 6, loc. cit.

6. Gladkikh and Loktev, *Sluzhba zdorov'ia*: 65, 68, 88-91.

7. Kazimiera J. Cottam, *Women in War and Resistance: Selected Biographies of Soviet Women Soldiers* (Nepean, Canada: New Military Publishing, 1998): 223-277.

8. Gladkikh and Loktev, *Sluzhba zdorov'ia*: 42.

9. Ibid.: 73.

10. Ibid.: 91-98.

11. Glantz, *Colossus*: 443.

12. Gladkikh and Loktev, *Sluzhba zdorov'ia*: 99.

13. Ibid.: 74-77.

14."Istoriia sanitarnykh avtomobilei Rossii i SSSR 1941-1945, http: // ambulances.ru/history_rus_41. shtml. Accessed 6/15/2006. I am very grateful to Professor Rustem Khaziev, Bashkortostan University, Ufa, for bringing this and other post-Soviet Russian language internet medical sites to my attention.

15. Moscow, February 21, 1938, "The Market in the Soviet Union for Dental, Surgical, Medical, and Hospital Equipment, Apparatus, and Supplies," in NAUSA, RG 489, Box 82, 11,100, BFDC, U. S. Dept. of Commerce.

16. Report of Medinstrumentprom for 1940, RGAE, f. 8009, op. 2, d. 123, ll. 2-4, 6-7, 17, 39, 39 ob., 40, 44-46, 60, 61 ob..

17. VNIKhFI, Report for 1940, RGAE, f. 8009, op. 2, d. 33, ll. 1-57.

18. Gladkikh and Loktev, *Sluzhba zdorov'ia*: 71.

19. Ibid.: 72.

20. Ibid.: 73.

21. Ibid.: 78-79.

22. Ibid.: 79.

23. State Archive of the Russian Federation [hereafter cited GARF], f. A 482, op. 51, d. 34, l. 6.

Chapter 3
Vaccines and Pharmaceuticals during the First Two Years of World War II

Soviet pharmacy specialists disparaged the pharmaceutical industry they found in eastern Poland, following Soviet invasion and annexation of the area in September 1939. Pharmacy specialists opined that in the "Western Ukrainian Provinces" the industry was "weakly developed." There was "a factory of patented and endocrine preparations, named Laocoon, and two or three *kustar'* (small-scale) galenical laboratories." However, firms in Warsaw—Speiss and Company, Klave, and others—or foreign firms supplied most medicines. Of course that was not a detriment while Poland was intact. Now, however, Warsaw was in German hands. But additionally, Soviet inspectors were disgusted by the enormous choice of "patented" medicines—"two or three thousand names"—that were being purveyed in the Western Provinces.[1]

Meanwhile, output and distribution of pharmaceuticals by Soviet pharmaceutical factories and output of vaccines, serums and antitoxins by Soviet institutes appeared to be problematical.

During the Winter War between the Soviet Union and Finland that broke out in November 1939 and was resolved by the Peace of Moscow in 1940, typhus, typhoid, paratyphus, dysentery, hemocolitis (or bacillary dysentery), and meningitis flared up amongst Soviet troops.[2] This might have signaled the Soviet Union's biological warfare program run amuck. An offensive biological weapons program had been established in 1928, according to foremost specialist Anthony Rimmington. "A wide range of agents, including plague, tularaemia, leprosy, foot-and-mouth disease, cholera, dysentery, typhus, paratyphoid, and tetanus were investigated both in the laboratory and in the field with a view to their use as offensive battlefield weapons."[3] Or the flare up might have been due to less sinister developments. Dysentery, marked by bloody diarrhea, is caused by amoebae or bacteria. Both agents "thrive in water contaminated by human feces." Amoebic dysentery is more a disease of the tropics. "Large outbreaks of bacillary dysentery," however, according to a contemporary health bulletin, "have occurred in communities where sewerage mixes with drinking water. Fruits and vegetables grown with contaminated water" also can cause the disease and it can be spread through poor hygiene—failure to wash hands after using the toilet.[4] The water in Leningrad was contaminated with the parasite Giardia as late as the 1990s. Typhoid also is spread through contaminated food and water. Thus, outbreaks of these two diseases indicated inadequate amounts of or inadequate use of hand soap, detergent, iodine to purify drinking water, and bleach. The prevalence of dysentery further pointed to inadequate administration of vaccines, available either in liquid form, tablet form or by subcutaneous injections and lack of bacteriophages, which were used in the 1940s against dysentery. Similarly, the prevalence of typhoid and paratyphus A and B pointed to inadequate inoculation against these diseases.[5] Additionally, it would appear that there were inadequate amounts of sulfa drugs, used to treat dysentery in the 1940s. Outbreaks of typhus, meanwhile, signaled insufficient amounts of the antiparasite soap, "Preparation K"; "antipedikulin"; and "piretrum" powder, all of which were used to counter the disease at that time.[6]

Touting a death rate from disease and wounds of 5 to 6 percent among Soviet troops and in the front regions during the Finnish War compared to losses "up to 11 percent"[7] among Russian and foreign troops during World War I, as a recent post-Soviet history does, is ridiculous, given the fact that World War I lasted three years for Russia and four years for foreign armies, that fighting took place over extremely long fronts, far from supply bases, and that far more population movements occurred, whereas the Finnish War lasted about four months and was fought close to Leningrad where there were major pharmaceutical factories and institutes.

Still, matters were not as bad for the Red Army as for civilians. Authorities were alarmed by serious defects in health care in the city of Leningrad in 1940. Early in the year the head of the Leningrad Health Department chastised the "medical profession" for not "reducing gastrointestinal diseases and infant pneumonia" in hospital wards and not providing proper inoculation "against diphtheria for children." The authorities attributed these failures to the fact that "'a large part of the medical team had been sent to serve the front in the last quarter of 1939 and the first half of 1940'," to "the poor discipline of medical workers [and their] "lack of clear guidance from the City Health Department," and to "the aloofness of research institutes from the practical needs of urban health care." Health authorities more accurately attributed the infestations of lice (which spread typhus) among the population of Leningrad to crowded living quarters and outbreaks of typhoid to the "unsatisfactory sanitary condition of the city." The last involved "inadequate capacity of the drainage system and piped water," "the shortcomings of the refuse-clearing and cleaning system," "unpackaged foodstuffs" sold on the street, and "the state of many canteens."[8]

Nowhere did health authorities mention that outbreaks of gastrointestinal diseases, pneumonia, typhus and typhoid might be due to lack of vaccines, serums and antitoxins and lack of soap, disinfectants, and sulfa drugs—in other words inadequacies in the institutes that produced the vaccines and antitoxins and deficiencies in the Soviet pharmaceutical industry. For, although nurses were needed in the neonatal wards to monitor the babies and although vaccinators, inspectors and sanitary workers also were needed, the kindest, best educated, best directed medical personnel require wherewithal to prevent and treat disease.

Indeed, Leningrad was not the only area affected by serious infectious diseases nor could the onus be put on disruption of personnel and supplies due to the Winter War. In the early 1940s, Soviet epidemiologists E. M. Ravikovich and O. E. Mayerman lamented the outbreaks of diphtheria and scarlatina among children in Soviet cities, noting that these had begun in 1938—well before the Winter War. They reached a peak in 1939 and 1940—in areas other than Leningrad.[9]

Dysentery also was a terrible scourge in the Soviet Union from the second half of the 1930s, propelling the epidemiological section of the All-Union Institute of Experimental Medicine to hold a conference on the subject in May, 1940.[10] Dysentery usually attacked in the summer months.[11] But in the Soviet Union between 1935 and 1939, a new type, "winter-spring" dysentery had become alarmingly prevalent and pernicious among children younger than three years of age and, more specifically, among infants in their first year. E. M. Rabinovich, from the Moscow City Bacteriological Institute, reported that 40 to 45 percent of those sick with dysentery were children younger than three. Tragically, their death rate was 85 percent. He urged that medics investigate another type of vaccine and apply bacteriophage therapy.[12]

Military physician V. K. Kirsenko advocated a two-pronged approach to prevent bacillary dysentery in 1940—vaccine, given by mouth, and "sanitary, hygienic measures." He provided case studies of young adult males in the military in 1934 and 1938 to prove the efficacy of these measures. When vaccination was not effective, Kirsenko opined that it was because of "inexact . . . or poor quality vaccination." But in general vaccination resulted in three to four times fewer cases in the cohort studied in 1938.[13] At the same time military physician V. Skvortsov recommended a three-pronged approach to eradicate dysentery—vaccination, also in tablet form and sanitary-hygienic measures to prevent the disease and bacteriophages for treatment. He claimed that the effects of vaccination lasted only two and a half to three or at the utmost four months. Thus it was necessary to isolate those stricken with dysentery and administer bacteriophages to them every four hours.[14] Skvortsov did not elaborate on the sanitary-hygienic measures to be used. However, in the 1930s and 1940 they involved water filtration and disinfectants such as iodine and chlorine.

On the basis of clinical studies in 1940 and 1941, military physician G. I. Samokhin maintained that the new sulfa drug, Sul'fidin, given in a mild dose every four hours for the first day and in a heavier dose the next two days, was the quickest, most effective therapy for those with dysentery. Additionally, he noted the importance of a near "starvation" diet—tea with sugar, bullion, and *kisel* (a starchy jelly)—for two days and then a normal diet that included "grey, Red Army bread."[15]

As for pneumonia in the infant wards, it is common in hospitals. It can be caused by viruses, by bacteria—either internal or external microbes in food, water and air, or by fungi. Bacteria or viruses normally present in the body are usually defeated in persons with a healthy immune system but in individuals in a weakened state they can lodge in the lungs, causing pneumonia. In Leningrad, in 1940, specialists attributed pneumonia in the infant wards to cold and also to the babies being in a weakened state due to early weaning. Liquid vitamins and infant formula could have helped (though admittedly the last depended upon clean water) so obviously these items were lacking. Additionally, it appeared that there were shortages of sulfa drugs, which were used to treat bacterial pneumonia in 1940. Discovered by the German researcher Gerhard Domagk in 1932, sulfa drugs were commonly applied in France, England and the United States against diseases caused by bacteria in 1937.[16] It is true that there were many different kinds of sulfa drugs, that not all sulfa drugs were equally effective, as a later chapter discusses in more detail, and that sulfa drugs may not have been appropriate for infants. Moreover, there was no surety that the pneumonia in Leningrad was the bacterial form. In cases of viral pneumonia, in the 1930s and 1940s, patients were treated with warmth, vaporizers and popular remedies—expectorants containing licorice, black cherry bark, raw onions, and honey. In fact, these remedies are still used today. But since it was difficult to ascertain the etiology of pneumonia, sulfa drugs often were administered lest the pneumonia be bacterial.[17] All these remedies could have been applied to the babies in Leningrad and the spread of pneumonia could have been countered with soap and disinfectants. That these measures were not taken suggested a dearth of simpler medicaments as well as state-of-the-art ones in Leningrad in 1939 and 1940.

That this was the case is proven by the fact that in December 1940 along with better heat in the hospital wards "3,000 hot water bottles," "123 incubators," and "supplies of sulfanilamides" were sent to Leningrad, alleviating gastrointestinal diseases and pneumonia among infants.[18] But this occurred some six months after the problem had first surfaced and nearly nine months after the end of the Winter War. Why had it taken so long?

The Soviet government's response to the flare up in infectious diseases, judging by an account of V. S. Chetverikov, was typical of bureaucrats and especially typical of Soviet bureaucrats. By decrees and threats, the Soviet government attempted to increase the number of qualified physicians involved with sanitary and antiepidemic work.

For example, in March 1940 a *Prikaz* of the USSR People's Commissariat of Health "established the post of state sanitary inspector (*gossaninspektor*) of a union republic [SSR], ASSR (Autonomous republic or subdivision of an SSR), *krai* (region), *oblast'*, and city." It was ordained that to this post could "only be appointed medical workers with higher education." Since a high level of training was a criterion, special courses were established in *medvuzy* (medical schools on the community college level) and in higher-level medical schools to prepare individuals for the new position. Additionally, physicians were drafted to fill the new posts—3,976 between 1938 and 1940 and 1,500 in 1941. Nevertheless, individuals involved in "sanitary work" lagged. Although the general number of physicians increased by 22,000 between 1936 and 1940, the number of "'sanitary' doctors remained without change, since a significant number of them voluntarily or by decision of organs of health protection transferred to clinics and administrative work." Obviously, the post was unattractive. For officials, the solution was to issue more decrees. *Prikaz* No. 104 of March 12, 1941, "suggested" to the health departments of union republics "to return to sanitary and anti-epidemic work all doctors finishing sanitary-hygiene studies . . . and clinical studies" or those on their way to finishing medical studies. This netted one hundred doctors. Additionally, firing, appointment and transfer of local state sanitary inspectors now required the agreement of people's commissars for health of the union republic. Two assistants were provided for each sanitary inspector—totaling around 300,000 people. Unfortunately, local authorities continued to undermine the central government's project. Despite the fact that the post of sanitary inspector was approved in local budgets, many officials at the *oblast'* and *raion* (district) levels of the union republics did not make the requisite appointments and thus many sanitary inspector posts remained vacant.[19]

But, in any case, although beefing up personnel reflected good intent, what was needed, in addition was an adequate supply of vaccines, antitoxins, phages, and pharmaceuticals. What was the situation in the agencies that produced these products?

Vaccines, Antitoxins and Bacteriophages

Soviet institutes had long produced antitoxins for diphtheria and scarlatina, a divaccine against typhoid, a vaccine against typhus and dysentery, and had recently developed bacteriophages—viruses bred to attack bacteria that are discussed at length in chapter 5. In 1940 there were eight such institutes. Obviously they were not producing the preventative items in sufficiency. The Ufa Bacteriological Institute was not representative of all the institutes. Problems in the Ufa Institute, however, go far to explaining the shortages of vaccines, antitoxins and bacteriophages in Leningrad and elsewhere.

The Ufa Bacteriological Institute supplied vaccines, serums, antitoxins, and bacteriophages to Moscow as well as to the new steel city, Magnitogorsk, situated in the Urals, and to Kuibyshev *oblast'*, the former Samara, situated on the middle Volga River, both of which were in closer proximity.[20] In 1938 the Ufa Bacteriological Institute had ten departments. In one report the Institute proclaimed that in 1938 it had "partially fabricated" dysentery vaccine, typhoid divaccine and bacteriophages in excess of the amount ordained by the Production Plan, which presumably was based on need, and had stored these products in a warehouse. Five hundred thirty-nine liters of diphtheria antitoxin were said to have been "partially fabricated," compared with 450 liters ordained by the plan, and 146 liters had been turned over to the warehouse.[21] In its Annual Report for 1938, though, the Institute admitted that a "whole range of preparations" in the Production Plan were not fulfilled. Diphtheria "anatoxin" was entirely not prepared in 1938; the production of bacteriophages was "late"; the quota for measles vaccine was "severely unfulfilled" —only 69.6 percent required by the Plan was produced. The plan for scarlatina antitoxin was fulfilled only 44.7 percent.[22]

Matters did not improve noticeably in 1939. Director of Production Kritskin's report for the first half of 1939 detailed the reasons for the shortages. The "plan for putting out the serums was not fulfilled . . . because of . . . [problems with] horses, absence of cadres (the serum department needed six doctors instead of three), and absence of a whole range of ancillary items . . . ampules . . . agar . . . caustic soda . . . notwithstanding prolonged requests in 1939 did not arrive." White mice also were lacking. The poor quality of the glass ampules on hand—50 percent were broken after transport and washing—thwarted production and distribution. Lack of forage for horses, in turn due to lack of funds, prevented immunizing them in "hard frost." Putting the Production Department on *khozraschet* was harmful financially and the institute also was deprived of necessary turnover monies (*oborotnye sredstva*).[23] More specifically, *brak* (spoilage) prevented fulfillment of plan targets for dysentery vaccine and bacteriophages. "The plan for scarlatina antitoxin was not fulfilled because of insufficient cadres. The diphtheria antitoxin plan was not fulfilled because of absence of a doctor in January", that specialist being "on a business trip (*kommandirovka*), and because of insufficiency of turnover monies."[24]

The Institute's problems continued in 1940. Director of Production Boichuk's report for the first quarter of the year detailed his achievements and also the challenges he faced. There was a "surplus" of scarlatina serum or antitoxin and "deliveries proceeded . . . according to requirements. The smallpox plan was fulfilled, a surplus [of half a million doses] being in the warehouse." However, "the plan for [typhoid] divaccine was not fulfilled" in the first half of the year "because of absence of chemically pure salt." The first half-year plan for dysentery vaccine was not fulfilled. Nevertheless, "the plan of deliveries was guaranteed, but in view of the Bashnarkomzdrav's [the Bashkir Commissariat of Health's] refusal of 1,215 liters, this amount remained in the warehouse of the Production Department." Additionally, there were "200 million AE doses" of dysentery serum in the warehouse. But, the bacteriophage plan was not fulfilled because "in the first quarter the Control Institute delayed its answer [to methods of production] for a long time." A "lack of guinea pigs" also contributed to nonfulfillment of the bacteriophage plan.[25]

The Institute obviously faced grave difficulties. Boichuk complained bitterly to the director of the Institute about the physical conditions in the Production Department. The "little" boiler in the unit did not produce a sufficient amount of steam and also "could result in *brak* since it was difficult to sterilize it." Deliveries of firewood were inadequate "in the absence of transport." The "vertical autoclave frequently needed to be repaired." "Lack of fully reliable autoclaves" for sterilizing [typhoid] divaccine, in fact had resulted in *brak* of this product to the amount of 270 liters. Quarantine quarters for the animals were lacking. The bookkeeping was "bad," "notwithstanding frequent requests to the Chief Bookkeeper of the Institute about verification." In conclusion, a weary Boichuk requested that if these matters were not resolved, "I ask to be freed from the post I occupy."[26]

He did leave that post, if not the Institute, because his successor signed reports for the second half of 1940. But that did not solve the Institute's problems. In the third quarter of the year the plan for smallpox vaccine was not fulfilled because of *brak* of over 641,000 doses. During that same third quarter only 9 percent of the plan for scarlatina antitoxin was fulfilled, only 60 percent of smallpox detrit was acquired, only 39 percent of divaccine was produced and, in addition, *brak* of divaccine occurred because of poor sterilization. This was due, in turn, to "absence of fully workable autoclaves."[27] On the last matter, one of the directors, Kniss-Plotnikov complained to the Russian Republic Commissariat of Health—on a little piece of brown paper—that a Commission had recommended a new autoclave and the Institute had "requested it from the Russian Commissariat of Health in the second quarter, but it had not been received. We ask you to send us the autoclave," he finished plaintively.[28]

By the end of 1940 the Institute registered both "fulfillment and overfulfillment" of some quotas but underfulfillment of other targets. In the third quarter, most successful was the production of typhus vaccine at 142 percent of Narkomzdrav's requirement and 76 percent of the Bacteriological Institute's requirement. The target for Gonovaccine was fulfilled at a little over 53 percent. However, the plan for whooping cough vaccine of both the Commissariat of Health and the Institute was fulfilled at only about 26 percent during the third quarter. Output of diphtheria anatoxin was fulfilled at a little over 87 percent for both plans, for that quarter.[29] This product did not reach its targets due to *brak*, absence of guinea pigs, and repair of the autoclaves.[30] The plan for scarlatina antitoxin was fulfilled at only 9 percent for the entire year. This was said to be of no consequence, however, because of "availability in the warehouse of the prepared product." At the end of 1940 the target for production of smallpox *detrit* remained fulfilled at 60 percent. While 641,000 doses had been spoiled during the first half of 1940, by the third quarter the number of doses had risen to 947,000.[31]

The Ufa Bacteriological Institute's failure to reach targets impacted public health negatively. Early in 1941 the Director of the Maternity Home in Kirov *raion*, the district where the giant steel plant Magnitogorsk was located, notified the Ufa Bacteriological Institute that "because of the absence of vaccine . . . newborns did not receive injections. On December 20, 1940, a communiqué had been sent by water to the director of the lab" including a "project of the contract for all of 1941. However, as yet there has been no answer." The communiqué was signed by

"Grinkevich, Chief Doctor of the *Roddom* (Maternity Home)."[32] The contract for 1941 between the Maternity Home in Kirov and the Ufa Bacteriological Institute for 4,800 to 5,000 doses of vaccines was finally concluded with the stipulation that "The Laboratory is obliged to send good-quality vaccine and without interruption—except for delays occasioned by hold-ups en route for which the laboratory cannot be responsible. The Maternity Home agreed to pay the shipping costs.[33] A complaint from another customer to the Ufa Bacteriological Institute—asking that there be "sent at once (*srochno*) diphtheria antitoxin" and other items— was written on green paper with purple ink.[34] Several disputes regarding payment for or holdups in the supply of vaccines and antitoxins as stipulated in contracts between the Ufa Bacteriological Institute and agents receiving its preparations were settled by *arbitrazh* (arbitration) in February 1941.[35] As for diphtheria and scarlatina, according to the general epidemiology report, these diseases did not disappear in the Soviet Union as a whole, although they began to subside by 1941, due to a concerted inoculation campaign. Thus matters must have improved.[36]

Pharmaceuticals

The upsurge in major infectious diseases also pointed to problems in the production and distribution of pharmaceuticals.

Stockpiling pharmaceuticals for the military might have shorted civilians. Little heed was paid to medical care for the tens of thousands of citizens of the Baltic States deported to Russia in the summer of 1940 after the Soviet Union annexed these countries.[37] Similarly neglected were the two million Poles shipped to the Soviet Arctic to toil in timber-felling camps,[38] despite the fact that such wholesale transports must have affected disease patterns. However, the Soviet government was concerned about the needs of the Red Army. The Plenum of the All-Union Vitamin Committee, which met in Moscow from October 11 through December 13, 1940, insisted on increasing vitamins for Red Army kits.[39] Articles on the toxicity of poisonous dust and chemicals peppered the pages of *Farmakologiia i toksikologiia* (Pharmacology and Toxicology) in 1940. Ostensibly the new science of industrial hygiene was being addressed but findings in this area also were germane to poison gases and pollutants from chemical warfare.[40] Medical supplies and pharmaceuticals, thus, were stored for the military.

This partially explained shortages for civilians. But what explained shortages for the troops?

Soviet versus German R&D

Soviet pharmaceutical research and development was *not* a problem. Soviet research and development was derivative. However, Soviet pharmaceutical scientists ably cloned German medicines, thus keeping pace with the German pharmaceutical industry. This was important because, despite the flight of Jewish scientists from Germany in the 1930s, German science continued to be first class.

Indeed, Hitler's regime brought positives as well as negatives to the German pharmaceutical industry. And the negatives never forced the German pharmaceutical industry to its knees. According to John E. Lesch, I. G. Farben, a conglomerate of Bayer, Hoechst, and three other enterprises, chafed at the National Socialists' prohibition on the use of animals in drug research, insistence on the benefits of folk medicine as opposed to chemotherapy, and requirement that the company submit applications to the government in case the product or the patent fell under the rubric of a biological weapon or state secret.[41] Gerhard Domagk one of the discoverers of Prontosil was not allowed to receive the Nobel Prize in 1939 and, moreover, was roughed up by the Gestapo and put in jail.[42] Farben also had to contend with competition from British and French pharmaceutical houses.[43] After 1939, with Germany at war, Farben's lab at Elberfeld suffered shortages of mice.[44] Nevertheless, Farben continued to do research on and produced many sulfa drugs, such as Streptozon (Prontosil Soluble) in 1933, and in 1937, Uliron, a drug against anaerobic bacteria that caused gas gangrene—partly because of the adroitness of a leading chemist and Farben director Heinrich Hörlein, who joined the Nazi party to protect the conglomerate from Nazi micromanagement.[45]

Christopher Kobrak, chronicles the financial hardships imposed on the German pharmaceutical company Schering because of Nazi insistence on high taxes, curtailment of overtime work, demands for hiring the unemployed, "restrictive dividend and investment laws," and limitations on "the export and foreign exchange allocation system." But he also emphasizes that Schering remained autonomous under the Nazis.[46]

Further, the Hitler regime subsidized and promoted German scientific research, including medical research, Richard J. Evans, an authority on the Third Reich, notes. Although the Nazi government meddled in German pharmaceutical companies to some extent, they were not expropriated. Nor was the German pharmaceutical industry cramped financially, curtailed by limited imports and excessive exports, forced to make do with obsolete equipment and insufficient reagents, and buffeted by purges, as was the Soviet pharmaceutical industry in the 1920s and 1930s. Indeed, Evans notes that "[M]edicine and biology benefited from the Nazis' encouragement in areas such as the improvement of crop yields, chemical fertilizers and synthetic fuels . . . government-funded research institutes and company research and development departments . . . continued to pioneer many scientific and technological innovations under the Third Reich." In addition to the discovery of " nuclear fission by Otto Hahn and Lise Mittner in 1938"[47] —never mind that Lise Mittner subsequently was forced to correspond with Otto Hahn from her safe haven in Norway[48]—German scientists invented a dizzying array of "technological developments like the jet propulsion engine, electron microscopes and the electronic computer . . . cold-steel extrusion, aerial infrared photography, power circuit breakers, tape recorders, x-ray tubes, colour film processing, diesel motors and intercontinental ballistic missiles"—and "important drugs like methadone and Demerol, and the nerve gas, sarin."[49]

The Soviets themselves acknowledged German technical superiority with full page advertisements of state-of-the-art German equipment in their chief pharmaceutical publications. In 1937 *Farmatsiia i farmakologiia* and in 1939 *Farmatsiia* portrayed shiny German machines, trumpeting them as "Machines for preparing salves. . . .Presses for preparing tablets . . . suppositories" and "Forms for . . . suppositories" and "lip pomades" from the "Factory of pharmaceutical machines" of "Robert Liebau, Chemnitz (Germany)" and a machine—"New [in]1937"—for making ampules from "Deutsche Rotawerke, Aachen (Germany)." The latter made "from 600 to 900" ampules "of all normal degrees and forms in an hour."[50]

But, by the late 1930s, Soviet pharmacologists could point to achievements of their own. Some were fairly prosaic but others constituted major breakthroughs. For example, in 1939, the Red Star Factory in Khar'kov modified its method of making benzolsulfuric acid, which "eliminated the poisoning of workers."[51] More importantly, in the core pharmaceutical industry as a whole, eighteen new drugs appeared, including the anesthetic Sovkain; ascorbic acid, and two new sulfa drugs, Sul'fidin and Bakteriotsid.[52]

The All-Union Vitamin Institute, the All-Union Institute of Experimental Medicine, All-Union Food Institute of Narkomzdrav, and USSR Institute of Food concentrated on mass-production of vitamins. Professor A. V. Lavrov, of the All-Union Scientific-Research Pharmaceutical-Chemical Institute (VNIKhFI), which was part of the core pharmaceutical industry, Khimfarmprom/Glavkhimfarmprom in Moscow, reported on the synthesis of Vitamin B1 or Thiamin, which had been synthesized four years earlier by foreign researchers. Other researchers worked on deriving Vitamin C from sweetbriar, on combining ascorbic acid with Rivanol, combining Vitamin C with Riboflavin or Vitamin B2, on Vitamin E, and on extracting keratin from carrots.[53] VNIKhFI scientists synthesized Vitamin K, prevention for hemorrhaging—crucial in front-line medical care—and Vitamin B6 and Vitamin E. The institute also synthesized nicotine acid, for treatment of pellagra, a chronic disease caused by niacin deficiency, the symptoms of which were skin eruptions, digestive and nervous disturbances, and eventual mental deterioration, and Anal'gin, deemed equal to Pyramidon in clinical tests for its antipyretic, analgesic, and anti-inflammatory properties. The Institute also developed a new psychiatric drug, Fenamin[54] and synthesized a new therapy to combat tuberculosis, a combination of gold and calcium dubbed "Krezanol." Although this product appeared bizarre, according to reports, "[T]ests in the Tuberculosis Institute showed it was not inferior to analogous foreign preparations."[55] Finally, VNIKhFI improved processes for making some medicines, using substitutes for *defitsit* materials.[56] The Soviet pharmaceutical industry was used to shortages and the need for import substitutes.

In wartime, methods to skirt deficits and, of course, vitamins could make the difference between life and death on a large scale.[57]

Very interesting and important for both wartime and peacetime medicine was the refining of an antiviral by a Doctor Fal'kovich, who had originally developed it in the Mechnikov Institute nearly ten years earlier. Although called an antiviral, Fal'kovich's remedy appeared an analogue to Streptomycin, derived by Selman Waksman of Rutgers University from soil organisms in 1943. Streptomycin combated certain types of streptococcus, staphylococcus, and other bacterial diseases resistant to sulfa drugs (and later to penicillin), such as tuberculosis, pneumonia, typhoid fever, infections of the urinary passage, dysentery, undulant fever, and gangrene—although in due time bacteria also developed resistance to Streptomycin and it was reserved for the treatment of tuberculosis. Coincidentally, its discoverer, Waksman, was a Russian immigrant whose real given name was Abraham. The development of Streptomycin had begun with one of his students in 1939 and was moved along by his own discovery of actinomycin, a peptide antibiotic, in 1940.[58] Fal'kovich's remedy, though an antiviral, was derived from staphylococci put in a peptone bullion, and after ten days, filtered through an infusion of earth and then through porcelain. The residue was again mixed with staphylococci and again filtered after a ten day period. The liquid, containing a "substance as yet unknown," inhibited the growth of staphylococci and also "other microbes, for example, streptococci." Ten to twelve drops of the remedy, given three times a day by a medical sister or even the patient, attacked grippe. The drops could also be given as a "prophylactic to combat grippe"—that is, a sort of "flu shot."[59]

Malaria was debilitating and one form that circulated in the Soviet Union—*plasmodium falciparum*—was fatal. Russia's main communicable disease in imperial times, malaria had reached epidemic proportions during and after the civil war, the last war on Soviet soil. Three new antimalarials appeared in 1940. Two, "Khinolin-52"and "Khinolin-60"were developed by VNIKhFI and one by the USSR Academy of Sciences, "Khinolin L-28."[60]

Anemia was a serious health threat world wide. In the 1920s The Eli Lilly pharmaceutical firm in Indianapolis, Indiana, had been spurred to produce liver extracts because the wife of the owner of the company, Josiah K. Lilly, had pernicious anemia.[61] Realizing that anemia would be especially problematical in wartime, in 1939 the Kirov Meat-Processing Plant in Leningrad produced "Ferro-Hematogen," which "showed good results in treating anemia."[62] Hematogen also was put out by the Voroshilovgrad Meat-Processing Plant.[63]

The medical historian John E. Lesch considers sulfa drugs "The First Miracle Drugs." The Soviet pharmaceutical industry had developed a sulfa drug named Streptotsid in 1937. It was produced in the Semashko Factory in Moscow. There was both a white and a red version. White Streptotsid was particularly effective against gonorrhea.[64] A number of new sulfa drugs or new methods of producing old ones appeared in the period 1939 to 1941. The Organic Chemistry Department at the Leningrad Pharmaceutical Institute developed a combination of White Streptotsid and Urotropin (a former Schering specific), named "Strepturin," which was said to be identical to a product sold in Germany under the name "Septurit." The foreign version had been described in an Austrian patent, "number 156368," but the Russians claimed to have used "a different method from that described in the patent." Clinical tests proved the Russian version was effective in combating streptococcus bacteria. The formula for the Russian product, a combination of sulfanilamide and hexamethylentetramin, was published.[65] VNIKhFI in Moscow developed a Soviet version of the sulfa drug Sul'fidin No. 32, which had "aroused great interest in the medical world" because, "[A]pplied in cases of croupous inflamation of the lungs it . . . quickly restored the normal condition of the organism." The formula for this drug also was provided.[66]

A number of coking-chemical plants churned out ingredients for sulfa drugs. The Voroshilov coking plant in the Ukraine installed equipment for producing "*timocheviny*," one of the basic ingredients for Sul'fazol, a replacement for Sul'fidin. The coking-chemical industry in Khar'kov, Ukraine, in conjunction with the local scientific research institute, worked out a new method of producing pyridine from concentrated ammonia water, pyridine being another basic ingredient for making Sul'fidin. The Sverdlovsk pharmaceutical factory in the Urals established a new shop for producing Sul'fidin, Streptotsid, Metizol and zinc, iron and calcium preparations. Korzina, a woman researcher at VNIKhFI in Moscow, worked out a new method of producing the antivenereal Novarsenol, "significantly raising its activity and liquidating *brak*" or spoilage. The Karpov Factory in Moscow implemented the new method in producing the drug. Less important, but perhaps also useful, the Karpov Factory worked out a new method of making Benzal'degid (benzaldehyde), which was used as a solvent in flavoring and in perfumery, and also benzoic acid by oxidizing toluol.[67]

A factory in the second-tier Russian Republic pharmaceutical industry, Medfarmprom, contributed to improving civilian medicine and preparing for possible war on Soviet soil with a "prophylactic anti-gonorrhea substance, 'Profilaktikum,'" sold in a tin tube in pharmacies for 1 ruble, 25 kopeks—two kopeks less than the journal in which it was advertised.[68] This item refuted some claims, made after the Great Patriotic War, that venereal diseases had been conquered in the Soviet Union during the 1930s but flared up after the war in territories occupied by the Germans after 1941—but so did special venereal-disease wards discussed in the medical press.

Caffeine, antiseptics and surgical equipment and instruments were crucial to front-line medical care and to civilians in the 1940s. The Tbilisi Chemical-Pharmaceutical Factory No.1, part of the Georgian pharmaceutical industry, worked out a quicker and better method of producing mercury salve.[69] The Scientific-Research Institute in Tbilisi helped the Tbilisi Caffeine Factory work out a method of producing caffeine from raw materials. The resulting product contained 11 percent caffeine.[70]

A third-tier pharmaceutical enterprise subordinate to the Saratov Regional Pharmacy Administration produced a new antiseptic, "Khloratsid," which was "widely applied in many clinics and hospitals."[71] The collective of the Surgical Workshop in the Saratov Pharmacy Administration prepared instruments and equipment for hospitals and in- and out-patient clinics. A new electric machine enabled the collective to turn out more than 100 surgical tables and glass vessels.[72]

Soviet medical researchers also did a lot of research on bacteriophages. Although their use was rejected at the time by Western researchers, bacteriophages, which will be discussed in chapter 5, were innovative both for prevention and treatment of certain diseases.

In sum, Soviet pharmaceutical research could not be faulted. Soviet pharmacologists were doing as well as researchers in France, Britain and the United States in developing sulfa drugs to compete with Germany.[73] The problem in 1939 and 1940, as earlier, was that the Soviet pharmaceutical industry could not bring prototypes downstream in adequate numbers. Nor were adequate amounts of sulfa and other drugs distributed. Unlike the German pharmaceutical sector, the Soviet pharmaceutical sector was flawed at the production end and distribution also was faulty.

Production Problems

Of the factories comprising the core Soviet pharmaceutical industry Farmakon in Leningrad, had the best excuse for failure to perform from November 1939 through the first half of 1940, since it was on the front line of the war with Finland. On January 26, 1941, one Bezrodnyi, Director of the Farmakon Factory in Leningrad, and the heads of several of the shops, reported on the state of the factory to a meeting of the Party-Economic *Aktiv.* Sixty persons attended the meeting. Farmakon produced basic items such as the protein products, Kollargol and Protargol; an iron product—Zhelatoza; protein compounds pepton and pepsin, for culture media; milk sugar; the febrifuges— phenacetin, Pyramidon, and Pirazolon; camphor, an ingredient in topical remedies for skin irritations and burns; the expectorant and local anesthetic guaiacol, and the reagent—lactose. A major problem in 1940 had been shortages of raw materials. "Supply was very bad . . . materials nearly did not arrive in connection with the Finnish situation," the enterprise report lamented.[74]

Farmakon's problems were not all due to the war with Finland, however. Another problem was "insufficient distribution of funds from [its parent trust] Glavkhimfarmprom for chief types of raw materials." As a result, the factory got only four-fifths of the gelatin that it needed to make capsules and suffered shortfalls of other raw materials. "The situation with fuel" also "was very difficult"—of six to seven thousand tons of coal only four thousand were distributed and 3,200 tons "were of such poor quality they could not be used."[75] Further, the water supply in the Farmakon Factory had not been reconstructed "since the factory was built in

1908 and was in a dilapidated condition." Farmakon had transportation problems. The factory lacked "an especially equipped garage and repair place" for vehicles.[76] In desperation, Farmakon used sleight of hand to balance its books. To defray "costs for some kinds if materials" and "transport," directors siphoned money from the payroll.[77]

Farmakon did compensate for some of the deficit materials. A method for producing Kollargol was developed to offset "deficit egg protein." A new installation allowed production of synthetic camphor from residues. The "new preparation Anal'gin"—touted as an excellent febrifuge, analgesic and anti-inflammatory—"was produced in an especially short time in 1940." The factory improved the use of warehouse space.[78] Production of Protargol and camphor were in the 97th percentile according to the Plan and two other planned preparations were produced in the 80th percentile.[79]

Nevertheless "unsatisfactory condition of the autoclave led to insufficient production" of some items—only half the amount of benzoic acid soda that was projected was actually made. And, in sum "absence of raw materials, insufficient supplies of fuel and electrical energy, and inability to preserve cadres of workers"[80] resulted in significant under-fulfillment of many important items. Only 52.2 percent of the Production Plan for the febrifuge Pyramidon, 48.1 percent of the febrifuge Phenacetin, 44.6 percent of the growth booster lecithin, and 29.9 percent of the reagent (or food supplement) lactose were produced.[81]

Thus shortages of food supplements in Leningrad in 1940 can be explained by Farmakon's troubles. However, shortages of sulfa drugs in Leningrad cannot be blamed on the tribulations of Farmakon, because the factory did not produce these new miracle drugs. The Akrikhin Factory in a village outside of Moscow did. So did the Red Star factory in Khar'kov—at least until 1940. These factories were far from Leningrad. Indeed, although there was some duplication of production in Soviet pharmaceutical factories, the attempt of higher officials to relegate production of certain products as much as possible to a few factories, which then were expected to supply the entire Soviet Union, was one of the primary factors causing shortages of pharmaceuticals. Other factors stemmed from conditions in the enterprises which, in turn, were caused by decisions made by higher officials and inefficiencies in the macroeconomy, as well as by failures at the ground level.

High government officials reorganized the industry five times during the 1930s. In 1939 the industry was reorganized yet again. The intent was to make the industry more rational. But frequent reorganization was disruptive and segregating production of pharmaceuticals in a few factories made distribution very complex.

In 1939 the core pharmaceutical industry Khimfarmprom USSR was named the Chief Administration of the Chemical-Pharmaceutical Industry—Glavkhimfarmprom.[82] More significantly, the factories in the industry's jurisdiction were realigned. The March 8 Bandaging Factory (the pre-Soviet Iakovlev Factory) was transferred back to (Glav) Khimfarmprom and the Construction Trust was transferred out.[83] Meanwhile, the new Akrikhin Factory, built to produce the antimalarial, Akrikhin and sulfa drugs, as well as other pharmaceuticals, was transferred from the Commissariat of Heavy Industry to the USSR Commissariat of Health. A Regulation (*postanovlenie*) of USSR Sovnarkom (Council of Peoples' Commissars), had ordered the transfer of the factory in June 1937. A *Prikaz* from the Assistant USSR Commissar for Health in April 1939, duly sanctioned by a decree (*rasporiazheniia*) of the commissariat in May 1939, established a commission of twelve, consisting of a chairman, five representatives from the factory plus the engineer for technical safety and five representatives from the Commissariat of Health to make an on-site inspection of Akrikhin. The Council of Labor and Defense (STO) and the Commercial Bank reviewed the commission's report, which was not submitted until the end of July 1939, ostensibly because of the thoroughness of the review process.[84]

Reorganization continued. In 1940, as a result of further pruning, the core pharmaceutical industry consisted of ten large factories. In addition to Farmakon, in Leningrad, there were six factories in Moscow: the Alkaloid Factory, Karpov, Semashko, Salicylate, the Endocrine and Vitamin Factory, and Akrikhin. The Dzerzhinskii Factory was thousands of miles away in Chimkent, Kazakhstan. The Ukraine was home to two first-tier factories: Red Star in Khar'kov and the Lomonosov Factory in Kiev. The core pharmaceutical industry also included three smaller factories—Artificial Teeth in Leningrad, Pharmacy Packaging in Tver' and the March 8 Bandaging Factory in Moscow as well as two research-scientific Institutes, VNIKhFI and VILAR (which concentrated on botanicals), and a research laboratory (LVEN).[85]

The finalized attachment of the Akrikhin Factory to the core pharmaceutical industry was potentially a plus. However, on the negative side, the industry took on the factory's debt. And, simultaneously, the industry lost some ancillary entities. The supply arm of the industry (Khimfarmsnab) was merged with the industry's sales' arm (Khimfarmtorg) to create an entity independent of and parallel to Glavkhimfarmprom. This "independent Glavk" was named "Glavpromsnabsbyt." And the office of Leksyr'e, the Botanicals Division, also was made into an independent trust. This reshuffling was disruptive and further fragmented the industry. The pharmaceutical industry lost control over supplies for and sales of its products and also the reorganization also made it more difficult for the industry to procure medicinal botanicals, which served as the base of many pharmaceuticals.

The republics that constituted the Soviet Union also had their own pharmaceutical factories. The Russian Republic had eighteen enterprises under the jurisdiction of its commissariat of health. The conglomerate, thus, was called Glavmedfarmprom Narkomzdrava RSFSR. The Ukraine had fifteen enterprises under the jurisdiction of Ukrmedfarmprom Narkomzdrava U[kr]SSR. The Georgian SSR had seven enterprises named Farmkhimprom Narkomzdrava Gruzinskoi SSR.[86] However, in the earlier 1930s, many crucial medicines were supplied to the people throughout the RSFSR and in the other republics of the Soviet Union not by their local factories but by the factories in the first-tier, core pharmaceutical industry,

Glavkhimfarmprom.

Another factor cramping output of pharmaceuticals was inadequate investment. In his 1967 history of the Soviet pharmaceutical industry, A. G. Natradze implied that the Soviet government pumped substantial investment into the pharmaceutical industry in the decade before the Great Patriotic War, leading to enormous increase in output. If the degree of capital investment in 1929-1930 was set at 100 percent, Natradze averred, then by 1941 investment had risen to 197.3 percent. If the value of the basic means [of production] in 1929 was 1.0, then value of production by 1941 was 13.7. As a result in 1940, Natradze trumpeted, the core Soviet pharmaceutical industry not only produced thousands of units of therapies for humans, amounting to 275 million rubles, like the antimalarial, Akrikhin; febrifuges such as Pyramidon, aspirin, and phenacetin; the anesthetic Anestezin; the vermifuge Santonin; and caffeine, crucial for operations, but also "new preparations for the livestock industry" like "Naganin and Fenotiazin" and preparations for combating agricultural pests like Anabazin, "a premier insectofungicide." Meanwhile, he alleged, Glavmedfarmprom RSFSR produced sixty-two million rubles' worth of galenical preparations, salves and bandages. Ukrainian enterprises produced synthesized and galenical preparations such as Pyramidon, Validol, chloroform, and bandaging materials. And Farmkhimprom Georgia produced codeine, tanin, Digaleneo [undoubtedly a cardiac preparation], and other items.[87]

Newly accessible archival materials of factories, in addition to Farmakon, paint a different picture. They struggled to fulfill their mandate and sometimes succeeded. But the factories had to cope with insufficient funds, antiquated equipment, lack of clean water and electricity, irregular deliveries of raw materials and ancillary glass and paper products, and a careless work ethic which resulted in improper use of machinery and spoilage of raw materials and finished products.

Production in 1939

In 1939 conditions in many Soviet pharmaceutical factories were not only poor but primitive. The new Akrikhin Factory, located in the village of Staraia Kupavna near Moscow, one of the producers of sulfa drugs, and the old nineteenth-century Dzerzhinskii Factory in Chimkent, Kazakhstan, both lacked clean water. In both cases pipe fitting did not arrive and lack of cement also held up pipe laying in the Akrikhin Factory. Pharmaceuticals must be produced in sterile conditions but the Badam River, source of water for the Chimkent Factory, was admitted to be "dirty."

"Canalization"—water supply and sewerage—was "in a satisfactory state in the other factories." However, enterprises across the board suffered from accidents and shortages of raw materials and fuel.[88] For example, quinine for Biokhinol did not arrive at the Karpov Factory and the Semashko Factory lacked steam in December 1938 and January 1939. The entire pharmaceutical industry was in an "exceptionally difficult position with supplies of fuel" in 1939. Twenty-seven thousand tons of coal had been allocated but due to problems with railway wagons less than half that actually arrived.[89] "Supplies of building materials, metals . . . also were difficult." The "normative" amounts of cotton and paper tissue ordered in 1939 "arrived only in 1940." Only a little over half the paper supplies arrived although the industry achieved gains in "lowering the requirements of paper." There was "absence of boxes in all factories."[90]

The picture was not completely bleak. Output of some items increased in 1939, as compared with 1938. These included the antimalarial Akrikhin; the Soviet Union's premier sulfa drug, Streptotsid; insulin; sodium salicylate; the vermifuge Santonin; Chloretin; narcotic ether; codeine; the anesthetic, Tiokain; glucose; Phenolphthalein; Bromural; chloroform; and Dichloramin. Output of "alkaloids of opium" almost doubled. Novocain overfilled its target as did the antivenereals Novarsenol and Neosalvarsan. Akrikhin, Streptotsid and insulin almost met their targets.[91] To repeat, it is assumed that Plan targets were based on need. However, while some pharmaceuticals were produced in sufficiency, "almost" meeting targets meant that others, unless there were stockpiles, were in short supply.

Additionally, many crucial products did not reach Plan targets at all. Among the items not produced in sufficiency were aspirin, which met 59 percent of its target, and salol and sodium salicylate, used for aspirin, which met about four fifths of their targets; mercury preparations, used against infections and venereal diseases at the time, which ranged from 21 percent to 82 percent of targets; Diuretin, applied against water retention, which fulfilled only 50 percent of its target; caffeine products, which were particularly important in field medicine, outputs of which ranged from 34 to 43 percent of plan quotas; the febrifuges Phenacetin and Pyramidon, which were put out at 41 percent and 75 percent of targets, respectively; and anesthetic preparations, crucial for field and civilian surgery, which met only 64 percent of plan targets.[92] Even more discouraging, output of aspirin; bismuth; caffeine; the barbiturates, Veronal and Liuminal; the febrifuges, antipyrine and Pyramidon; and "a range of other preparations"—was lower in 1939 than in 1938.[93]

Insufficiency of raw materials was the excuse most often cited for nonfulfillment of targets.[94] But *brak*—breakage or spoilage—also contributed to inadequate output. *Brak* or breakage of glass for chloroform particularly held up anesthetic products.[95] This problem could not be attributed to inadequate investment or an inefficient macro economy. Rather, it indicated poor management at the enterprise level.

Production in 1940

Matters did not improve noticeably in 1940. The "Report" for the entire industry especially focused on *brak* and attendant losses, decrying that there had been "significant rise in internal factory *brak* in 1940, compared with 1939."[96] For example in the Red Star Factory in Khar'kov, whereas only 800 kilograms of Dichloramin were spoiled in 1939, 6, 360 kilograms of Dichloramin were spoiled in 1940—almost an eight-fold increase. Losses for Streptotsid were analogous: the amount of 90 kilograms ruined in 1939 escalated to 388 kilograms ruined in 1940—a greater than four-fold increase. Losses of Pyramidon more than doubled from 162 kilograms in 1939 to 375 kilograms in 1940.[97] The Alkaloid Factory in Moscow was praised for "improving the quality of production and reducing internal *brak* in money terms from 56,728 rubles' worth spoiled in 1939 to only 30,925 rubles' worth spoiled in 1940. However, some of the factory's products suffered from *reklamatsiia* or rejection by purchasers because of "unsatisfactory work of" its "analytical laboratories."[98] Officials urged the Alkaloid factory to enforce quality control and make more careful analyses. Huge losses from *brak* prompted the Presidium (the permanent committee) of the Supreme Soviet, the Soviet parliament, to issue an *Ukaz* (Edict) June 10, 1940, "About Responsibility for Putting Out Poor-Quality Products."[99] Additionally, the industry report berated workers for not properly oiling machines and otherwise not taking proper care of machinery, for not fulfilling their work norms, and for unsatisfactory organization of warehouses."[100] As for the last, for example, although Farmakon in Leningrad "paid great attention to organizing its warehouse . . . in 1939," nevertheless "warehouse space was insufficient" and, as a result, "iron and part of the building materials sat in the courtyard."[101]

The losses of Streptotsid at the Red Star factory in Khar'kov and the shockingly inadequate production facilities and worker conditions at the Akrikhin and Endocrine and Vitamin factories explain the shortages of sulfa drugs, disinfectants and food supplements in Leningrad.

The Akrikhin Factory in Moscow was one of the producers of sulfa drugs for the entire Soviet Union. It had "existed as an independent economic entity since January 1939," but "began its activity in 1940 in exceptionally difficult conditions," its report complained. There was no mention, however, whether the purge of the former director Ivan Grigor'evich Shuvalov had helped or hurt matters.

The members of the due-diligence commission supervising the transfer of Akrikhin from the USSR Commissariat Ministry of Heavy Industry to the USSR Commissariat of Health, who initially inspected the eight buildings, electrical substation, warehouses, water supply, and fire depot comprising the factory, pronounced that the enterprise had "good access for supplies," because it had been built thirty kilometers from Moscow, on the Gorky railway line, and thirty-nine kilometers via the Moscow-Noginsk Highway. However, the commission criticized other features of the Akrikhin enterprise. The commission noted that "the factory operates in conditions of unending construction." Expenditures for dwellings and cultural facilities ate up 53 percent of the budget because "full absence in the villages of available living space" made it "necessary to build living quarters for almost all workers of the factory in view of the 40 kilometer distance from Moscow and *absence of passenger trains to the factory* [underlined in the original]." The factory also was forced to make "great expenditures because of poor natural conditions . . . swampy conditions required draining (*drenirovaniia*)" and "the level of subsoil water was high." Additionally, since the Akrikhin Factory sat on the territory of a former chemical factory, "built 100 years earlier . . . the area was contaminated . . . and drinking water was not potable." The factory needed more capitalization. Still, the commission believed the factory had good potential. Costs of production had been lowered, allowing "the possibility of severely lowering the distribution price of the antimalarial Akrikhin from 1,200 thousand rubles per ton to 600 thousand rubles per ton in 1938"and the factory's production of "100 tons of Akrikhin, fully realized in the USSR, gave the possibility of treating the millions sick with malaria and severely cutting imports of quinine, saving hard currency, and justifying the building of the factory of synthetic antimalarial preparations."[102]

The Akrikhin Factory's own report for 1940 noted strides made in research and development, but also stressed supply problems and inadequacies with the physical plant that held up production and endangered workers. On the positive side, during 1940 work was accomplished on standardizing the sulfa drugs, Red and White Streptotsid and Sul'fidin, and also narcotic, medicinal, and vinegar-ethyl ethers. Additionally, "the telephone network was in good condition."[103]

However, the "absence of fuel and raw materials in the first quarter had negative impact" on output.[104] Because of "interruptions in supplies of raw ethyl acetate" production of some products was lower in 1940 than in 1939. Because "machines worked on the [antimalarial] Akrikhin, no work was done on [the key water purifier] Pantotsid." Even so production of Akrikhin—the raison d'etre for establishing the factory—reached only about half its target because of "interruptions" in supplies of a major ingredient. Similarly, "interruptions" of two major ingredients "negatively affected production" of Streptotsid, the Soviet Union's premier sulfa drug.[105] Output of four chloride products, important for disinfecting, remained the same as in 1939 or increased only fractionally.[106] These problems explain, to a large extent, the shortages of sulfa drugs and disinfectants in Leningrad in 1940.

The factory's unpublished report also complained that the water supply "was extremely strained."[107] Additionally, there had been seventy-one cases of "unfortunate incidents," a number of which involved serious eye injuries, as was the case with a laboratory worker who got sulfuric acid in his eyes.[108] A published report of the activities of the Akrikhin Factory lamented the "severe insufficiency of fuel," the "difficulties with electrical energy," and the "deficit of raw materials" experienced during 1940.[109]

Poor conditions at the Red Star Factory in Khar'kov in 1940 led to losses of Streptotsid, cancellation of the factory's production of that drug, and, in turn, to shortages in Leningrad. The Red Star Factory achieved some successes but had to surmount many hurdles. Production of some preparations, including medical antipyrine, for quelling fevers, and ether, for operations, decreased in 1940 compared with 1939. Output of technical antipyrine, calcium gluconate, and the febrifuges, Pyramidon, and Salipirin, remained virtually unchanged. But *brak* decreased the amount of antipyrine, Pyramidon and Hydrokhinon available for shipping.[110]

Some decreased output had positive implications, for it resulted from the adoption of "more exact processes," which while initially disruptive would have long-term benefits. In the case of medical antipyrine, "lessened supplies at the end of the year, followed application of supplies that guaranteed higher quality of the product" and efforts had been made to further improve production of the preparation and other products. For making technical antipyrine the factory had adopted the new "Reiter method." This "improved work [conditions] in the shop by eliminating toxic dichloritan" and "lowered costs" although the financial benefits might have been offset by the fact that the factory "increased work days." Additionally, the Red Star Factory installed some new equipment which increased output. Replacing an old iron apparatus with a stainless steel one plus a longer work day led to increased production of one chloride product. Production of a sulfate had increased by replacing a wooden apparatus with a stainless steel one and production of calcium gluconate had increased—though minutely—by replacing a wooden apparatus with a porcelain one. Output of the water purifier chloramine had risen by "increasing the space for drying" the product, although that robbed Peter to pay Paul, since it was achieved "at the cost of using the former dryer of Pirazolon." [111]

On the whole, however, the Red Star Factory complained of obsolete equipment, power outages and irregular deliveries of raw materials. Factory managers were able to compensate for some of these problems. For example, the factory's two boilers, which dated to 1900, "did not satisfy the rising needs of the factory for steam" and, additionally, the old boilers plus lack of ventilation constituted a health hazard for workers, allowing dichloritan, chlorine, toluol, ammonia, and other gases to circulate. The electrical system was inadequate, although electricity had been installed in the garage and warehouse. The factory water supply came from the city of Khar'kov and its volume was "insufficient from May to October." To compensate, the management of the Red Star Factory devised a special cooling system for the refrigerator and other apparatus. But macroeconomic inefficiencies and exogenous policy decisions hampered deliveries of raw materials. The Red Star report complained that "[T]he quantity was above annual requirements but the materials came with great interruptions. For example, aniline came to the factory only in April and chromnik in the second half of March" and "in November there were no guarantees of raw materials" at all. Part of the reason for the erratic deliveries was that until the second half of 1939 some materials like chlorosulfuric acid came predominantly from Leningrad. Sourcing then was switched—obviously by higher authorities and without consent of the Red Star managers—to the Konstantinovskii Factory in the Donbass. Unfortunately, acid from this factory "gave significantly lower outputs of benzosul'fo chloride." The factory also lacked railway wagons.[112] And Dichloramin was "taken from the [Red Star production] program in 1940 because production was not profitable." Although the factory had developed improved methods for producing the sulfa drug Streptotsid in 1940, production of the drug also was "removed from the program."[113]

The Red Star Factory had been fined over fifty thousand rubles by the Akrikhin Factory for not supplying pirazol and had been penalized for not paying for purchases in time.[114] The factory also suffered both from lack of qualified workers and, until June 1940, an insufficient labor force. The latter problem mainly resulted from lack of dormitories and was solved by a government decree (*Ukaz*) of June 6, requiring workers to stay at their current workplace. The former problem was eradicated by a training program, described below.[115] So, despite the fines, the impression one gets from reading the Red Star Factory reports is that the managers took initiative and were fairly successful in grappling with problems.

The Factory of Endocrine and Vitamin Preparations in Moscow successfully produced the growth product Pituikrin and Vitaminol.[116] However, many products were held up in 1940 by shortages of raw materials, glass, and the like. Adrenalin was "entirely not produced in August," and "was produced in insignificant amounts in March and April because of the absence of orange flagons—250 thousand were required and only 192 thousand were received. The factory tried to increase the output of insulin but interruptions of fuel and iron, spirits, sulfuric ammonia, and other items "did not allow the factory" to do so. Output of the biologicals, Ovarin and Spermine, were held up by lack of flagons, eggs and semen, and lack of eggs held up Ovarin in tablets. Production of Follikulin (Folliculin)—for menstrual and conception problems and an important diuretic—was stymied by "receiving ingredients for them of low activity." Output of three Vitamin A preparations was held up "following insufficient [supplies of] petroleum ether." Production of Vitamin C was held up "because of insufficient equipment and absence of space." Output of cholesterin was retarded because "obtaining the product from brains required a great amount of . . . ether, acetone . . . which was impossible [to procure]." Another insulin preparation was "removed from the [production] program" because "technical documentation" for production was "not guaranteed." Fire danger prevented production of a new hormone preparation.[117]

Conditions for workers at the factory of Endocrine and Vitamin Preparations "were extremely poor" in 1940. "Dust from wood material circulated in the packaging section" and although "ventilation was introduced in the packaging section . . . in connection with the transfer of electricity from 220 volts to 380 volts the ventilation system operated with interruptions." Although "part of the motors" were received at the end of 1940, "because of insufficient electricity, interruptions in the operation of the ventilation [system] continued."[118] The one bright spot here was that only two accidents occurred, "because the apparatus was cold." The "loss to the factory was charged to the account of the responsible" worker.[119]

The only unambiguously positive report for 1940 for a core factory was that from the Salicylate Factory in Moscow. It dwelled mainly on financial matters. Products were sent all over the USSR. But such extreme centralization was problematical in 1940 and would be worse if war came to Soviet soil. Nevertheless, stock in the factory appeared healthy and loans from the commercial bank had enabled the factory to build housing for workers.[120]

Second- and third-tier pharmaceutical factories supplied about a quarter of the pharmaceuticals used in the Soviet Union. These supplemented pharmaceuticals produced and distributed by the factories that comprised the core pharmaceutical industry and the other quarter that were imported. However, the second-tier manufactories, grouped under Medfarmprom in the Russian Republic, also suffered from outmoded physical plants, poor workmanship and shortages of raw materials. For example, the chief mechanic of Factory No.1 in Leningrad (the former Factory of Medical Preparations) lamented in 1940 that "[I]t is not an anecdote but a fact that a significant part of the apparatus of our . . . factory dates back to 1861."[121]

Stalingradskaia pravda (Stalingrad Truth, in its literal translation) reported on April 9, 1940, that because the local Pharmacy administration, under the direction of one Dikkerman, had not fulfilled its production plan for 1939, four pharmacies in the center of Stalingrad were "deprived of . . . cotton, aspirin . . . turpentine, gauze, and other materials."[122]

In the Perm Gypsum Factory in 1940, violation of "work discipline" and "financial discipline" prompted the Commissariat of Health of the Russian Republic to investigate.[123] The pharmacologist M. Orekhov, who had led expeditions to find native medicinal plants in the 1920s and early 1930s, criticized other pharmaceutical factories under the jurisdiction of the RSFSR Commissariat of Health for losses due to *brak* in 1940.[124] A. M. Sorokin, Head of "Medfarmprom" the agency that supervised pharmaceutical enterprises in the RSFSR Commissariat of Health, castigated the Khar'kov Production Artel "Sanhygiene" ("Sangigiene" in the Russian), for manufacturing "packaged medicines—mint, valerian drops, iodine infusions, aspirin, Pyramidon, and others in extremely unsanitary conditions."[125] The Russian Republic Commissariat of Health conducted an investigation to ferret out the "significant amounts of non-liquid raw materials, supplies and equipment in all enterprises, which other enterprises need."[126]

In the spring of 1940, Dr. F. Khodorkov, head of the Treatment Department of the Sanitary Administration of the Red Army, published an "open letter" to the USSR Commissariat of Health requesting "swift distribution of Sul'fidin" in adequate amounts through production on a factory scale. Dr. Khodorkov praised the quality of the new Soviet sulfa drug, Sul'fidin, which resulted in "massive demands for it." However, he complained that "these demands cannot be satisfied because, until now, Sul'fidin is only produced by laboratory methods in the Chemical-Pharmaceutical Institute. . . ."[127]

This accusation and the problems thwarting production of other sulfa remedies explain why it took so long for these miracle drugs to reach Leningrad.

Finances

No matter what difficulties the Soviet pharmaceutical industry had to overcome, Soviet officials did not relax their attention to the bottom line. Factories' finances were as important to the Soviet government as output. Reduction of costs was praised. Over-spending was condemned.[128]

Waste at the enterprise level justified this hard-nosed business approach in part. However, it ignored the macroeconomic difficulties with which factory managers had to cope. For example, the beleaguered Farmakon Factory in Leningrad touted lowering costs by 650,000 rubles in 1940 through rationalization. But the factory was forced to submit to arbitration for not paying one of its creditors, the Vinnitsiia Spirit Trust, 789 rubles, 51 kopeks in 1939 and to ask forgiveness for leasing expensive dwelling space because "it had not been guaranteed the means" to build "its own living quarters" for workers.[129] Factories increasingly resorted to Bank credit to defray expenses[130]— costs of raw materials, fuel and electricity; higher costs for workers; and increased *nakladnykh* (or re-distributive) costs, and to shore up their own finances.

Although the Soviet pharmaceutical industry supposedly was planned, because factories did not receive raw materials in time, they had to improvise. Factories weakly adhered to the manufacturing plan, willfully producing "expensive" items "outside the plan" and "little working" on some items mandated by the Plan.[131] This impacted intermediary consumers, the pharmacy administrations, which supplied pharmacies, and ultimately Soviet citizens, who were the final consumers.

Government officials' remedies for these problems were to impose fines, issue directives,[132] and to reorganize. But these measures did not solve the underlying systemic problems. And they certainly did not improve Soviet health care. In 1939, the sixtieth year of Stalin's birth, the Soviet pharmaceutical journal, *Farmatsiia,* presented a sympathetic portrayal of his rise from a humble background; his education in the seminary in Tiflis—"My parents were not educated people but my education was not bad"; his conversion to Marxism at the seminary and subsequent work as a labor organizer in Batum and Baku; and his successful defeat of the White General Anton Denikin in the civil war, after removing the nefarious Trotsky. Lauded were Stalin's leadership of the Soviet Union after Lenin's death, particularly, his work on the 1924 USSR Constitution; his courageous "direction of the party against Trotskyism" and "mobilization of the party in the struggle against the right deviation (Bukharin, Rykov, Tomsky)"; his fight for collectivization of agriculture and issuance of the new Constitution of 1936.[133]

But Stalin's opponents in the pharmaceutical industry were not so laudatory of his leadership, at least in the health care sector. In 1937, the Old Bolshevik Izrail I. Levinshtein had criticized shortages and problems in the pharmaceutical sector. For his outspokenness he was labeled a "Trotskyite" and vilified.[134] By 1940 he was back on the scene. He countered colleagues who disparaged the pre-Soviet pharmaceutical industry, insisting that there was a viable pharmaceutical industry in Imperial Russia.[135] This contention could have been relegated to the realm of academic squabbling. Or it might have been another, albeit somewhat veiled criticism of the Soviet pharmaceutical industry.

A. G. Natradze's criticism of the industry in 1940, delivered in 1945, was not veiled. Undoubtedly shaken by wartime experiences, Natradze, then Assistant Commissar for Health,[136] forthrightly acknowledged that "before the war the 'medical industry' did not satisfy in full measure the requirements of our country for medicines. In 1940, for example, the need for aspirin was satisfied 46 percent, for sulfuric barium 30 percent, for Novarsenol 76 percent, for Streptotsid 44 percent, for ephedrine, 6 percent, and so on."[137] Iodine was insufficient, as were antimalarials, malaria reaching epidemic proportions during the war.[138] Henry Sigerist, William H. Welch Professor of the History of Medicine at Johns Hopkins in the 1930s and an unabashed promoter of Soviet medicine before the war, confirmed Natradze's appraisal. He ruefully admitted in 1947 that "[I]t cannot be said . . . that the output of the Soviet pharmaceutical industry was producing in 1941 at what we would consider an adequate level for civilian needs."[139]

War, particularly on one's own turf, forces innovation and production. We soon shall see whether this happened in the pharmaceutical and medical/surgical instruments industries during the Great Patriotic War. Before examining how the pharmaceutical and medical instruments industries responded to the challenges of war on Soviet soil, however, the next chapter investigates the availability of pharmaceuticals for civilians during the first two years of World War II, while the Soviet Union was still on the offensive. The chapter after that examines what pharmacologists recommended for prevention and treatment of disease on the eve of the Great Patriotic War.

Notes

1. L. E. Babich, "Aptechnoe delo v zapadnykh oblastiakh Ukrainy," *Farmatsiia*, vol. 3, no. 11(1940): 13-14.

2. Gladkikh and Loktev, *Sluzhba zdorov'ia*, p. 39.

3. Rimmington, "The Soviet Union's Offensive Program," in Wright, ed., *Biological Warfare and Disarmament: New Problems/New Perspectives*: 106-107. On tularaemia, see also Wolfgang Eckart, " 'Creating Confidence': Heinz Zeiss as a Traveller in the Soviet Union, 1921-1932," in Solomon, *Doing Medicine Together: Germany and Russia Between the Wars*: 221-224. Tularaemia is also spelled tularemia. See "Health Beat," Illinois Department of Public Health, http://www.idph.state.il.us/public/hb/ybtulare.htm. Accessed 6/19/2007. See also Jonathan A. Edlow, MD et al, "Tick-Borne Disesase, Tularemia," http://www.emedicine. com: 17. Accessed 6/19/2007.Washing the hands after touching infected rabbits can prevent spread the disease. Coming into contact with infected animals is one of the normal methods of communication rather than use of the disease as an aerosolized bioweapon.

4. "A Healthy Me. Ills and Conditions: Dysentery," http:// www.ahealthyme.com/ topic/dysentery. Accessed 6/20/2007.

5. Gladkikh and Loktev, *Sluzhba zdorov'ia v Velikoi Otechestvennoi Voine*: 39-41, 67-69.

6. Ibid.: 39-41.

7. Gladkikh and Loktev, *Sluzhba zdorv'ia* : 44.

8. Nadezhda Cherepenina, "Healthcare on the Eve of War," in Barber and Dzeniskevich, eds. *Life and Death in Besieged Leningrad, 1941-1944*: 20-21.

9. E. M. Ravikovich and O. E. Mayerman, "Materialy po epidemiologii difterii i skarlatiny v gody otechestvennoi voiny," *Zhurnal mikrobiologii, epidemiologii, i immunobiologii*, (1945): 15-16.

10. A. L. Siroko, "Novoe v bor'be s dizenteriei," *Voenno-sanitanoe delo*, no. 10 (1940): 100.

11. V. Skvortsov, "Bor'ba s batsilliarnoi dizenteriei (gemokolitami) v vesenne-letnii period," *Voenno-sanitarnoe delo*, no. 4 (1940): 22-24.

12. Siroko, "Novoe v bor'be s dizenteriei," loc. cit.

13. V. K. Kirsenko, "O techenie dizenterii u vaktsinirovannykh protiv nee po Bezredka," *Voenno-sanitarnoe delo*, no. 8 (1940): 75-77.

14. Skvortsov, "Bor'ba s batsilliarnoi dizenteriei (gemokolitami) v vesenne-letnii period," loc. cit.

15. G. I. Samokhin, "Lechenie batsilliarnoi dizenterii sul'fidinom," *Voennaia Meditsina Glubnogo Tyla*, Tashkent (1943): 567-571.

16. John E. Lesch, *The First Miracle Drugs*: 40, 51-67, 81-91, 104-106, 122-157.

17. On pneumonia see Answers.com: Pneumonia: 1-33; Botanical remedies: 2. See also Pediatric Advisor 2006.2: Pneumonia Admission Information and Discharge Instructions, www.med.umich.edu/1libr/pa/pa_dpneumon_hhg.htm. Donald Filtser mentioned the possible inappropriateness of sulfa for infants at the annual meeting of the American Association for the Advancement of Slavic Studies, Washington, D. C. (November 2006).

18. Cherepenina, "Health Care on the Eve": 21.

19. V. S. Chetverikov, "Sanitarnoe delo v SSSR vo vremia period pervykh dvukh let voiny," *Gigieia i sanitariia*, vol. 8, no. 10 (1943): 31-32.

20. TsGIA, RB, R f. 1203, op. 1, d. 17, ll. 75, 77 (Dogovor [Contract], Rodilnyi dom [Maternity Home], Magnitogorsk, Kirov *oblast'* 1941); l. 70 (Copy: Kontora Rosmedsnabtorg, Moscow, July 1940); l. 69 (Dorsanotdel, upravlenie zheleznodorogi, [Railroad], Kuibyshev, *oblast'*, 28 August, 1941) and l. 79 (Missive about vaccinating children, Kuibyshev *oblast'*, 22 November 1940); l. 65, TubInstitute, Kazan', 26, November 1940).

21.TsGIA RB, R f. 1203, op. 1, d. 35, l. 6. In absolute numbers the amount of dysentery vaccine "Partially Fabricated" was 2,810 liters compared with 2,000 liters ordained by the Plan. "Given to the Warehouse" were 2,551.06 liters. Compared with 1,000 liters of divaccine ordained by the Plan, 1,220 liters were produced and 1,031.73 "Given to the Warehouse." Compared with 250 liters of bacteriophages ordained by the Plan, 270 liters were produced and 226.55 turned over to the Warehouse.

22. TsGIA RB, R. f. 1203, op. 1, d. 33, l. 1 (Protokol sanitarno-epidemicheskoi Upravleniia Narkomzdrava BASSR o rassmotrenii i utverzhdenii godovogo otchete Bakteriologicheskogo Instituta za 1938 god., 20 May 1939.) There is some inconsistency with terminology and amounts in the two accounts about production for 1938. Another source cites scarlatina serum (*syvorot*) partially fabricated to the amount of 43 percent of Plan, with

33 percent "Given to the warehouse"; diphtheria serum (*syvorot*) partially fabricated to the amount of 60 percent of Plan, with 30 percent given to the warehouse; and dysentery serum (*syvorot*) partially fabricated at 50 percent. TsGIA RB, R F. 1203, op. 1, d. 35, l. 6.

23. TsGIA RB, R f. 1203, op. 1, d. 43, l. 86.

24. TsGIA RB, R f. 1203, op. 1, d. 43, l. 86.

25. TsGIA RB, R. f. 1203, op. 1, d. 43, l. 59.

26. TsGIA RB, R. f. 1203, op. 1, d. 43, l. 2. On the issue of the *brak* of divaccine, see TsGIA RB R. 1203, op. 2, d. 14.

27. TsGIA RB, R. f. 1203, op. 2, d. 14, ll. 42, 45. Report of Director of the Institute Golikov and new Head of Production Kochergin, with Head of the Plan group Kniss-Plotnikov.

28. TsGIA RB, R. f., R. F. 1203, op. 2, d. 14, l. 55.

29. TsGIA RB, R f. 1203, op. 2, d. 12, ll 31, 58.

30. TsGIA RB, R. f. 1203, op. 1, d. 43, l. 10.

31. TsGIA RB, R f.1203, op. 2, d. 14, ll. 42, 45; TsGIA RB, R1203, op. 1, d. 43, l. 10.

32. TsGIA RB, R. f. 1203, op. 2, d. 17, l. 75 (January 25, 1941).

33. TsGIA RB, R. f. 1203, op. 1, d. 17, l. 77 (Dogovor [Contract], January 1, 1941 to 31 December, 1941, signed by Grinkevich, Chief Doctor of the Maternity Home, Kirov raion, Magnitogorsk oblast').

34. TsGIA RB, R f. 1203, op. 1, d. 17, l. 24 (February 18, 1941).

35. TsGIA RB, R f. 1203, op. 1, d. 17, ll. 44, 47.

36. Ravikovich and Mayerman, "Materialy po epidemiologii difterii i skarlatiny v gody otechestvennoi voiny," *Zhurnal mikrobiologii, epidemiologii, i immunobiologii* (1945): 15-16.

37. Tens of thousands of citizens of the three Baltic States were shipped to the Soviet Union, along with the presidents of Estonia and Latvia, Pats and Ulmanis, respectively, following rigged elections for parliament and executive posts in the summer of 1940. Romuald Misiunas and Rein Taagpera, *The Baltic States: Years of Dependence, 1940-1990* (Los Angeles and Berkeley: University of California Press, 1993): 15-45. Deportations of the presidents: 22; of other citizens: 40-43.

38. In 1940 and 1941, some two million Poles were shipped to timber-cutting and other labor camps in the Soviet far north, including Andrew Rej, longtime friend and colleague of the author. See also Neal Ascherson, *The Struggles for Poland* (New York; Random House, 1987): 90-93.

39."Soobshchenie o rabote plenuma v vsesoiuznogo vitaminogo komiteta prokhodivshego v Moskve s 11 X po 13 XII 1940," *Farmakologiia i toksikologiia*, vol. 4, no. 2, (1941): 80.

40. For example, P. L. Braginskii, "Deistvie protravitelia 'kupfermeritol'na zhivotnyi organizm," *Farmakologiia i toksikologiia,* vol. 3, no. 6 (1940): 12-16, discussed the danger of a fungicide being ingested by collective-farm cattle. A mixture of orto and paranitrokhlorbenzol was studied and reported on by N. S. Pravdin, "K voprosu ob otsenkestepeni toksichnosti iadovitykh proizvodstvennykh pilei," ibid.: 17-20. The effects of poisoning with nitrochlorbenzol— chloroform and nitric acid are used in chemical warfare—was reported on by Ia. A. Levin, of the Biochemical Department of the Khar'kov Medical Institute, in "O kharakteristike okislitel'nykh protsessov pri otravlenii nitrokhlorbenzolom," ibid.: 28-38. See also P. Ia. Mytnik, "O roli nervnogo komponenta v mekhanizme khronicheskikh otravlenii promyshlenymi iadami," ibid.: 39-46. The conclusion of the study, conducted at the

Moscow Institute of Experimental Medicine, was that poisoning with a mixture of benzol and carbontetrachloride altered "the reaction of the experimental animal to either of these poisons." (46).

41. Lesch, *The First Miracle Drugs*: 72-81, 93.

42. Lesch, ibid.: 100-103.

43. Lesch, ibid.: 82-83, 91.

44. Lesch, ibid.: 97.

45. Lesch, ibid. : 83, 85, 94, 109-119.

46. Kobrak, *National Cultures and International Competition: The Experience of Schering AG, 1851-1950*: 217-254.

47. Richard J. Evans, *The Third Reich in Power* (New York: The Penguin Press, 2005): 310-311. On the benefits of Hitler's regime for the entire German economy, see Werner Abelshauser, "Germany: guns, butter, and economic miracles," in Mark Harrison, ed., *The Economics of World War II: Six great powers in international comparison* (Cambridge: Cambridge University Press, 1998): 122-176. For the travails of the Soviet pharmaceutical industry in the 1920s and 1930s, see Conroy, *The Soviet Pharmaceutical Business During Its First Two Decades, 1917-1937*, passim.

48. Discussion with John Anderson, physicist, Denver, September 6, 2006.

49. Evans, *The Third Reich in Power*: 311.

50. Advertisement, endpaper of *Farmatsiia i Farmakologiia*, no. 2, 1937 and endpaper of *Farmatsiia*, vol. 2, no. 1, 1939. The advertisement noted that ordering these machines could be done "only on the basis of existing rules in the USSR about the monopoly of foreign trade."

51. RGAE, f. 8009, op. 2, d. 5, l. 3.

52. RGAE, f. 8009, op. 2, d. 5, l. 35.

53. A. I. Travin, "Sinticheskii vitamin B1 (Tiamin)," *Farmakologiia i toksikologiia*, vol. 4, no. 1(1941): 79-81. Also, "Obzory: Voprosy farmakoterapii ," V. I. Skvortsov, "Ocherk I: Vitaminoterapiia," *Farmakologiia i toksikologiia*, vol. 4, no. 2 (1941): 77-78; V. V. Vasil'eva, "Soobshchenie o rabote plenuma vsesoiuznogo vitaminogo komiteta prokhodivshego v Moskve s 11 X po 13 XII 1940": 79-82; .M. Mashkovskii, "Vitamin K," ibid.: 82-85.

54. "Po soiuzu," *Farmatsiia*, vol. 3 , no. 9-10 (1940): 56. The chemical structure of Vitamin B1 had been discovered in 1936. Professor A. V. Lavrov studied the vitamin, as noted above.

55. "Po soiuzu," *Farmatsiia*, vol. 3, no. 11 (1940): 46.

56. VNIKhFI, Report for 1940, RGAE, f.. 8009, op. 2, d. 33, ll. 1-57.

57. On the importance of vitamins during the Great Patriotic War see K. S. Petrovskii, "Pitanie Voisk Sovetskoi Armii: Normirovanie vitaminov v sutochnom ratsione," in Smirnov, gen. ed., *Opyt sovetskoi meditsiny v Velikoi Otechestvennoi Voine*, vol. 33 (1955): 135-138.

58. For concise information on Streptomycin see *World Book Encyclopedia*, vol. 18, (1976): 796. Reuben and Wittcoff provide additional information on the drug and on actinomycin in *Pharmaceutical Chemicals in Perspective*: 158-159, 162.

59. "Chto takoe antivirus voobshche i v chastnosti protivogrippoznyi antivirus," *Farmatsiia*, vol.3, no. 9-10 (1940): 30-31.

60. "Po soiuzu," *Farmatsiia*, vol. 3, no. 12 (1940): 42.

61. James H. Madison, *Eli Lilly: A Life, 1885-1977* (Indianapolis: Indiana Historical

Society, 1989): 65-67, 83.

62. "Po soiuzu," *Farmatsiia*, vol.3, no. 9-10 (1940): 55.

63. "Po soiuzu," *Farmatsiia*, vol. 3 , no. 11 (1940):46.

64. Streptotsid and the use of White Streptotsid and sulfanilamide against gonorrhea are discussed in Conroy, *The Soviet Pharmaceutical Business During Its First Two Decades*: 251.

65. P. I. Astrakhantsev and S. M. Vasil'ev, "Molekukiarnoe soedinenie belogo streptotsida i urotropina (Strepturin)," *Farmatsiia*, vol. 3, no. 9-10 (1940): 24-28.

66. V. Ivanova, "Analiz Sul'fidin No. 32," *Farmatsiia*, vol.3 , no 9-10 (1940): 28-29.

67. "Po soiuzu," *Farmatsiia*, vol. 3, no. 11 (1940): 46.

68. Advertisements on endpages of *Farmatsiia*, vol. 3 , no. 7-8, 9-10 (1940).

69. "Po soiuzu," *Farmatsiia*, " vol. 3, no. 11 (1940): 47.

70. "Po soiuzu," *Farmatsiia*, vol. 3, no. 12 (1940): 43.

71. "Po soiuzu," *Farmatsiia*, vol. 3, no. 11 (1940): 46.

72. "Po soiuzu," *Farmatsiia*, vol. 3, no. 12 (1940): 42.

73. Lesch, *The First Miracle Drugs*: 122-157.

74. Report of the Farmakon Factory, 1940, RGAE, f. 8009, op. 2, d. 13, l. 90. For early twentieth-century uses of camphor in medicine and photography, see Kobrak, *National Cultures and International Competition: The Experience of Schering AG, 1851-1950*: 44-46.

75. RGAE, f. 8009, op. 2, d. 13, ll. 39, 90, 91. In absolute terms, as a result of lack of funds, of 48.3 tons of gelatin ordered only 39.3 tons were received. Of 55.6 tons of vinegar anhydride requested only two thirds of that amount were received—34 tons. Of 157.2 tons of caustic ordered, only about two-thirds were received—100 tons. Less than one third of the 98 tons of paranitrochlorbenzol requested were received, less than one half the amount of sodium bromide requested was received.

76. Report of the Farmakon Factory, 1940, RGAE, f. 8009, op. 2, d. 13, ll. 3, 17, 26.

77. RGAE, f. 8009, op. 2, d. 13, l. 2.

78. RGAE, f. 8009, op. 2, d. 13, ll. 13, 40, 41, 90.

79. RGAE, f. 8009, op. 2, d. 13, l. 38.

80. RGAE, f. 8009, op. 2, d. 13, l. 38.

81. RGAE, f. 8009, op. 2, d. 13, ll. 38-39.

82. Natradze, *Ocherk*: 139.

83. RGAE, f. 8009, op. 2, d. 5, preface and l. 1.

84. RGAE, f. 8009, op. 20, d. 211, ll. 1-17, 137.

86. RGAE, f. 8009, op. 2, d. 7, l. 1.

86. Natradze, *Ocherk*: 140-141.

87. Natradze, *Ocherk* : 139-141.

88. RGAE, f. 8009, op. 2, d. 5, ll. 2-6, 9-11, 17.

89. RGAE, f. 8009, op. 2, d. 5, ll. 35-41, 95. Of 27,000 tons allocated only 11,463 tons arrived.

90. RGAE, f. 8009, op. 2, d. 5, ll. 96, 98.

91. RGAE, f. 8009, op. 2, d. 5, ll. 30-33.

92. RGAE, f. 8009, op. 2, d. 5, l. 34.

93. RGAE, f. 8009, op. 2, d. 5, ll. 33-35. One other preparation was Benzonaftol. Only 56 percent of paper supplies arrived.

94. RGAE, f. 8009, op. 2, d. 5, ll. 35, 43, 95, 96, 98.

95. RGAE, f. 8009, op. 2, d. 5, ll. 30-34.

96. RGAE, f. 8009, op. 2, d. 7, l. 5.
97. RGAE, f. 8009, op. 2, d. 7, l. 5.
98. RGAE, f. 8009, op. 2, d. 7, l. 5.
99. RGAE, f. 8009, op. 2, d. 7, l. 6.
100. RGAE, f. 8009, op. 2, d. 7, ll. 6, 9, 18.
101. RGAE, f. 8009, op. 2, d. 13, l. 113.
102. RGAE, f. 8009, op. 20, d. 211, ll. 1-17, 137.
103. Report on the Akrikhin Factory, 1940, RGAE, f. 8009, op. 2, d. 11, ll. 22, 36.
104. RGAE, f. 8009, op. 2, d. 11, ll. 7-10.
105. RGAE, f. 8009, op. 2, d. 11, ll. 10, 18. Interruptions of raw ethyl acetate affected production of ethyl acetate, aceto-vinegar-ether, paranitroanizol, and trichloric-phosphorus. The major ingredient for Akrikhin that arrived irregularly was vinegar-ethyl ether. In exact terms, production of the antimalarial Akrikhin reached only 57.18 percent of its target. The ingredients lacking for Streptotsid were an acetate and chlor-sul'furic acid.
106. RGAE, f. 8009, op. 2, d. 11, ll. 14, 17, 18. These were chlortoluidin, chlornitroanilovic acid, dichlortoluol, and dichlorbenzoic acid.
107. RGAE, f. 8009, op. 2, d. 11, l. 21.
108. RGAE, f. 8009, op. 2, d. 11, ll. 39, 41, 44.
109. Narkomzdrav USSR, Glavnoe upravlenie khimiko-farmatsevticheskoi promyshlennosti: Zavod Akrikhin, *Biulleten' po obmenu opytom na pravakh rukopisi*, 1-2 (1940): 23.
110. Report of the Red Star Factory, 1940, RGAE, f. 8009, op. 2, d. 25, ll. 1, 15, 2. Another product whose output was lower in 1940 than in 1939 was benzosul'fochloride, partially due to "the amount of days spent on repair." The ether product was methylene ether.
111. RGAE, f. 8009, op. 2, d. 25, ll. 1-3. Production of benzosul'fo-chloride had already increased 9 percent in comparison with 1939 and was slated to increase in the 1940 work year because the old iron apparatus had been replaced with a stainless steel one "that significantly increased output and lowered repair." The sulfate was paraaminophenolsulfate.
112. RGAE, f. 8009, op. 2, d. 25, ll. 3, 3 ob, 10 ob, 11, 48.
113. RGAE, f. 8009, op. 2, d. 25, ll. 1-2.
114. RGAE, f. 8009, op. 2, d. 25, l.16.
115. RGAE, f. 8009, op. 2, d. 25, ll. 36-38.
116. RGAE, f. 8009, op. 2, d. 22, l. 17.
117. Report of the Endocrine and Vitamin Factory for 1940, RGAE, f. 8009, op. 2, d. 22, ll. 1, 18, 19. Mamofizon would seem related to breast milk production. The important diuretic was Adiurekrin. The vitamin A products were Karatol, Karaton, and Kortin. The insulin product was "Giston-zinc-insulin." Also removed was Gravidan.
118. RGAE, f. 8009, op. 2, d. 22, ll. 4, 10.
119. RGAE, f. 8009, op. 2, d. 22, l. 7.
120. RGAE, f. 8009, op. 2, d. 17, ll. 24-26, 31, 33, 42.
121. Narkomzdrav RSFSR, Upravlenie mediko-farmatsevtich. promyshlennosti, "Medfarmprom," *Informatsionnyi biulleten'*, Moscow, no. 1 (1940): 17.
122. "Po soiuzu," *Farmatsiia*, vol. 3 , no. 9-10 (1940): 54.
123. Narkomzdrav RSFSR Upravlenie mediko-farmatsevtich. promyshlennosti, "Medfarmprom," *Informatsionnyi biulleten'*, no. 2 (1940): 21.
124. Orekhov, *Informatsionnyi builleten'*, no. 3 (1940): 5-7.

125. *Informatsionnyi biulleten'*, no. 3 (1940): 24 and ibid., no. 4 (1940): 1.

126. *Informatsionnyi biulleten'*, no. 3 (1940): 27.

127. *Informatsionnyi biulleten'*, no. 4 (1940): 20-21.

128. RGAE, f. 8009, op. 2, d. 7, passim, especially ll. 12, 13, 16, 18.

129. RGAE, f. 8009, op. 2, d. 13, ll. 2, 112-113.

130. RGAE, f. 8009, op. 2, d. 7, l. 17. The use of bank credit increased from 76.6 percent in 1939 to 83 percent in 1940.

131. RGAE, f. 8009, op. 2, d. 7, ll. 8-9.

132. RGAE, f. 8009, op. 2, d. 13, ll. 2, 92.

133. "Privet tov. Stalinu," *Farmatsiia*, vol. 2, no. 12 (1939):1- 10.

134. Conroy, *The Pharmaceutical Business During Its First Two Decades*: 239-242.

135. Levinshtein gave perspective on the pharmaceutical industry of Imperial Russia through his study, *Istoriia farmatsii i organizatsiia farmatsevticheskogo dela* (History of Pharmacy and the Organization of the Pharmaceutical Business). This book was lauded at the February 1940 meeting of the Moscow Scientific-Pharmaceutical Association as "the first of its kind," a possible textbook, because of its rich survey of the pharmaceutical literature. Levinshtein asserted, in a discussion on his paper, "The Life and Work of Gregory Dragendorff" [nineteenth-century pharmacologist at Iur'ev (Dorpat) University] that "it was not possible to affirm," as one F. Ivanov had, "that before the [First World] war the [Russian] pharmaceutical industry did not exist." (Ivanov apparently had made this comment in the course of reviewing a text by L. L. Semov, *Handbook of Pharmaceutical Chemistry.*) Levinshtein's insistence on historical accuracy gave notice that, despite having been purged, he was resuming his role as industry watch-dog. I[srail] L[evinshtein], "V Moskovskoi nauchno-farmatsevticheskoi assotsiatsii," *Farmatsiia*, vol. 3, no. 9-10 (1940): 45-47. One Professor V. V. Nikolaev reviewed Levinshtein's book He did make note of some misprints and mistakes. There was negative reaction to Levinshtein's paper about Dragendorff on the part of some members but, nevertheless, it was slated to be published in a Ukrainian journal.

136. RGAE, f. 8009, op. 2, d. 36, l. 42.

137. A. G. Natradze, "Zadachi khimiko-farmatsevticheskoi promyshlennosti v 1945 g.," *Farmatsiia*, vol. 8, no. 1 (1945): 12-13. Though he repeatedly used the term chemical-pharmaceutical industry, an anachronism in 1941, this sentence reads "*pered voinoi meditsinskaia promyshlennost' ne udovletvoriala v polnoi mere potrebnosti nashei strany v medikamentakh.*" (13)

138. Smirnov, Chief Editor. *Opyt sovetskoi meditsiny v Velikoi Otechestvennoi Voine, 1941-1945 gg.*, vol. 31 (1955): 136; vol. 32 (1955): 16.

139. Henry Sigerist, *Medicine and Health in the Soviet Union* (New York: the Citadel Press, 1947): 105. His earlier book, *Socialized Medicine in the Soviet Union* (New York: W. W. Norton, 1937), uncritically presented Soviet data that portrayed a rosy picture of Soviet medical care.

Chapter 4
At the *Apteka* during the First Two Years of World War II

What was the availability of medicines and health-care products at the grass-roots level, for Soviet citizens living in various parts of the Soviet Union during the first two years of World War II but prior to the Great Patriotic War?

For new Soviet citizens, residing in areas newly annexed by the Soviet Union, pharmacy ownership and dispensing were changed to conform to the Soviet system. In 1940, pharmacies (*apteki*) in the former eastern Polish provinces, taken by the Soviet Union in 1939, were nationalized—96 in Belostok, 66 in Baranovicheskaia province, 63 in Vilna, 35 in Brest, and 21 in Pinsk were taken from their owners. Hundreds of *aptekarskie magaziny*, "drug stores" which sold sundries and packaged medicines but which could not prepare medicines, also were nationalized.[1]

Soviet inspectors found much to criticize in the "bourgeois" Polish pharmacies. They considered the number of pharmacies inadequate. Three hundred seventy-six pharmacies served 8.3 million inhabitants, including 3.4 rural dwellers. This meant that, on average, one pharmacy served 22.7 thousand people whereas in the Soviet Ukraine one pharmacy served 15.8 thousand. Most of the pharmacies were located in cities and 26 "*raions*" had no pharmacies.[2] This assessment, however, ignored the "hundreds" of drug stores which, in an era of factory-prepared medicines efficiently supplemented pharmacies, where medicine were still made up by hand on the premises. But Soviet pharmacy specialists dismissed the drug stores as "commercial" establishments because they purveyed "patented" or "specific" remedies, implying that such remedies were snake-oil medicines.[3] They also asserted that, as all but four of the pharmacies were privately owned, they too were more businesses than medical entities. Pharmacy owners focused on profits and the average price for medicines, according to the inspectors, was two-and-a-half to three times higher than in the

Soviet Ukraine. Following nationalization, Soviet authorities reduced prices from 10 to 80 percent. Additionally, Soviet pharmacy administrators declared that reception rooms in Polish pharmacies—which were reminiscent of pre-Soviet Tsarist pharmacies, particularly the Ferrein flagship pharmacy, now Pharmacy No. 1—were too lavish. They were richly decorated with "beautiful cases, many with stained glass in various forms and colors, statues of Greek gods and goddesses, busts of Hippocrates, Galen, Socrates and other ancient physicians and philosophers—all this to create an impression of a scientific and solid institution."[4] Soviet authorities opined that such luxurious appointments signified that money was stinted on work rooms. Although pharmacies were open twenty-four hours, Soviet inspectors declared that they rarely found stools for assistants; most of the work was done standing. They claimed that the infusion apparatus was good but sterilizers were lacking. Boiled water was frequently used in place of distilled water. Analytical cabinets were good but inspectors noted a "thick film of dust" in many. Soviet inspectors found fault with the fact that most pharmacists were Polish and quotas limited the number of Ukrainian and Jewish pharmacists. They were outraged that in January 1939, three Jewish students had been killed in the highest educational institution in L'vov (L'viv).[5]

On the other hand, Soviet inspectors admired the excellent preservation of materials as well as their clear, attractive labeling. Providing illustrations, they admitted that such bottles and labels could be used with good effect in the Soviet Union. The former Polish pharmacies also contained a wealth of reference literature from Merck and Bayer, in addition to the Polish pharmacopoeia and pharmaceutical encyclopedia.[6]

Meanwhile, Soviet pharmacists and some pharmaceutical administrators complained about defects in Soviet pharmacies, not only in their private reports but also in pharmaceutical journals.

A major one was lack of access in certain areas. In Tsarist Russia, in the first decade of the twentieth century, urbanites were fairly well served by some 4,804 pharmacies whether they lived in the European parts of the Empire, in Central Asia, or in Siberia. On average, in European Russia a pharmacy served 10,300 city dwellers. In St. Petersburg the ratio was 1:16,000; in Moscow the ratio was 1:22,800. In Siberian and Central Asian cities the ration was less favorable. One pharmacy served, on average, 20,000 city dwellers. Pharmacies were monitored by government authorities for cleanliness, proper preservation of drugs, the caliber of the pharmacists that managed them and dispensed medicines, and so forth. Furthermore, pharmacies were supplemented by about 10,000 "drug stores" which were not allowed to make-up medicines on site but purveyed pre-packaged medicines and soap, disinfectants and sundries. In rural areas, in late Imperial Russia, pharmacies and drug stores were few and far between. On average one pharmacy served 100,000 people. Additionally, the stock in rural pharmacies was minimal compared to urban pharmacies and often only a partially trained pharmacist or an individual not trained as a pharmacist at all was in charge.[7]

Soviet authorities continued the practice that had obtained in Imperial Russia of dividing the venues where medicines were dispensed into pharmacies and drug stores. Pharmacies, deemed to be scientific, were authorized to fill prescriptions. "Stores of Sanitation and Hygiene," the Soviet name for the "drug stores (*aptekarskie magaziny*) of Imperial Russia, sold sundries along with factory-prepared medicines, disinfectants and the like. Soviet pharmacy authorities supervised dispensing as had tsarist pharmacy officials. Indeed they used many of the same rules and regulations as in the imperial period, adding additional ones. Unlike the pharmacies and "drug stores" of Imperial Russia, however, the pharmacies and "drug stores " in the Soviet Union were not privately owned or even leased after the late 1920s but, rather, were owned by local governments. Furthermore, Soviet pharmacies did not purchase their own wares. These were supplied by Pharmacy Administrations (*Aptekoupravleniia*).

The number of both pharmacies and drug stores declined drastically after the October Revolution and during the civil war. They then made a comeback during the New Economic Policy of the 1920s. By the end of the NEP the number of free-standing pharmacies in the entire Soviet Union approximated the number in the Tsarist Empire. There also were pharmacies in hospitals and other institutions, as in the imperial period. While in some cities the number of pharmacies remained the same, other cities lost out. For example, there were far fewer pharmacies in Kherson than before the revolution. Also the number of supplementary drug stores declined. Some rural areas sported more pharmacies than before the revolution, on the other hand.[8]

During the 1930s, the Soviet pharmacy network increased spectacularly in the Caucasian and Central Asian republics. In the Uzbek Republic there had been only 24 pharmacies before 1917; in 1940 there were 63 urban pharmacies and 98 rural ones, supplemented by 77 "stalls" selling medicinal herbs and packaged medicines, 77 sanitary stores, 163 pharmacy "points," and 4 chemical-analytical laboratories. Nevertheless, one pharmacy still served 40,000 people, on average. Ratios in Georgia and the Ukraine were more favorable. One pharmacy served an average of 16,300 people in the Ukraine and 8,500 in Georgia. Between 1925 and 1940 the number of pharmacies increased from 13 to 61 in the Armenian Republic, from 6 to 59 in the Kirghiz Republic, and from 30 to an amazing 300 in the Kazakh Republic.[9]

By January, 1941, 2,175 urban pharmacies and 1,881 rural pharmacies, supplemented with 583 [drug] stores, 1,951 kiosks, and 5,292 pharmacy "points" operated in the Russian Republic (RSFSR). However, there were still 159 *raion* centers without pharmacies.[10] One pharmacy served, on average, 22,700 people. And in Moscow and Leningrad, in particular, matters had worsened since prerevolutionary times, for one pharmacy in these cities served, on average, 35,000 people.[11] In terms of quantity, the inhabitants of the Soviet Ukraine were better off than the inhabitants of the newly acquired Polish provinces but the inhabitants of the Russian Republic were not.

In addition to a need for more pharmacies per capita, the quality of dispensing also was uneven in Soviet pharmacies of the 1930s. Poorly trained *praktikanty* rather than fully- or even partially-trained pharmacists often dispensed medicines on the eve of the Great Patriotic War, as they had during the 1930s. In the United States in 1943, with a population roughly commensurate with that of the Soviet Union, there was a total of 70,449 pharmacists available for retail practice.[12] In 1940, in the RSFSR, the largest republic in the Soviet Union, there were less than 38,000 dispensers. More significant, fully qualified pharmacists (*provisory*) in the RSFSR in 1940 numbered fewer than 1,814. There were 15,760 partially qualified assistant pharmacists, whereas minimally trained *praktikanty* amounted to a sizable 19, 261.[13] In 1931, some *praktikanty*, who enrolled in a course on the use of medical instruments, were said to be virtually illiterate.[14] Undoubtedly the education and training of the *praktikanty* improved during the 1930s but, nevertheless, they were not fully certified, even by Soviet standards.

The stock in Soviet pharmacies and drugstores during the 1930s also often left much to be desired. Lacking complete inventories, we can only make educated guesses about the availability of various kinds of medicines in *apteki* in various areas. Nevertheless, insufficiencies were implied in advertisements of the time and alluded to in published materials of the era.

In 1939 the All-Union Ministry of Health and Khimfarmtorg proudly announced a number of "new" pharmaceuticals "sold in all pharmacies." These included "Papaverin solianokislyi" (Papaverinum hydrochloride), an antispasmodic, analgesic, depressant alkaloid of opium. It was recommended for diseases of the digestive tract, bronchial asthma, in gynecology and some other problems. Because it was a narcotic, this product required a doctor's prescription. "Adalin" (bromdiethylacetylcarbamid) was a soporific (sleeping potion) and was recommended for the headaches of those suffering from nephritis (acute or chronic inflammation of the kidneys). This drug also required a doctor's prescription. "Calcium gluconate," which could be dispensed over-the-counter, was recommended for rickets, tuberculosis of the lungs, asthma, and other cases where calcium therapy was indicated. It was alleged to be "analogous to the foreign preparation, calcium chloride" but "more easily digested and less toxic." [15] "Ammargen (a water-ammonia solution containing 2.5 percent silver)" was a new "antiseptic substance" for "ulcerous" conditions and for surgery, gynecology, "venerology," and dermatology that was "sold in all pharmacies."[16] "Atofan" (phenylkhinolincarbolic acid) was an analgesic, an anti-inflammatory, and a febrifuge. The Soviet pharmaceutical industry had cloned this product in the 1920s from Schering's Atophan, which that house had produced from before World War I. [17] The advertisement recommended it for arthritic rheumatism, neuralgia, and other painful conditions, asserting it could be acquired over-the-counter, not only "in all pharmacies" but in all "sanitary and hygiene stores."[18] However, while all these substances were claimed to be readily available, a disclaimer on the advertisements' page instructed patrons "in [cases of] absence [of these products] in pharmacies to turn to . . . the regional (*krai* or *oblast'*) department of the pharmacy administration.[19]

Similarly, while more than a dozen May and Baker remedies and chemicals for photography were advertised in *Farmatsiia* in 1939, the fine print at the bottom noted that "foreign wares must be distributed only on the bases of existing USSR rules about the monopoly of foreign trade."[20] These disclaimers raise red flags.

Pharmaceutical officials admitted that some pharmacies lacked basic remedies. In 1939, the Pharmacy Administration of the Ukraine blamed managers of pharmacies. They were said to be neglecting their responsibility to serve the people's health needs in order "to quantitatively fulfill trade-financial plans." Instead of providing medicines and medical wares, which authorities claimed were produced in sufficiency by the pharmaceutical industry, some pharmacy managers were selling "mirrors, glue, shoe cream, hair nets" and other sundries that more properly belonged in drug stores, or as they were called in Soviet parlance, sanitary and hygiene stores. Pharmacy managers were further accused of refusing to dispense medicines even when they were available in sufficiency in the warehouses. Officials sternly listed twenty-two sundries that were not in future to be allowed in *apteki*. But they also resolved "to strengthen supplies of medicines and medical wares to the pharmacies, to widen the assortment of medical wares, to introduce new medicinal substances," as well as to prosecute pharmacy managers derelict in their duty."[21]

An additional problem was a lack of containers. A report from the American Embassy in Moscow in 1938 noted that

> As a rule, foreign medicinals are imported in bulk only, and repackaged in the pharmacies and laboratories under the Administration of Pharmacies of the People's Commissariat of Health. Exceptions are perhaps made in regard to certain biologicals which require preservation in hermetically sealed vials or other small containers.
>
> Medicine containers of all types used in the Soviet Union are of domestic manufacture. Official Soviet statistics do not indicate any imports of such items. The containers have no standard form and consist mostly of bottles, jars, and cartons of all shapes and sizes. The population is encouraged to return empty bottles and jars to the drugstores. Metal tubes are very seldom used, and fancy or patented tin containers are not used at all. [22]

Now, of course pharmacy managers could not be blamed for the lack of containers. It also appeared unfair that they were chastised for selling sundries. People may well have needed and wanted items for cleaning their dwellings, washing their hair and their clothes and so forth. Further, pharmacy managers' eagerness to sell lucrative wares resulted from authorities' insistence that pharmacies make profits. Nevertheless, from his own experiences, dictated to me in his study in Denver some sixty years after the fact, Dr. David Genis agrees that managers of pharmacies and managers of pharmacy administrations that supplied them were partly responsible for poorly stocked pharmacies. Dr. Genis' father was the manager of a pharmacy administration in Kazakhstan after the war. He phoned authorities up the chain of command to get items needed by the pharmacies in his jurisdiction. After he died, a new manager, much less committed, did not bother to pull strings and pharmacies and consumers were not as well provided for as during the tenure of Dr. Genis' father.[23]

Although hospitals had their own pharmacies, some apparently were not as well-equipped as they ought to have been. Dr. Genis' older sister died of scarlatina in the 1930s at the age of eleven months, while incarcerated in the infectious ward of a large hospital in the city of Khar'kov, in the eastern Ukraine, apparently from lack of treatment.[24] It is true that, in the United States today, many people catch serious infections in hospitals and some die. Moreover, scarlatina or scarlet fever, caused by a streptococcal bacterium, was a serious disease before penicillin became available in the 1940s, at the end of World War II. Symptoms included a red rash, sore throat, fever, chills, rapid pulse and vomiting. Scarlatina could take a mild form or it could kill or maim. However, in the 1930s a serum or antitoxin (from the blood of an infected animal) was available to both immunize and treat the disease. In the United States the antitoxin was patented by George and Gladys Dick. An American physician, Alphonse Dochez, working at Johns Hopkins and Columbia University, also developed an antitoxin, receiving a British patent in 1924 and an American patent in 1926. However, George and Gladys Dick, husband-and-wife physicians, whose combined training included Rush Medical College in Chicago, Johns Hopkins, the University of Chicago, and medical schools in Vienna and Berlin, developed their scarlatina antitoxin and received their American patent in 1925, thus capturing the American market for their scarlet-fever screening test and scarlet-fever antitoxin, used both to treat the disease and also to immunize.[25]

Ironically, Russian scientists may actually have pioneered the scarlatina antitoxin. The Bacteriological Institute in Ufa, Russia, founded in 1905, prepared a *syvorotka* (serum or antitoxin) against scarlatina from 1916 through the 1920s. In the 1930s, though, the scarlatina serum, made from the hearts of children who had died from the disease, was prepared according to the method of Dick and other Western scientists. In any case, the Ufa Institute had trouble preparing enough of the serum and other serums and vaccines in the early 1930s, due to shortages of pharmaceuticals and other ancillary items.[26] It certainly was absent when Dr. Genis' sister succumbed. As a result of this disaster, when Dr. Genis himself came down with scarlet fever a few years later, his mother refused to let him go to the hospital, even when the militia threatened her and threatened their father with loss of his factory job.[27]

Pharmacists and pharmacy officials continued to express concern about the stocks in pharmacies in 1940 and 1941. In 1940 one A. N. Sorokin lamented, in an article in the journal *Farmatsiia*, that pharmacies had to have "hidden reserves" to compensate for outmoded equipment in the factories and unsatisfactory distribution channels. He asserted that "the need for prepared medicines was great."[28]

More significant was the report from the Chief Pharmacy Administration of the Russian Republic (*Glavnoe Aptechnoe Upravlenie Narkomzdrava RSFSR*) in January 1941, a scant six months before the onset of the Great Patriotic War, that complained to higher officials about "interruptions" and sometimes complete absence in some pharmacies of basic items like ether, cocaine, Novocain, caffeine, Liuminal [the Soviet version of the barbiturate Luminal], pilocarpine, barium for x-rays, ice bags, autoclaves, x-ray machines, needles and syringes, boxes, dental wares, and eyeglass lenses.[29]

As noted in the previous chapter, the scarcity of these items for civilians might have been due in part to stockpiling them for the military. Difficulties in pharmaceutical and medical factories—problems in acquiring raw materials, *brak* or spoilage, and insufficiency of package materials—also accounted for the interruption and absence of such basic items in the pharmacy. Dr. David Genis elaborated on other factors causing difficulties for consumers trekking to pharmacies to acquire pharmaceuticals. One was that pharmaceutical and ancillary glass factories did not produce enough ampules, capsules and medicines in tablet forms. Dearth of containers forced Soviet pharmacists to give out prescribed medicines in powdered form. As specialists had noted in the nineteenth century, powders were not as accurate as medicines contained in preordained doses. But neither Soviet pharmacists nor patients had a choice. The powders were distributed in folded paper. This necessitated their being diluted with water. If patients brought bottles or jars to the pharmacy sterilized water was mixed with the powder on site. If not, patients had to mix them up at home. Powders not in capsules were bitter. This necessitated their being mixed with honey or jam to disguise the taste, obviously affecting compliance.[30]

Criminals also were responsible for scarcities. Dr. Genis noted that pharmaceuticals not available in pharmacies sometimes were sold at markets and bazaars—for high prices. They arrived there via theft on the part of pharmacy workers or those somewhere along the distribution chain. Finally, high prices made it difficult for ordinary Soviet citizens to get their prescriptions filled.[31]

Not all Soviet citizens had problems acquiring medicine in pharmacies or complained about Soviet medical care before the Great Patriotic War. Several former Soviet citizens responding to an *anketa* (questionnaire) querying their reminiscences about prewar and wartime pharmaceutical experiences, noted with pride that Soviet medical care was free of charge (*besplatno*). Some respondents remarked that they could not remember what medical care was like before the war, implying no difficulties stood out, or explained that were not ill and had no need to visit the pharmacy for medicine prior to the war. For example, Raisa Kuskina who lived in the city of Mogilev, Belorussia, stated that "before the war, I don't remember."[32] Lidiia Rakhshmut, who lived in Kiev, was "already a mama before the war, but" she "did not think there was any problem with medicine before the war."[33] Maina Tsirkina, who was twelve years old before the war and lived with her family in the town of Bobriusk in Belorussia, averred that "medical help was extended. . . .Before the war medical help was normal."[34] Yefim Kheyster, who also lived in the city of Bobriusk, agreed that "before the war the medicine provided was basically not bad (*ne plokhoe*)."[35]

Use of *Narodnaia Meditsina*

Generally those living in urban areas fared pretty well. But it was commonplace for Soviet citizens, urbanites as well as rural dwellers and those living in the European part of the Soviet Union as well as in Siberia, Kazakhstan or the Central Asian republics, to supplement factory-produced medicines with *narodnaia meditsina*—home-made or traditional remedies. For example, Esfir' Falkovich, who lived in the city of Elektrostal', Moscow *oblast'*, before the war and who now is in her nineties, recalled that in the late 1930s and early 1940s there was aspirin, Red Streptotsid and Sul'fidin. Those with malaria received quinine and Akrikhin. But "basically" people used "extracts" made from "botanicals," [Vishnevskii's] "fish oil, cupping, mustard [plasters], and botanical medicines, *narodnaia meditsina*."[36] Of course, mustard plasters were commonly used in the United States in the 1930s. However, medicinal botanicals were far less used in the United States by this time, as the following chapter enumerates. And cupping would not have been familiar to Americans in the 1930s. This was an old Oriental or Arabic procedure in which heated class cups are applied to the skin, particularly on the back, to create a vacuum. According to a contemporary website, "blood stasis is formed and localized healing takes place." It has been asserted that cupping causes "tissues to release toxins, activates "the lymphatic system," and clears "colon blockages."[37] These popular practices, subsumed under the name of *narodnaia meditsina*, continued to be a major part of the self-treatment regimen of Soviet citizens because pharmacies were not always convenient or did not carry needed remedies.

One "Mark," for example, lived in Odessa before the war. He admired the fact the "medical help" was rendered "*besplatno*." But, although he lived in a major city, like Esfir', the remedies with which he was familiar were a mixture of botanicals, perhaps collected, perhaps purchased in the pharmacy, and factory-made or patented products. Colds were treated with aspirin and medicinal botanicals. "[h]eart-vascular diseases and stomach-intestinal diseases" were treated with botanicals—"naperstanka (digitalis) . . . landysh (lily-of-the-valley), romashka (chamomile)." For laxatives, "castor oil" was used, for malaria quinine and Akrikhin. "At the end of the 1930s Red Streptotsid, then White Streptotsid appeared. Sulfi'din appeared before the war," Mark recalled. He wisely observed that medical care "differed" according to whether the individual lived "in the village, where there was a fel'dsher or *akusherka* (midwife)"; in a "*raion* center, where there was a hospital and lying-in hospital"; or in "a larger town, where there was a medical auditorium [that was affiliated with a teaching hospital]."[38]

Mariia Sergeevna Kuznetsova lived on a remote state farm (*sovkhoz*) in eastern Siberia before the war. Her family members were pioneer farmers in Imperial Russia, having migrated to Siberia in the early twentieth century, lured by P. A. Stolypin's program to encourage resettlement in Siberia, in part to alleviate "land hunger" in Russia and Ukraine. The farmers were given tax breaks and implements but life was hard.[39] By the late 1920s or early 1930s Mariia Sergeevna's family farmstead was part of a state farm comprised of about twenty families. The *sovkhoz* grew vegetables; there were milch cows and aviaries.

Born in 1925, Mariia Sergeevna attended primary school ten kilometers from home in the small village of Ust'-Tala, which she reached by boat, crossing the River Kondom. The village had amenities of sorts—a soviet (council) of party officers, village administrators, a post office, a police station, and a basic medical station (*medpunkt*). Today a physically and mentally lively, beautiful and gracious woman in her eighties, Mariia Sergeevna recalled that when young she had a "strong Siberian constitution" and "practically was never ill." She needed little medical help. When she did get a cold, she relied on traditional remedies, described in a later chapter.

Many Americans also treated minor ailments with home-made remedies. However, Americans did not make their own soap in the late 1930s. The peasants of Siberia did. They suffered a shortage of factory-made soap, an everyday necessity. As a result, Mariia Sergeevna's mother and the other women in their village made soap, known as *domoroshchennoe mylo*. "From the stove they took ashes for preparing alkaline. The ashes were poured into a canvas bag, the bag was tied up, then it was put into a wooden box and boiled water was poured in. This process was called washing linen in lye."[40] It was an arduous process, reminiscent of nineteenth-, early-twentieth century American pioneers and considered archaic in the United States by the Second World War.

Some Soviet citizens, living in less remote areas of the Soviet Union in the late 1930s and early 1940s, had problems acquiring other pharmaceuticals as well. The mother of Mariiam Samoilovna Tartakovskaya, who lived in the Ukraine, was a dentist. Nevertheless, she had trouble acquiring Novocain.[41] Anna Konetspolskaya also lived in the Ukraine, in the city of Dnepropetrovsk, before the war. She had allergies and when she was twelve years old developed boils over her entire body. Her mother "lubricated her with vinegar greens" to alleviate the problem.[42] Polina Savranskaya lived in the Ukraine before the war. She recalled that "before the war it was very difficult (*tiazhelo*) with medicines." Nevertheless, she was treated for malaria with Akrikhin, [43] the new Soviet antimalarial produced by the Moscow-area factory of the same name. Liudmila Ravvina, who lived in Vitebsk *oblast'* in Belorussia, was eight years old before the war. She claimed she "could say nothing" about medical care before the war, giving the impression that all was well. On the other hand she did recall that "they treated her throat with the steam of boiled potatoes"[44] thus implying use of home-made rather than factory-prepared remedies. Tat'iana Petrishche, a historian of pharmacy who teaches at the Medical Institute in Vitebsk, has served as a conduit for responses from war survivors now living in Belarus who wish to remain anonymous. Tat'iana's neighbor, now living in the city of Vitebsk—Marc Chagall's natal city—was born in 1922 and lived in a village in Vitebsk *oblast'* before the war. In the 1930s she and her family "had no medicines." A basic treatment was honey. When she became ill with Botkin's disease (viral hepatitis), she drank a decoction of carrots. She and her family did have soap, however. It was brought to them by an itinerant (and quite possibly underground) trader. She recalled that a "man came to the village, who exchanged—for rags—matches, thread, soap" and other household items.[45]

At this point it is germane to note that there were illnesses for which no medicines were available in the late 1930s and early 1940s, in the United States as well as in the Soviet Union. In these cases anything that alleviated suffering was used. For example, Anna Konetspolskaya suffered from asthma. There was no effective remedy for that disease on the eve of and during World War II nor was there much to even alleviate the problem. In the Crimea Anna was treated with medical mud.[46]

Tat'iana Petrishche's paternal grandfather lived in the countryside in Lepel'skii *raion*, Vitebsk *oblast'*, where medicines were scarce. In addition, he suffered from a stomach ailment, which Tat'iana theorizes was an ulcer. Not only was the etiology of ulcers mistakenly diagnosed until recently when it was discovered they were caused by bacteria, but there was no cure until recently, although there were remedies and diet that alleviated symptoms of the ulcer. So Tat'iana's paternal grandfather was on his own in more ways than one.

He obviously was a resourceful and independent-minded individual. In the 1930s he lived on a *khutor*—an independent farmstead. Only about one forth of peasants had lived on a *khutor* in Imperial Russia and most were located in the western provinces of the Empire. Most peasants—about 75 percent in Imperial Russia and over 90 percent in Soviet Russia of the 1920s—lived in *obshchiny.* In these communes, the village owned the arable land and parceled it out to families in scattered strips. Each family owned its own house, garden, sheds, tools and animals. The community shared pastureland. During the reign of Nicholas II, the government had attempted to convert the *obshchiny*, a combination of socialistic and private agriculture, into separated, private farmsteads *(khutory)*, through a program known as the Stolypin Agrarian Reforms, for Minister of Internal Affairs P. A. Stolypin, who began implementing the program in 1906. It was difficult to demolish communal ownership and carve off a farmstead, however, so most peasants continued to live in the *obshchina.* In the 1920s, following their seizure of private estates, most farmland was organized in *obshchiny.* During the civil war period of 1917/1918-1920 the Soviet government had attempted to combine two or three *obshchiny* into a collective farm or *kolkhoz*. The *kolkhoz* was distinguished from the *obshchina* because it eliminated the practice of allotting separated strips to families in favor of large open fields. Theoretically the entire collective owned the farmland and ideally it could use state-of-the art agricultural machinery.[47]

Many peasants resisted change both in Imperial and in Soviet Russia. However, at the end of the 1920s, Stalin determined to forcibly replace both *khutory* or private farms and *obshchiny* or semi-socialistic farms, with completely collectivized *kolkhozy* or big agricultural units run like factories, the *sovkhozy*. A war between the Soviet government and the peasantry ensued. The government won. After executions, resettlement and harsh treatment of many peasants; after the peasants had destroyed many of their animals; after crop failures (some a result of bad weather), famine, and food rationing by the mid-1930s most farmland was either in a *kolkhoz* or a *sovkhoz*. Some peasants (about 7 percent) held out.[48] Tat'iana Petrishche's paternal grandfather was one. The government ordered him to move his house and shed to the village. But the outbreak of World War II nullified this *diktat*. So Tat'iana's grandfather moved his buildings back on his *khutor* and lived there during the war.

Tat'iana Petrishche's grandfather not only defied the Soviet government. He defiantly treated his stomach ailment—probably an ulcer—by "eating a piece of chalk." He also used a remedy that combined "fresh cucumbers and honey." He had his own honey because he kept bees.[49]

Results

Thus we see that, well before the Great Patriotic War, Soviet citizens' experiences with pharmaceutical help varied. Some were satisfied. Others, however, had difficulties in acquiring factory-produced medicines and soap. As a result, some suffered pain and discomfort. Some Soviet citizens died as a result of inadequate supplies of vaccines, antitoxins, sulfa drugs, and the like. Those that survived exemplified the theory that the fittest survive.

Soviet citizens who had difficulties acquiring medicines and vaccines and antitoxins attempted to compensate with home remedies. Thus, *narodnaia meditsina* remained a part of their lives. Although popular, traditional, home-made remedies were not effective against all diseases and medical problems, they were effective in many cases. The next chapter illustrates that Soviet pharmacologists also turned to *narodnaia meditsina* before World War II came to Soviet soil, in order to compensate for shortages of sulfa drugs and other state-of-the art medicines, shortages of medical apparatus, and shortages of vaccines, serums and antitoxins. In this way, Soviet medicine took a different path from American medicine, even before the Great Patriotic War began.

Notes

1.Narkomzdav RSFSR Upravlenie mediko-farmatsevtich promyshlennosti "Medfarmprom," *Informatsionnyi biulleten'*, no. 2 (1940): 20 and no. 3 (1940): 23. Also "Po soiuzu," *Farmatsiia*, vol. 3, no. 9-10 (1940): 54.

2. Babich, "Aptechnoe delo v zapadnykh oblastiakh Ukrainy," *Farmatsiia*, vol. 3, no. 11 (1940): 11.

3. Ibid.: 12-13.

4. Ibid.: 12.

5. Ibid.: 12-14.

6. Ibid.: 13.

7. Conroy, *In Health and In Sickness: Pharmacy, Pharmacists and the Pharmaceutical Industry in Late Imperial and Early Soviet Russia*: 39-76. See also Conroy, *The Soviet Pharmaceutical Business During Its First Two Decades*: 23-24.

8. For details see Conroy, *The Soviet Pharmaceutical Business During Its First Two Decades*: 139-148.

9. Mary Schaeffer Conroy, "Pharmacy in Soviet Russia before the Great Patriotic War (1941-45)," *Pharmacy in History*, vol. 40, no. 1 (1998): 14-15.

10. GARF, f. A482, op. 51, d. 15, ll. 4, 6.

11. V. M. Salo, "Deiatel'nost' aptechnykh upravlenii v predvoennyi period (1936-1940 gg.)," *Farmatsiia*, vol. 28 (1979): 17.

12. Dennis B. Worthen, "Selective Service and the Pharmacist: Necessary Men in WW II," *Pharmacy in History*, vol. 43, no. 4 (2001):126.

13. Original notes in Conroy, "Pharmacy in Soviet Russia before the Great Patriotic War," : 16-17.

14. I. Ia. Bychkov and A. Chelidze, "K itogam kursov po meditsinskomu instrumentariiu," *Sovetskaia farmatsiia*, vol. 2, no. 4 (1931): 25.

15. Advertisements, endpaper, *Farmatsiia*, vol. 2, no. 1 (1939).

16. Advertisement, endpaper, *Farmatsiia*, vol. 2, no. 4 (1939).

17. Kobrak, *National Cultures*: 56-57, 364; Discussion on Soviet production of this product in Conroy, *The Soviet Pharmaceutical Business*: 134-135.

18. Advertisement, endpaper, *Farmatsiia*, vol. 2, no. 1 (1939).

19. Loc. Cit.

20. Endpaper, *Farmatsiia*, vol. 2, no. 4 (1939).

21. Document No. 18, "Obizhnik aptekoupravlinnia ukraini shchodo pokrashchannia likars'skogo zabezpechennia naselennia i viluchennia z aptek tovariv nemedichnogo priznachennia," 27 grudnia 1939 r., Siatinia, *Istoriia farmatsii*: 408-409.

22. "Memorandum on the Market for Medicinals in the U.S.S.R": 2. Enclosure to dispatch No. 1456 of July 8, 1939, from the American Embassy, Moscow, U.S.S.R. in NAUSA, RG 489, Box 82, 10,300, BFDC, U. S. Dept. of Commerce. Pharmacies still lacked containers in the 1980s and 1990s.

23. Interview with David Genis, Denver, CO (September 11, 2006).

24. David Genis, Denver, CO, responses to *anketa* (August 20, 2006) and e-mail communiqué (September 27, 2006). The scarlatina antitoxin may not have been entirely effective. Dr. Genis stated that in the 1930s in Khar'kov "there was no medicine against scarlatina" (Response to *anketa* August 20, 2006). He reiterated, on September 27, 2006,

that despite the antitoxin produced in Ufa from 1916, the doctor had none of it in the infectious ward of the hospital in Khar'kov in the 1930s when his sister died.

25. WWW.bookrags.com/Scarlet_fever, pp. 1-11. Accessed 9/24/2006. For a 1930 account of serious complications of high fever and delirium from scarlet fever affecting a Canadian woman who lived on a remote farm and had just given birth, see H. R. Clouston "Puerperal Fever or Scarlet Fever," *The Canadian Medical Association Journal*, (1930): 705-707. The woman recovered after being given scarlatina antitoxin. Clouston also noted that "*large amounts of scarlet fever antitoxin will prevent these infections* [angina]." (707) Heart complications or rheumatic fever sometimes resulted from untreated scarlet fever.

26. Conroy, *The Soviet Pharmaceutical Business During Its First two Decades*: 12, 154, 165.

27. David Genis, e-mail communiqué (Denver, CO, September 27, 2006). Dr. Genis' father moved out of their apartment to prevent losing his factory job during a period of "significant unemployment."

28. A. N. Sorokin, "Puty razvitiia farmatsevticheskoi promyshlennosti," *Farmatsiia*, vol. 3, no. 7-8 (1940): 9-11.

29. GARF, f. A482, op. 51, d. 15, ll. 11-13, 48-51.

30. Interview with David Genis (September 11, 2006).

31. David Genis, responses to *anketa* (Denver, CO, August 20, 2006).

32. Raisa Kuskina, responses to *anketa* (Denver, CO, August 28, 2006).

33. Ludiia Rakhshmut, responses to *anketa* (Denver, CO, September 2006).

34. Maina Tsirkina, responses to *anketa* (Denver, CO, August 28, 2006).

35. Yefim Kheyster, responses to *anketa* (Denver, CO, August 29, 2006).

36. Esfir' Falkovich, responses to *anketa* (Denver CO, October, 30, 2006).

37. For details, see "What is Cupping Therapy," http://www.chinajnbook.com/ cupping/intro.htm, 2 pages. Accessed 11/21/2006. Also, Michelle Roberts, "What Caused Gwyneth's Spots," BBC News Online health staff, 2 pages, http://newsvote.bbc.co.uk/ mpapps/pagetools/print/news.bbc.co.uk/1/hi/health/3879447.stm. Accessed 11/21/2006.

38. "Mark," responses to *anketa* (Denver, CO, October 30, 2006).

39. Mary Schaeffer Conroy, *Peter Arkad'evich Stolypin, Practical Politics in Late Tsarist Russia* (Boulder: Westview Press, 1976): 47. See also Thomas Porter and William Gleason, "The Zemstvo and The Transformation of Russian Society," in Mary Schaeffer Conroy, *Emerging Democracy in Late Imperial Russia* (Boulder: University Press of Colorado, 1998): 81-83.

40. Mariia Sergeevna Kuznetsova, e-mail communiqué (Ufa, Russia, June 20, 2006).

41. Mariiam Samoilovna Tartakovskaya, responses to *anketa* (Denver, CO, September 2006).

42. Anna Konetspolskaya, responses to *anketa* (Denver, CO, August 25, 2006).

43. Polina Savranskaya, responses to *anketa* (Denver, CO, September 2, 2006).

44. Liudmilla Ravvina, responses to *anketa* Denver, CO, August 29, 2006.

45. Anonymous neighbor of Tat'iana Petrishche, Vitebsk, Belarus, e-mail response to *anketa* via Petrishche (September 25, 2006). On the Soviet government's crackdown on private traders during the second half of the 1920s NEP, particularly in Belarus, see Alan M. Ball, *Russia's Last Capitalists: The NEPmen, 1921-1929* (Berkeley: University of California Press, 1987): 98-108. See also Rustem A. Khaziev, ed., *Bubliki dlia respubliki* (Ufa: Bashkir State University, 2005), passim. On the government's clamp-down on

private trade see Julie Hessler, *A Social History of Soviet Trade* (Princeton; Princeton University Press, 2004): 145-154, 198-201,205 (cosmetics in the 1930s), 251-266.

46. Anna Konetspolskaya, responses to *anketa* (Denver, CO, 2006). The author suffered terribly from bronchial asthma as a child in the late 1930s and 1940s and, in fact through the 1960s. There was no cure, nor even effective therapies. I took some sort of bitter-tasting tablets which my mother ground up in grape jelly to disguise the taste. The medicine made me nauseas but did not ease my breathing. My Austrian grandmother made me drink hot tea and the steam helped somewhat.

47. The literature on peasant agriculture is voluminous. The following are some selected sources. Paul R. Gregory, *Before Command: An Economic History of Russia from Emancipation to the First Five-Year Plan* (Princeton: Princeton University Press, 1994) includes a review of peasant agriculture and living standards in late Imperial and Early Soviet Russia. For peasant agriculture in the 1920s, prior to collectivization, see Moishe Levin, *Russian Peasants and Soviet Power: A Study of Collectivization* (New York: W. W. Norton and Company, 1968).

For Sergei Witte who drafted the "agrarian reform," see Sidney Harcave, *Count Witte and the Twilight of Imperial Russia: A Biography* (Armonk: M.E. Sharpe, 2004). For an analysis of the "Stolypin Reforms" see Stephen F. Williams, *Liberal Reform in an Illiberal Regime: The Creation of Private Property in Russia, 1906-1915* (Stanford: Hoover Institution Press, 2006). On Stolypin and his other policies see Conroy, *Peter Arkad'evich Stolypin: Practical Politics in Late Imperial Russia,* passim. and Abraham Ascher, *P. A. Stolypin: The Search for Stability in Late Imperial Russia* (Stanford: Stanford University Press, 2001). Hundreds of books about Stolypin have appeared in post-Soviet Russia where he has become an icon. Some of these are plagiarized from Western books. For a high quality, post-Soviet Russian work on Stolypin (and his relatives) see Boris G. Fedorov, *Petr Arkad'evich Stolypin* (Moscow: Rosspen, 2002). On the agricultural reforms, specifically, see 249-293. An interesting source book on Stolypin, with much material dealing with agricultural issues, is *P. A Stolypin: Grani talanta politika* (Moscow: Rosspen, 2006).

48. For selected sources on collectivization see Robert Conquest, *Harvest of Sorrow: Soviet Collectivization and the Terror Famine* (New York: Oxford University Press, 1986); Sheila Fitzpatrick, *Stalin's Peasants: Resistance and Survival in the Russian Village After Collectivization* (New York: Oxford University Press, 1994); Lynne Viola, *Peasant Rebels Under Stalin: Collectivization and the Culture of Peasant Resistance* (New York: Oxford University Press, 1999) and Steven Shabad, Lynne Viola, V. P. Danilov, and N. A. Ivnitskii, eds. *The War Against the Peasantry, 1927-1930: The Tragedy of the Soviet Countryside*, Vol. I (New Haven: Yale University Press, 2005).

49. Paternal grandfather of Tat'iana Petrishche (anonymous), e-mail responses to *anketa* (September 25, 2006) and e-mail communiqué (October 6, 2006).

Chapter 5
Pharmacologists Investigate *Narodnaia Meditsina* and Phages during The First Two Years of World War II

Hitler's National Socialist government tried to replace chemotherapy—and indeed the use of serums to some extent—with "natural" remedies and folk medicine during the 1930s but the German pharmaceutical industry successfully resisted.[1] And although Hitler's government interfered in the operations of Schering and the conglomerate I. G. Farben, these entities remained privately owned, fairly autonomous and leaders in the development and production of pharmaceuticals.

The Soviet government owned Soviet pharmaceutical factories. However, although higher authorities interfered in the Soviet pharmaceutical sector far more than Hitler and his cohorts in Germany did, Stalin and his entourage never attempted to eliminate chemically synthesized medicines and indeed touted the scientific, cutting-edge quality of Soviet pharmaceuticals. Nevertheless, heavy exporting of chemicals and the inefficiency of the Soviet macro economy enhanced the use of traditional remedies in Soviet medical practice. To compensate for deficits of chemically synthesized medicines, disinfectants and soap pharmacologists investigated botanical and traditional remedies that ordinary people had been using in lieu of factory produced pharmaceuticals. Some of the folk remedies were sensible. Some remedies, like phages, had potential. Other remedies were bizarre. But this trend pushed Soviet mainstream medicine onto a different trajectory from American medicine. *Narodnaia meditsina*—loosely translated as popular, folk, or traditional medicine—was used not only by ordinary citizens but treated seriously by Soviet scientists. Soviet pharmacologists and pharmacists not only tolerated but advocated cupping, the use of botanicals, and other therapies that in the United States were relegated to allopathic practitioners by the late 1930s. Although Americans in small towns and farming communities or urbanites "in a pinch" resorted to their grandparents' remedies, mainstream American physicians and pharmacists relied on state-of-the-art machinery and chemically synthesized medicines. [2]

Medicinal Botanicals

The Soviet pharmaceutical industry paralleled West European and American pharmaceutical houses in research and development of antimalarials, sulfa drugs, vitamins, and hormones. Soviet research on vaccines, antitoxins and serums was equal to and in some cases in advance of western European and American. Nevertheless, the use of botanical remedies and traditional therapies continued to be much more significant in the Soviet Union than in the United States at the end of the 1930s.

This is not to say that the American pharmaceutical industry did not utilize botanicals. Quinine would be an important therapeutic for the American army during World War II, despite the availability of synthetic antimalarials like Atabrine. And in the 1930s, the United States produced "700,000 to 900,000 pounds" of peppermint oil per year. Indeed, while "total imports of peppermint oil" were "very small in comparison with . . . domestic production," the Soviet Union supplied almost all of them; "imports of peppermint oil into the United States for 1939" amounted to "5,466 pounds, of which 4,452 pounds were credited as coming from Soviet Russia." The United States actually worried that "Russian oil" would "become a serious competitor of the domestically produced product," for in May 1939, the "S.S. Rodina from Leningrad brought in 375 cases totaling . . . 24,750 pounds," which was consigned to the Amtorg Trading Company and "47 cases arrived on the S.S. Kuznetz Leskov from Murmansk in March, 1939," along with 113 cases on the S. S. Chelvuskinetz from Leningrad, each case containing either 40 or 66 pounds.[3]

Further, belladonna leaves, aconite roots and some other plants were important to American pharmacology. Indeed, penicillin was made from molds, sometimes found on fruits. Nevertheless, in the 1930s, American scientists developed a process to mass-produce molds and although the catalyst was corn-steep liquor, the machinery used in the process, crucial to mass-producing penicillin during World War II, was state of the art.[4] By the late 1930s, in fact, in the United States heavy reliance on medicinal botanicals was associated with eclectic practitioners, called by John Haller "Medical Protestants."[5] Soviet pharmacologists, in contrast, viewed botanicals as equal partners with chemically synthesized therapies.

In the Eleventh U. S. Pharmacopoeia of 1936, for example, 15 and a half percent of articles were devoted to "natural products," that is, botanical raw materials. By 1942 coverage of these items would drop to a mere 10 percent. In the Seventh Soviet Pharmacopoeia of 1937, on the other hand, over 20 percent of the articles discussed "natural products." Conversely, "preparations of organic chemistry" were accorded a little over 22 percent of articles in the Soviet Pharmacopoeia of 1937, whereas these products received 30 percent of coverage in the U.S. Pharmacopoeia of 1936. Preparations of inorganic chemistry received about the same amount of coverage in both pharmacopoeias: 14 percent in the American and about 16 percent in the Soviet. Hormone (*Organo*) preparations and vitamins were covered by over two percent of the articles in the US Pharmacopoeia as were serums and vaccines. In the Soviet Pharmacopoeia these items were addressed by only one-half a percent of articles and one-third a percent of articles, respectively. Meanwhile, 34 percent of articles in the Soviet Pharmacopoeia discussed galenical and "prepared forms" of medicine but in the American only 30 percent of articles did so.[6]

We can hypothesize that Soviet scientists focused more assiduously on medicinal botanicals, traditional and alternative remedies than their American counterparts because the Soviet government limited imports and aggressive exporting of chemicals by Soviet foreign trade officials led to shortages of these materials for pharmaceutical factories and, in turn, shortfalls of chemically synthesized medicines.[7]

During the 1920s and early 1930s Soviet scientists made expeditions to Kazakhstan, Eastern Siberia, Central Asia, and the Caucasus to study the inhabitants' uses of local medicinal botanicals. They interviewed people and collected specimens which were then researched in the Alkaloid department of the All-Union Scientific Research Chemical-Pharmaceutical Institute. *Sovkhozy* or state farms were established in various republics to cultivate medicinal botanicals on a large scale for internal use and for export.[8] The pharmaceutical factories of the Georgian Republic "produced a large amount of preparations from local medicinal botanicals."[9] In 1940 the Scientific-Research Chemical-Pharmaceutical Institute of the Georgian SSR, founded in 1932, was transferred to Glavkhimfarmprom. The institute "looked for and studied medicinal botanicals in Georgia, Azerbaijan and Armenia and worked out methods of producing new preparations from local raw materials," such as "teal'bin, filiksan, sukradbell, digalen-neo, and others" and also worked out new methods of producing old staples, such as tannin and caffeine.[10]

Nevertheless, in their inaugural meeting in June 1937, the First All-Union Congress of Pharmacologists and Toxicologists lambasted Soviet pharmacologists for being "too preoccupied with theoretical issues to satisfy issues of public welfare." They criticized the industry's lack of attention to the rich store of indigenous medicinal plants. "Of the 20,000 forms of plants, produced in the USSR from the subtropical to the polar regions" speakers at the rostrum of the All Union Congress harangued, "from the point of view of medicine, only about twenty are used." Soviet pharmacologists were reproved because, aside from attention to digitalis, ipecacaunha, and a few other plants, they had made "entirely insufficient pharmacological study of plants used in popular medicine."[11] On the other hand, a report at the September 1937 Conference, rather contradictorily, praised the enormous growth in the use of medicinal plants in the USSR during the Second and Third Five-Year Plans.[12]

In any case, between 1938 and 1941, Soviet pharmacologists investigated large numbers of plants and plant-based remedies that were staples in popular medicine.

For example, the entire issue of *Farmakologia i toksikologia* (Pharmacology and Toxicology) volume 2, number 4, 1939, dealt with articles on botanicals. The following issue, number 5, contained an article on the nineteenth-century pharmacologist N. P. Kravkov; the other four of ten articles in the issue discussed botanicals. Thus, only sizable chunks of published research can convey pharmacologists' and pharmacists' obsession with investigating every possible botanical and traditional remedy. Unfortunately, we have little information on the amount of medicines actually developed and officially purveyed as a result of this research. Esfir' Falkovich recalled that the young people constructing Komsomol'sk in Siberia in 1934 suffered from scurvy because of lack of vitamins. They were given a decoction of boiled pine syrup to combat their debility. However, she observed that boiling may have destroyed the potency of the vitamins.[13] This is meager evidence. But the fact that pharmacologists expended so much effort on botanicals and traditional remedies indicates that they considered them significant. The researchers' thoroughness also suggests that conventional therapies were not abundant and that, therefore, alternatives, were necessary. Additionally, reports about pharmacological research on botanicals and unusual remedies provide information on what conditions and diseases were especially troubling in the Soviet Union on the eve of the Great Patriotic War.

Research: 1938

Quite a bit of research focused on anesthesia. In 1938, Dr. N. G. Poliakov and his colleagues at the Military Medical Academy in Leningrad—a venerable institution established in the imperial period, now under the jurisdiction of the Red Army and named after Sergei M. Kirov, following his assassination—studied the activity of vegetable poisons, ascetylcholine, arecholine, "fizostizmin," and atropine on breathing.[14] Metil anabazin (Methyl Anabasine) was reviewed as an improvement on anabasine, an alkaloid derived by Orekhov and S. P. Men'shikov from the plant *Anabasis aphylla*, common to Kazakhstan. Methyl Anabasine's effect as a respiratory stimulant was compared with lobeline, caffeine, ephedrine, and pilocarpine.[15] L. G. Merkulov of the Leningrad branch of the Institute of Experimental Medicine, reported on the creation of a new anesthetic that combined ether paraaminobenzoic acid and the alkaloid lupinine. The anesthetic was said to be more effective than cocaine in ophthalmology.[16] In Perm, Professor A. K. Sangailo investigated the influence of series number 13 of Garmin, an alkaloid of *Peganum Harmala*, produced in the Alkaloid Factory in Moscow, on spinal-cerebral activity.[17]

Three botanical cardiac remedies were investigated in 1938. Cytisin (tsitizin), derived from the seeds of *cytisis laburnum,* which was grown in the Nikitskii Botanical Garden in Baku, was researched as a substitute for nicotine in cardiac and ganglion therapies. Methylcytisin (Metiltsitizin) was a synthetic combination which produced cytisin and also was found naturally in some medicinal plants, such as

Thermopsis lanceolata, discovered by the botanist A. P. Orekhov. Soviet pharmacologists were excited, in 1938, by the fact that both cytisin and methylcytisin had been discovered in *Thermopsis alterniflora.*[18] *Hamamelis virginianis* also was being studied for its effect on coronary vessels. Further, the roots of *vincetoxicum offinalis* were researched as an analog to Strofantin, a cardiac therapy.[19]

During 1938, chereda, botanically known as *Bidens tripartitus chereda,* research on which had first been conducted in 1912, was again researched in Omsk, for a variety of applications. In popular medicine, the stem, leaves and flowers of *Herba bidentis* were brewed and used as tea for internal application or for bathing to treat scrofula or tuberculosis of the lymph nodes. In the Altai region chereda was used as an abortifacient and the pre-World War II research focused on that aspect of the drug.[20]

A potential breakthrough in 1938, considering the ongoing threat of malaria, synthetic antimalarials notwithstanding, was a new method of cultivating the cinchona tree. "Large experimental cinchona plantations," particularly focusing on *Cinchona Succiruba,* a species which had been "imported from the mountainous tropical regions of Bolivia," and grew "rapidly," with "good frost-resisting properties," had "been laid out in the warmer regions of Georgia." When two years old, "the entire tree-trunk, leaves, and roots" and not just the bark, was used to extract "quinine alkaloids by a chemical process."[21]

Research: 1939

By 1939 Soviet pharmacologists were captivated with the possibilities of lobelia. In the nineteenth century, lobelia, the emetic herb, had been one of the key plants in the system of natural remedies developed by the American "eclectic" Samuel Thompson. His followers in the United States used the drug in their arsenal of therapies from the early nineteenth century through the 1930s. In the 1930s American eclectic physicians still used two hundred specific medicines, most made from plants. As did Soviet pharmacologists they favored lobelia, aconite, buckthorn bark, canabis indica, camphor, belladonna, black cohosh, spearmint, convallaria, and strophantus. However, in the United States at this time, eclectics constituted a tiny minority of medical practitioners in the United States. Following advances in bacteriology, mainstream American physicians of the 1930s—allopathic physicians—disagreed with the "eclectics'" reliance on plant-based medicine.[22]

There seems to have been no similar cleavage among medical practitioners in the Soviet Union. In the 1930s many divergent therapies were used in Soviet allopathic medicine. Along with use of synthesized medicines, hormones, vitamins, and other therapies, some plant-based medicines were produced by core pharmaceutical factories and Soviet pharmacologists endorsed greater use of medicinal plants.

The forms of cultivated and wild lobelia researched in 1939 in the Soviet Union included *Lobelia inflata L., Lobelia syphilitica L., Lobelia sessilifolia Lamb., Lobelia dortmanna L.* Lobelia was cultivated by the All Russian Institute of Plant Production near Leningrad. The Institute derived the alkaloid lobelin from the plant, conducting a number of tests on the substance alone and in compounds during 1939. They concluded that the natural substance had less toxicity than the German synthetic preparation and determined to increase cultivation of *Lobelia inflata*, in particular.[23] In somewhat related research G. N. Pokrovskii, of the Voronezh Medical Institute, reported on the use of the Khava rhubarb, first researched in 1900 and grown in the Voronezh *Sovkhoz* (State Farm) for Medicinal Plants, as a laxative.[24]

Oleander and Magnolia, long-time staples in popular medicine, attained renewed significance in 1939 when V. I. Sila, at the Khar'kov Medical Institute Department of Pharmacology, investigated the glycoside Folinerin, derived from the Oleander tree (*Nerium oleander*) as a cardiac treatment. Folinerin had been derived in 1935, first by foreign pharmacologists and then in the Ukrainian Institute of Experimental Pharmacy. In the Soviet Union, the Oleander tree was native to the Caucasian Shore of the Black Sea and the southern shore of the Crimean Peninsula. Oleander leaves had long been used in popular medicine as a distillation, an infusion, a powder, and other medicinal forms as a treatment for skin diseases, such as chronic eczema and skin parasites. Therapies derived from oleander also were taken internally as a laxative, for menstrual problems, as an abortifacient, as an antimalarial, and as a diuretic. Indeed, in 1851, the Russian pharmacologist Lukomskii had derived an alkaloid he called "oleadrin" from the leaves of the tree and used it to treat epilepsy. In 1883 Oleadrin was shown to be a cardiac stimulant similar to foxglove.[25] The new cardiac glycoside developed from Oleander roots in 1939 was called "Kotenerin."[26]

In 1939 Orekhov and Proskurnin isolated two alkaloids of *Magnolia Fuscata,* Magnolin and Magnolamin, for use as cardiac remedies. This enlarged the significance of the plant which grew wild on the south shore of the Crimean Peninsula, the Black Sea Shore of the Caucasus and in Turkmenistan and was cultivated in Batum and Sukhum. It long had played a role in popular medicine as an antimalarial and diuretic.[27] The Boiarka tree (*Crataegus altaica*) provided another innovative cardiac therapy. A. A. Liubushin, working in the Experimental Laboratory of the Kazakh Commissariat of Health in 1939, reported on infusions made from the roots and leaves of the tree, which grew widely in the mountainous regions of southern and eastern Kazakhstan and was used by locals for heart problems. The berries of the Boiarka were used as food.[28] All these remedies were standardized by VILAR (the Institute of Medicinal Plants), which was part of the core industry, Khimfarmprom.[29] And more botanical remedies were touted.

The French scientist Duquesnel had discovered aconitine, derived from aconite, in 1871. In the late 1930s the All-Union Scientific-Research Chemical-Pharmaceutical Institute touted "Soviet Aconitine," so-called because it was derived from *Aconitum napellus,* which grew in Siberia, east of Lake Baikal. Local inhabitants referred to it as *volkoboi,* having long used it for poisoning wolves (*volkvy*). VNIKhFI also derived two other aconitine-like alkaloids from aconite growing in the Altai mountains, *Aconitum Tianschanicum F.* and *Aconitum Anthora L.*, called by locals "Issyk-Kul Root" and "Poisoning Swine" (*iadovityi svinets*). According to N. G. Poliakov-Stanevich, at the Military Medical Academy, "Soviet-Russian aconitine preparations" had the same effect on guinea pigs as that described in the American pharmacopoeia. [30]

Imperial Russian as well as Soviet plant researchers were praised for their discoveries. The alkaloids of Seneca had first been noted in 1895; one Bocharov had reported on them in *Russkii vrach* in 1904. In the early 1930s, A. P. Orekhov, at the Alkaloid Department of Pharmaceutical Chemistry in Moscow, discovered another alkaloid named Platyfyllin, derived from Seneca (also known as Krestovnika), which grew in the Caucasus. In 1939, G. S. Gvishiani, in the Department of Pharmacology of the Military Medical Academy, reported on his research of the characteristics of Platyfyllin.[31] In 1939, E. Shass enthusiastically reported on the recent Soviet discovery of Sal'solin, as a remedy for arteriosclerosis. Four years earlier Professors Orekhov and Proskurnina, at the Scientific-Research Chemical Pharmaceutical Institute in Moscow, had derived two alkaloids, Sal'solin and Sal'solidin, from the Central Asian forms of Salsola (called in Russian "Sol'ianka"), namely *Salsola Ricteri* and *Salsola subaphylla.* Tests on rabbits showed that sal'solin resulted in "small (up to 15-20 percent) and unusually quick lowering of blood pressure." The alkaloid also resulted in "lessening and sometimes complete disappearance of head ache and dizziness."[32]

For would-be mothers, A. A. Miazdrikova, of the Pharmacology Department of the Moscow Medical Institute, reported on positive results from combining Yohimbine with the female hormone Folliculine, in cases when even very large doses of Folliculine failed to stimulate ovarial function.[33]

Researchers in the non-Russian republics received publicity for finding treatments for serious medical problems and diseases. The Pharmacology Department of the Ukrainian Institute of Experimental Medicine investigated the benefits to the heart muscle of discrete, small doses of the glycoside Strophantin.[34] An interesting antidysentery remedy was made from *Rumex confertus willd,* long used in popular medicine, especially in Ukraine, but not investigated scientifically. The plant also grew in the Caucasus, western Siberia, Central Asia, and Central America, but the plants scrutinized during the first two years of World War II were collected in the village of Kurilovka, in Dnepropetrovsk *oblast'*.[35] The laboratory in the Ukrainian Experimental Culinary Institute developed another innovative remedy made from apple powder to be applied for children's diarrhea that turned out to be dysentery.[36] Dysentery, as we have noted was a serious problem in the Soviet Union at this time.

G. D. Allakhverdibekov at the Azerbaijan Medical Institute in Baku, researched infusions made from *Stigmata maydis* (corn hairs), a plant which grew in the Caucasus and which locals used to treat liver and kidney diseases. He found that the infusions "increased hepatic bile secretion . . . the rate of bile secretion into the doudenum" and thus that infusions "from corn stigmata can be considered as a good choleretic and cholagogue." [37]

G. T. Sevast'ianov, at the Kazakh Branch of the Academy of Sciences, named after Molotov, was excited about the possible uses of *Glaucium fimbrilligerum*, a member of the poppy family, which grew widely in the wild state in Kazakhstan. The plant had a high alkaloid content. From January 1938, tests of 10 percent infusion of the plant were conducted on seventy-seven animals, including frogs, dogs and rats. The effect was similar to alkaloids of opium. Sevast'ianov urged further study of the plant, but the implication was that, since the morphine content of Soviet opium poppies fluctuated, the new plant might serve as a substitute or at least complement use of the traditional poppy.[38]

Research: 1941

The entire first issue of *Pharmacology and Toxicology* for 1941 reported on research conducted on plants, many of which were staples of popular remedies. For example, five plants from Central Asia and Kazakhstan, brought back from expeditions in 1939, were studied at VNIKhFI in Moscow. Of them, *Daucua carota*, which grew wild in Kazakhstan, produced a vermifuge or worm expellant that was used in popular medicine. *Tithymalus gapula* was used in contractions of the womb.[39] A number of plants and plant-based remedies used for cardiac problems were studied at Medical and Pharmaceutical Institutes in Moscow and in Khar'kov. They included Far-Eastern Lily-of-the Valley (Landysh); Amur Adonis; Soviet crystallized Periplotsin, derived from the bark of Caucasian *Periploca*; *Stachys sylvatica*, Neriofolen, from the leaves of Caucasian Oleander; and a new heart glucoside, Folinerin, from Nerium Oleander. Periplotsin was an old remedy from the 1890s, resurrected in the 1920s; Neriofolen was said to "occupy an intermediate position between adonilen and convallen"; Folinerin was deemed similar to Digitalis. [40] The roots of *Rotentilla Tormentilla* were studied at the Odessa Medical Institute for use as an astringent. [41] The silver mimosa was studied at the Leningrad Scientific Research Pharmaceutical Institute as a replacement for scarce gum arabic in medical practice.[42] There were further reports on the new alkaloid "Galostochin," said to be similar to ephedrine in increasing blood pressure.[43] The old standby *Thermopsis Lanceolata* was also studied as a respiratory and circulation stimulant.[44] A number of plants, *Tagetes erutes, Trifolium arvense, Amarantus paniculatus*, *Callendula officinalis*, "long used in popular medicine for liver diseases," were studied at the Dnepropetrovsk Pharmaceutical Institute for their cholagogic action, that is, increase of bile and effect on cholesterol. [45] Again, various species of *Folia sennae—Cassia acutifolia, Cassia sofora,* and *Cassia obovata*—were studied for use as laxatives.[46] *Folio sennae*, commonly called "Alexander Leaves" had been part of the popular materia medica in the nineteenth and early twentieth centuries.

Collection and Cultivation

Medicinal plants were not only researched, they were collected and, as noted in the case of cinchona and magnolia, were cultivated. In 1939 the Commissariat of Health recruited pharmacy workers to collect plants for the pharmaceutical industry. The commissariat advertised for pharmacists to help "strengthen medical help to workers" by contracting with one of ten regional offices for the collection and preparation of wild medicinal plants. Pay was scaled according to the importance of the plants—dried valerian root was worth the most—and included living expenses.[47]

In 1939 the All Russian Office of the Union of Medicinal Plants (Soiuzlek-syr'e), located at the former Ferrein headquarters, no. 12 Krivokolennyi pereulok, in Moscow, informed "all pharmacy administrations and pharmacies" that it had begun producing subtropical and tropical plants, among them "kassiia" (Alexander's Leaves), aloe, Indian konopla (canabis), gum arabic, asafetida, "smola gal'ban," "istod uzkolistnyi," "as a fully valuable replacement for imported senega" and "tragacanth," yielding a gum used in pharmacy. The warehouses of the Union of Medicinal Plants claimed to have a full assortment of medicinal plants, which were distributed to clinics and treatment institutions. The Union also reminded pharmacy personnel that it produced cut and powdered medicinal plants, packaged "shalfeia" and pharmaceutical chamomile which were distributed in packaged weights of 25 and 50 grams. All products were analyzed.[48]

Plants were discussed in books during 1940 and 1941.[49] Plants were cultivated in Georgia. Some were cultivated in a monastery; this cultivation had begun in 1932. Foreign botanicals were cultivated in a state farm in Abkhazia.[50] Children in the pioneer camp connected with the Shcherbakov factory in the Chkalovsk station were put to work preparing chamomile flowers during the summer of 1940.[51]

Snakes

Snakes of the Soviet Union were studied in addition to plants. In 1938 medicinal uses for the venom of a viper found in the Ussuri region—Ancistrodon Blomhofii ussuriensis s Emelianoff—was studied for effects on the respiratory system. One A. E. Feoktistov had first researched the medicinal properties of this snake venom in 1888.[52] In 1939, G. A. Mednikian, of the Department of Parasitology and

Experimental Pharmacology, Leningrad Branch of the Gorky Institute of Experimental Medicine, reported on effects to intestinal and uterine capillaries and wider blood vessels, of the application of venom from this snake. In small doses, the venom dilated the capillaries and vessels, slowing blood flow; in larger doses, the venom "stimulated the uterine horn, showing anticoagulatory and slightly hemolytic properties." [53] Also in Leningrad, G. I. Tsobkallo reported on the hemostatic properties of venom from the viper Lebetina L., found in the Caucasian and Turkmen republics.[54] And F. F. Talyzin of the Gorky Institute of Experimental Medicine in Moscow, reported on the effect of combining the venom of a viper widespread in Armenia with acetylcholine and atropine.[55]

Strange remedies in 1940 and early 1941 dealt with the venom of vipers—(Raddae BTTG and Renadae ursini Christ), the effect of extracts of flatworms on the intestine, and extracts of the male fern. Regarding the last, it was determined that "commercial preparations were less active than required by international standards" and less active than those prepared in the laboratory. [56] This indicated that the last item was commercially prepared.

The active ingredients in these botanical and animal products, long a part of *narodnaia meditsina*, had strong scientific foundation particularly for combating viral diseases or diseases for which there were no therapies in existence

Phages

One remedy that was futuristic and innovative was the bacteriophage. Lytic bacteriophages, or phages as they came to be more familiarly called, are now regarded as viruses that attack bacteria. A contemporary internet website explains these as "bacteria-specialized viruses" and portrays them as tadpole-like with "a head filled with genetic material, a syringe-shaped tail, and several fibers that selectively attach themselves to specific receptors on the host bacterial surface." As for how they work, according to the site "phages bore into their respective host bacteria and inject them with the phage's own genetic material . . . phage DNA is replicated and then incorporated into bacteria-infectious particles that are manufactured from chemical components stolen from the bacterial host. These 'virions' are then released . . . via a process known as 'lysis,' which kills bacterial cell."[57]

In 1943, in the thick of the Second World War, Military Doctor J. G. Scadding asserted in the British Medical journal, *The Lancet*, "That sulphonamide drugs have a beneficial effect on bacillary dysentery is now generally accepted, although convincing statistical evidence is not yet available." Noting that there were different types of dysentery and that not all sulfa drugs were equally effective, he tested three sulfa drugs available to him on 358 cases of mild dysentery receiving "equally efficacious results." But he acknowledged that some of the drugs had unpleasant side effects such as "vomiting . . . troublesome enough to interfere with treatment and also that sulfa drugs were not so helpful in cases of severe dysentery "where the colonic mucosa may be grossly thickened and partly converted into highly vascular granulation tissue oozing pus. . . .And in severe Shiga infections there is no doubt of the great value of concentrated antitoxic serum." [58]

We have seen in Chapter 3, that Soviet physicians recommended vaccination and sanitary-hygienic measures to prevent dysentery and sulfa drugs—particularly Sul'fidin—and a nourishing liquid diet to treat those who had come down with bacillary dysentery. But from 1939 they also placed great faith in bacteriophages.

Bacteriophages had been discovered and originally used by foreign physicians. "About 25 years ago," *Time* magazine reported in May 1941, "bacteriophage was first isolated by a British scientist from a dead germ colony."[59] In 1919, a 1940 Soviet publication reported in more detail, one "Dr. Erell [sic] first applied bacteriophages" to quell dysentery "in children." After studying "10 thousand cases," one "De Kosta Kruts . . . came to the conclusion that the bacteriophage was a good remedy for bacillary dysentery." Three other foreign physicians also received "positive results." But four foreign physicians did not and therefore they dismissed the therapy. Bacteriophage therapy was resurrected in 1939 by eight Soviet physicians—Mel'nik, Ruchko, Orbant, Ruchkovskii, Iashchenko, Suknev, Olisko, and Mikhailov. During July, August and September bacteriophages were tested on 243 men and 23 women. Most (85 percent) were between 20 to 30 years of age; 13 percent were between 31 and 40 years, and 2 percent forty-one and older. The physicians noted "positive and quick effects" using bacteriophages to treat dysentery.[60]

As for children, several institutes applied bacteriophages—the Mechnikov Institute in Moscow, the Pasteur Institute in Leningrad, the institute in Sverdlovsk, and others," lowering the incidence of dysentery among young children from two to six times.[61]

By the spring and summer of 1941 bacteriophages were touted as the new panacea not only for dysentery but for other diseases and medical problems. Soviet physicians especially considered phages "magic bullets." Soviet military doctors O. E. Bauer and M. A. Velik announced that "tests for the activity of dry bacteriophages in treatment of dysentery" had been authorized by "order of the Sanitary administration of the Red Army." Dry bacteriophages to attack dysentery had been produced in the Institute of Microbiology of the USSR Academy of Sciences, from mixing bullion of bacteriophages with vaccines and serums produced at the institute and the Central Institute of experimental Medicine, the Mechnikov Institute, and the Khar'kov and Tbilisi Medical Institutes.[62]

American physicians were intrigued with the possibilities of phages as well. In its may 1941 article, *Time* magazine informed readers that "[L]ast week doctors hailed an old conqueror of the dread staphylococcus germ. Considered by some scientists a virus, by others an enzyme, this germ-eater . . . a bacteriophage" is "found in the human intestinal tract, in urine, pus, blood and sewage" although "it can scarcely be seen under a high-powered microscope. And must be cultured on a special nitrogen compound called asparagines." Sinclair Lewis had "dramatized" the bacteria killing properties of the bacteriophage in his novel *Arrowsmith* the *Time* article continued, but in 1941 his work seemed "conservative." In early May a "Dr. Ward J. MacNeal of Columbia University" described to the "New York State Medical Society" in Buffalo "how he had used bacteriophage in treating osteomyelitis (an infection of bone often caused by the staphylococcus" and "had saved not only limbs, but lives." MacNeal had tested the bacteriophage on "500 patients with severe infections" and had "cured 34%—a high proportion." MacNeal sent "a sample of the blood or pus containing the bacteria to special laboratories" and had "the bacteriophage made to order." He then "injected it into the veins, as much as a quart in eight hours." MacNeal concluded that the bacteriophage "first weakened bacteria with special enzymes, then most probably" joined forces with the white blood cells which eat the invaders." [63]

He considered bacteriophage "particularly useful for deep-seated bone infections which are difficult to open and drain." One of Dr. MacNeal's patients had been a surgeon "who had an abcess in his shinbone. Instead of an operation, he asked for bacteriophage," receiving "daily injections. In 48 hours his excruciating pain was relieved, in three weeks he was walking, in six he was playing tennis."[64]

So it appeared that Soviet physicians were in the avant-garde with their use of bacteriophages. Today, phages are regarded by some medical specialists as useful for treating bacterial diseases where bacteria have become immune to antibiotics. Yet, although nowhere was it stated in the Soviet medical literature of 1939-1941, Soviet scientists probably were infatuated with bacteriophages not so much because of problematical side effects of bactericides and antibiotics but because the Soviet pharmaceutical industry was problematical. The Soviet Union was embroiled in offensive wars and was being warned that a defensive war was looming. Bacteriophages appeared a panacea given shortages of sulfa drugs, soap, disinfectants and other conventional pharmaceuticals.

The "K-R" Cancer Cure

In contrast to phages, the bizarre "K-R" cancer cure appeared more the whim of its creator, Grigory Roskin than a sensible therapy. In the late1920s Roskin had become convinced that a South American protozoan could cure cancer. His research escalated in 1929 but slackened in the 1930s due to funding and political problems. After marrying Nina Kliueva, a famous researcher in her own right, in 1939, the new couple fixated on *Trypanosoma cruzi* as a cancer cure.[65]

Other dubious remedies would surface during the next phase of World War II. Thus, while keeping one foot planted in mainstream medical science, due partly to exigencies, the Soviet pharmaceutical industry began to investigate and employ unconventional therapies. Some might tolerantly be called innovative. Others would have to be relegated to the rubric of charlatanism.

The Results

In conclusion, preventive medicine, like the pharmaceutical industry, made strides during the late 1930s. But this sector of health care suffered from shortages as did the pharmaceutical industry. Soviet researchers thoroughly reexamined traditional folk remedies. This appears ironical in a country that worshiped science. After reviewing the pharmaceutical industry one cannot but speculate that sourcing problems and shortfalls prompted this research as much as concern over the side effects of chemically synthesized drugs. Some traditional popular remedies did have therapeutic value. However, others were only partial palliatives and patients would need sulfa drugs, which were proven bactericides. Still other alternative remedies were dubious. But the research was in place to supplement conventional medicine.

The next plateau for the Soviet health care system was to meet the challenges generated by the Great Patriotic War.

Notes

1. Lesch, *The First Miracle Drugs*: 74, 79, 80, 106-107.

2. Soviet citizens living in post Soviet Russia and other republics of the former Soviet Union and those now living in the United States still apply and often prefer cupping, botanical and other traditional remedies even when chemically synthesized, "scientific" remedies are available. E-mail from Professor Rustem A. Khaziev, June 15, 2006 and conversations with émigrés from the former Soviet Union now living in Denver, 2005-2006.

3. Harry J. Schnell, President, Oil, Paint and Drug Publishing Co, Inc., to Mr. Charles C. Concannon, Chief, Chemical Division, Department of Commerce, Bureau of Foreign and Domestic Commerce, May 26, 1939, NAUSA, File RG 151, 231, Box 1004, BFDC, U. S. Dept. of Commerce.

4. On the importance of botanicals see Worthen, *Pharmacy in World War II*: 7, 80. American pharmacologists' experimentation with molds, which had been progressing since 1917, led, in 1935, to development of a "'submerged' fermentation process in which a mold was grown throughout the medium." In 1937, the regional U.S. Department of Agriculture Laboratory in Peoria, Illinois, extended this process by using corn-steep liquor to enhance the growth of the mold, a method which would be used to mass-produce penicillin during World War II. Peter Neushul, "Science, Government, and the Mass Production of Penicillin," *The Journal of the History of Medicine and Allied Sciences, Inc.*, vol. 48 (1993): 374-377. These issues are discussed further in chapter 6 of this work.

5. John Haller, *Medical Protestants: The Eclectics in American Medicine, 1825-1939* (Carbondale: Southern Illinois University Press, 1994).

6. M. Kh. Bergol'ts, "Galenovye preparaty v novykh izdaniiakh farmakopei (XII) i natsional'nogo fomuliara (VII) SShA," *Farmatsiia*, vol. 8, no. 6 (1945): 36 and Bergol'ts,

"Osnovnye puti razvitiia galenovogo proizvodstva SSSR," *Farmatsiia*, vol. 8, no. 4 (1945): 18.

7. For details see Conroy, *The Soviet Pharmaceutical Business During Its First Two Decades*: 201-209 and 246-249.

8. For details see Conroy, ibid.: 210-212.

9. A. G. Natradze, *Ocherk razvitiia khimiko-farmatsevticheskoi promyshlennosti SSSR*: 140.

10.Natradze, *Ocherk*: 140-141.

11. "Pervaia vsesoiuznaia konferentsiia farmakologov i toksikologov, 1-5 iunia 1937 g.," *Farmakologiia*, vol. 1, no. 1 (1938): 84-85.

12. "Vsesoiuznaia konferentsiia farmakologov i toksikologov, 1-5 iunia 1937 g. , Po dokladu ot VILAR: Sovremennoe sostoianie i perspektivy osnoveniia lekarstvennogo syr'ia SSSR," *Farmakologiia*, vol.1, no. 2-3 (1938): 173.

13. Esfir' Falkovich, interview (Denver, Colorado, May 21, 2004).

14. N. G. Poliakov, "Deistvie nekotorykh vegetativnikh iadov na sosudistyi sykhatel'nyi i vagustnyi tsentry," *Farmakologiia i toksikologiia,* vol. 1, no. 2-3 (1938): 25-34.

15. Iu. I. Syrneva, "K vlianiiu na dykhanie metil-anabazina per se i v kombinatsii s drugimi veshchestvami, vozbuzhdaiushchimi dykhanie," *Farmakologiia*, vol. 1, no. 1, (1938): 27-36. In 1975 anabasis was used in the USSR as an insecticide and to counter parasites. G. N. Kotukov, *Kul'tiviruemye i dikorastushchie lekarastvennye rasteniia* (Kiev, 1975): 117-118.

16. L. G. Merkulov, "K probleme-sviaz' mezhdu khimicheskim stroeniem a farmakologicheskim deistviem: Mestnoanestezirushchie svoistva efira praaminobenzoinoi kisloty i alkaloida lupina," *Farmakologiia*, vol. 1, no. 1 (1938): 37-45.

17. A. K. Sangailo, "Vliianie garmina na spinomozgovuiu reflektornuiu deiatel'nost'," *Farmakologiia*, vol. 1, no. 1 (1938): 96.

18. P. Kh. Iuzbashinskaia, "Farmalogicheskaia kharakteristika metiltsitizina," *Farmakologiia*, vol. 1, no. 2 and 3 (1938): 66-75.

19. I. I. Sivertsev, "Deistviia Hamamelis Virginiana na coronarnye sosudy i rabotu izolirovanogo cheloveka i zhivotnykh," *Farmakologiia* , vol. 1, no. 2-3 (1938): 105-112. 116

20. Z. I. Ivanova, "K farmakologii cheredy," *Farmakologiia*, vol. 1, no. 1(1938): 64-65.

21. "Soviet Production of Quinine," *Bulletin of the Russo-British Chamber of Commerce*, No. 70 (March 15, 1938): 9 in NAUSA, File RG 489, Box 82, 10,300, BFDC, US Dept of Commerce.

22. Thompson pioneered the use of *Lobelia inflata*, "found in most areas of the United States" and adopted from the Indians by early settlers. Haller, *Medical Protestants*: 37-38, 187, 193-194, and passim.

23. V. P. Kalashnikov, "Biologicheskoe ispytanie lobelin, vydelennogo iz odutloi lobelii, kul'tirovannoi pod leningradom," *Farmakologiia i toksikologiia*, vol. 2, no. 4 (1939): 3-14.

24. G. N. Pokrovskii, "O slabitel'nom desitvii khavskogo revenia," *Farmakologiia*, vol. 1, no. 1 (1938): 80-83.

25. V. I. Sila, "K farmakologii novogo serdechnogo gliukozida folinerina (iz Nerium Oleander)," *Farmakologiia i toksikologiia,* vol. 2, no. 4 (1939): 15-26.

26. M. N. Varlakov, "Kotenerin—novyi gliukozid iz kory oleandra," *Farmatsiia*, vol. 3, no. 11 (1940): 27-31.

27. E. S. Komissarova, "O deistvii alkaloidov magnolii (*Magnolia Fuscata*) na serdechno sosudistuiu sistemu," *Farmakologiia i toksikologiia*, no. 1 (1945): 17-20. The Magnolia plant had more than twenty forms.

28. A. A. Liubushin, "Farmakologicheskoe deistvie kornei i list'ev boiarki," *Farmakologiia i toksikologiia*, vol. 2, no. 4 (1939): 37-39.

29. M. N. Varlakov, "Kotenerin—novyi gliukozid iz kory oleandra," *Farmatsiia*, vol. 3, no. 11(1940): 27-31.

30. N. G. Poliakov-Stanevich, "O toksicheskom deistvii sovetskogo akonitina chuvstvitel'nosti k nemu razlichnykh zhivotnykh," *Farmakologiia i toksikologiia*, vol. 2, no. 4 (1939): 50-56. Quote from English synopsis: 56.

31. G. S. Gvishiani, "O nekotorykh farmalogicheskikh svoistvakh platifillina," *Farmakologiia i toksikologiia*, vol. 2, no. 4 (1939): 39-46.

32. E. Shass, "Sal'solin," *Farmakologiia i toksikologiia*, vol. 2, no. 4 (1939): 87. Sal'solin had the chemical formula C11 H15 NO2. Sal'solidin had the formula C12 H17 NO2.

33. A. A. Miazdrikova, "Vliianie iokhimbina na spetificheskoe deistvie follikulina," *Farmakologiia i toksikologiia*, vol. 2, no. 5 (1939): 97-101.

34. A. I. Cherkes and M. A. Angarskaia, "Eksperimental'nye issledovaniia po farmakologiia sertsa: desitvie strofantina na uglevodnyimobmen serdechnoi myshnyi," *Farmakologiia i toksikologiia*, vol. 2, no. 5 (1939): 60-71.

35. R. L. Khazanovich, "Izuchenie konskogo shchavelia Rumek confertus willd," *Farmatsiia*, vol. 3 , no. 11 (1940): 31-36 and ibid., no. 12: 24-28.

36. "Po soiuzu," *Farmatsiia*, vol. 3 , no. 12 (1940): 42.

37. G. D. Allalkverdibekov, "Farmakologiia Stigmata maydis," *Farmakologiia i toksikologiia*, vol. 2, no. 4 (1939): 57-62. Quote from English synopsis: 62.

38. G. T. Sevast'ianov, "Fiziologicheskaia otsenka rasteniia Glaucium fimbrilligerum," *Farmakologiia i toksikologiia*, vol. 2, no. 6 (1939): 43-46.

39. N. V. Sapezhinskaia, "K farmakologii narodnolekarstvennykh rastenii," *Farmakologiia i toksikologiia*, vol. 4, no. 1 (1941): 5-9.

40. V. I. Zavrazhnov (Voronezh Medical Institute), "Deistvie dal'nevostochnogo landysha na sertse krolika," *Farmakologiia i toksikologiia*, vol. 4, no. 1 (1941): 10-15; N. V. Pereslegin, "Biologicheskoi aktivnosti amurskogo goritsveta," ibid.: 16-17; I. M. Subbotin (Leningrad Research Pharmaceutcial Institute), "Deistvie na sertse liagushki i toksichnost' lesnogo chistetsa (Stachys silvatica)," ibid.: 26-29; S. E. Abramovich (Ukrainian Institute of Experimental Pharmacy), "Eksperimental'no farmakologicheskoe issledovanie sovetskogo periplotsina," ibid.: 52-58; A. D. Turova (Moscow Pharmacology Institute), "Materialy k farmakologii nerifolena," ibid.: 59-64; V. I. Sila (from the Faculty of Pharmacology of the First Khar'kov Medical Institute and the Ukrainian Institute of Experimental Pharmacy), "K farmakologii novogo serdechnogo gliukozida folinerina (iz Nerium Oleander)," ibid.,: 65-72.

41. K. V. Gribova, "Kharakteristika viazhushchikh svoitstv preparatov kornia tormentilly," *Farmakologiia i toksikologiia*, vol. 4, no. 1 (1941): 18-21.

42. S. I. Meerovich, "O kamedi serebristoi mimozy (gummi acaciae dealbata) kak zamenitele araviiskoi kamedi," *Farmakologiia i toksikologiia*, vol. 4, no. 1 (1941): 73-77.

43. Iu. I. Syrneva, "K farmakologii novogo alkaloida galostokhina," *Farmakologiia i*

toksikologiia, vol. 4, no. 1 (1941): 45-51.

44. M. D. Mashkovskii (All Union Scientific Research Chemical-Pharmaceutical Institute, Moscow), "Preparaty iz Thermopsis Lanceolata kak vozbuditeli dykhaniia i krovoobrashcheniia," *Farmakologiia i toksikologiia*, vol. 4, no. 1 (1941): 34-44.

45. N. A. Naumenko, "K farmakologii rastitelnykh zhelchegonnykh sredstv," *Farmakolgiia i toksikologiia*, vol. 4, no. 1 (1941): 22-25.

46. I. E. Mosgov, "Sravnitalnaia otsenka farmakologicheskoi aktivnosti raznykh vidov senny," *Farmakologiia i toksikologiia* , vol. 4, no. 1 (1941): 30-33.

47. Advertisement: "Attention all pharmacy workers!" (back cover of *Farmatsiia*, no. 7, 1939). Addresses were provided for the ten local departments; headquarters of the project were at Soiuzleksyr'e, located in the Karpov (former Ferrein) plant, Krivokolennyi Lane. First cited Conroy, "Pharmacy in Soviet Russia before the Great Patriotic War" : 12, 23,

48. Advertisement, last page, *Farmakologiia i toksikologiia*, vol. 2, no. 3 (1939).

49. For example, see the review of E. Shass by V. P. Kalashnikov, *Posobie po chastnoi retsepture* (Medgiz, 1940 g., 163 str., tirazh 3,000, tsena, 9 rub.), in "Bibliografiia," *Farmatsiia*, vol. 3, no. 11 (1940): 42-44. This was a handbook for the Red Army. The review criticized the lack of attention to new remedies. Some mistakes were noted. One was that opium was cultivated not in Turkestan, but in Kazakhstan, and formulated not in the form of briquets but in the form of round clumps, and without covered leaves of poppy. Another book Shass reviewed in the same issue was that by Professor L. M. Krechetovich, head of the chair of the botanicals in the Military-veterinary Academy of the Red Army. 136 pp, 164 drawings, price 6 rubles, 50 kopeks. The book discussed poisonous plants. Ibid.: 45.

50. "Po soiuzu," *Farmatsiia*, vol. 3 no. 11 (1940): 46.

51. "Po soiuzu," *Farmatsiia*, vol. 3, no. 12 (1940): 42.

52. G. A. Mednikian, "Farmakologicheskie svoistva iada zmei shchitomordnika (Ancistrodon Blomhofii ussuriensis s Emelianoff)," *Farmakologiia i toksikologiia*, vol. 1, no. 2-3 (1938): 135-149.

53.G. A. Mednikian, "Farmalogicheskie svoistva iada zmei zhitomordnika (Ancistrodon Blomhofii ussuriensis s. Emelianoff," *Farmakologiia i toksikologiia*, vol. 2, no. 6, (1939): 47-58.

54. G. I. Tsobkallo, "Farmalogicheskaia kharakteristika iada giurzy (Vipera Lebetina L)," *Farmakologiia i toksikologiia*, vol. 2, no. 6 (1939): 59-65.

55. F. F. Talyzin, "Farmalogicheskie svoistva iada gadiuki raddae (Vipera Raddae BTTG, 1870)," *Farmakologiia i toksikologiia*, vol. 2, no. 6 (1939): 66-69.

56. P. P. Perfil'ev (Branch of All Russian Institute of Experimental Medicine in Suhum), "Opyt po izucheniiu deistviia iada gadiuk raddae i stepnykh gadiuk na zhivotnykh," *Farmakologiia i toksikologiia*, vol. 4, no. 2 (1941): 53-56; F. F. Talyzin, "Deistvie ekstraktov nekotorykh paraziicheskikh ploskikh chervei na kishechnikh," ibid.: 57-61; T. Ia. Chertskovskaia, "O biologicheskoi aktivnosti i stoikosti ekstraktov muzhskogo paporotnika," ibid.: 62-68.

57."What are Lytic Bacteriophages?" in Phage Biotech Ltd., "Phage Therapy," http://www.phage-biotech.com/links.html, accessed December 6, 2002.

58. J. G. Scadding, "Comparative Effects of Sulphonamide Drugs in Mild Bacillary Dysentery," *The Lancet* (June 17, 1944): 784-786; quote: 785. Scadding tested Sulphaguanidine, Sulphapyridine and Sulphanilamide. Sulphathiazole was on the market but was not available to him.

59. "Phage v. Staph," *Time*, vol. 37, no. 19 (May 12, 1941): 43.

60. S. I. Koifman, "Opyt lecheniia batsilliarnoi dizenterii bakteriofagom," *Voenno-Sanitarnoe delo*, no. 8 (940): 72-73.

61. Siroko, "Novoe v bor'be s dizenteriei," *Voenno-santiarnoe delo*, no. 10 (1940): 100-101.

62. O. E. Bauer and M. A. Velik, "Nabliudeniia nad deistviem sukhogo dizenteriinogo bakteriofaga," *Voenno-sanitarnoe delo*, no. 9 (1941): 35.

63. "Phage v. Staph," *Time*, vol. 37, no. 19 (1941): 43.

64. "Phage v. Staph," loc.cit.

65. Nikolai Krementsov, *The Cure* (Chicago: University of Chicago Press, 2002) and V. D. Esakov and E. S. Levina, *Delo KR* (Moscow: Institut rossiiskoi istorii, 2001).

Part III

The Great Patriotic War: June 22, 1941-1945

Chapter 6
Production of Pharmaceuticals During the First Two Years of the Great Patriotic War, 1941-1943

From September 1939 to June 1941 Germany and the Soviet Union shared a border. Germany had annexed about two thirds of Poland. The Soviet Union had subsumed the eastern portion of Poland and the states of Estonia, Latvia, and Lithuania. Despite manifold warnings from diplomats and spies and disquieting observations of German hostility, cartographers of the Twenty-first Soviet Motorized Topographical Brigade, Pribaltiiskii VO (Division), mapping the new borders of the USSR in Lithuania, were unprepared for the three-pronged German advance across the newly annexed Soviet territory, toward Leningrad, Moscow, and into the Ukraine that began in the early morning hours of June 22, 1941. The Soviet Union's ally had metamorphosed into a vicious enemy. World War II had become the Great Patriotic War. Between 1941 and 1943 Leningrad would be encircled; Moscow bombarded, though not taken; and German armies would reach as far east and south as Stalingrad on the Volga and the Crimea and North Caucasus.

One of the cartographers in Lithuania that June morning was twenty-two year old Boris Zakaliapin. He later recalled that his Red Army officers were panic-stricken. His unit was given two canisters of benzene to burn their maps, lest they fall into enemy hands, and ordered to retreat to Libau and then to Riga, Latvia.[1] According to the account of one chief military topographer, the U.S.S.R. lost "a hundred million maps . . . at the border. The Germans saw piles of burning maps . . . two hundred wagons full of maps were lost in the first few days of the war."[2]

The swift advance of the enemy also impacted medical care. Two hundred wagon-loads of medicines were lost at Dvinsk alone. Medical facilities and pharmaceutical factories in the newly acquired territories of the Baltic States were now in German hands.[3] Worse, the pharmaceutical industry situated in the Soviet heartland was not fully prepared for the cataclysm that was to cost an estimated 25 million lives, mostly civilian.

Diseases

What medical problems were unleashed by war on Soviet soil? What pharmaceuticals were needed to combat them? The thirty-five volume work *Opyt sovetskoi meditsiny v Velikoi Otechestvennoi Voine, 1941-1945*, published under the general editorship of Minister of Health E. I. Smirnov in the 1950s, doled out morbidity and mortality statistics parsimoniously. However, it provided interesting information on the chief medical problems and the most important pharmaceuticals needed at the front. Surgery was precarious. Geksenal and Dikain, synthesized in 1936, and Sovkain, synthesized in 1937, were the chief anesthetics used.[4] Anaerobic infections in wounds were fatal without amputation. Even with surgery, mortality was high, but applying chloramine following surgery lessened mortality to 43.1 percent; use of sulfa drugs lowered fatalities to 22.5 percent.[5]

The Smirnov volumes emphasize that during the first two years of the Great Patriotic War, 1941through 1943, less than two thirds of Red Army troops who perished died from wound complications while diseases felled the rest.[6] Dysentery, typhus, and malaria were most pernicious. Dysentery constituted two thirds of the infectious diseases affecting the Red Army. Typhus afflicted over another quarter (26.14 percent),[7] with pneumonia as a possible complication.[8] Following development of a new vaccine by Professor M. K. Krontovskaia and Dr. Maevskii in 1942,[9] the Smirnov volumes asserted that most of the troops were immunized.[10] If administered early, the vaccine mitigated the disease and lessened its epidemiological impact. Typhoid affected a mere 7.3 percent of the troops. Hepatitis afflicted only about 5 percent of the general number of sick.[11]

A recently published work, *Sluzhba zdorov'ia v Velikoi Otechestvennoi Voine*, authored by two military officers, using newly available materials from Communist Party and other official archives, attempts to present a more honest and accurate recital of illnesses among the Red Army and the civilian population during the Great Patriotic War. The authors imply that pharmaceuticals stored in military warehouses prevented epidemics among the troops during the first year of the war.[12] They claim that the anti-parasite substances "SK-9" and the anti-parasite soap "K," in particular, played a major role in preventing epidemics of typhus.[13] Despite epidemics of typhus among the German forces, until April 1942, the authors allege that there were only 7,930 cases of typhus among the Red Army and over 58.54 percent of them were in the three most active fronts (out of ten). "Naturally" there were "deficiencies" in the war on typhus, the authors concede, but baths and clean linen helped greatly.[14]

During the second half of 1942 and the first half of 1943, the authors of *Sluzhba zdorov'ia* note that communicable diseases increased among the troops. Typhus among the troops rose to 71,331 cases in 1942 waning to 38, 654 cases in 1943.[15] As for typhoid, the authors vaguely remark that in 1941 its prevalence among the troops remained the same as before the war, with a flare up at the beginning of 1942.[16] As for dysentery, they claim its incidence was lower in 1941 than in 1940.[17] But the hiatus in the spread of both diseases was over by 1942. In 1942, 95,962 Red Army troops were sick with dysentery and 6,898 with typhoid. In 1943 the respective figures were 51,814 and 6,465. Thus there was some improvement. More than half those sick with dysentery in the army were on the Leningrad front.[18]

The authors of *Sluzhba zdorov'ia* affirm that typhus was widespread during the second half of 1942 and first half of 1943.[19] Civilians were particularly hard hit, although the entire population was not affected. Outbreaks of typhus occurred in the liberated regions of Kursk, Khar'kov and Voronezh in 1943.[20]

Articles published during the war, archival materials, and the recollections of individuals who lived during the war add texture to this story. For example, in 1943 an article by V. S. Chetverikov referred to "worsening sanitary-epidemic conditions at the beginning of 1942 in some union republics."[21]

Dr. David Genis, who experienced the war first-hand, notes that typhus, typhoid and scarlatina were major problems for civilians, particularly those evacuated from the western parts of the Soviet Union. He explains why typhus, in particular, erupted. "The number coming down with typhus, especially among the evacuated, pouring monthly into the hinterlands" and interacting "with the local populations, in schools . . . was very great," he recalled. "[P]eople did not have the possibility to wash their hands or to bathe, there was no soap, there were no clothes so for months people could not change, they lived in close proximity; therefore there was a great increase in lice and typhus."[22] For example, he and his family were evacuated from Khar'kov, in the eastern Ukraine in September 1941. They wended their way to Kazakhstan in a "*teplushka*," a heated railway car for commodities, surrounded by open platforms on which excess refugees perched. The journey took a month. "The train moved slowly, halting for a long time at little stations, and sometimes standing in a field, waiting for "sanitary trains" bringing wounded from the front to go eastward and trains with soldiers and military materiel to go to the west. The trains with evacuees," he recalled, "were always last in line for permission to go on; therefore many died en route from starvation, the absence of timely medical assistance, cold or heat—from the absence of elementary conditions of life." One of the worst problems, confirmed by other evacuees in a later chapter, was lack of water. Dr. Genis remembered how, when their train stopped at some station, hordes "of people rushed out of the wagons with vessels, pushing each other, to be first to get to the water containers at the station, to drink and carry back some water. All feared that while the train might stand for hours it might unexpectedly leave quickly, so they could not wait their turn in line for water and meanwhile in the wagon waited their family, children and all wanted to drink." People tried to bathe under the pumps. But compounding their distress was the fact that at Russian railroad stations there usually were two separate pumps. One issued cold water. The other issued boiling water, to allow passengers to brew tea. Therefore, all washing and bathing was done with cold water.[23]

Outbreaks of tularemia (also spelled tularaemia) also occurred during the Great Patriotic War and they have caused contention amongst medical historians. Tularemia is caused by the bacterium *Francisella tularensis.* It is spread by deer flies or ticks and thus naturally infects animals. The disease can occur in humans who handle or eat infected rabbits. It is not spread from person to person. The plague-like symptoms of tularemia were first noted in Japan in 1837. The disease itself was named for an outbreak in Tulare County, California, that occurred in 1911. Tularemia is widespread in the United States. For example, a contemporary Internet website for the state of Illinois explains how to protect against it. Nevertheless, many Western medical historians have asserted that a highly contagious and lethal, aerosolized form of the disease had been developed through the Soviet biological weapons program of the 1930s. They remark that an outbreak of tularemia occurred before the Battle of Stalingrad, which began late in 1942, and they attribute it to sinister actions on the part of the Soviet government—a deliberate attempt on the part of Soviet officials and military officers to infect invading German forces before the battle of Stalingrad—Soviet civilians and troops unfortunately getting caught up in the process.[24]

The authors of *Sluzhba zdorov'ia* devote several pages to the epidemics of tularemia that erupted among the civilians of Rostov, Stalingrad and Voroshilovgrad. They date the initial appearance of the disease to the fall and winter of 1941-1942[25]—that is a *year before* the Battle of Stalingrad. They do admit that tularemia spread to the military between November 1942 and April 1943 and that the incidence of this disease rose alarmingly from a mere 35 in October to 3,962 in November to 9,165 in December to 10,121 in January 1943. But they assert that 65 percent of the cases were among the troops on the *western front* with about 25 percent of cases being among the troops on the southwest and Don fronts.[26] Tularemia remained a problem until 1945.[27]

The authors of *Sluzhba zdorov'ia* , P. F. Gladkikh and A. E. Loktev, are military men who presumably had access to secret military archives. By their own admission they are committed to setting the World War II Soviet health record straight. However, they make no mention of the use of biological weapons. Rather they depict the flare-up of tularemia to natural causes. They blame the initial outbreaks of tularemia to bacteria in mouse droppings and the subsequent epidemics of tularemia to large numbers of bombed-out civilians and Red Army troops living in dugouts (*zemlianki*) infested with mice. Further, instead of blaming the government they praise government edicts of August 1943 ordering ramped up efforts to cope with tularemia and the application of "prophylactic chemicals—carbonic barium and sodium floride—to disinfect living quarters and kill the mice.[28] Gladkikh and Loktev's account, in sum, counters the conspiracy theory.

Both Glakikh and Loktev's version of the flare up in tularemia and those of Western medical historians could be correct. Typhus, typhoid and dysentery also were investigated in the Soviet biological weapons program and epidemics of these diseases might also have been part of an offensive plan which caught up Soviet citizens as well as the enemy. On the other hand, Soviet bioweapons specialist Anthony Rimmington has concluded that Stalin's purges and his support of Lysenko's biology theories that rejected genetics caused major setbacks in the Soviet Union's biological weapons' program.[29] Additionally, perfectly natural causes—poor hygiene, lack of soap and other disinfectants and, in the case of tularemia, living quarters overrun by rodents and eating infected rabbits—could have spawned the diseases just as well. Natural causes certainly were responsible for the geometrical rise in malaria cases and infectious diseases like scarlatina which were not part of the biological weapons program.

Malaria was Russia's chief infectious disease in the nineteenth, early twentieth centuries. Three forms of the disease are debilitating since the parasite sucks iron from red blood cells. One form of malaria, which causes the walls of blood vessels to thicken, is fatal. Malaria was endemic and often epidemic, not only in the Caucasus and southern areas but along the Volga River.[30] The Smirnov volumes and *Sluzhba zdorov'ia* agree that malaria remained a scourge both for troops and civilians during the war. The Smirnov volumes state that over 25 percent of Red Army troops were sick with malaria in August 1942. In 1943, the peak year, 30 percent were sick with malaria in July, 29 percent in August, and 21 percent in September. In 1944, some 20 percent suffered from the disease in July and September and a whopping 41 percent were hit in August.[31] Malaria diminished around Leningrad during the siege, but it flared up again in 1945, affecting 5 percent of the population. Malaria was seven times more prevalent in Belorussia in 1945 than in 1940, six times more prevalent in Karelia, six times more prevalent in Smolensk, twelve times more in Pskov, and twice as prevalent in Ukraine.[32]

Sluzhba zdorov'ia relates that in 1942 the incidence of malaria escalated but they do not give specific percentages of Red Army troops affected, as do the Smirnov volumes. These authors merely note that 83.8 percent of cases were on the home front.[33] Malaria hit civilians in the Don region of southeastern Ukraine, particularly hard; 80 percent were afflicted with the disease. The authors of *Sluzhba zdorov'ia* blame insufficient measures against the anopheles mosquito.[34]

Dr. David Genis, who lived in Kzyl-Orda in the south of Kazakhstan during the war and practiced medicine there after it, becoming a noted parasitologist who received awards for his parasitology texts, confirmed that malaria, especially its fatal form, *Plasmodium falciparum*, racked Kazakhstan and Central Asian Republics like Uzbekistan where many evacuees from the western parts of the Soviet Union landed during the war. Genis' brother died from malaria shortly after the war in 1948. He was twelve years of age.[35]

The Caspian-steppe geopolitical region abounded in other parasites, Dr. Genis notes. One caused a dreadful disease called *Leishmania tropica*. Carried by sand flies, the disease produced ulcers on the body and head, particularly the eyes of dogs and other wild animals. In humans, the severe form of the disease (*Leishmania donovani*) resulted in high fever, enlarged liver, pneumonia, and ultimately death. It was especially harmful to infants. Individuals did recover from the milder form of the disease (*Leishmania brasiliensis*) with resultant immunity.[36] Amoebic dysentery was another killer in Kazakhstan. "Many were infected with this disease," Dr. Genis recalled.[37] The fatal form, spread by feces, traveled from the intestine to the liver, lungs, brain and other organs.[38] But humans could recover from the non-pathogenic, bacterial form without treatment, as he did.[39]

Dr. Genis further adds that there were all manner of worms that lowered the appetite and particularly attacked children, in European Russia, as well as the Caucasus, Central Asia and the Far East.[40] Tapeworms lived in dirty soil.[41] Trichanosis was common, caused by improperly cooked meat.

The Smirnov volumes described other medical conditions that affected the troops and were debilitating but not fatal. Skin diseases "were insignificant"—at least "in comparison with other diseases during . . . the war." [42] Scabies, or "the itch," caused by a parasite, amounted to "21.7 percent of all skin diseases"[43] Eczema constituted 10 percent of skin diseases during the war; dermatitis, about 2 percent.[44]

Obviously inadequate sanitary measures were greatly responsible for many of the diseases racking the Soviet Union during the war. And the job of the state sanitary inspectors (*gossaninspektory*), a post newly established in March 1940, was indeed mind-boggling. They now had to grapple with large contingents of evacuated civilians who were housed in makeshift dwellings. This in turn strained the sewer and water systems, already inadequate before the war. Complicating the problem, the great mass of sanitary workers and physicians, whose numbers were already precarious before the war, were drafted into the Red Army.

Even so, according to V. S. Chetverikov—admittedly only one source— the USSR Commissariat of Public Health focused mainly on increasing the number of state sanitary inspectors and other sanitary personnel and the number of sanitary stations. And, as before the Great Patriotic War, they wielded the stick. In many areas the post of state sanitary inspector was unfilled when the Great Patriotic War began. This was because there was "lack of attraction" on the part "of clinical physicians to sanitary work." Thus, in early 1942 the representative of the GKO (State Committee on Defense) G. A. Miterev issued Decrees (*Prikazi*) 1, 7, and 11ordering that "at once, all posts of local sanitary inspectors to which there had been made no appointments, be filled, particularly in rural areas." Feldshers and also medical students enrolled in sanitary courses were pressed into the position. (Student enrollments plummeted by 60 percent.) *Prikazi* ordained that physicians in hospitals and clinics assist the sanitary inspectors. Great effort was expended on establishing sanitary stations. By 1942 there were more than 600 in the Russian Republic (RSFSR), 58 in Azerbaijan, 28 in the Turkmen SSR, 132 in the Uzbek SSR, and 100 connected with water transport. In the summer of 1942 brigades of student-medics were organized to combat severe diseases, especially typhus, with baths, laundries and disinfectants and to implement "prophylactic measures" against intestinal diseases. A decree of May 29, 1942, ordained that railway sanitary inspectors were authorized to serve as "state sanitary inspectors."[45]

All these efforts were necessary. But to adequately cope with widespread infectious diseases—whether precipitated by the upheavals of the war and population movements or by high Soviet government officials, and Stalin in particular, infecting Soviet citizens with contagious microbes from secret laboratories to use them as human bullets—decrees, threats and increased medical personnel were not enough. Vaccines, serums, antitoxins, bacteriophages, and pharmaceuticals were needed. Producing the products for treating wounds and preventing and containing epidemics was the challenge of scientists in institutes and managers and workers in pharmaceutical factories. Acquiring and distributing the needed items was the challenge of pharmacists at the grass-roots level.

Prevention and Remedies

Special institutes produced vaccines and antitoxins to prevent communicable diseases. At the outset of the war there were vaccines against typhoid and antitoxins to combat diphtheria and scarlatina, as described in chapter 3. In 1942 a new vaccine for typhus was developed.[46] In 1942 a new method of preparing dysentery vaccine, using ultra-violet light, also was developed. Further, it was determined that giving dysentery vaccine in conjunction with other vaccines such as a typhus-paratyphus trivaccine was more effective than using the dysentery vaccine alone.[47] In 1943 output of vaccinations against typhus, tularemia, typhoid, paratyphoid A and B, dysentery, cholera, tetanus, and Siberian plague (anthrax) was ramped up at twenty institutes.[48] Directives for containing diseases on railroads were issued. There were increased attempts to isolate the sick. Staff was increased in certain localities.[49]

The disinfecting chamber (*dezkamera*), a little stove with high heat to kill lice and their eggs infesting people's clothes, was a further measure to control typhus. *Dezkamera* were set up at railway stations. While their clothes were being disinfected, people showered or bathed with a sliver of soap, after which the clothes were returned. Travelers could not get tickets without getting a "sanitary *propusk*"—a certificate ascertaining that they had gone through this process, Dr. Genis emphasized. Students in dormitories also visited the bathhouse and *dezkamera* every couple of weeks.[50] This system seems to have been put into place after the first panic subsided and the evacuation process became more orderly. In 1942, for example, Ia. A. Frenkel' noted that the most important measures to prevent typhus were bathhouses and disinfecting chambers; after outbreak, isolation in hospitals was required.[51]

The bathhouses were problematical, however. Dr. Genis recalls that although in the countryside families sometimes had their own bathhouses, in the cities and towns, at least Kzyl, Kazakhstan where he lived during the war, there were few public bathhouses. Further, they were expensive and not hygienic. Kzyl was an *oblast'* city (county seat) with a population of over 50,000. Yet there were only two bathhouses, one belonging to the city and the other to the railway station. Moreover, they were dirty and his family had no money to go to the baths. Therefore they bathed at home, in a basin, with water heated on the stove.[52]

Aside from the *dezkamera* and soap, produced by the soap trust TEZhE or by local slaughterhouses, and the vaccines and serums produced by special institutes, products of the pharmaceutical industry were used to prevent typhus and also typhoid, malaria, and many other communicable diseases. What were the chief pharmaceuticals used to attack diseases and medical problems?

Disinfectants were extremely important. According to the Smirnov volumes, iodine was one disinfectant/antiseptic that was consistently used throughout the war[53] to purify water, to treat wounds, and to combat infections in surgery.[54] Chloramine and Pantotsid also were used for water purification.[55] In addition important antiseptics and disinfectants included Lysol, Pantosept, Neopantotsid, sodium chloride, phenol, and Rivanol.[56] The Smirnov volumes noted that DDT (discovered by a Swiss scientist in 1939) and Diphenilamine were valuable pesticides in eliminating fleas and flies that spread many infectious diseases and the anopheles mosquitoes that spread malaria. The Pharmacy Committee of Scholars of the Medical Council, a subdivision of the USSR Commissariat of Health, approved the use of DDT in 1943, but there is no information on how much of this valuable insecticide was available in the Soviet Union during the war.[57]

Tamara Nikolaevna Khazieva was lucky enough to be able to stay put during the Great Patriotic War. She lived in Ufa, far from the fighting. During the war she assisted her mother who "worked in a disinfecting station (*dezotstantsiia*)." She "brought disinfectants to those quarters where there were infectious diseases: typhus and typhoid, scarlatina, diphtheria. The linen of the sick was soaked in chloride. The rooms were washed with the solution." However, "chloride was available **only** [bold in original] at the disinfecting station"; it could not be acquired by the general public during the war.[58]

In his parasitology textbook, Dr. Genis noted that "prophylaxis" was important to combating amoebic dysentery—in particular, washing dirty linen in Lysol.[59] Similarly, he opined that soap—careful washing the hands after using the toilet—was the best prevention for worms. He urged disinfecting with chloride.[60] Also important were more baths and laundries and scrutiny of workers in food preparation, measures that were implemented to some extent.[61]

The authors of *Sluzhba zdorov'ia* cite phages as the main treatment for bacillary dysentery.[62] However, we have seen in Chapter 3 that physicians also advocated sulfa drugs, isolation and a nourishing liquid diet to combat this form of dysentery.[63] Food shortages (alimentary dystrophy) were said to have prevented epidemics but weakened constitutions also made people susceptible to communicable diseases. Thus, attempts were made to improve diets[64] and to increase the output of vitamins. Infant formula, made with clean water, would have helped babies who were nursing withstand dysentery but accounts of the time do not mention it.

To contain tularemia, the authors of *Sluzhba zdorov'ia* emphasize that in the summer of 1943 over 58,000 *zemlianki* (dugouts) and wells were disinfected with carbonic barium and sodium floride.[65] The Soviet Union had a drug that appeared analogous to Streptomycin, the drug of choice to treat tularemia (and other gram-negative bacterial infections), but it was not being produced on a factory scale at this time.[66]

There was little hope of preventing malaria or leishmaniasis because window screens and bed-netting were not used in the Soviet Union and DDT may not have been available. The treatments for both diseases also were problematical. Trivalent antimony, used against leishmaniasis in the early twentieth century, was very toxic although more effective pentavalent antimonials were coming into use. There still is no cure for malaria, either the three enervating forms or the fatal form. However, Soviet pharmaceutical factories were capable of producing the antimalarials, Plazmotsid and Akrikhin, the former cloned from the German Plasmochin (or Plasmoquine) in the early 1930s and the latter synthesized in 1936, to quell the strong fevers and chills that accompanied the action of the parasite in the red blood cells if quinine was not available.[67]

The Smirnov volumes noted that belladonna, atropine, hydrochloric acid, bromine soda, as well as the new product Liuminal (Luminal), synthesized in the mid-1930s, were important for treating gastritis and stomach ulcers.[68] Treatment for hepatitis was based on diet, 100 grams of protein, Vitamin B 1, glucose, and insulin.[69] Dr. Genis remarked that killing a tapeworm in the intestine was done by imbibing airplane fuel.[70]

Meanwhile, old topical remedies like formalin, fish oil, and the petroleum product, Naftalan, were valuable for treating frostbite, according to the Smirnov volumes.[71] Familiar products like tannin, morphine, atropine, adrenaline, chloral hydrate and Novocain, as well as new products like Rivanol, Pantopon, Geksenal and Sovkain were used to treat shock in cases of severe burns from bombs and shells.[72]

Popular remedies for scabies included kerosene and benzene; health professionals relied on Peruvian balsam, benzylbenzoate, sulfuric salves and hydrochloric acid.[73] "Personal prophylactic kits" and "illustrated talks" were used to preclude venereal diseases.[74] If these failed, treatment included daily doses of arsenic, bismuth and sulfanilamide preparations. Trade-named antivenereals included Arsenoxide, Sal'varsan, Malforsen, and Arsphenamine.[75] Both traditional topical, coal-tar based salves and sulfanilamide preparations were used to treat eczema.[76]

Since penicillin was produced on a factory scale only in the last year of the war,[77] sulfa drugs were crucial. The new Soviet sulfa drugs, Sul'fidin and White Streptotsid, and also hydrogen peroxide and calcium chloride were used to treat ulcerous staphylococcus and streptococcus skin diseases.[78] One of the most important sulfa drugs was Gramitsidin, according to the Smirnov volumes.[79]

Sulfa drugs were especially needed to combat dysentery. However, British military physician J. G. Scadding cautioned that many different forms of bacilli caused dysentery and, conversely, not all sulfa drugs were equally effective. "Sulphaguanidine is commonly regarded as the drug of choice," he wrote in 1944, "because it is relatively poorly absorbed from the gut, reaching a high concentration in the intestinal lumen without a correspondingly high blood-concentration and thus having little tendency to cause systemic toxic effects." In the Middle East in 1942 and 1943, this drug had good results against "'acute, subacute and chronic bacillary dysentery.'" Other physicians, Scadding reported, preferred sulphapyridine and sulphathiazole, while still others claimed in 1943 that "'suphanilamide in the form of crushed tablets does not have any definite effect in the disease.'" To sort out the claims and counter claims, Scadding made tests "during the summer of 1943 at a large desert base hospital . . . to estimate the relative efficacy of such sulpha [sic] drugs as were readily available at that time—which unfortunately did not include sulphathiazole."[80]

Scadding's observations underscore the fact that, while Soviet military and civilians greatly suffered during the Second World War, for their British and American allies, North Africa and the Middle East were hotbeds of disease and the Pacific theater was particularly a hell-hole for American troops. His remarks further underscore the fact that neither sulfa drugs nor other therapies could be randomly applied to serious diseases. On the other hand they saved many lives.

Evacuation and Other Hurdles in 1941

How well did the Soviet pharmaceutical industry do its part to produce the essential items noted above? How well did the industry do its part, along with the institutes that produced vaccines, serums, antitoxins, and phages, to prevent and contain outbreaks of communicable disease, to treat infections and other medical conditions, to restore and maintain the health of both civilians and the military?

First, we need to remind ourselves that the pharmaceutical industry, like other key industries, was under stress. We also need to remind ourselves that the American pharmaceutical industry had to grapple with shortages of packaging and raw ingredients for materials in 1941, even before the United States officially entered the war. The reasons for the shortages at that time were enemy control of raw materials or processing plants and lend lease to Britain and the Soviet Union. For example, Japan "controlled 70 percent of the world's" tin sources, located largely in the Dutch East Indies and China, and the United States "received 90 percent of its supply" of tin from Holland, which was under German occupation. Other items identified in short supply and inadequately stockpiled in 1941 were aconite root, belladonna leaves and roots, henbane leaves, red squill, ergot of rye, Santonin, and quinine. The sources of the first six items were Europe, and in some cases more specifically Germany, England and Russia; the main source of quinine was the Dutch East Indies. After the United States entered the war in December 1941, the needs of the military and the drain of items to lend lease created potential shortages for American civilians. For example, in May 1942, Dennis Worthen, historian of American pharmacy, notes that the "military had reportedly ordered 100,000 vials of tentanus antitoxin, 40 million quinine tablets, 25 million sulfathiazole tables, and 10 million sulfapyridine tablets. The sulfas alone represented the civilian needs of the entire country for two or three months." Additionally, he continues, "[C]hemicals needed in the production of medicines were being requested for use in war production, especially alcohol, phenol, glycerin, and potassium." Sugar also was among the items in short supply. "Within the first five months of America's entry into the war," Worthen comments, the "list of shortages for the manufacture of medicines was already over 200 items." He details how the National Pharmacopoeia and National Formulary were accordingly adjusted; a massive hunt for tin was undertaken; domestic sources of some items, such as belladonna, were established; and substitutes were used. As a result, Americans trekking to the pharmacy to fill prescriptions or buy over-the-counter pharmaceuticals did not suffer greatly. [81]

The western parts of the Soviet Union and the Ukraine, of course, were under enemy occupation in 1942. Thus, common sense dictates that pharmaceutical production would have been more difficult than in the United States. However, although some difficulties confronting the Soviet pharmaceutical industry were caused by the war, others were caused by longstanding and systemic factors.

In the summer of 1941 the core pharmaceutical industry Glavkhimfarmprom produced up to two thirds of the Soviet Union's pharmaceuticals. Under the jurisdiction of the USSR People's Commissariat of Health, the core pharmaceutical industry included ten factories, two scientific institutes, and three manufactories.[82] Nine of the ten key factories were potentially at risk after June 22. They were Akrikhin, Karpov, Semashko, Alkaloid, Salicylate, and the Factory of Endocrine and Vitamin Preparations in Moscow; two factories in the Ukrainian SSR: the Red Star Factory in Khar'kov and the Lomonosov Factory in Kiev; and Farmakon in Leningrad. The Dzerzhinskii Factory was out of harm's way in far off Kazakhstan. The main scientific institutes in the core pharmaceutical industry—the All-Union Scientific Research Chemical-Pharmaceutical Institute (VNIKhFI),which developed new drugs; VILAR, specializing in plant-based medicines; and the laboratory, LVEN, also were potentially in danger of coming under siege.

During 1940 the Factory of Artificial Teeth in Leningrad, the March 8 Bandaging Manufactory (the pre-revolutionary Iakovlev Factory) in Moscow, and a Packaging plant in Torzhok, old Tver' Province had been added to the system. Although this restored some natural affinities, the benefits were offset by the fact that higher authorities removed a caffeine factory, two iodine factories, and the Office of Medicinal Plants. Entities that produced some crucial ingredients, therefore, were outside the industries control. Additionally, as before the war, a number of ancillary entities—marketing and supply offices, chemical factories, and medical instruments' manufactories were located in separate administrative divisions making it difficult for the pharmaceutical industry to interact with them.[83]

The government continued to restructure the core pharmaceutical industry during the war. Three glass factories were added to the system. Two were located just north of Moscow, in Solnechnogorsk and in Klin, where Peter Tchaikovsky had summered. The third was in Smolensk *oblast'*, west of Moscow. [84] Initially, these additions were positive because the pharmaceutical industry had no previous direct connection to glass ampules and containers. Unfortunately, the Germans soon took over Smolensk and Klin. In the second quarter of 1942, the core pharmaceutical industry, Glavkhimfarmprom, and the medical instruments' industry, Glavmedfarmprom, were briefly merged. This resulted in more cohesion but working out a collaborative program was time-consuming.[85] Further, the core pharmaceutical industry still remained separated from many ancillary industries.

Evacuation proved to be a major problem for the core pharmaceutical factories located in Moscow. According to popular histories, moving machinery and workers from Moscow factories along railway lines to safe havens in the east helped "save" the Soviet Union in World War II. *Sluzhba zdorov'ia* admits that this was not the case with regard to hospital and medical equipment.[86] Archival materials show that the process of evacuating pharmaceutical factories, in particular, was chaotic and counterproductive. It led to further reorganization and decreased productivity in factories still operating near the front. Production in the new factories established in Siberia and Central Asia did not meet expectations. And in a few years much equipment was sent back westward, causing further dislocation.

Evacuation of pharmaceutical factories began in mid-October 1941 in accordance with a decree issued by the "Committee on Evacuation" established in Sovnarkom, the Soviet Government.[87] Moscow factories were temporarily closed for the move and a portion of the equipment was dismantled to be sent eastward with workers and their families.[88] This cost valuable production time at the outset. At the same time, some factories in the Ukraine were added to the core enterprises of Glavkhimfarmprom, which added to the confusion.[89]

Equipment evacuated from the Alkaloid Factory was transferred to the Dzerzhinskii Santonin Factory in Chimkent, southern Kazakhstan. Otherwise equipment from Moscow factories was dispersed to six newly created branch factories, several in an area radiating out in a semicircle from Tomsk. Materials and equipment of The March 8 Bandaging Factory were transferred to the city of Tomsk; those from the Endocrine and Vitamin Factory were sent to the city of Novosibirsk, to form Factory No. 35. Much equipment from the Salicylate Factory was sent to Kemerovo, south of Tomsk, to form Factory No. 36; that from the Semashko Factory was sent to Anzhero-Sudzhensk, also south of Tomsk, to form Factory No. 37. Equipment and materials from the Akrikhin factory were shipped to Irbit, to form Factory No.38; those from the Karpov Factory were sent to the city of Tiumen, western Siberia, to form Factory No. 39.

The Health of Workers' Factory and Factory of Artificial Teeth from Khar'kov were relocated to Frunze, in the Kirghiz SSR. The Lomonosov Factory in Kiev was moved to the city of Kazan'. It was, however, transferred out of the jurisdiction of Glavkhimfarmprom and put under the authority of Glavmedfarmprom. Thus, the incessant tinkering that had destabilized the industry throughout the 1930s continued, even as war raged.

The Institute of Endocrinology in Khar'kov was moved to the city of Biisk, in the Altai region south of Tomsk. The Institute of Endocrinology from Kiev was set up in Frunze. The Ukrainian branch of the Scientific Pharmaceutical Research Institute from Khar'kov also was relocated to Frunze. A branch of the Scientific Chemical-Pharmaceutical Research Institute in Moscow was established in the city of Sverdlovsk in the Urals.[90]

Evacuation of pharmaceutical factories, though perhaps necessary and heroic, was extremely disorganized and disruptive. Stores on hand were wasted and machinery was not apportioned properly between the factories remaining in production in Moscow and their branches in the east.

Industry reports confirmed that in the fourth quarter of 1941, as a result of evacuation, there was "scarcely any production." There were "losses of raw materials and finished products" and unforeseen "expenditures for dismounting and evacuating equipment, workers and their families." In December the government issued a *prikaz* halting the evacuation process. Equipment which had not been loaded for shipping was reinstalled. The Akrikhin factory in Moscow and Farmakon in Leningrad operated, "putting out a small amount." The core industry suffered financial strain. Purchasers did not pay for wares, credit from Gosbank was lower than stated in the plan, lowered tempos and losses from evacuating enterprises lowered revenue, and expenditures for evacuating enterprises were high.[91]

The Farmakon Factory and the manufactory of Artificial Teeth in Leningrad faced the gravest hurdles because of the nine-hundred-day siege of the city, but by dint of necessity they managed to function and even produced for other cities, as we shall see momentarily. The seven factories that continued to operate in the city of Moscow—Akrikhin, Alkaloid, Karpov, Semashko, Salicylate, Endocrine and Vitamins, and March 8 Bandaging Materials—were in danger in 1941-1942, but not under such dire threat. In the spring of 1942, Soviet physician Maxim Pavlovich Murov, sent to Moscow from the front for a conference, "found Moscow curiously unchanged." 'It'" was "still the same . . . the people were grimmer. . . . There" was "less food about. . . . And there" was "a curfew, which" had "put a stop to all night life." But there were "few enough signs of the siege and the raids. One" had "to search for them. Here and there buildings have been damaged. But," Murov mused, "I imagined that compared with some of the English towns—even London—Moscow would pass unscathed."[92]

Evacuation, thus, rather than war damage hampered Moscow pharmaceutical factories during the war. Much equipment was obsolete before the war. With evacuation, the best equipment was sent eastward, forcing Moscow pharmaceutical factories to work with the rudimentary remnants, even "defective apparatus." "Technological troubles" particularly affected the Akrikhin and Salicylate factories during the first year of the war.[93] In 1941, the Akrikhin Factory produced White Streptotsid, considered extremely valuable to prevent high temperatures and ulceration from wounds, in Shop No. 1 with skeletal equipment and crew, including fifteen-year old Lida Dmitrieva and two husband and wife teams.[94]

Meanwhile, evacuated materials did not always reach their destination. Premises designated for the new factories sometimes were occupied. It took time to install the equipment. For example, materials and equipment for Factory No. 39, from the Karpov Factory, were scheduled to be installed in space vacated by a former beer brewery in the city of Tiumen. However, when the equipment arrived it was discovered that the brewery was occupied. Thus, the equipment was sent to "the less suitable" furniture factory, *Pobeda.* Factory No. 38 was designated to use materials and equipment from the Akrikin Factory. These were scheduled to be installed in one half of the Irbitsk vodka factory. More room was needed but only belatedly was the whole liquor factory allocated for production of pharmaceuticals. "The greatest difficulty" was experienced with Factory No. 37, which was to operate with equipment from the Semashko Factory. Only one and a half months after being on the road did the factory acquire the space allotted for it in the city of Anzhero-Sudzhensk.[95] Some of the newly established factories in the east performed fairly well, after a time. In 1942, Factory No. 35, the branch of the Endocrine and Vitamin Factory out in Novosibirsk, fulfilled its plan by more than 95 percent, producing ascorbic acid, insulin, and adrenalin. Failure to perform at 100 percent was due to late installation of equipment in the case of ascorbic acid and interruptions of supplies in the case of insulin and adrenalin.[96] Factory No. 36, the branch of the Salicylate Factory in Kemerovo, produced aspirin, ether salicylate, and sodium salicylate. Factory No. 38 in Irbit, satellite of the Akrikhin Factory, produced 10.9 tons of White Streptotsid and 17.3 tons of narcotic ether. Only one third of a ton of Sul'fidin was produced, however, due to "interruptions of raw materials, steam, and electrical energy." In the second quarter of 1942 the Irbit factory began to manufacture White Streptotsid chiefly from semi-manufactured amounts sent from the Akrikhin factory in Moscow! From the third quarter, however, the factory began to produce Streptotsid on the basis of raw materials.[97] Factory No. 37, the branch of the Semashko Factory finally got into gear in the autumn of 1942.[98]

Nevertheless, in 1943, the burden of producing pharmaceuticals still rested on factories remaining in the heart of Russia. The "weight of production from eastern factories rose in comparison with 1942," but "the weight of eastern preparations in the general volume [of output] was insignificant."[99] For example, the eastern factories produced only 4.3 percent of the ascorbic acid produced in 1943, a little over one third of the total amount of iodine preparations (compared with over half in 1942), 30 percent or so of salicylate preparations and sulfa drugs, Streptotsid and Sul'fidin-sulfazol, and only 18 percent of narcotic ether. The last preparations were among those for which contributions from the eastern factories rose as compared with 1942. [100]

Furthermore, the negative aspects of evacuation resurfaced at the end of the war. Because eastern factories did not perform as well as expected—for example they produced only a little over 3 percent of the total amount of narcotic ether, only 13 percent of ascorbic acid, 27 percent of iodine preparations, less than a third of Streptotsid, and 43 to 44 percent of salicylate and Sulfidin-Sul'fazol preparations[101]—they possessed "superfluous" equipment. Therefore, in 1944 the excess machinery was shipped back from the eastern satellite factories to Moscow factories. Nine wagons of 66 engines were sent back to the Karpov factory; the Chimkent factory sent back 66 units of equipment, including 36 electric motors; the Akrikhin factory received two wagon loads of equipment from Factory No. 38; the Dzerzhinskii factory received a diesel from Factory No. 38.[102] It must have been depressing for factory directors to realize what they had done without. Further, the process of reinstalling the equipment must have been disruptive and the equipment may have been the worse for wear.

Life was difficult for workers in pharmaceutical factories during the Great Patriotic War. On the other side of the coin, untrained workers impeded productivity. Throughout the NEP and 1930s working in pharmaceutical factories was hazardous to one's health. After 1941, the advent of new, hastily trained workers, mainly women, the use of obsolete equipment, lack of special shoes and clothes and, conversely, use of inappropriate outfits, such as "paper uniforms in the shops working with acids" and added pressures resulted in a "high number of unpleasant accidents." Some "resulted in death" but severing of fingers and hands was more common. Factories were praised in these cases for not "sending the maimed to easier work." For example, the "head of the garage at the Alkaloid Factory cut off his hand and only after three months was he transferred" to another position. [103] Further, perquisites promised to pharmaceutical workers did not arrive in 1942. "Milk had been guaranteed for all harmful occupations," but "the Akrikhin Factory did not receive milk for four months."[104] The Akrikhin Factory also suffered from "lack of staff in the laboratory" as well as "the poor condition of apparatus."[105]

Industry executives particularly fretted about the caliber of workers in 1944. The Glavk had twenty enterprises with 7,574 workers, of which 6,396 were women. Over 1,000 people had higher educations, but specialists with requisite middle and lower education "were insignificant." Various factories, particularly Karpov, had in-house technicums to train workers. Interestingly, most of the personnel in the Glavk Administration were engineers—twenty five. There were seven economists, six accountants, four inspectors, only two provizors (fully-qualified pharmacists) and only one pharmacist.[106]

The sourcing dysfunctionalities that plagued executives and managers in the core pharmaceutical industry during the 1930s persisted during the Great Patriotic War. Some Moscow factories and those in other areas experienced "interruptions in supplies of raw materials." "Technological troubles" hindered the glass factories as well as the Akrikhin and Salicylate factories in Moscow. [107]

On the other hand, some "enterprises had significant stores of raw materials, resulting from evacuation and not used because of conserving for future need (*zakonservirovaniia*) or because of lack of increase in corresponding production. Such stores of materials were in the Semashko, Dzerzhinskii, Health of Labor and other factories."[108]

Production in 1942

The authors of *Sluzhba zdorov'ia* emphasize that in the fall of 1941 and the spring of 1942 the nomenclature of pharmaceuticals was reduced from 236 to 120 items, implying that this streamlining aided production. They aver that the pharmaceuticals produced in January and February 1942 exceeded Plan targets, they provide figures for large amounts of basic pharmaceuticals produced in 1942, and they claim that in December 1943 three months of "sanitary and pharmaceutical supplies" were available in military warehouses and three to six months worth of supplies were available in surrounding warehouses.[109] The products they cite for 1942 included adrenalin, glucose, caffeine, morphia, and codeine—all important for field surgery; fish oil, which perhaps was needed to supplement food shortages and also to make the Vishnevskii antibacterial salve; camphor oil, a disinfectant; chlorethyl apparently an anesthetic; liquid ammonia, a disinfectant; Utrotropin, an old anti-infectant, made from formeldehyde and ammonia by Schering from 1894 and cloned by the Soviets in the 1920s; Pantapon, an old Roche product, consisting of an alkaloid of opium in the form of hydrochloric salts, also cloned by the Soviet pharmaceutical industry; bismuth, manganate salts, salve against the itch; calcium chloride and Lobelin.[110] The amounts of these products appear in Table 6.1.

Table 6.1 Production in Thousands of Units (*Shtuk*) and Tons, 1942. Information from the Central Archive of the Ministry of Defense

Adrenalin	224.42	Chlorethyl	2,032.81
Glucose	371.54	Urotropin	58.90
Caffeine	4,109.91	Pantopon	270.60
Morphia	5,038.37	Bismuth in tablets, tons	11.27
Lobelin	409.03	Salts of manganate, tons	3.50
Calcium chloride	81.46	Codeine,salts in tablets,tons	7.33
Camphor oil	11,075.10	Fish oil, tons	81.75
Liquid ammonia	99.00	Anti-mite salve, tons	20.80

Source: Figures quoted in Gladkikh and Loktev, *Sluzhba zdorov'ia*, pp. 169-170

These production figures are based on information in the Central Archive of the Ministry of Defense. Noticeably, iodine the most commonly used antiseptic and disinfectant; sulfa drugs, "K" soap, Novocain, and aspirin are missing from the production list.

How did the pharmaceutical factories themselves report their output in 1942? For one thing, the industry report was more specific. Only some items corresponded with those in the Ministry of Defense statistics. Secondly, fulfillment of Plan targets, presumably based on needs of civilians as well as the military, fluctuated from very good to very bad.

Table. 6.2: Production, Percent of Plan Fulfilled, Industry Report, 1942

Akrikhin	22.8	Ascorbic acid	14.6
Medical Glucose	99.7	Liuminal	0.0
"K" Soap	43.1	Novocain	132.5
Pantotsid	169.0	Preparations of bismuth	100.8
Preparations of iodine	98.6	Iodine sublimate	98.3
Preparations of mercury	81.0	Aspirin	54.6
Salol	27.5	Rivanol	35.7
Streptotsid	56.4	Sul'fazol	39.6
Sul'fidin	105.7	Urotropin	140.0
Narcotic chloroform	92.9	Narcotic ether	91.9

Source: RGAE, f. 8009, op. 2, d. 36, 1.35.

Reports from individual factories give texture to the gross figures. Output fluctuated considerably from factory to factory due to various stresses. In 1942, output of the Karpov Factory was said to be "satisfactory" with regard to 126 products, among them basics like permanganate, chlorethyl, special reagents, milk acid, sublimate, calomel, iodine sublimate, potassium, calcium iodide, barium for x-rays, mercury salts, Urotropin, and so forth. The Semashko Factory was said to have produced Sul'fidin, Streptotsid, narcotic chloroform, and the barbiturate, Liuminal. The Alkaloid Factory produced Novocain, Sul'fazol, and Pyramidon. The target for Sul'fazol was not met in 1942, however, because the partially manufactured ingredient Sul'fochloride did not arrive from the Semashko Factory (probably because of spoilage as noted above) and the plan for Pyramidon was not fulfilled because bisulfate was not received. The plan for codeine was not fulfilled because the specifications for the methodological process arrived too late. The Vitamin section of the Endocrine and Vitamin Factory in Moscow "entirely did not perform" and the Endocrine shops did not produce ephedrine and insulin because of lack of spirits.[111]

The Dzerzhinskii factory, already safely located out in Kazakhstan, should have performed better than it did in 1942. However, the factory only fulfilled half—13 of 26—the items projected in the plan. The reasons for this were that some semi-manufactured ingredients from the Alkaloid Factory did not come, "resulting in the plan for codeine not being fulfilled" as well as the plan for phosphorous. "Non-fulfillment of Santonin "[112] was caused by "interruptions in the supply of Darmin." There were "significant complications in supplies of sulfuric acid" and "fuel."[113]

In addition to the sourcing difficulties, medicines and supplies were spoiled because of carelessness. In 1942, a tremendous amount of medicines were lost through *brak* (rejection because of defects). For example, 1,571 kilograms of the sulfa drug, Red Streptotsid, and 347 kilograms of White Streptotsid; 650 kilograms of Dikhlorakridin; 488 kilograms of Fenetidin; 160 kilograms of tablets of the anti-malarial Akrikhin; 478 kilograms of Sul'fochloride; 547 kilograms of Diethylamine; and so on.[114] Factories were penalized for putting out defective products, as they had been before the war. Therefore, they appealed to higher authorities to help them prevent *brak* and incurring fines.

Nevertheless, it is axiomatic that wars stimulate innovation and output. This occurred in the American pharmaceutical industry, as Dennis Worthen amply relates.[115] As for the Soviet defense industry, Mark Harrison has demonstrated that the Soviet Union won the war mainly because it produced more tanks, airplanes and fuel than Germany and the tanks and airplanes were first-rate, although to accomplish these feats consumer goods were cut to the barest minimum.[116]

To some extent, the Soviet pharmaceutical industry, at least in R&D, rose to the occasion, creatively coping with the exigencies of wartime. Before the tide of war began to turn with the battle of Stalingrad in late 1942 and the battles of Kursk and Khar'kov in the summer of 1943, new processes and products emerged to compensate for shortages. Some were developed in scientific institutes and some in the factories themselves.[117] However, some substitutions had deleterious effects.

New Processes

USSR Assistant Commissar of Health Natradze permitted the Karpov Factory to put out packets of sodium chloride of 14 to16 percent, to distribute nitric acid bismuth with sodium chloride up to 0.25 percent, and to distribute caffeine benzoic soda with carbonate content "up to 0.2 percent." The new boiling temperature for Red Streptotsid caused "massive *brak*," so VNIKhFI (the Scientific Chemical-Pharmaceutical Research Institute) helped the Akrikhin Factory to adjust the temperature. The Institute assisted the Semashko Factory in producing Geksenal with higher sodium. The Institute worked out new methods for the Endocrine and Vitamin Factory to produce hydrochlorate of morphium and ascorbic acid and helped the branch of the Endocrine Factory in Novosibirsk to change the methods of producing Phytin, and ampules of calcium chloride, ephedrine, and decholine. The Salicylate Factory decided to distribute two series of aspirin tablets with lower boiling temperature. The Pharmacological Committee allowed the factory to put out methylsalicylate with a mixture of chloroform for "orders of necessity."[118]

Factories themselves took the initiative to alter methods in order to compensate for deficits. In 1942, the Karpov Factory replaced salicylic acid with common salt and sulfuric acid in the production of chloretin, rectified spirits with raw spirits for production of chlorethyl, pure potash with technical potash for production of potassium iodide, and Urotropin was crystalized with water instead of spirits. Factory No. 39, the branch of the Karpov Factory in Tiumen produced iodoform without acetone and chlorine. The Semashko Factory substituted sulfate of ammonia for salicylic acid in the production of the barbiturate Liuminal and for both salicylic acid and ammonium in the production of Sul'fidin. Factory No. 37, the branch of the Semashko Factory in Anzhero-Sudzhensk, used oxide of calcium to produce Streptotsid.[119] The Endocrine and Vitamin Factory produced medical glucose with re-crystallized water.[120]

In 1942, managers in several factories altered production methods in order to utilize equipment remaining in the factories. The Karpov Factory used a ceramic retort in the absence of a quartz one to produce sublimate and calomel and an enamel apparatus in place of a porcelain one to produce sublimate of iodine. The old autoclave in the Akrikhin Factory was used with lower pressure. The Semashko Factory produced aminopyridine with a temperature four degrees lower than previously to use reagents on hand.[121]

Factory laboratories worked feverishly in 1943 to develop new methods of production that did not use "deficit forms of materials" and "used less fuel and electrical energy." Dozens of new methods were developed, many reusing residues of products. Some new methods had the added bonus of making production safer.[122] Nevertheless, accidents continued.[123]

Some new methods developed in laboratories were successfully implemented on a factory scale. One of the most important was devised to put out nicotine acid—"use of which on the part of the Red Army and civilian population" was "very large"—using "airplane gasoline" from the Pyramidon base of the Kemerovo Factory. The new methods were implemented in the Chimkent Dzerzhinskii Factory and a factory in Sverdlovsk. There were several attempts to produce Streptotsid from residual materials.[124]

Before the war shortages of paper and cartons plagued factory managers. During the war cotton was severely deficit. The Sanitary Institute of the Red Army assisted in developing substitute ingredients for bandaging materials for the Bandaging Factory in Moscow and the Tomsk, Dzerzhinskii, and Health of Labor factories. The composition of cotton was modified and, in lieu of sterile paper, it was distributed in "any kind of white paper packets with 10 pieces of kraft paper." [125]

Thus directors of pharmaceutical factories exhibited creativity and heroism. But, while some substitutes worked well or were harmless, others may have rendered items less effective or even dangerous. As noted in the Introduction, Dr. David Genis has remarked that Red Streptotsid was extremely toxic.[126] The processes developed during the war might have been responsible. Or perhaps the drug was defective from the start.

New Products

The new products developed during the war veered from cutting edge to prosaic to downright questionable. Some breakthroughs were variations—one might say imitations—of foreign products. Some products were applied on a wide scale. Other prototypes never reached the public. Some appeared dubious or precarious to health.

During 1941-1942, pharmacologists developed a new sulfanilamide, "Preparation 805," which was successfully used to treat tuberculosis patients and for surgery at the front in 1943.[127] A congress of pharmacologists, which convened in September 1943, was lauded for assisting the Red Army and preventing epidemics that had occurred in other wars.[128] The laboratory of sanitary-chemical defense of the USSR Commissariat of Health conducted research on the application of "khlorsuktsinimid" as a bactericide for drinking water.[129]

Despite the development of "Soviet Penicillin," Metilkofein (Methyl-caffeine) won the Stalin prize in 1943. In Soviet sources methyl-caffeine was touted as a crucial product that was less toxic than caffeine. In accounts published for American consumption it was emphasized that methyl-caffeine was a fitting substitute for natural caffeine, because derived from uric acid, it required only "16 kilos of raw material" to produce one kilo whereas natural caffeine, made from tea leaves and tea powder, required "320 kilograms" of the raw material.[130] Other new drugs from

1943 included Disul'fan, deemed "similar to the American Dizulon"; Sul'fatsil, "analogous to the foreign albutsid"; Gramitsidin, "similar to an American product" for ulcerous wounds; Tannidgen, acetylized Tannigen, to combat dysentery, especially in children; and Ferroaskorbin, to combat anemia.[131] Disul'fan or "Preparation No. 19" was considered especially effective for stomach-intestinal infections and chronic gonorrhea. Shop No. 1 of the Akrikhin Factory near Moscow began production of the drug in 1944.[132] A third new sulfa drug, "Preparation 063," developed by pharmacologists in the Sverdlovsk branch of the Scientific-Research Chemical-Pharmaceutical Institute, appeared strikingly similar to the May and Baker therapy for bacterial pneumonia, "M& B 693,"which, though discovered in 1938, became famous when used to treat Churchill during the war. "Churchill's cure, not once but twice in 1943" made "M & B a household word in Britain."[133] The chemical structure of the Russian sulfanilamidmethylpyrimidine, [134] however, differed from the British acetyl sulfapyridine.

Penicillin

The major wonder drug of World War II was penicillin. The mass-production of penicillin, the first true antibiotic, offers one of the best examples—along with DDT, used by American forces to quell a typhus epidemic in Italy[135]—of how wars stimulate innovations in the pharmaceutical sector as well as the arena of weaponry and of how vital a robust economy is to the production of pharmaceuticals. For a British scientist, Alexander Fleming, had discovered the bacteria-killing properties of penicillin in 1928—though he had not made use of his discovery—and other British scientists under the leadership of Howard W. Florey, had begun "work on antibiotic substances in 1936, when" they "received a Rockefeller grant . . . for the purchase of equipment." Simultaneously, in the period 1935 to 1937, American scientists, including James Currie, who went to work for Pfizer, and researchers at the U. S. Department of Agriculture, "patented a 'submerged' fermentation process in which a mold was grown throughout the medium; devised instruments—rotary fermenters or cylinders "of high purity aluminum"—capable of making large batches of *Penicillium* strains; and, finally, discovered "an effective" medium 'for growing molds in submerged culture," namely "corn steep liquor, a byproduct of the wet corn milling industry." [136] But it took the war to bring the British and American researchers together and it took the war and money to speed up the process of developing a drug that could effectively attack bacterial diseases in humans.

The British made the first clinical tests on humans in 1941while Britain was under bombardment. Although the siege of Britain forced Florey to come to the United States and appeal to American pharmaceutical companies to produce the drug, it would seem that he might have had to do this, war or no war, because the Americans had the equipment and the knowledge to make penicillin on a large scale. But the war certainly propelled research on the best strains of *Penicillium* to use—*notatum* and *chrysogenum* were preferred—and more productive strains of these were sought, including a type of bread mold. Wartime experience jettisoned the theory that penicillin could be synthesized. Although synthesis was accomplished in 1959, fermentation is still the best method of producing the drug. Wartime needs also convinced major pharmaceutical companies—Pfizer, in particular, but also Merck and Squibb—to make mass quantities of penicillin. Fifteen thousand strains of *Penicillium* had been tested by the summer of 1944. The costs were astronomical. And both research and production involved multiple government agencies—the U. S. Office of Scientific Research and Development, the U. S. Department of Agriculture, the War Production Board's Office of Production Research and Developments—universities and pharmaceutical companies.[137]

Mass production began only in 1943. By March 1943, in the "defunct Rubel Ice Plant" in Brooklyn, using cobbled-together equipment, Pfizer "was producing five times more penicillin than originally anticipated" and estimated that it would "soon be able to produce up to 45 million units a month."[138] Yet, although by February 1944 "twenty-one government assisted plants" were "over ninety percent" outfitted and output had leapt from 100 million units to 18,726 million units, there were still "technical problems" to be overcome.[139]

Interestingly, in 1924, a Soviet scientist named Butkevich noted the antibacterial properties of *penicillium*, used from 1893 by one A. Wehner to produce citric acid. Unfortunately, this did not lead to production of penicillin.[140] And Soviet attempts to mass-produce penicillin during the Great Patriotic War were fraught with difficulties. Later Soviet accounts blamed hostility on the part of the allies toward the Soviet Union. But there were plenty of internal problems as well.

In 1942, one version of the development of "Soviet penicillin" asserts that the Soviet government instructed Zinaida Vissarionovna Yermol'eva, who had organized the Laboratory of Biochemical Microbes in 1925 in the Institute of Biochemistry, to produce penicillin on a large scale.[141] It seems, however, that T. I. Balezina, who had been directed to organize a penicillin laboratory at the beginning of 1942 in the Institute of Experimental Medicine, actually was the more hands-on director of the project. One N. I. Grashchenkov the Director of the Institute of Experimental Medicine ordered the mold *Penicillium notatum* from England but, to the consternation of Yermol'eva and Professor V. V. Parin, at the Commissariat of Health, it did not arrive. Thus, Balezina began to gather fungus locally in the spring of 1942. According to Balezina's later reminiscences, the fungus gathered was less lively than Flemming's by four to six times but showed the possibility of active production of penicillin. The group under Balezina then extended their efforts, getting mold from clean potatoes. The 93rd strain of fungus, grown in a bombed-out building, finally showed greater (four to eight times more) activity. It was identified by L. I. Kursanov as "similar to *Penicillium crustosum*." Meanwhile, Yermol'eva, who got credit for the discovery in later encyclopedia entries, was distracted with trying to deal with a cholera epidemic in Stalingrad.[142]

Soviet scientists considered their penicillin different from the British and American product. Their first accounts stated that work on "Soviet penicillin" began "independently from English scientists." Soviet articles in pharmacological journals of the wartime period did not refer to foreign research and developments on penicillin.[143] They noted merely that at the end of 1942 Kursanov produced penicillin with greater antibacterial activity, similar to *Penicillium crustosum*" and it was tested, first on mice and rabbits, and then clinically, on humans, with good results. [144]

However, although Soviet scientists were able to replicate penicillin production on a small scale, they had difficulty producing the new wonder drug on a large scale. Yermol'eva surveyed the effects of the antibiotic on a wide variety of diseases—syphilis, meningococcal meningitis, influenza, the common cold, encephalitis, tuberculosis, staphylococcal "bacteremia," septicemia and others, but because of the very small amounts on hand, only a small number of cases were involved in each test. According to one later account, industrial production began in the summer of 1943 at the factory of Endocrine Preparations. [145] Another later account avers that, "[A]t the end of 1943 the Soviet Government decided to organize a shop to produce penicillin in Factory No. 13 according to the "dry" method worked out by Professor P. G. Strelkov. Simultaneously, Assistant Commissar for Health A. G. Natradze resolved to produce penicillin at the Endocrine Factory, "the director of which was R. I. Kogan . . . according to the deep method of producing the mold in 10-15-ton volumes devised by one Professor N. I. Gel'perin (Helperin)."[146] An official Soviet encyclopedia versions claims that in January 1944, production was transferred to the Karpov Factory—the old Ferrein Factory—and that Professor Florey, one of the British scientists who had discovered penicillin, came to Moscow to oversee comparative evaluation of Soviet, American and British penicillin.[147]

In any case, clinical trials continued though 1944 on very small numbers. Americans reported that in the spring of 1944 only fourteen cases of syphilis were treated.[148] Russians later confirmed that tests were made on eighteen individuals, then wider clinical trials on twenty-five "hopeless" cases, wounded men with septicemia.[149] A report from 1945 described in detail tests on fifty-seven soldiers with ulcerous infections and forty soldiers with sepsis in the summer of 1944. Of the first group penicillin combined with surgery gave good results. Of the second group, thirty six regained health and four died.[150]

Although A. G. Natradze later recalled that "I]n 1944 we organized production of penicillin in Factory No. 40, in the Karpov Factory and in meat factories, and penicillin began to be sent to hospitals" and Balezina recalled that the new drug was sent to "the front" in 1944, the Soviet government also dispatched delegations to France and England to purchase a license to produce penicillin on a mass scale according to foreign methods.[151] Purchasing a license was somewhat of a departure for the Soviet pharmaceutical industry. During the 1920s and 1930s the industry produced brand name and patented products "formerly imported" but there are no records of licenses.[152] Now, according to the later Soviet version, the government offered to pay the 10-million dollar price to produce penicillin by the deep fermentation method. Unfortunately, negotiations took a while and the price jumped to 20 million dollars. Assistant Commissar for Health Natradze subsequently claimed that the Soviet government then learned that "the sellers were American as well as British and that they would not sell, even for 30 million dollars." [153]

As the saying goes, necessity is the mother of invention. Despite the fact that one Soviet version, stated that a "dry" method of producing penicillin was worked out at the end of 1943—and not by Yermol'eva—a Soviet press release of May 1945 announced that "the experimental laboratory attached to the All-Union Institute of Experimental Medicine controlled by Prof. Yermol'eva produced Soviet penicillin from moulds in 1944"—it would seem in conjunction with the licensing problem. Her "laboratory," the press release continued ,"discovered new media for producing the fungi from which penicillin is obtained . . . grown from easily-acquired products—wheat-bran and maize. A chemical method" was "devised of obtaining dry penicillin which" did "not require complicated installations and apparatus. This . . . enabled penicillin to be produced on a mass scale in Moscow, Leningrad, Baku, Minsk and Tomsk." The press release also credited Yermol'eva with an "inter-nasal method of using penicillin" for "children's infectious diseases" and "in collaboration with Urazova" of producing "anti-penitelaz, which safeguards penicillin from destruction by microbes."[154]

Whichever version of the origin of Soviet penicillin is correct, since mass production began when the tide of war had already turned in Soviet favor, only a small number of Red Army and Navy men benefited from penicillin during the war.[155] From archival information it appears that very little penicillin was produced during the war.[156] Nor do civilian war survivors remember penicillin. Thus, no civilians benefited, although penicillin would have helped quash scarlatina and other bacterial diseases.

It is true that in the United States in 1943 penicillin was not easy to make or for civilians to acquire. Since the new wonder drug could not be synthesized, as noted, in some cases moldy fruits were collected to produce penicillin. The American government relegated penicillin to the war effort. It was strictly rationed for civilians and some died, despite pathetic requests to President and Mrs. Roosevelt for the release of new antibiotic. There also was confusion at that time and later about the sorts of illnesses for which penicillin was efficacious. Nevertheless, some American citizens, civilians as well as troops, were saved by the fact that the American pharmaceutical industry was able to mass-produce penicillin.[157]

In the Soviet Union, meanwhile, the main drugs used during the war were bactericides rather than antibiotics— sulfa drugs. Gramitsidin, in particular, was effusively praised.[158] By 1948, penicillin was produced in Moscow, Riga, and Minsk. Methods of production had improved and output had increased in the first two factories but not in the third.[159]

While the Cold War apparently affected penicillin production, the United States did send large quantities of pharmaceuticals and medical supplies, as described in the next chapter. Additionally contact between the Soviet pharmaceutical industry and the United States and Soviet efforts to emulate American penicillin production continued because Soviet factories apparently continued to have difficulty mass-producing the new antibiotic. The Red Army seized carloads of "trophy" pharmaceutical equipment from Eastern Europe at the end of the war. However, the industry had difficulty installing the equipment. Thus, in 1946, Soviet officials resolved to import equipment from the United States.[160] Discussion also ensued as to whether to locate production in the Ministry of Health or the Ministry of Food. One Professor Bukin, who had just returned from a trip to the United States, advocated the latter, since the U. S. Department of Agriculture headed production of penicillin. After the war Zinaida Vissarionovna recommended that production be located in the Ministry of Health.[161]

Output from the Core Industry in 1943

As for production of other needed pharmaceuticals during 1943, in Moscow the Alkaloid and Karpov factories performed best. The Akrikhin Factory "worked poorly." The factory did not fulfill the first quarter plan until December and also did not fulfill the mix (*nomenklatura*) of items. The Salicylate Factory did not fulfill its plan in the first half of the year but did produce the designated mix in the second half.[162]

Over all, fulfillment of the plan was lower in 1943 than in 1942. Of twenty-six planned "important products," production of twelve was fulfilled but the plan for fourteen was not fulfilled. Some products were seriously under plan targets, although from statistics it is difficult to say whether absolute production was disastrously low.[163]

Reasons for poor performance varied. A number of raw materials were severely deficit. Of acetanilide, 312.2 tons were needed and only 131 tons were available. Of paranitrotoluol, 108 tons were needed and only 16.8 tons were available! Of vinegar anhydride, 132.8 tons were needed but only 36.6 tons were available.[164]

As was depressingly clear before the war, during the first two years of the conflict, the interconnection of factories in the Soviet system created a domino effect which accentuated shortages. For example, in 1943, the target for sterile cotton production was not fulfilled because of "lack of [raw] cotton," production of glucose was not fulfilled because of "lower power in connection with transfer of production from maize to glucose sugar"; "ascorbic acid did not reach its target because of late output from Factory No. 35." The plan for Phenacetin was not fulfilled because the output of Factory No. 37, the branch of the Semashko Factory, was late.[165]

And the chain reaction of supplies went on and on.[166] It was less dramatic than the atomic fission experiment, which had recently occurred at the University of Chicago and was being replicated by Soviet scientists.[167] But, erratic deliveries (*uzkikh mest v proizvodstvo*) and production portended grave consequences for the welfare of Soviet citizens.

Finances

Despite the problems with which the pharmaceutical industry grappled, government officials continued to be as concerned about the health of the industry's finances as about the health of the populace. The management of the industry and managers of individual factories dutifully sent reports to higher government officials in 1942 and, along with production figures, they itemized the "Number of cases of *brak*," stating the "amount in kilograms" and "the cost in rubles." Factories were fined for sending out defective products but there is no record of what punishments they incurred for losses. The losses certainly were partly responsible for shortages for final consumers, however, whether military or civilian. But not all these losses may have been due to the need for substitution or even worker carelessness but rather to more sinister and unpatriotic reasons, namely theft and profiteering by workers.

At the Akrikhin Factory near Moscow, for example, 63 cases of *brak* resulted in 1,571 kilograms of Red Streptotsid being ruined at a cost of 57,473 rubles, far exceeding the 14 cases and 347 kilograms of White Streptotsid ruined at a cost of only 10,482 rubles. Loses from Sul'fidin at the Akrikhin factory were even higher at 75,978 rubles even though the cases of *brak* were far fewer (9) and the amount affected less (207 kilograms). Losses from Diethilamin and Dikhlorakridin were higher still at 88,493 rubles and 93, 416 rubles respectively. Fortunately, for the Akrikhin Factory, losses from tablets of the antimalarial Akrikhin, with Plazmotsid, were minimal, with 160 kilograms and 23,353 rubles' worth being ruined in one episode.[168] However since malaria was a grave threat this was a serious loss for the citizenry, if not for the factory and government coffers.

At the Bandaging Materials Factory in Moscow, 120,181bandages of various kinds, including 120, 217 sterile bandages; 14, 220 first-aid packets; 5, 536 "indo" [individual] packets; and 290 units of hygroscopic, sterile cotton were spoiled. "Massive *brak*" was listed as the cause. No ruble amount was stated in the report. Fortunately, 27 percent of the bandages and all but some 900 first-aid packets were "redeemable." However, none of the "indo" packets and the hygroscopic sterile cotton pieces was salvageable.[169]

Dr. David Genis has averred that, in the post-war period, workers stole pharmaceuticals from the factories and sold them at the bazaars for exorbitant prices.[170] Perhaps some of the bandages and the first-aid packets and all of the "indo" packets and hygroscopic cotton, mentioned in the reports above, actually disappeared because of worker pilfering. The same may have been the case with "410 thousand' sterile bandages at a cost of 30,944 rubles ruined at the "Health of Workers" Factory. The 4,620 rubles' worth of glucose spoiled at the factory was not onerous for the government coffers but 300 kilograms of glucose ruined would be detrimental for those wounded or requiring surgery.[171]

Similarly, although the 27, 977 rubles' worth of iodine drops (300 in absolute amounts) ruined at Factory No. 39 in Tiumen was not terrible, the loss to the public was serious. Monetary losses of sulfuric acid barium and sodium chloride at the factory were less at 545 rubles and 1,336 rubles respectively, but the physical amount of sodium chloride lost—740 kilograms—was not negligible. Nor was the 2,001 *shtuk* (units) of glucose ampules, at a cost of 11,221 rubles, ruined in four episodes at the Endocrine and Vitamin Factory, Moscow. All these losses and the 870 kilograms of aspirin ruined at the Salicylate Factory in Moscow, at a cost of 26,813 rubles, would have increased the hardships of the Soviet people. So too would the astounding 140,000 *shtuk* of camphor-salve ampules ruined at the factory at a cost of 2, 744 rubles.[172]

Nevertheless, factories proudly reported the monetary savings they achieved by new processes or use of substitutes. For example, changes in the method of cleaning one ingredient for Akrikhin and semifinished Rivanol, as well as replacing bisul'fide with re-cleaned ammonia, led to annual savings of 185,400 rubles in 1942. Changes in making "sorbit" by replacing medical glucose with meat sugar amounted to a savings of 213,500 with subsequent change in making "sorbit" netting an additional 350,000 rubles.[173] A new method of making White Streptotsid at Factory No. 37 saved 82,000 rubles in 1942. A "method of receiving iodide drops from technical instead of pure potash" resulted in "annual economy of 143,600 rubles" at Factory No. 39. Both *brak* and expenditures for fuel were lessened at the Solnechnogorsk Glass Factory for "annual economy of 500,000 rubles" in 1942—a definite plus for both the Red Army and civilians since glass products were sorely needed for medicines. And modernization of the steam boiler resulted in savings of 126,500 at the Health of Workers Factory that year.[174]

Indeed, the industry reported fulfillment of its financial plan for 1942 as if in peacetime. It noted, for example, that payments "to the State Budget were established at 13,588 thousand rubles"; "actual payments from profits amounted to 11,434 thousand rubles." Additional payments from "turnover" of 2,647 thousand rubles" and "overpayments *(pereplata)* from 1941" of 1,066 thousand rubles" increased the sum paid to the State Budget to 15,147 thousand rubles. Therefore "overpayment amounted to 1, 559 thousand rubles."[175]

The industry also itemized payments to the Central Credit Bank for various categories, including the Amortization Fund for capital repair. The industry reported debts (*debitory*) and "non-payments (*tovary neoplach*)." for wares. It explained that some factories—like Semashko—had overpaid in 1941, thus accounting for lower payment in 1942, and that Factory No. 37 in Anzhero-Sudzhensk, suffered from the fact that "the local division of the Bank, incorrectly understanding a telegram of the Central Credit Bank about permitted limits of capitalization in the third quarter of 1942, demanded from the factory payment from turnover at 370 thousand rubles." [176]

The industry reported loans, turnover, and elaborate "active" and passive" balance statements just as if no war was raging.[177] Most interesting was the industry's emphasis that profits (or "turnover monies" as the Soviet accounting system termed them), wildly fluctuated from year to year—and the reasons for the fluctuation. One would have thought that State Budget officials and the Central Credit Bank officials would have been knowledgeable about both facts.

But, apparently they needed reminding, for the industry report for 1942 duly noted that "turnover" plummeted from 7,308 thousand rubles in 1941 to 3,288 thousand rubles in 1942. There had been an even worse dip down to 2,024 thousand rubles in 1940. "Proper turnover and equalization . . . of means amounted to 94, 846 thousand rubles and raised the established norms to 6,026 thousand rubles," the report intoned. The reason for "Superfluous turnover monies against the norms, in significant part, is accounted for by wares, shipped and not paid for on time by purchasers, which in the chemical-pharmaceutical industry systematically from year to year, results in significant sums." Thus, in 1938 turnover had amounted to 4,066 thousand rubles, in 1939 to 3,246 thousand rubles, and so on. In 1942, "superfluous turnover monies" was not the result of selling more. Rather it resulted from "insufficient supplies to the chemical-pharmaceutical industry of raw materials and other materials in the fourth quarter" —for which the industry had not paid. "Indebtedness," in the figures, meanwhile, was "explained by absence of sufficient turnover monies in the wares-sales network" —that is the *aptekoupravleniia*. In other words the Pharmacy Administrations that purchased from the industry for pharmacies did not have enough funds in some years.[178]

Secondary and Third-Level Factories

The physical and financial problems of the core pharmaceutical industry, which had dominated production and sales before the war, promoted decentralization. Secondary and third-level factories tried mightily to fill the breach. A number of them contributed interesting products and processes, particularly "sanitary-technical" items, although physicians noted that "the quality could have been better."[179]

Pharmaceutical enterprises in Leningrad (some of which were part of the core pharmaceutical industry) were cut off from Moscow to some extent for a year and a half after September 1941. Nevertheless, thirty factories produced more than sixty important products during the winter of 1941-1942, in due time supplying some to other cities. Anesthetics were particularly needed in Leningrad in the fall and winter of 1941 as bombs felled the citizens and the blockade prevented imports from outside. Chemists Shaikind, Vovsi and Zhel'vis organized production of ether, chloroform and chlorethyl that were said to be sufficient for the more than 100,000 operations performed during the blockade. Two individuals, Istomin and Kliukin prepared more than 500,000 kilograms of surgical gypsum needed for surgery. N. I. Volynkin in the Leningrad Pharmaceutical Institute devised a method of making glucose for blood transfusions, netting 20,000 kilograms. Technician Kalinskaia, with the help of Volynkin put out diuretin and theobromine in pharmaceutical factories. Chemist Novosil'tsev devised a method of making nicotine acid in the Leningrad tobacco factory. Lemon acid soda was prepared in the besieged city and Docent Volova discovered a method of producing zinc peroxide to use in cases of gangrene.[180] Other important products included a salve to combat lice, an antigrippe (flu) preparation called Kal'tseks, and a hemostatic for the front called Ambrin.[181]

Manufactories in other areas also developed some useful new remedies in 1943. The Molotov Institute produced a salve—Gandrofil'naia—to protect the skin against poisonous gases.[182] Thermopsis, discovered in 1933 by one Dr. Varlakov, was used in Molotov *oblast'* in 1943 as a replacement for ipecacuanha both in infusions and in Dovers Powders.[183] In western Siberia the root of the perennial *Sanguis orba officinalis*—Krovokhlebka in local parlance—was used as a treatment for diarrhea. From this root, extracted with boiling water into wooden receptacles, transferred through a vacuum apparatus and filtered through flannel and an acid solution, was derived a new medicine, Sanal'bin. Chemical tests conducted in Tomsk (no numbers were provided) showed the preparation was effective in treating enteritis, enterocolitis, and hemocolitis.[184] The Ukrainian Research Chemical-Pharmaceutical Institute developed a vascular-cardiac therapy, Strofantin K, from seeds of *Strofantus Kombe Oliver*. The product, which treated chronic insufficient blood flow and heart "weakness" was applied to sixteen patients with positive results.[185] Gidroksal, a colloidal solution in water of hydrate oxide ammonia, was developed to treat stomach disorders.[186]

There is no information on how many of these innovative remedies were produced. But what was clear was that in 1943, despite concerted efforts, the availability of pharmaceuticals was still precarious. The bulk of these products were channeled to the troops at the Front or to favored groups like musicians from the Bol'shoi Theater, evacuated to Kuibyshev. The tide of war began to turn in 1943 in favor of the Soviet Union.[187] But institutes and the pharmaceutical industry were far from conquering the problems that had impeded them even before the war. We now examine developments in the last two years of the war, how ordinary citizens survived and how pharmacologists and physicians compensated for lack of pharmaceuticals.

Notes

1. El'vira Yershova, "XX vek v sud'bakh rossiiskikh provintial'noi sem'i," *INFOR: Veter Vremeni*, no. 1 (11) (June 2005): 30-31.

2. Marius Broekmeyer, *Stalin, the Russians, and Their War*, trans. by Rosalind Buck (Madison: University of Wisconsin Press, 2005; first published in Amsterdam in 1999): 45-71.

3. Ibid.: 115-116.

4. Smirnov, gen. ed., *Opyt sovetskoi meditsiny*, vol. 3: 467.

5. Smirnov, *Opyt sovetskoi meditsiny*, vol. 2: 151, 167, 179.

6. Smirnov, ed., *Opyt sovetskoi meditisny*, vol. 35, Table 2 : 27. During the first year of the war, of military in treatment institutions, 65.1 percent died from wounds (71.7 percent in the fighting zone, 70 percent in the army region, 60.2 in the front region) and 28.3 percent died from diseases (33.3 percent in the front region, 23.5 percent in the army region, and 11.4 percent in the fighting zone.) In the second year of the war, of military in treatment institutions, 58.7 percent died from wounds. In turn, 4.1 percent died from wounds . . . and 31. 6 percent died from diseases (40.7 percent in the front zone). In the third year of the war, percentages were reversed. Eighty one and 3 tenths of troops in treatment institutions died from wounds (93 percent in the fighting zone). Three and 2 tenths percent of the wounded died from diseases and 13.2 percent of the military, in general, in treatment institutions, died from diseases (23.9 percent in the front region). In the fourth year of the war, 85.8 percent of troops in treatment institutions died from wounds (96.8 percent in the fighting zone). Two and 5 tenths percent of the wounded died from diseases (mostly in the front region) and 9.6 percent of the military in general died from diseases (20.4 percent in the front region).

7. Smirnov, ed., *Opyt sovetskoi meditsiny*, vol 32, part 1: 65; also vol. 32, part 2: 12, 13, 15.

8. Smirnov, ed., *Opyt sovetskoi meditsiny*,vol. 31: 105.

9. Smirnov, ed., *Opyt sovetskoi meditsiny*, vol. 31: 104-105, 106, 109 (light-heavy forms of typhus): 123, 125.)

10. Smirnov, ed., *Opyt sovetskoi meditsiny*, vol 2 : 229, 231.

11. Smirnov, ed., *Opyt sovetskoi meditsiny*, vol. 23-24: 17.

12. Gladkikh and Loktev, *Sluzhba zdorov'ia*: 151-153.

13. Gladkikh and Loktev, ibid.: 155.

14. Gladkikh and Loktev, ibid.: 156-157.

15. Gladkikh and Loktev, ibid.: 262.

16. Gladkikh and Loktev, ibid.: 158.

17. Gladkikh and Loktev, ibid.: 159.

18. Gladkikh and Loktev, ibid.: 266.

19. Gladkikh and Loktev, ibid.: 258.

20. Gladkikh and Loktev, ibid.: 261.

21 V. S. Chetverikov, "Sanitarnoe delo v SSSR vo vremia pervykh dvukh let

voiny," *Gigiena i sanitaria*, vol. 8, no. 10 (1943): 34.

22. David Genis, e-mail communiqué (Denver, CO, September 21, 2006).
23. David Genis, e-mail communiqué (Denver, CO, September 27, 2006).
24. Edlow, "Tick-Borne Diseases, Tularemia," www.emedicine.com/emerg/topic591.htm: 2, 10, 15, 17. Accessed 6/19/2007. See also "Illinois Department of Public Health: Health Beat," www.idph.state.il.us/public/hb/hb/ tulare.htm: 1-3. Accessed 6/19/2007. For tularemia in the Soviet biological weapons program see Rimmington, "The Soviet Union's Offensive Program," in Wright, *Biological Warfare*: 106-107 and Eckhart, "Zeiss in the Soviet Union," in Solomon, *Doing Business Together*: 222-224.
25. Gladkikh and Loktev, *Sluzhba zdorov'ia*: 157.
26. Gladkikh and Loktev, ibid.: 263.
27. Gladkikh and Loktev, ibid.: 157.
28. Gladkikh and Loktev, ibid.,:157, 264-265.
29. Rimmington, "The Soviet Union's Offensive Program": 107.
30.For information on malaria in nineteenth-, early twentieth-century Russia, when it was the Empire's chief communicable disease, see Mary Schaeffer Conroy, "Malaria in Late Tsarist Russia," *Bulletin of the History of Medicine*, vol. 56, no. 1 (1982): 41-55.
31. Smirnov, ed., *Opyt sovetskoi meditsiny*, vol. 32: 16.
32. Smirnov, ed., *Opyt sovetskoi meditsiny*, vol. 31: 136.
33. Gladkikh and Loktev, *Sluzhba zdorov'ia*: 159-160.
34. Gladkikh and Loktev, ibid.: 268-269.
35. D. E. Genis, *Meditsinskaia parazitologiia*, 2nd edition (Moscow: Meditsina, 1979): 47-63 and responses to *anketa* (August 20, 2006).
36. Genis, *Meditsinskaia parazitologiia*: 16-21.
37. Genis, responses to *anketa* (August 20, 2006).
38. Genis, *Meditsinskaia parazitologiia*: 33-41, esp.: 36.
39. Genis, responses to *anketa* (August 20, 2006).
40. Genis, *Meditsinskaia parazitologiia*: 26-28, 112-120.
41. Genis, *Meditsinskaia parazitologiia*: 88-98.
42. Smirnov, ed., *Opyt sovetskoi meditsiny*, vol. 1: 13.
43. Smirnov, ed., *Opyt sovetskoi meditsiny* , vol. 27: 14.
44. Smirnov, ed., *Opyt sovetskoi meditsiny*, vol. 27: 102.
45. Chetverikov, "Sanitarnoe delo": 32-38.
46. S. A. Kolesnikov, "Sovetskoe zdravookhanenie v dni otechestvennoi voiny," *Sovetskaia meditsina*, vol. 7, no. 7-8 (1943): 4.
47. V. L. Troitskii, "Predokhranitel'naia vaktsinatsiia protiv dizenterii," *Dostizheniia sovetskoi meditsiny v otechestvennoi voine* , no. 1 (1943): 84, 91-95.
48. Gladkikh and Loktev, *Sluzhba zdorov'ia*: 266.
49. Gladkikh and Loktev, ibid.: 266-267.
50. David Genis, e-mail communiqué (Denver, CO., September 21, 2006).
51. Ia. A. Frenkel', "Zadachi sel'skikh vrachebnykh uchastkov v usloviiakh voennogo vremeni," *Fed'dsher i akusherka*, [no volume or edition numbers] (1942): 36-38.
52. Genis, e-mail communiqué (Denver, CO, September 21, 2006).
53. Smirnov, ed., *Opyt sovetskoi meditsiny*, vol. 1: 169.
54. Ibid., vol. 2 :. 48
55. Smirnov, ed., *Opyt sovetskoi meditsiny*, vol. 31: 95.

56. Smirnov, ed., *Opyt sovetskoi meditsiny,* vol. 1:. 86, 169, 175; vol. 32, part 2: 162, 164.

57. Smirnov, ed., *Opyt sovetskoi meditsiny,* vol. 32, part 2: 162, 177. Information on the approval of DDT for use in the Soviet Union is given in "Iz otcheta farmakologicheskogo komiteta uchenogo meditsinskogo soveta NKZdrava o rabote za 1943 g.," *Farmakologiia i toksikologiia*, vol. 7, no. 3 (1944): 4.

58. Tamara Nikolaevna Khazieva, Ufa, Russia, e-mail communiqué (June 15, 2006).

59. Genis, *Meditsinskaia parazitologiia*: 39.

60. Genis, ibid.: 114, 120.

63. Gladkikh and Loktev, *Sluzhba zdorov'ia*:159.

61. Gladkikh and Loktev, ibid.: 266.

63. See Chapter 3 of this work

64. Gladkikh and Loktev, ibid.:177. For the contrary phenomenon of "the lack if susceptibility of the emaciated organ to infection. The reduction of infectious morbidity in nutritional dystrophy" similar to "absence of disease in hibernating animals" observed during the siege of Leningrad see Svetlana Magaeva, "Physiological and Psychosomatic Prerequisites for Survival and Recovery," chapter 5 in Barber and Dzeniskevich, *Life and Death in Besieged Leningrad*: 146 and passim.

65. Gladkikh and Loktev, *Sluzhba zdorov'ia*: 264.

66. See Chapter 3 of this work.

67. Smirnov, ed., *Opyt sovetskoi meditsiny,* vol. 31: 157. For information on Charles Donovan's work on leishmaniasis in the early twentieth century and the use of trivalent antimony (a heavy metal) until this remedy was superseded by pentavalent antimonials see Bern, Caryn, Chowdhury, and Rajib,"The epidemiology of visceral leishmaniasis in Bangladesh: prospects for improved control," *Indian Journal of Medical Research* (March 2006) in http://findarticles.com/p/articles/mi_qa3867/is_200603/ai_nl16522864. Accessed 7/2/2007. This article claims that "pentavalent antimonials introduced between 1915 and 1939 resulted in a 95 percent cure rate, and treatment regimens not very different from those used today in Bangladesh. DDT and pyrethrum were known to be effective for sand fly control by the 1940s." (2) However, a second article by Nina Ulrich, University of Hanover, Germany, claims that pentavalent antimonials were not used until the 1950s and that "Nowadays, mainly sodium stibogluconate (pentostam) and meglumine antimonite (glucantime) are used." "Antimony," http://pubs.acs.org/cen/80th/print/antimony.html. Accessed 7/2/2007.

68. Smirnov, ed., *Opyt sovetskoi meditsiny*, vol 23: 62, 151-152.

69. Smirnov, ed., *Opyt sovetskoi meditsiny*, vol. 24 : 17, 65.

70. Genis, Interview and responses to *anketa* (August 20, 2006).

71. Smirnov, ed., *Opyt sovetskoi meditsiny,* vol. 1: 285.

72. Smirnov, ed., *Opyt sovetskoi meditsiny,* vol. 1: 365; vol. 3: 467.

73. Smirnov, ed., *Opyt sovetskoi meditsiny,* vol. 27: 80.

74. Smirnov, ed., *Opyt sovetskoi meditsiny*, vol. 27: 130, 131, 135, 138-140.

75. Smirnov, ed., *Opyt sovetskoi meditsiny*, vol. 27: 134, 138, 139, 146.

76. Smirnov, ed., *Opyt sovetskoi meditsiny*, vol. 27-28: 56.

77. Smirnov, ed., *Opyt sovetskoi meditsiny*, vol. 1: 174; for venereal disease, vol. 27: 198-199.

78. Smirnov, ed., *Opyt sovetskoi meditsiny*, vol.27: 48.

79. Smirnov, ed., *Opyt sovetskoi meditsiny*, vol. 1: 175. Gramitsidin was effective only

as a local bactericide applied to the surface of wounds. However, it was 32 times more effective than Chloratsid, 16 times more effective than chloramine, and 4 times more effective than Rivanol.

80. J. G. Scadding, "Comparative Effects of Sulphonamide Drugs in Mild Bacillary Dysentery," *The Lancet*, June 17 (1944) 784-786; quotes: 784.

81. Worthen, *Pharmacy in World War II*: 7, 78-98. Chart on shortages in 1941: 80; hunt for supplies of tin and use of glass containers: 80-84, 98; hunt for quinine: 84-90; competing needs of the army, lend lease and civilians: 94-95; substitutions: 96-99.

82. Some eighty medium and smaller pharmaceutical enterprises produced a quarter or less of the pharmaceuticals used in the Soviet Union. These entities were under the jurisdiction of republic commissariats of health.

83. See previous chapters.

84. RGAE f. 8009, op. 2, d. 36, l. 27.

85. RGAE, f. 8009, op. 2, d. 36, l. 30. They were ordered "to establish a united plan for the whole chemical-pharmaceutical industry."

86. Gladkikh and Loktev, *Sluzhba zdorov'ia*: 116-117. Without giving details, the authors note that after the attack on Moscow was repulsed, in the second half of 1942, the Moscow pharmaceutical factories worked on the base of old equipment. (167)

87. RGAE, f. 8009, op. 2, d. 36, l. 27.

88. RGAE, f. 8009, op. 2, d. 34, l. 18.

89. RGAE, f. 8009, op. 2, d. 36, l. 27.

90. RGAE, f. 8009, op. 2, d. 36, ll. 28, 29.

91.RGAE, f. 8009, op. 2, d. 34, ll. 1-3, 18; RGAE, f. 8009, op. 36, l. 27, 28, 29.

92. Maxim Pavlovich Murov, quoted in George Borodin, *Red Surgeon* (London: Museum Press Limited, 1945): 98-99.

93. RGAE, f. 8009, op. 2, d. 36, ll. 27, 36.

94. V. Afanas'ev et al, *Zhivi "Akrikhin"!* : 34-36. Production of White Streptotsid had begun in the factory on a small scale in 1938 and ramped up in the spring of 1939.

95. RGAE, f. 8009, op. 2, d. 36, ll. 29, 30, 36.

96. RGAE, f. 8009, op. 2, d. 36, l. 157.

97. RGAE, f. 8009, op. 2, d. 36, ll. 168, 177.

98. RGAE, f. 8009, op. 2, d. 38, l. 17.

99. RGAE, f. 8009, op. 2, d. 38, l. 21.

100. RGAE, f. 8009, op. 2, d. 39, l. 32.

101. RGAE, f. 8009, op. 2, d. 39, l. 32.

102. RGAE, f. 8009, op. 2, d. 39, l. 92.

103. RGAE, f. 8009, op. 2, d. 36, l. 55.

104. RGAE, f. 8009, op. 2, d. 36, l. 55

105. RGAE, f. 8009, op. 2, d. 36, ll. 146-148.

106. RGAE, f. 8009, op. 2, d. 39, ll. 118-125.

107. RGAE, f. 8009, op. 2, d. 36, l. 36.

108. RGAE, f. 8009, op. 2, d. 36, l. 59

109. Gladkikh and Loktev, *Sluzhba zdorov'ia*: 167, 273.

110. Gladkikh and Loktev, ibid., pp. 169-170. For information on Urotropin see Kobrak, *National Cultures and International Competition*: 117. The clones are discussed by Conroy, *The Soviet Pharmaceutical Business*: 129, 131. For Pantapon, see Renate A. Reidl,

"A Brief History of the Pharmaceutical Industry in Basel," in Jonathan Libenau, Gregory Higby, and Elaine C. Stroud, eds. *Pill Peddlers: Essays on the History of the Pharmaceutical Industry* (Madison, WI: American Institute of the History of Pharmacy, 1990): 54, 56. Russian imitation of the product is discussed in Conroy, *The Soviet Pharmaceutical Business*: 15, 129, 131, 133.

111. RGAE, f. 8009, op. 2, d. 36, ll. 120-121, 127 -141.

112. On the importance of Santonin see chapter 1.

113. RGAE, f. 8009, op. 2, d. 36, ll. 155-156.

114. RGAE, f. 8009, op. 2, d. 36, l. 149.

115. World War II forced the American pharmaceutical industry to be creative in acquiring quinine in 1942 and in producing penicillin in 1943. In 1942, in the United States, retail stocks of quinine were collected from around the country to supplement quinine stockpiled before the war and the synthetic antimalarial, atabrine, which soldiers disliked. Dennis B. Worthen, "The National Quinine Pool: When Quinine Went to War," *Pharmacy in History*, vol. 38, no. 3 (1996): 143-147. Also, Worthen, *Pharmacy in World War II*: 84-90.

Penicillin needed to be produced in a mass scale during the war, but it could not be synthesized. To make the process more efficient, in 1943 Robert Coghill and a groups of scientists at Northern Illinois Regional research laboratory in Peoria, "discovered a new fermenting media" made of corn steep liquor "that produced a significant increase in penicillin mold." They gathered up spoiled fruit from grocers to obtain the mold. Milton Scoutaris, "'Moldy Mary' and the Illinois Fruit and Vegetable Company," *Pharmacy in History*, vol. 38, no. 4 (1996): 175-177.

See also the use of penicillin to combat syphilis in 1943. John Parascandola, "John Mahoney and the Introduction of Penicillin to Treat Syphilis," *Pharmacy in History*, vol. 43, no. 1 (2001): 3-13.

116. Mark Harrison, *Accounting for War: Soviet production, employment, and the defense burden, 1940-1945* (Cambridge: Cambridge University Press, 1996).

117. In 1945 the names of some scientists who worked out new processes were publicized, more fully than in the factory reports of the preceding three years, in P. I. Astrakhantsev, "Pomoshch' VNIKhFI farmatsevticheskoi promyshlennosti v god otechestvennoi voiny," *Farmatsiia*, vol. 8, no. 4 (1945): 12-16:

Sul'fanilamide Preparations: (12) A substitute for deficit acetanilide was developed in 1942. A method of producing Streptotsid from formanilide was developed by G. I. Braz (senior scientific associate). A new method of receiving sul'fanilamine: A. M. Grigorovskii (senior scientific associate) and K. I. Znaeva (senior chemist). The method given for chlorbenzol, etc.

In the production of Sul'fidin in factories, the water method of receiving it was worked out by E. S. Golovchinska under the direction of Prof. Magidson. She received second prize in an All-Union competition of Narkomzdrav USSR

In a branch of VNIKhFI, scientific director I. Ia. Postovskii, worked out and introduced into Factory No. 8 of Glavmedfarmprom a method of receiving norsul'fazol (sul'fatiazol) from a new raw materials, more aavailable in the area, and vanilla ether.

In the Alkaloid Factory there was worked out by Candidate of Chemical Sciences V. N. Sokolova a method of receiving 2-aminotiazol by means of chorinization of acetal'degide (12).

Penicillin: A new method of making this new antibiotic was worked out by L. M. Utkin

(13). Yermoleva was not mentioned)

Akrikhin: Senior scientific associate of VNIKhFI, I. Kh. Fel'dman, worked out new method of producing this antimalarial. Also A. M. Grigorovskii worled out a method avoiding deficit material.

Antipyrine and Pyramidon: Into the factory was introduced a method worked out by Senior Scientific Associate I. E. Gorbovitskii with another associate of immediately producing nitrozirovaniia toluosul'fonate antipyrine without preliminary separation of the latter, replacing muric acid. The method won first prize of Narkomzrav USSR

Ascorbic acid: was worked out in VNIKhFI and applied in Factory No. 40 (13)

118.RGAE, f. 8009, op. 2, d. 36, ll. 41, 42.

119. RGAE, f. 8009, op. 2, d. 36, ll. 37, 41.

120. RGAE, f. 8009, op. 2, d. 36, l. 141.

121. RGAE, f. 8009, op. 2, d. 36, l. 38.

122. RGAE, f. 8009, op. 2, d. 38, ll. 44-50

123. RGAE, f. 8009, op. 2, d. 38, l. 63.

124. Other new methods applied on a factory scale involved, production of Sul'fidin, in the absence of a pyridine base, using acetanaminobenzolsulphochloride, without recrystallization of it, from dichloretan. Because some factories possessed formailid, a method was worked out to obtain Streptotsid from formailid. The method was introduced in the factory in Sverdlovsk and Factory No. 38 in Irbitsk. Methods of producing Streptotsid from chlorbenzol were going on in 1943. Other methods using substitutes were developed to produce antipyrine and Pyramidon. RGAE, f. 8009, op. 2, d. 38, l. 42.

125. RGAE, f. 8009, op. 2, d. 36, l. 45.

126. Interview with David Genis, Parasitologist (Denver, CO, 18 August 2006).

127. L. V. Borodkina, "Opyt primeneniia preparata '805' v klinike legochnogo tuberkuleza,"*Farmakologiia i toksikologiia*, vol. 6, no. 3 (1943):15-17 and Prof. S. I. Banaitis, "Preparat '805' v khirugicheskoi praktike fronta," ibid.: 18-20.

128."Stenogramma soveshchaniia farmakologov, 16 sentiabria 1943 g.," *Farmakologiia i toksikologiia*, vol. 7, no. 1 (1944): 3 , 5, 28-29.

129. V. F. Gladkikh, " Dannye farmakologicheskogo obsledovaniia khlorsuktsinimida," *Farmakologiia i toksikologiia*, vol. 6, no. 1 (1943): 39 (pp. 38-43).

130."Iz ocheta farmakologicheskogo komiteta uchenogo meditsinskogo soveta NKZdrava o rabote za 1943 g.," *Farmakologiia i toksikologiia*, vol. 7, no. 3, 1944, pp. 3-11. Composition of methyl-caffeine in "Economic News Bulletin No. 144, November 15, 1945 , NAUSA, RG 489, Box 82, File 10,300, BFDC, U. S . Department of Commerce.

131. "Iz ocheta ": 3-11. Other new drugs included sul'fodiamin (a dusting powder for wounds and applied internally), bistal'bin, and sikkoplatsentin, ibid.: 1-9.

132. Afanas'ev, *Zhivi , "Akrikhin"!* : 36-37.

133. John E. Lesch, "The Discovery of M&B 693 (Sulfapyridine)," in Gregory Higby and Elaine C. Stroud, eds., *The Inside Story of Medicines* (Madison, WI: American Institute for the History of Pharmacy, 1997): 111.

134. N. I. Yefimov, "K farmakologii preparata sul'fanilamidmetilpirimidina, ego natrievoi soli, '063,'" *Farmakologiia i toksikologiia*, vol. 6, no. 1 (1943): 61-64.

135. Paul A. Dahm, "DDT," *World Book Encyclopedia* (Field Enterprises, 1976), vol. 5: 48-49.

136. Peter Neushul, "Science, Government, and the Mass Production of Penicillin," *The*

Journal of the History of Medicine and Allied Sciences, Inc., vol. 48, no. 4 (1993): 371-395. American mycologists' experimentation with molds, such as that of James Currie, who first worked in the USDA and then at Charles Pfizer and Co., Inc., began in 1916.Neushul, "Science, Government, and Penicillin": 372-375. At Pfizer Currie "helped develop methods for mass-producing gluconic acid using mold fermentation. Currie's research and Pfizer's experience with large-scale fermentation, helped the company become the world's largest producer of penicillin during WWII." (375) By 1935, USDA scientists patented "a 'submerged' fermentation process in which a mold was grown throughout the medium." Rotary fermenters using aluminum aided the process. In 1936, fermenters were installed at a USDA lab in Ames Iowa; in 1938 they were moved to a lab in Peoria, Illinois, "where they were used to test submerged growth of various *Penicillium* strains." In 1937, Andrew Moyer's use of corn-steep liquor in the growth medium accelerated the process. Neushul, "Science, Government and Penicillin": 377-379.

137. Neushul, ibid.: 371-395, passim.

138. Jeffrey L. Rodengen, *The Legend of Pfizer* (Write Stuff Syndicate,1999): 65.

139 Neushul, ibid.:. 394-395.

140. Vl. Saposhnikov, "Limonnaia kislota i limonokisloe brozhenie," *Kimiko-farmatsevticheskii zhurnal*, no. 6-7 (1924): 17-19.

141. The laboratory named for one A. N. Bakh, had already developed "a range of preparations considered valuable—lizotsim, ekmolin, ekmonovotsillin, piophagy and choleraphage." T. I. Balezina, "K istorii polucheniia Z. V. Yermol'evoi penitsillina," *Antibiotiki i khimoterapiia*, vol. 43, no. 5 (1998): 7.

142. Baleznina, "K istorii polucheniia Z. V. Yermolevoi penitsillina," *Antibiotiki i khimoterapiia*, vol. 43, no. 5 (1998): 7-8.

143. "Iz otcheta," *Farmakologiia i toksikologiia*, vol. 7, no. 3 (1944): 8.

144. Balezina, "K istorii polucheniia Z. V. Yermol'evoi penitsillina": 8.

145. "Penitsilliny," *Bol'shaia meditsinskaia entsiklopediia* (Moscow ,1982) vol.18: 460.

146. Balezina, "K istorii polucheniia" : 8.

147. "Penitsilliny," *Bol'shaia meditsinskaia entsiklopediia* (Moscow, 1982) vol. 18: 460.

148. Interview conducted by the US Naval Attaché in Moscow (May 29, 1944) in NAUSA, File 489, Box 82, 10,300 (Jul 13, 1944) BFDC, U. S. Dept. of Commerce.

149. Balezina, " K istorii polucheniia Z. V. Ermol'evoi penitsillina" : 8.

150. S. O. Portugalov, "Opyt primeneniia penitsillina pri tiazhelekh formakh gnoinosepticheskoi infektsii," *Voenno-meditsinskii zhurnal* (1945) : 29-37.

151. A. G. Natradze, "K istorii otkrytiia otechestvennogo penitsillina," *Antibiotiki i khimoterapiia*, vol. 39, no. 1 (1994): 21-22; Balezina, "K istorii polucheniia" : 8.

152. Details in Conroy, *The Soviet Pharmaceutical Business during Its First Two Decades*: 129-132.

153. Natradze, "K istorii otkrytiia otechestvennogo penitsillina": 21-22.

154. "The Mass Production of Penicillin: Successes achieved at Prof. Ermolova's [sic] laboratory," *Vech[ernaia] Moskva* (May 18, 1945) as quoted in "Joint Press Reading" (May 19, 1945) in NAUSA, RG 489, Box 82, BFDC, U. S. Dept. of Commerce.

155. Report of interview of the Director of Division of Higher Education of the Red Navy Medical Service, Dr. Gregory Blaustein. Report of US Assistant Naval Attache in

Moscow (May 15, 1944): 6, NAUSA, File RG 489, Box 82, BFDC, U. S. Dept. of Commerce.

156. RGAE, f. 8009, op. 2, d. 59, (1945) l. 42 (Karpov Factory) and l. 45 (Factory No. 40).

157. David P. Adams, "Wartime Bureaucracy and Penicillin Allocation: The Committee on Chemotherapeutic and Other Agents," *Journal of the History of Medicine and Allied Sciences*, vol. 44 (1989): 196-217, denials: 202-205. On the collection of moldy fruit see note 115, above.

158. For example, Smirnov, ed., *Opyt sovetskoi meditsiny*, vol. 14: 314. Gramitsidin in ampules was mentioned as a new substance, produced in 1943. "Iz otcheta," : 7.

159. RGAE, f. 8009, op. 20, d. 176 (1948), l. 15 (Moscow No. 40) and Riga; l. 16 (Minsk).

160. A. G. Natradze, "O dal'neishem razvitii meditsinskoi promyshlennosti," *Farmatsiia*, vol. 8, no. 6 (1945): 5.

161. A. G. Natradze in "K istorii otkrytiia otechestvennogo penitsillina": 22.

162. RGAE, f. 8009, op. 2, d. 38, l. 17.

163. RGAE, f. 8009, op. 2, d. 38, l. 17.

164. RGAE, f. 8009, op. 2, d. 38, l. 19.

165. RGAE, f. 8009, op. 2, d. 38, l. 20.

166. In 1943, methyl caffeine did not reach targets because of interruption in supplies of vinegar anhydride. Novocain did not reach targets because of "interruptions in supplies of paranitrobenzoic acid in the Akrikhin Factory," in turn, resulting from "absence of paranitrotoluol." There were "technical difficulties" in producing Pyramidon. Salicylate was held up by "construction of a second autoclave in the Salicylate Factory and interruptions in supplies." Rivanol was held up by interruptions in the supplies of paranitrotoluol and Streptotsid by interruptions in supplies of acetanalide. The target for Sul'fazol was not fulfilled because of interruptions in supplies to the Alkaloid Factory of sul'fochloride from the Semashko Factory, in turn due to absence of acetanalide. Preparations of mercury were not fulfilled because of lack of chlorine, preparations of bismuth because of lack of metallic bismuth, Pantotsid because of lack of paratoluol sul'fochloride. RGAE, f. 8009, op. 2, d. 38, l. 20

167. See David Holloway, *Stalin and the Bomb* (New Haven: Yale University Press, 1994): 74-95.

168. RGAE, f. 8009, op. 2, d. 36, ll. 41-42, 149. Indeed, the report for 1942 stated that the "lower percentage of internal *brak* (in ratio to cost) against 1940 cannot be explained by better production methods but by poor accounting." (l.41)

169. RGAE, f. 8009, op. 2, d. 36, ll. 42, 207.

170. Interview with David Genis (Denver, CO., August 18, 2006).

171. RGAE, f. 8009, op. 2, d. 36, l. 42.

172. RGAE, f. 8009, op. 2, d. 36, l. 42.

173. RGAE, f. 8009, op. 2, d. 36, ll. 56, 57.

174. RGAE, f. 8009, op. 2, d. 36, l. 57.

175. RGAE, f. 8009, op. 2, d. 36, l. 60.

176. RGAE, f. 8009, op. 2, d. 36, ll. 61-62.

177. RGAE, f. 8009, op. 2, d. 36, ll. 61- 66, 116-117, 120-126..

178. RGAE, f. 8009, op. 2, d. 36, l. 63.

179. Smirnov, ed., *Opyt sovetskoi meditsiny*, vol. 32, part 2: 128-129. The Smirnov volumes were more discussing laundry items and criticized the "armature of boilers."

180. Iu. Ia. Kaganovich, "Medikamentoznoe snabzhenie v dni otechestvennoi voiny v Leningrade," *Farmatsiia*, vol. 8, no. 6 (1945): 14-16.

181.Dmitriev, G. "Vse dlia nuzhd leningradskogo fronta," *Farmatsiia*, vol. 6, no. 1, (1943): 42.

182. A. L. Katalkherman, "Gidrofil'naia mazevaia osnova, bystro zasykhaiushchaia na kozhe," *Farmatsiia*, vol. 6, no. 1 (1943): 28-31.

183. D. M. Shcherbachev, "K anatomicheskomu issledovaniiu travy termopsisa (Thermopsis Lanceolata R. Br.)," *Farmatsiia*, vol. 6, no. 2 (1943): 32-33.

184. M. M. Rubinshtein, V. A. Ioffe, "Novye lekarstvennye sredstva: Sanal'bin," *Farmatsiia*, vol. 6, no. 2 (1943): 36-37.

185. L-n, "Strofantin K," *Farmatsiia*, vol. 6, no. 2 (1943): 38-39.

186. L-n. "Gidroksal'," *Farmatsiia*, vol. 6, no. 2 (1943): 37.

187. See, for example, David M. Glantz and Jonathan M. House, *The Battle of Kursk* (Lawrence: University Press of Kansas, 1999).

Chapter 7
Points of Light? Production and Foreign Assistance, 1943-1945

Foreign physicians making short visits to the Soviet Union in early 1943 uncritically lauded Soviet medicine and surgery. However, they did imply shortages of anesthetics, disinfectants, and surgical instruments.

Gordon Gordon-Taylor, member of a British-American-Canadian Surgical Mission visiting the front at Vyaz'ma, situated midway between Moscow and Smolensk, near the Soviet Union's western borders, raved about various types of surgery—neurological surgery, gastro-intestinal and gastro-duodunal surgery (performed by one Professor Yudin) and genito-urinary surgery. He noted in particular that "employment of corpse blood . . . under the supervision of Professors Bagdasarov and Bogovmoletz [sic] . . . probably was a transient phase in the history of the organization of blood transfusion in Russia, designed to meet urgent need for blood . . . and although the machinery for its collection is still present in at least one hospital, this type of blood and this mode of collection has now been superseded by the most modern methods, *perhaps even surpassing in carefulness of ritual those employed in Britain* [italics in original]."[1]

An account of the same mission—"a two-day visit to front line hospitals in the Vyasma [sic] area of the Western Front" by Canadian Wilder Penfield was more balanced. Although it ended on the utopian call to "our friendship in science, in life and in the world," it implied scarcity of certain items. Penfield acknowledged the "staggering" casualties "approaching 6 million" of Red Army troops and cautiously repeated the official statistic that "70% of the injured are said to have been returned to the fighting line," a claim that peppered every account of Russian frontline medical care. Penfield appreciated the "strongly built" hospital huts, partially erected by nurses who "appeared in correct uniform on duty" and some of whom appeared in the evening "in fancy dress, singing and doing folk dances." But he also noted that "no antiseptics and no ointments" were used "in preparing the wound for suture" and that

"[B]acteriological examination was made of the 'flora' of the wound, and the presence of streptococci was taken as an indication for more frequent washing and further delay in closure," thus implying shortage of antiseptics and disinfectants. He either noticed or was told that magnesium sulfate 20 percent or sodium chloride 10 percent was used to irrigate wounds and that streptocide [sic] was inserted before suturing. He cited one Professor Lebedenko's account that local anesthesia was used for head wounds and, perhaps testifying to other shortages, that the brain wound was "washed out" but "left open," sulfonamide being "applied locally as a powder or in suspension, and given by mouth or vein." Lauding the work of Professor Bogomoletz [sic] and others, Penfield praised Soviet methods of collecting and preserving blood for transfusions. "Five-hundred to eight hundred donors" were "bled daily at the Central Institute and large stocks of blood pass through it from filial institutes and collection points." The donor's name was noted on the bottle, sometimes stimulating "correspondence and friendship between donor and recipient" [!] Blood was stored in absolutely sterile conditions and, "preserved in 5% sodium citrate and 25% glucose solution," was "sent to the front by air in well insulted boxes" to protect it for "6 hours against a temperature of 40" degrees below zero. "Serum was preferred to plasma" and "[D]ried serum" was "used as well as liquid." That sodium and potassium chloride "with magnesium chloride and glucose" were used for serum transfusine implied sufficiency of these items. On the other hand, that "[C]olloid infusine," prepared from "the casein of milk, the antigen having been removed" seemed "as useful as plasma" and that "[C]adaver blood" was "still utilized," the method of removing "3 litres of blood from each cadaver" as "described in medical literature before the war," perhaps testified to shortages of living donor blood or inadequate methods of packaging and transporting it. Penfield was quick to add, however, that this affected only civilians since "living-donor blood" rather than cadaver blood was used at the front.[2]

Penfield also recommended "Bogomoletz' [sic] antireticular cytotoxic serum" for treating gastric ulcer that had escalated "among the women at home," ostensibly "due to the increased strains of wartime." (We now know that ulcers result from bacterial infection.) Penfield further suggested that the serum be used in small doses to "accelerate callus formation about fractures" and to increase the healing of wounds. He praised an innovative treatment devised for fractures by one Professor Friedland of the Botkin Hospital. Friedland used movement and massage and also an "alcohol-novocaine [sic] injection into the tissue about the fracture" thus implying sufficiency of these items.[3]

Penfield saw x-rays. He praised genito-urinary surgery, particularly replacement of "external genitalia," triage and so on. "[S]trong antiseptics" were not used for wounds, he affirmed, but rather "iodine," underlining the importance of iodine, which was obtained with great difficulty in the Soviet Union in the 1920s and 1930s. And, although sulfonamides were employed, Penfield remarked that "[T]hese drugs are not given to the soldiers to carry," perhaps indicating scarcity for they were "used enthusiastically in the U.S.S.R. as in other countries."[4]

Sir Ernest Rock Carling, Consultant in Surgery, noted in 1943 that "in Moscow there is, judging by experience in Great Britain, little sign of bombardment." He admitted that "[O]perative surgery on the central and peripheral nervous systems . . . is perhaps lacking in refinements now the rule in American and British units" and accepted with reservations the claims of the People's Commissar for Health that "the U.S.S.R. have practically abolished" gas gangrene and typhus, as well as cholera. But he praised the expertise of physicians and surgeons, the system of blood transfusions and care of military wounded, and approved the use of potassium phosphate and calcium to prevent "shock" after blood transfusions.[5]

Bernard Koten's "Soviet Medicine in Wartime," replete with staged photos of physicians and soldiers, a comely nurse on skis and a "blood transfusion in a field hospital," was a puff piece. He reiterated that 70 percent of wounded were returned to the front, lauded huge amounts of medical graduates and physicians, referred vaguely to Stalin prizes for hemostatic preparations and freezing blood plasma, ointments "to speed the healing of wounds and ulcers" and a "method of preparing vinvlic ethers, which stimulate the growth of tissue and whose oils can be successfully applied to the treatment of wounds." Koten noted, however, that surgical "instruments" though "good" were "jealously guarded and cleaned by nurses," thus suggesting that these were in short supply.[6]

The account of a three-week visit of "four British Surgeons" to the same frontline hospitals in Vyazma noted that "young Russian surgeons would benefit from a study of our best hospital practice" although they conceded that "our young surgeons would learn much from the Russian clinics," particularly Professor Yudin's "remarkable operation for replacement of the obstructed oesophagus by the jejunum" and his use of "skin-tight plaster for the treatment of war wounds," a method said to have been first used by Pirogov in the Crimean War when sailcloth was dipped in plaster. The British surgeons found that "neither Soviet nor European anesthetic practice is so good as it is in Great Britain or the United States" but acknowledged that the "Soviet system of blood transfusion" was "beyond criticism." They praised clearing stations behind the front as "well-equipped" and also "the tough Russian constitution [!]" for the fact that "70 percent" of the wounded were returned "to the firing line" and that Soviet nurses did construction work along with their medical duties. On a more professional note they praised emergency medical services in Moscow and military ophthalmology.[7]

Daniel Halpern gushed about many facets of frontline medical-surgical care particularly the bravery and devotion of surgeons and other medical personnel. He asserted that frontline medical facilities were well equipped. However, he also remarked that "Chemists devote their time searching for substitutes for balsam of Peru" and noted that when the "supply [of blood] has run out, blood is donated by the medical personnel[!]." Indeed "Professor Alexander Vishnevski," [sic] having performed "over 400 difficult operations in field hospitals, once drew blood from his own veins during an operation" for transfusion to a small girl, wounded when an air raid shelter was hit by a bomb, thus strongly implying that civilians were perhaps not so well supplied as the military. Halpern recounted new preparations and procedures—a "synthetic oil of balsam"; "a method for producing anti-typhus vaccine in large quantities"; "[S]pecial plants in Kirghizia for the large scale production of vitamins A and C"; "[A]n improved hemostatic preparation called 'trombin';" a "new method" which facilitated "freezing blood plasma"; new methods "for preparation of vinyl ethers, which stimulate tissue growth"; a "drug" for the "treatment of dysentery"; and, of course, the anti-reticular cytotoxic serum of Bogomolets, which had "important application in cases of sclerosis and hypertony of the vascular system." He cited the same statistics as others on the medical mission, regarding numbers of medical personnel who had graduated but also gave a disturbing tidbit of medical information on care of children in boarding institutions, emphasizing that large-scale preparation of wholesome foods had cut cases of scarlet fever "by 38% in 1940."[8]

Two English translations of articles by Russian physicians, one in *The South African Medical Journal*, the other in the *Journal of the American Medical Association*, presented Russian medical advances in glowing tones. Professor N. Graschenkov discussed bacteriophagy; the use of ultra-violet rays; short waves to treat frostbite (developed in the Finnish War); sulphonamides (which were implied to be available in sufficiency); vitamin B-1 and nicotine therapy; vaccinations to combat "spotted or historical typhus" and measures to protect against cholera. Graschenkov repeated that 70 percent of wounded men were returned to the front.[9] Professor Lavrentiev stressed the "prompt diagnosis of typhus"; the use of bacteriophages, sometimes combined with sulfapyridine and sulfathiazole (thus implying shortages of both therapies); transplants of animal and human nerves to replace defects of the nerve stems and injuries of the brain; heat and light treatments; and Vishnevsky's [sic] treatment for wounds "by means of plugs soaked in an emulsion of balsam, tar and similar substances, with an admixture of xeroform"—the last treatment also implying shortages of conventional chemotherapy.[10]

The anonymous "U.S. Correspondent" reporting to *The Australian Journal of Pharmacy* in March 1943 took everything he witnessed or was told by his Soviet colleagues at face value, for example that "only 1.5 per cent of their wounded had died . . . an unprecedented record, surpassing even that of American military surgeons who saved 96 out of every 100 men wounded at Pearl Harbor." He accurately noted that in the Great Patriotic War most military casualties were "due to bombing, mortar fire and grenades . . . 95 per cent of wounds were caused by shrapnel," but recounted Soviet accomplishments in the context of the First World War without apparent reflection that medical care amongst all belligerents had improved. For example, "[M]ortality from brain wounds" was only "about 5 per cent," as compared to "35 per cent" in World War I; "deaths from stomach wounds" had "dropped 33 per cent;" deaths "from head, jam and thorax wounds 50 per cent; and from spinal column injuries 80 per cent." [11]

The U. S. Correspondent opined that Soviet battlefield medicine had perfected plasma transfusions. In comparison to Halpern, the correspondent averred that acquiring blood for transfusions was "an easy matter for any hospital" because "[A]ll Soviet citizens have regular periodic blood tests for reasons of social hygiene." Therefore the hospital needing blood had only to "call up one of the organizations with which it is in permanent contact, and ask for the required number of blood donors." The correspondent related the innovations contributed by Soviet physicians, enlarging on "the method of obtaining the coagulating agent Thrombin" developed by one "Dr. Kudryashev of Moscow." Thrombin had been "first obtained in 1912" and isolated by "American scientists," but Kudryashev discovered how to mass produce it in "thousands of quarts, and it is now being used in many hospitals in Russia." Amazingly, Red Army nurses were able to give transfusions right on the battlefield, all of them being provided with "200 cc of blood of the 'universal' type" and "sterilized rubber tube, needle and filter," implying complete sufficiency of these items.[12]

The anonymous U. S. War Correspondent noted that "[S]ulfa drugs and tetanus serum have reduced danger of infections." Yet the Soviets did not use sulfa drugs to combat the anaerobic bacteria that caused gas gangrene. I. G. Farben had developed the sulfa drug Uliron between 1935 and 1937.[13] Perhaps this was because the Soviets did not have enough sulfa drugs—or perhaps medics simply preferred another method. "[I]n use of antitoxin for gas gangrene Russia claims to be well ahead of other nations," the U. S. Correspondent commented, repeating a claim apparently verified by "a famed Boston surgeon . . . Dr. Hugh Cabot." "Tetanus" was rare due to a serum. "Anti-tetanus and Anti-gangrene Injections" were administered "at field stations as soon as possible."[14]

Sulfa drugs such as "streptocide, sulfadine, sulfazol, and other variants of sulfanilamide" appeared to be plentiful at the Soviet front in the account published by *The Australian Journal of Pharmacy*, as were morphia, alcohol and various heart stimulants. "The standard of medical services in Russia undoubtedly" was deemed "high, and cleanliness" had "become almost a fetish." However, some improvisational procedures implied severe shortages. For example, "[G]aping wounds" were "healed by covering them with the treated peritoneum of an animal, a method developed by Professor V. Krause." And, according to "Dr. B. A. Petrov, chief surgeon of the Black Sea Fleet," field surgeons "now apply a cast directly on the open wound." This facilitated "removal of the patient and" significantly effected "tremendous saving in dressing materials."[15]

Veterans who survived the Great Patriotic War and their wives also give high marks to medical care for soldiers at the front and in military hospitals. Mariia Sergeevna Kuznetsova, who now lives in Ufa, Russia, remembers that her husband, "Anatolii Vasil'evich, was severely wounded in the war. He stumbled on a mine and the mine tore two fingers from his left hand. He told me that military medicine was very, very good." The treatment was "[S]pectacular . . . not only in the hospital but also in the medical train, in which . . . he was transported from the front to the hospital in the rear." "The bed linen was very clean." Anatolii Vasil'evich "remembered all his life, the ideal cleanliness in the train and in the hospital and the solicitous care of the doctors and medsisters (medical sisters, nurses) for the wounded soldiers." [16]

Mark Nulevich himself served at the front during the Great Patriotic War. Subsequently, he emigrated from the Soviet Union and now lives in Denver, Colorado. Although he was at odds with some aspects of life in the Soviet Union, nonetheless, he considers "the medical care in the Red Army" during the war "better than that in the German and French military." The method of evacuating the wounded, the medsisters, the dogs used to find the living wounded, the auto transport, the medical care the wounded received was exceptionally good.[17]

Liudmila Ravvina, evacuated from Belorussia to Fergana, Uzbekistan, during the war, helped her mother in a military hospital, distributing medicines to the patients, among them Streptotsid and aspirin. Her brother had scarlatina and measles and he was appropriately treated.[18]

Dr. David Genis praised the skill of surgeons, particularly those dealing with difficult military wounds. His uncle in Sverdlovsk did excellent reconstructive facial surgery on soldiers whose jaws were destroyed. But he was dubious about the availability of medicines and apparatus in Soviet hospitals.[19]

Indeed, the critical issue in the medical care of Soviet citizens, both military and civilians, was the amount of pharmaceuticals and vaccines, serums and antitoxins available. The Soviet Union won the war in part because Soviet factories outproduced German planes, tanks and firepower. The Soviet Union did not do the same in terms of medicine. German pharmaceutical houses did not produce penicillin during World War II. However, it appears that they produced large amounts of pharmaceuticals. According to John Lesch, during World War II the major sulfa drugs "Prontosil, Uliron [against gas gangrene] and Marfanil were made and sold in quantity. In the war years 1940-1945 alone, he continues, "I. G. Farben took in more than 48.5 million marks on sales of Prontosil, exclusive of veterinary medicine. . . .I. G. Farben manufactured Marfanil powder, which was used in the treatment of wounds in quantities up to ten tons per month. Some of this fell into Allied hands in North Africa, but before the chemical formula had been published."[20] Christopher Kobrak comments the same about Schering. Although Schering had pared down its list of products during the war, he notes, "it still offered approximately fifty pharmaceutical products, less than forty fine chemicals, fifteen plant protection products, five x-ray products" and other essentials.[21] It is true that acquiring pharmaceuticals was problematical for some German citizens. Ernestine Bradley recalls that in 1944 there was a shortage of soap powder. And in 1945 her mother suffered greatly from a lack of sulfa drugs and anesthesia.[22] So Germany had some problems producing and distributing pharmaceuticals. But they came at the tail end of the war.

The Soviet Union had problems earlier and of greater magnitude. David Glantz, renowned war historian, alleged—in broad brush strokes—that "medical support and health care provided to Red Army soldiers remained weak throughout the war." Out of "22 million Red Army and Fleet medical cases treated . . . 7.6 million resulted from various diseases. This grim toll of sickness was clearly excessive," he opined, "and was a direct result of poor field sanitary conditions, mediocre medical treatment, and the general shortage of medicines and other medical equipment."[23] His source was a 1993 Russian-language publication.[24] He noted that 2.3 million Red Army men "were lost to illness and infectious disease."[25] However, he does not relate this statistic to those of other World War II armies, nor does he provide any more details about production and distribution of pharmaceuticals and medical-surgical supplies.

Survivors of the Great Patriotic War explain away any problems suffered by civilians with the slogan "All for the Front." But if the troops did not have the best of medical care what must the situation have been like for civilians? An examination of the performance of the medical/surgical instruments' industry during the war and the pharmaceutical industry during its last two years helps us to flesh out the picture of Soviet medical care.

The tide of war turned in 1943, impacting the pharmaceutical industry to some extent. Reports emphasized "significant amount of repair and renovation went on in Moscow pharmaceutical factories," because they had received "95 percent of funding [they] needed." There was "significant repair in the second shop of the Akrikhin Factory." The Endocrine and Vitamin Factory "installed a new Shtein-Muller steam boiler system." In the Farmakon Factory in Leningrad a large boiler was replaced with a small one, giving electric motors additional power of 50 kilowatts. Factory No. 37 received a new transformer and windows were repaired to save on fuel. Workers' productivity increased by 1943. Industry reports noted that costs for some items were lower and fewer defective products were sent out, reducing fines. They decried the fact that accounting reports still arrived late, particularly from the eastern factories. Indeed, wartime or not, officials' preoccupation with the financial health of the industry did not stint. Almost half the industry's report for 1943 dealt with costs, profits and losses.[26]

The 1943 reports celebrated "significant improvement" of sulfa drugs, iodine, Novocain, and Khloretil (Chlorethyl). However, they also admitted deficits in production, complaining about the "limited range" of Bromural, Phenacetin, Pyramidon, antipyrine, and Biokhinol.[27] In general, the scarcity of crucial pharmaceuticals available in 1943 was sobering. Only half of the medicaments, technical chemical preparations, ampules and tablets produced in 1940 were produced in 1943. Only one fifth of reagents produced in 1940 were produced in 1943. The industry report for 1943 frankly acknowledged that "the country did not receive such important medicines as Novarsenol (from the Karpov Factory), Phenacetin (from Factory No.37), [and] medical glucose (from the Factory of Endocrine and Vitamin Preparations)."[28]

The Medical Instruments' Industry

Production of medical equipment and surgical equipment arguably was more precarious. The Medical Instruments' industry was in a worse state than the pharmaceutical industry and for many of the same reasons. In 1941, Glavmedinstrumentprom saw manufactories under its jurisdiction increase from nineteen to twenty three. Five enterprises dated to before the revolution, emphasizing, as in the pharmaceutical sector, the debt the medical/surgical industry owed to its imperial base. A medical instruments' plant in Gorky (former Nizhninovgorod) *oblast'* had been founded in 1914, the Sacco and Vanzetti Dental Equipment plant in Stalingrad (former Tsaritsyn) in 1912, the State Factory of Disinfecting and Sanitary Equipment in Penza dated to 1848. The Suksunskii Sanitary Equipment Factory in Molotov *oblast'*, in the Urals, dated to 1728 and the Red Guard Medical Instruments Factory in Leningrad dated to 1760! Two enterprises—a medical instruments' plant in Gorky and a medical equipment plant in Moscow had been built during the NEP. A factory to produce electrical medical apparatus was established in 1930. Five sanitary equipment plants had been built during the thirties—one in Leningrad, one in Penza *oblast'*, one in the Odessa auto body factory, one in the Kazan' auto body plant, one in Leningrad. Two more medical instruments' plants also were built in the 1930s, one in Moscow *oblast'* and the second in Gorky *oblast'*. Another dental equipment plant also was established.[29]

The reshuffling and evacuation of medical instruments' manufactories paralleled the pharmaceutical sector. In 1941, the Vitebsk eyeglass manufactory was added to the system. The Kazan' Experimental Factory, Tiumen Factory No. 14, and Nizhni-Tagil Factory were newly organized. A repair workshop was shifted into the jurisdiction of the Commissariat of Enlightenment. Of the twenty-three enterprises in the medical instruments' industry in 1941, six were evacuated. A factory from Svoboda, on the Dzerzhinsk Railway in Penza *oblast'*, was moved to the city of Kuznetsk, also in Penza *oblast'*. The Odessa Auto-body Factory was moved to the city of Tomsk, the Sanitary Equipment factory in the city of Moscow was shipped to Tiumen, the Moscow Experimental-Mechanical Factory was moved from Moscow to Sverdlovsk in the Urals, the Kiev Factory of Dental Equipment was moved to the city of Kazan', the Vitebsk Eyeglass Factory was moved to Molotov *oblast'* in the Urals.[30]

Some enterprises in the system found themselves in enemy territory at the end of 1942 and the beginning of 1943, such as the Mariupolskii Machine Building Factory in the city of Mariupol and the Factory of the Fourteenth Anniversary of October in Moscow *oblast.'*[31]

By 1943 there were twenty-five enterprises under the administration of the Medical Instruments' Industry. The industry was, perhaps, getting too big and cumbersome.[32]

Sluzba zdorov'ia, the new publication based on recently accessible materials in the Central Archive of the Ministry of Defense and other government and Communist party archives, notes the failure of factories to meet targets for bandages in the second half of 1941. Only the locations of the bandaging factories were provided—Leningrad, Riazan' *oblast'*, Uzbekistan, etc. and it was not clear that the March 8 Bandaging Factory was included. In any case, output of sterile bandages, for example, met only 48.7 percent of target, non-sterile—66.7 percent, "ordinary" gauze bandages—49 percent, and individual bandaging packets—41.2 percent. Seven hundred fifty tons of hygroscopic cotton and 250 tons of compressed cotton were produced—meeting only 39.5 percent and 25.6 percent of Plan targets, respectively.[33]

Reports from the individual factories in the Medical Equipment and Surgical Instruments' industry give details to these skeletal figures and information about production of other items during the whole of 1941.

The Sacco and Vanzetti factory in Stalingrad fulfilled its plan in 1941. Others did not, due to lack of materials and electricity, inadequate work force, absence of materials, and the transfer to new forms of production. Steam pipes in the Lenin Factory in Gorky and Kazan' "worked with great difficulty." Additional boilers were installed. A generator was installed in the Fourteenth of October Factory and transformers in the Dental Factory in Kazan'. Three evacuated factories did not work at all. In Leningrad factories worked "under special conditions and could not fulfill the plan."[34]

Work discipline plummeted during the first year of the war, partially due to new, less trained workers. It was estimated that 233,323 rubles' worth of instruments were ruined during evacuation. Nevertheless, the industry was penalized for sending out defective goods.[35] Thus, the war took its toll on the Medical Instruments' Glavk budget.

Government authorities, though, did not let the industry off the hook with regard to prompt financial reporting. Accounting had been "fully centralized in 1941, resulting in balances being presented to the Glavk in shorter time," industry reports assured the government. But, "[A]fter the war began and especially after evacuation, the situation severely worsened." Many accountants in the Kazan', Gorky, and Moscow factories were called into the Red Army. Nevertheless, the Red Guard and MSTO factories in Leningrad were reproved for "especially poor" accounting and the Glavk was reproved for cuts in inspection, resulting from the war.[36]

Output of some items did increase in 1942. *Sluzhba zdorov'ia* presents very positive statistics for production of essential medical/surgical instruments during the second half of 1941 and the first half of 1942. This information is displayed in Table 7.1. The two sets of figures appear to refer to base factories and their evacuated branches.

Table. 7.1 Medical, Surgical Production, Second Half of 1941 and First Half of 1942, Central Archive of the Ministry of Defense

Item	Aggregate	Percent of Plan	Aggregate	Percent of Plan
Small operating apparatus	568	189.5	505	84.2
Large operating apparatus	522	104.4	100	100.0
Bandaging apparatus, small	4200	171.5	2495	104.0
Bandaging apparatus, large	1260	132.7	2450	100.0
Autoclaves	1361	185.6	1201	85.5
Needles for Rekord syringes	1290.72	88.8	484.1 thousand	38.0
Various surgical needles	1931.28 thousand	76.0	3557.9 thousand	79.8
Various pincers	188.7 thousand	74.4	383.6 thousand	67.0
Various medical knives	82.37 thousand	65.7	572.2 thousand	62.8
Various scalpels	143.4 thousand	94.5	174.8 thousand	95.7
Sterilizers	12, 358	152.3	9,050	58.2
Various syringes	155.23 thousand	88.0	112.5 thousand	89.3

Source: Quoted in Gladkikh and Loktev, *Sluzhba zdorov'ia*, p.168

Industry reports for calendar years, on the other hand, show increased production for 1941 but decreased as well as increased output of some crucial items in 1942 as the chart below illustrates. Details in the industry reports explain the reasons for the lag if not the reasons for the discrepancies between the charts.

Table 7.2 Medical/Surgical Instruments' Production, 1940-1942, from Reports of the Medical /Surgical Instruments' Industry

Medical/ Surgical Items	1940	1941	1942
Pincers	862,000	1,306,400	1,606,400
Knives	361,000	927,000	Approx. 600,000
Syringes	327,600	514,300	174,000
Scalpels	304,500	541,400	500,000+
Autoclaves	2,836	3,167	2,367
Disinfecting Chambers		344	2,389

Sources: RGAE, f. 8009, op. 2, d. 126, ll. 37-38; f. 8009, op. 2, d. 127, ll. 90, 90 ob., 91, 94, 96, 96 ob..

The industry figures in Table 7.2 indicate that in 1941, despite the outbreak of war, evacuation of factories, and the blockade of Leningrad, output of medical/surgical items in general increased markedly over 1940.[37] But in 1941 the output of disinfecting chambers—the chambers with a little stove to kill lice and prevent typhus—rose minimally,[38] despite the fact that the Smirnov volumes emphasized their role in preserving the health of the Red Army. The quality of some surgical instruments, such as "Rekord" syringes and pincers, was said to have improved in 1941. Reports averred that the "struggle with *brak*" was successful. "Great attention was paid to . . . the optical section . . . especially to endoscopic apparatus."[39]

In 1942, on the contrary, output of some items increased as compared to 1941, but that of others decreased. For example, the number of disinfecting chambers increased almost seven times. Production of "Shimmelbush" boxes doubled and nearly reached the planned output of 50,000; 300,000 more pincers were produced in 1942 than in 1941, and 10,000 more sterilizers were produced. On the other hand, production of knives in 1942 was only two thirds that in 1941 and amounted to only about 58 percent of the plan (which was presumably based on need) and 800 hundred fewer autoclaves were produced in 1942 compared with 1941. Although over 500,000 scalpels were produced in 1942, the amount was approximately 20,000 fewer than in 1941. The discrepancy in the output of syringes cited in Table 7.1 and the output of syringes cited in Table 7.2 is explained by the following information in the industry report. The Lenin Factory was the sole producer of syringes and needles. The factory produced 174,000 syringes in the first half of 1942 but production "of syringes and needles," ground "to a halt" in the second half due to absence of stainless steel. Lack of various other types of steel also accounted for diminished output of other products. Only a little more than one fourth of the amount of eyeglass lenses called for in the plan were produced because of severe delays in shipments of glass. The majority of factories were forced to collect their own firewood and other forms of fuel used locally. There were problems obtaining railway cars for shipment, thus shorting consumers.[40]

The industry continued to report uneven output in 1943. The Sacco and Vanzetti, Red Guard, and No. 4 factories fulfilled their production plans. But many factories suffered "interruptions of raw materials" and "50 percent of machines needed capital repair." "Transportation was one of the worst problems."[41]

Imports and Help from Abroad

The deficits of medical equipment and surgical instruments and also of medicines, anesthetics, disinfectants, and analgesics necessitated outside help. Henry Sigerist averred that "large quantities of foreign drugs along with medical instruments were supplied to Red Army hospitals under lend-lease—and by private agencies."[42] A public thank-you from Sergei Kolesnikov, head of the Soviet Red Cross and Red Crescent Society, tendered in English through the Soviet

Embassy in Washington in 1943, admitted that "[T]he first supply of surgical instruments, hospital clothing, bandaging material and insulin was sent . . . from the United States . . . as early as September 20, 1941 . . . and has been constantly increasing." The aid ostensibly was tendered by the American Red Cross and also by an organization called the "Russian War Relief, headed by one Professor Carter . . . formed in New York in 1941." The name of the latter was significant for it downplayed the Communist origins of the Soviet Union and highlighted pre-Soviet, Imperial Russian traditions. The timing of the aid underscored the fact that the Roosevelt administration sided with the Soviet Union against Germany before the United States entered the war. And the aid to the Soviet Union was indeed sizable. "Up to March, 1943," the Embassy's statement continued, "the American Red Cross had sent to the USSR 90 consignments consisting of 100,000 packages and weighing about 4,000 tons." In addition to pharmaceuticals, detailed shortly, "[P]ortable X-ray apparatus, electric sterilizers and tubes for blood transfusion have been particularly useful. . . ." This medical equipment from abroad explains why military men and their families praised Soviet wartime medical care, for according to the Embassy's statement "W]e have 1,718 evacuation hospitals and 268 base hospitals fully or partially equipped with American material."[43]

Within the Soviet Union, pharmacy journals did not publicize the medical/surgical equipment sent from abroad. However, industry reports acknowledged the aid. Records in the Central Archive of the Ministry of Defense testify to large amounts of items "imported" in 1942—over 68,000 syringes, 801,686 needles, 129,936 pincers, 1,033 scalpels, over 10,387 sterilizers, and other items.[44] Reports of the Chief Pharmaceutical Administration, now in the State Archives of the Russian Federation, noted that in 1943 "the arrival of imports significantly improved supplies of surgical items for specialized hospitals."[45]

Enormous amounts were "imported" in that year: 1,200,000 needles and syringes plus 32,700 "needles Diufo" and 26,000 other types of syringes; 26,000 anatomical pincers, 21,000 surgical pincers, 21,000 Kozhera and Peana pincers, and 122,000 pairs of surgical gloves. The Chief Pharmacy Administration of the RSFSR complained that "the factories of Glavrezinprom USSR unsatisfactorily distributed (*otovarivali*)" important medical/surgical items in 1943. For example, 16,800 oxygen pillows were allocated but only 9,200 obtained. "Imports," thus, made up the difference, as the following table illustrates:[46]

Table 7.3 Materials from Abroad, 1943

Items Needed	Allocated	Obtained	"Imported"
Hot water bottles	191,000	36,000	116,000
Bladders for ice	76,000	50,200	23,000

Source: Reports of the Chief Pharmacy Administration , GARF, f. A482, op. 51, d. 42, ll. 15-17.

Deficits of crucial medicines and other materials needed in 1943 "to supply treatment institutions and to satisfy the needs of the population" also were compensated for with "imports."

The Soviet Red Cross and Red Crescent thank-you to the American public in 1943 noted that "[T]he majority of [the 100,000] packages [from the American Red Cross] contained . . . sulfapyridine, sulfanilamide, lanolin, strophanthin, caffeine, adhesive plaster and bandages. . . .In addition we have received powdered milk, soap and a million sets of clothing and footwear for children . . . woolen underwear was sent to 28 regions in the USSR, including Voronezh, Stalingrad, Kursk, Kalinin, Moscow, Smolensk and Orel. American underclothing has been provided in 213 children's homes and 23 invalids' homes." For consumption of the American public the Embassy added that "We deeply appreciate the friendly help which the American people are affording the peoples of the USSR who have been dealt Hitler's heaviest blow and who have made more sacrifices than anyone else in the struggle of the United Nations against Nazi aggression." And there was a dose of defiant propaganda, affirming that "[T]he Soviet pharmaceutical industry has achieved great successes since the war."[47]

Internal reports acknowledged the largesse of the United States. But they more honestly admitted shortfalls in the pharmaceutical industry's output—all the while referring to the aid as "imports," as the following chart shows: [48]

Table 7.4 Amounts of Materials (in Tons, Except Ampules) from Abroad in 1943, Report of the Chief Pharmacy Administration

Item	Required	Allocated	Obtained	"Imported"
Aspirin	180	34.7	7.4	17.1
Barium, x-rays	200		60.0	0
Bismuth	40		46.0	0
Calcium chloride	120		36.0	0
Novocain	3		0.84	0.384
Caffeine	37		2.51	2.6
Salicylic acid	60		1.75	10.9
Streptosid	150		12.41	16.0
Sul'fidin	60		12.44	3.2
Glucose	180		13.0	26.0
Insulin ampules	600		159.0	26.0

Source: GARF, A482, op. 51, d. 42, l. 14

The Medical Instruments' Industry in 1944

By 1944, stronger downstream performance was visible in the Medical Instruments' industry. It was not as significant as the English-language bulletin "from Moscow" trumpeting that "medical instruments plants" completed "105.5

percent . . . of their ten months' plan for 1944," with the coda that the Leningrad medical instruments' plant had "resumed" production.[49] Still industry reports were bullish, averring that only six of twenty-two factories did not fulfill their production plans and stressing that output of some items had improved markedly—for example, production of "obstetrical" stethoscopes increased 15 times over 1943, "Diursen" pincers increased 370 times; and 65 percent more tooth drills were churned out than the previous year. The quality of some instruments also was said to have improved, specifically surgical and anatomical pincers. Eyeglasses were more modern. A handbook on surgical instruments was published. Ventilation in the Lenin factory was improved and, in general a certain amount of *remont* (renovation) took place in factories. [50]

But industry reports noted negatives as well as positives. "Plans to establish special instruments, apparatus, and equipment were not fulfilled. Of 86 new implements planned, only 57 were produced." "The chief instruments not fulfilled were gynecological." This had little impact on the Red Army but posed problems for the civilian population. Both military and civilians, however, were impacted by other failures in other areas. There was lack of quality control over syringes and needles manufactured in the Lenin Factory. As in the previous year, production of syringe glass was subject to "a great amount of *brak*." Delays in deliveries of green glass held up syringes. In two of the eastern factories, absence of steel resulted in the plan for pincers "remaining unfulfilled." Sterilizers also were held up because of lack of steel. Additionally, "the work of preparing cadres was insufficient." Although 1,100 new workers were given training, and the quality of 1,500 workers was improved, engineer- technical cadres "did not receive needed attention." Further "the average output of workers did not increase." The "treatment network" was only partially supplied, due to insufficiency of railway cars. [51] Obviously, industry problems were not all due to the war.

Nevertheless, higher Soviet officials continued to be as focused on sales and profits as on deliveries of goods to the populace. In 1944, they took pride in the fact that the medical, surgical instruments' industry "realized 147,452 thousand rubles, or 96.2 percent of plan."[52]

The Pharmaceutical Industry in 1944

By the summer of 1944 Red Army troops had retaken the western parts of the Soviet Union and were in East-Central Europe. Soviet reports for foreign consumption were upbeat about the pharmaceutical sector. "Mass production of medicines has been organized in Uzbekistan, Kirghizia, Armenia and Azerbaijan," a dispatch "from Moscow" emphasized late in 1944, adding that pharmaceutical plants were "being restored in Khar'kov . . . Voroshilovgrad and Kiev," that "[P]harmaceutical plants completed 104 percent of their ten month's plan" for 1944 and that "[P]roduction of highly-active preparations has increased greatly." Among the last were methyl-caffeine, phenamine, "'norsuifazol' which is considerably more potent than 'sulfidin,'" "500,000 units of . . . penicillin, "manufactured by the laboratory of the All-Union Institute for Experimental Medicine and two factories of the People's Commissariat for Health," and the development of "a new anti-tuberculosis drug, 'rubrokol' [sic]." The dispatch did admit, however, that "demand for medicines and medical equipment is still unsatisfied."[53]

The English-language reports stressed "gains in the production of biologicals," such as adrenalin, insulin, peptone and pepsin, both in meat and dairy enterprises and in the reconstructed factory in Moscow and a new factory in Semipalatinsk [Kazakhstan]. "Worn out" equipment, corroded enameled cast iron equipment, lack of vacuum pumps and equipment for regenerating alcohol, ether and other dissolvents" were lamented.[54] Nevertheless, the reports remarked that in 1944, "The Moscow Organo-Therapeutic Drugs factory . . . started in 1942," produced five and a half million rubles' worth of pantocrin, "extracted from the antlers of the spotted deer," and "campalon, made from animal livers."[55]

English language bulletins trumpeted attention to vitamins. A USSR level vitamin trust, Soyuzvitaminprom" [sic] already existed but in 1944 the USSR People's Commissariat for Food established a Vitamin Trust on the RSFSR level. This trust, Rosvitaminprom, "organized the production of vitamins in Moscow, Leningrad, Kalinin . . . Vologda . . . Gorky and Cheboksary" that was slated to "produce more than 1,500,000,000 doses of vitamins." They were mainly for the Red Army and hospitals but "a large proportion of them" was "to be sold to the population. Increased production of juices "rich in vitamin C" made from "wild berries" also was on the drawing board and "[P]lantations of currants and gooseberries" were "to be laid down." [56]

Internal pharmaceutical industry reports similarly trumpeted increased output but detailed shortfalls as well. In addition to penicillin, industry reports touted the development of caffeine, made from tea residue at the Dzerzhinskii Factory, Rubrakol and Vitamin B1, but lamented that production of the latter "was not possible because it depended upon imported equipment, which did not arrive." Much renovation had occurred in Moscow factories. New methodologies using substitute materials or outmoded apparatus were continuing. The work environment had become safer for workers.[57]

Indeed, progress in the medical pharmaceutical sector was not as spectacular as on the battlefront. As did the reports of the medical/surgical instruments' industry, pharmaceutical industry reports admitted that output was uneven. Some items were produced in quantities that far superseded output both in 1943 and in 1940. Production of other items fell short of 1943 but was significantly higher than in 1940 as Table 7.5 illustrates.

Table 7.5 Production in 1944 in Terms of Percentage,
Pharmaceutical Industry Reports

Pharmaceutical		Percent of 1940	Percent of 1943
Ascorbic acid, kg.			316.1
Bismuth preparations, tons		216.5	77.0
Chlorethyl	"	513.4	78.4
Methyl-caffeine	"	0	421.7
Narcotic ether	"	187.6	96.6
Novocain	"	160.0	111.6
Streptotsid	"	113.2	159.4
Sul'fidin-sul'fazol	"	35 times	100.9

Sources for chart: RGAE f. 8009, op. 2, d. 39, l. 31

Apparently, the experiments to increase output of Streptotsid had been successful. This was particularly welcome, since production of that item had satisfied less than half of need in 1940.

On the other hand, output of some pharmaceuticals was lower in 1944 than in 1943 and in 1940. Output of others was higher than in 1943, but lower than in 1940, as the following table shows:

Table 7.6 Production in 1944 in Terms of Percentage,
Pharmaceutical Industry Reports

Pharmaceutical	Percent of 1940	Percent of 1943
Akrikhin, tons	50.5	328.9
Glucose, tons	77.2	132.9
Luminal, kilograms	28.9	117.3
Merkuzal 10%, kg.	13.5	0
Bromide preparations, tons	0.7	0
Iodine preparations, tons	48.7	83.7
Phenacetin, tons	0.3	0
Pyramidon, tons	15.5	190.5
Salicylate prepartions, tons	29.5	183.3

Sources for chart: RGAE, f. 8009, op. 2, d. 39, l. 31.

Particularly in dire straits were salicylate preparations, for before the war, in 1940, they had satisfied less than half of need. And, insufficiencies of iodine were serious, since this was a chief disinfectant and antiseptic.

Additionally, in 1944 there still were severe shortages of laboratory vessels, reagents and equipment. Nor were laboratories guaranteed gas and water in 1944. Further, whereas quantity of any caliber was most important in the first two years of the war, pharmacy executives now complained about *quality*. *Reklamatsiia* or rejection of products remained the same as in 1943. In 1943, though, 60 percent of rejections had related to production and 40 percent to packaging. In 1944 the reverse was true—"60 percent of products were rejected because of poor packaging and only 40 percent because of the quality of the products themselves." Packaging flaws were serious, nevertheless. "Particularly bad was the quality of production of the glass factories Klinsk and Solnechnogorsk, about which there were complaints regarding containers for blood . . . [and] flagons for ether and chloroform, because of [poor] quality . . . great interruptions in delivery . . . poor packaging . . . [and] lack of packaging." Production of ampules barely met plan in 1944. The fault of the poor performance of the glass factories in terms of both quality and quantity lay in poor quality apparatus and an "accident" that ruined a stove at the Klinsk glass factory in November 1944.[58]

Obsolete enameled apparatus presented a specific problem. There was an attempt to get enameling apparatus from the Leningrad Food Kombinat—despite the fact that the city had been blockaded—which emphasizes disabilities Moscow factories suffered due to evacuation. However, "the enamel . . . was so defective that it had to be discarded." Lack of enameled apparatus impeded production of the antivenereal Novarsenol. Attempts were made to quickly produce enameled equipment but the main solution was to attempt repair.[59] Some equipment was ordered from abroad.

Electrical energy, too, "was very uneven in 1944 and amounts were insufficient." Further, "the fuel that arrived was of poor quality." Factories organized their own repair workshops. The boilers were old, "requiring serious reconstruction and partial replacement."[60]

Finances

Notwithstanding industry problems, for the Soviet government in 1944, as before, the finances of the pharmaceutical industry as the finances of the medical instruments industry, were very important, perhaps more important than production and distribution of pharmaceuticals. As they had earlier, industry executives explained the core industry's poor financial performance, attributing it to "lack of responsible control" and "over expenditure on raw materials . . . because of "the poor state of equipment."[61] Once again we see that industry problems were not solely due to the war, but also to systemic flaws.

1945

If the pharmaceutical industry's performance had matched that of the defense industry, its report would have been glowing. In 1945 Glavkhimfarmprom employed over 8,000 workers. Sixty-six percent were female. A woman, A. P. Grishakova, was Head of Glavkhimfarmprom USSR; another, Anna Nikolaevna Adova, was Director of the Moscow Pharmacy Institute; and still another, Kh. M. Sheveleva, was head of the Chief Pharmacy Administration in the Ukraine. Four women and fifteen men were directors of core pharmaceutical factories. Most were in their forties and had been in the industry prior to the war. All were party members. Two women and fourteen men served as chief engineers. [62]

English-language bulletins accentuated progress in the pharmaceutical sector. "Restoration of the first section of the very large Minsk pharmaceutical plant, the only one in Belorussia [Belmedtorg], has been completed," an English translation of *Vechernaya* [sic] *Moskva* (Evening Moscow) announced in July 1945. "The plant occupies a three-storey building. Several departments are in operation, and the plant is making tincture of iodine, zinc ointment, bandages and other things."[63] Meanwhile, a penicillin plant had been established at Kislovodsk to prepare the drug for use in hospitals in the Caucasus.[64] According to an English-language press release, production of penicillin was "expected to be three times as high as in 1945, output of phenacetin doubled, and of atabrin [sic], increased by 50 percent. Production of aspirin, sodium salicylate, salol, and sulfa drugs" was "constantly increasing. The manufacture of thiocol and guaiacol, two anti-tuberculosis drugs" was "soon to be resumed in a plant in Leningrad," the new "anti-tuberculosis drug, 'rubrikol'"(as this press release spelled the drug) having been developed "during the war." "Menthol, lead-bismuth preparations and resrocinal are slowly coming back into production," this bulletin concluded.[65]

There were some disquieting notes about actual production, however, even in the publicity for public and foreign consumption. For example, it was admitted that "[O]utput of infusions, drops, ointments, plasters, methyl caffeine, bismuth preparations, and ether is lagging. In spite of notable progress made by the Soviet drug industry, supplies are still well below demand."[66] And quality lagged. According to A. G. Natradze, USSR "Vice Commissar for Public Health Protection" in 1945, it was "planned to curtail production of sulfidin because of complications when large doses are given."[67] For endocrine preparations, "new methods of" clinical tests and "physical, chemical and biological control" had to be implemented. "Careless packing" had to be eliminated. And renewed "experiments in the use of the glands of fish, sea animals and birds" and study of "the new modifications in the method of producing insulin . . . published abroad" had to be undertaken."[68]

The pharmaceutical industry's reports for internal consumption confirmed that output was still very spotty at the end of the war. Production of methyl caffeine, salicylic acid, the sulfa drug Streptotsid, glucose, codeine, and penicillin were said to have increased in 1945 as compared with 1944. But production of other crucial pharmaceuticals fell short. These included aspirin, sulfuric barium, the febrifuge Pyramidon, diuretin, insulin, iodine products, Liuminal, and the antimalarials Plazmotsid and Akrikhin.[69] And, while reports for public and foreign consumption implied that the industry's problems stemmed from the war, internal reports made it clear that the reasons for the industry's underperformance were mainly the government's insistence on maintaining a poorly functioning macroeconomic system and implementing policies inhospitable to the pharmaceutical sector.

Lower output of pharmaceuticals in 1945 was connected with the war in only three factories. In the majority of other factories underproduction had no relationship to the conflict from which a victorious Soviet Union was emerging, though scarred and with millions dead, maimed and sick. Lower output in the Moscow Bandaging Factory resulted from a deliberate decision to cut production of bandages now that the war was over.[70] The Solnechnogorsk and Berezicheskii glass factories, caught up in the thick of the fighting, understandably performed worse in 1945 than in 1944. But Factory No. 35, the branch of the Moscow Endocrine and Vitamin [Preparations] Factory in Novosibirsk, and the Dzerzhinskii Factory in Kazakhstan, both of which also performed worse in 1945 than in 1944, had been far removed from the theater of war.[71] Similarly, output of iodine was lower in 1945 than in 1944, yet iodine factories had not been in the war zone.[72] Meanwhile, Farmakon in Leningrad, which had undergone the "nine-hundred-day siege," nearly quadrupled production in 1945 compared with 1944[73] and surmounted inadequate supplies of coal, as well.[74]

As before the war, the factors hindering production stemmed from a dysfunctional macro economy—irregular deliveries of raw materials and unpredictable energy supplies[75]—and government decisions that undercut the industry. Poor management also contributed. Factory No. 36 produced a mere 28.5 tons of aspirin in 1945 versus the 70 tons called for in the plan because of shortages of vinegar anhydride.[76] Interruptions of sulfate to the Berezicheskii Glass Factory and shortages of fuel and electricity in other glass factories were responsible, in part, for inadequate output of ampules and glass.[77] But whereas factories received too little of some materials they received too much of others.[78]

Due to effective administrators and creative and determined workers, some factories were able to overcome difficulties. The Klinsk Glass Factory, near Moscow, was short of electric power and had to rely on its own generator because it was excluded from the city electricity grid. Nevertheless, workers managed to make glass ampules.[79] Other factories also produced needed items, on their own, using available supplies or residue.[80]

The Dzerzhinskii Factory in Kazakhstan, where many evacuated civilians continued to live, on the other hand, was in a worse state at the end of the war than before it and there did not appear to be light on the immediate horizon. The physical plant was dilapidated.[81] The Kirghiz office of the Medicinal Plants' Trust, Lekrastrest, supplied the factory with poor quality botanicals that were cultivated locally—anabasis, darmin, and ephedra—and poor quality imported opium.[82] The factory lacked adequate electricity because high voltage lines had not been installed. Further, it received inadequate funds for coal.[83]

Brak was as big a problem at the end of the war as during it when many untrained workers first entered the factories. Administrators of the pharmaceutical sector blamed *brak* on "lack of insufficient attention by management and workers, failure to reward lack of *brak* with premiums and failure to punish those guilty of *brak*.[84] Some factories managed to grapple constructively with carelessness and a poor work ethic, however. The management of the Karpov Factory in Moscow, for example, established an on-site technicum to improve workers' skills.[85]

Theft by workers in pharmaceutical plants was a major problem at the end of the war.[86] So was corruption on the part of the management. In 1945 stocktaking revealed sizable differences between supplies of special clothing, instruments and other saleable items listed in the books and actually stocked in warehouses. Indeed, stocktaking in the warehouses was declared to be "chaotic," resulting in losses of some hundreds of rubles to over 10,000 rubles, Seven individuals deemed guilty of unauthorized removal and sale of materials from the Svoboda Factory, who altered the books to cover their tracks, were punished in 1945.[87] Further, careless management in warehouses combined with lack of space for packaging and shortages of packing materials held up distribution of pharmaceuticals that had been produced.[88]

Soviet pharmaceutical factories received confiscated (*trofeinoe*) equipment from pharmaceutical factories in Hungary and other East Central European states making reparations to the Soviet Union in 1945. However, not as much arrived as anticipated—100 railway wagons arrived in place of the 300 to 400 wagons scheduled—and inadequate instructions and lack of qualified workers held up installation and proper servicing of the "imported" apparatus.[89]

The Soviet government appeared to appreciate the commitment and the contributions that pharmaceutical specialists had made to the health and well being of civilians and Red Army troops during the war. In 1945 Narkomzdrav USSR awarded fifteen workers, some individuals, some combined into teams, six prizes for their suggestions about "rationalizing" work in the pharmaceutical factories. Workers in Factory No. 40 won prizes for the best installations four times during 1945. The Semashko Factory in Moscow won three prizes in this category. The Karpov Factory won three prizes, the Akrikhin and Alkaloid factories won two, and the Salicylate Factory and Factories No. 36, No. 37, and No. 38 each received one prize.[90]

Farmatsiia,one of the main journals of the industry, publicized other awards in 1945. Thirty-four men and women, mainly directors of factories, chief engineers, and heads of shops—sprinkled with a few ordinary workers and including Alexander Grigorevich Natradze, Deputy USSR Commissar of Health—received these awards and were wished further success in "the attainment of producing and supplying medicaments" and "raising the qualifications of cadres." Among the grantees were G. S. Budagov, Director of the Red Guard Factory in the Ukraine; A. A. Kagan, Director of the Alkaloid Factory in Moscow; R. I. Kogan, Director of the Moscow Endocrine and Vitamin Preparations Factory; and M. G. Brodsky, Director of Factory No. 37. E. V. Svetsova, head of a shop in the Akrikhin Factory and M. A. Vorob'ev, Chief Engineer of the Salicylate Factory made the cut, but not the directors of these Moscow factories, despite heroic wartime work. Second-tier specialists receiving awards included V. P. Labzin, head of Glavmedfarmprom; E. A. Meerson, Directory of Factory No. 17; G. A. Slutskii, Director of Factory No. 3; I. I. Manchenko, head of the Administration of Khimfarmprom, Ukraine; and S. I. Yemlianinov, Director of the medical instruments' factory Medapparatura in the Ukraine.[91]

Yet several government policies worked against the industry. Fines levied on workers for *brak* had some justification since losses from breakage and spoilage had risen from 781,000 rubles in 1944 to 908,000 rubles in 1945.[92] However, government demands that other costs be pared appeared excessive, considering the fact that enterprises had no control over many variables.[93] The financial policies of Gosbank (the State Bank) were as hard-nosed as those of any bank in a capitalistic country. Because shipments came irregularly, enterprises were forced to stretch their lines of credit with the State Bank to pay for "seasonal and imported materials" dumped on them all at once, above and beyond, moreover, what they had ordered. "Severe financial difficulties arose," the enterprises informed government officials, "with large, one-time shipments of raw materials."[94] Despite the inability of enterprises to control these shipments, in 1945 Gosbank ruthlessly closed their accounts.[95]

Desperate to improve their finances, pharmaceutical enterprises, in turn, took to producing and distributing "highly profitable items, such as sulfonamide preparations, outside the plan," regardless of whether their customers, the pharmacy administrations that supplied pharmacies, had ordered these items or could afford them.[96] In theory such increased production of sulfa drugs should have benefited Soviet citizens, the final consumers. But in actuality, this might not have been the case.

The Soviet government's obsession with profits also led to turning much land over to the production of essential oils which then were to be exported. Some of this production was in the Ukraine, which had been devastated by war. The purpose was to fill government coffers. Foreign perfumers were desperate to get essential oils by the war's end. Major sources in France, Italy and North Africa had been cut off in 1940 by the British blockade and then suffered from lack of labor, neglect and climatic reverses. The Soviet government offered to satisfy the perfumers' needs even if the Soviet pharmaceutical industry and Soviet citizens should be shortchanged in the process.

In January 1945 *The American Perfumer and Essential Oil Review* reported that "production of oils for perfumes, thymol, and a substitute for glycerine [sic] are being successfully produced in a plant in Kirghizia in the Chu River Valley, Soviet Russia."[97] The international perfume and cosmetics community was excited that *Ocimum canum*, from which an essential oil akin to camphor was distilled, had been successfully cultivated in the Ukraine in the 1930s.[98] And now the plant was again being produced. It is true that camphor had medicinal uses. However, it also was used in cosmetics and had non-pharmaceutical applications, synthetic camphor having been one of Schering's major products in the first three decades of the twentieth century.[99] So *Ocimum canum* might have sourced any one of these areas.

It was understandable that the Soviet government wanted to replenish the country's finances. But what are we to make of the notice in *The American Perfumer and Essential Oil Review* in February 1945 that "the [American] War Food Administration has purchased 1,000 lemongrass plants in Florida for the Russian government. It is not known to what use they will be put" since the "climate is too cold for commercial production of lemongrass oil."[100] (Ironically that issue carried a photograph of "individual sachets in tablet form" bearing "the heraldic device of the Russian Court" sold as the "essence of the House of Imperial Russe."[101])

In March 1945 *The American Perfumer and Essential Oil Review* noted that "Russia undercut U.S. prices [of coriander] before the war and now was "not shipping coriander seed . . . but" the "essential oil." "The price has more than quintupled since the war began." Russia was "now asking $28-$30 per pound against a prewar price of $4 per pound."[102] In April 1945 *The American Perfumer and Essential Oil Review* noted that "[A]ll factories of Ukraine's prewar essential oils have been restored to production according to the Soviet press." The first crop of coriander [sic], mint, cumin and lavender had been harvested in "many of the Ukrainian agricultural areas" and "during the spring season the planting of roses and lavender will begin in the Izmail Province bordering on the Danube River." "Before the war" readers were informed, the Ukraine "devoted 27,000 hectares to raising oil-bearing plants" that produced "more than 300 tons of essential oils." [103]

Now, it must be noted that much of this production was being made in the newly acquired western provinces of the Ukraine. Also such production had taken place before the war. Additionally, some essential oils are used in the production of medicaments. However, this was not peacetime. The Soviet Union should have addressed the production of essential items before luxuries. Rose and lavender oil are mainly used for perfumes, Grasse, France having become wealthy from this production.[104] So it would appear that just as grain was exported to Eastern Europe in 1946, despite famine in the Soviet Union,[105] production of essential oils for export to foreign perfumers took precedence over production of medicaments in the Soviet Union at the end of the Great Patriotic War. Of course, it could be hypothesized that export revenues might go to modernizing the factories of the core pharmaceutical industry. But, then again, they might not, judging from the Soviet government's record of overly aggressive exporting in the late 1920s and 1930s that shorted the industry and output of many important pharmaceuticals.[106]

To conclude, in the last two years of the Great Patriotic War, the Soviet pharmaceutical industry had to struggle with the same impediments as in the inter-war period. The Great Patriotic War imposed burdens upon the industry, no doubt about it. But as, if not more burdensome, was the economic system in the Soviet Union and government policies which were at cross-purposes with the pharmaceutical industry. What impact did this situation have on civilians? The pharmaceuticals and medical care that were available for them during the war are related in the following chapters.

Notes

1. Gordon Gordon-Taylor, "The Anglo-American-Canadian Surgical Mission to Russia, July, 1943," *The British Journal of Surgery*, vol. 31, no. 123 (January 1944): 205-207.

2. Wilder Penfield, "The British-American-Canadian Surgical Mission to the U.S.S.R.," *The Canadian Medical Association Journal*, vol. 49, no. 6, Toronto (December, 1943): 455-461; call to friendship: 461.

3. Penfield, ibid.: 459. Bogomolets' anti-reticular [spelled with and without the hyphen in contemporary accounts] cytotoxic serum is described in detail in Chapter 9 of *Medicines for the Soviet Masses*.

4. Penfield, ibid.: 460-461. For Soviet Russia's difficulty in producing iodine from seaweed, and the importance of this product, see Conroy, *The Soviet Pharmaceutical Business During Its First Two Decades* : 83, 85-86, 134, 194-196, 200.

5. E. Rock Carling, "Medical and Surgical Achievement in the U. S. S. R. during the War," *Nature*, vol. 133, no. 3884 (April 8, 1944): 419-424 and Sir Ernest Rock Carling, "Medical Mission to Moscow," *Inter-Allied Conferences of War Medicine: Unclassified Subjects*, Convened by the Royal Society of Medicine (n. d.): 404-405.

6. Bernard Koten, "Soviet Medicine in Wartime," *Hygeia* (American Medical Association), vol. 21 (1943): 268-270, 280.

7. "Soviet War-Time Surgery, *Nature*, vol. 152 (December 25, 1943): 756.

8. Daniel Halpern, "Russian Medicine in Wartime," *Quarterly of the Chicago Medical School*, vol. 3 (1942-1943): 7-8, 36-37.

9. Prof. N. Graschenkov, "Soviet Medicine in War-time," *South African Medical Journal*, vol. 17 (June 26, 1943): 185-187.

10. Professor Lavrentiev, "Experimental Medicine in Russian in the War," *Journal of the American Medical Association* (Chicago), vol. 121 (February 6, 1943): 436-437.

11. Anon., "From Our U. S. Correspondent: War Medicine and Pharmacology in Russia," *The Australian Journal of Pharmacy*, vol. 24 (March 30, 1943): 150.

12. Anon., "From Our U. S. Correspondent" : 150.

13. Loc. Cit. and Lesch, *The First Miracle Drugs*, p. 94- Germany developed Uliron in the mid 1930s. It was approved "for marketing and medical use" by Hitler's government in May 1937.

14. Anon, "From Our U. S. Correspondent: War Medicine and Pharmacology in Russia" : 150.

15. Cited in Anon, "From Our U. S. Correspondent," ibid.: 150.

16. Mariia Sergeevna Kuznetsova, Ufa, Russia, "Vospominaniia," e-mail, communiqué (June 20, 2006).

17. Mark Nulevich, responses to *anketa* and phone conversation, September 2006.

18. Liudmila Ravvina, responses to *anketa*, Denver, CO, September 2006.

19. David Genis, interview, Denver, CO, September 11, 2006.

20. Lesch, *The First Miracle Drugs*, p. 107.

21. Kobrak, *National Cultures*, p. 303.

22. Ernestine Bradley, *The Way Home* (New York: Pantheon Books, 2005): 60, 64-65.

23. Glantz, *Colossus Reborn: The Red Army at War, 1941-1943*: 442.

24. Glantz, *Colossus Reborn*, pp. 695-696.

25. Glantz, *Colossus*, ibid., pp. 623, 695.

26. RGAE, f. 8009, op. 2, d. 38, ll. 71-134. RGAE, f. 8009, op. 2, d. 38, ll, 64, 65, 68, 69-134.

27. There was "significant improvement" in supplies of bismuth, calcium chloride, Streptotsid, Sul'fidin, Urotropin, iodine, Novocain, khloretil, "and other items." On the other hand, there was a "limited range" of bromide salts, Bromural, Phenacetin, Pyramidon, Tiokol, menthol, antipyrine, Biokhinol, chloral hydrate, Protargol, and Kollargol. Some items "did not come at all." GARF, f. A482, op. 51, d. 42, l. 13.

28. RGAE, f. 8009, op. 2, d. 38, ll. 21, 133.

29. RGAE, f .8009, op. 2, d. 126, l. 100.

30. RGAE, f. 8009, op. 2, d. 126, l. 29

31. RGAE, f. 8009, op. 2, d. 126, l. 30

32. RGAE, f. 8009, op. 2, d. 129, l. 131.

33 Gladkikh and Loktev, *Sluzhba zdorov'ia*: 167-168.

34. RGAE, f. 8009, op. 2, d, 126, ll. 32, 33, 36, 37.

35.RGAE, f. 8009, op. 2, d. 126, ll. 59, 97-99.

36. RGAE, f. 8009, op. 2, d. 126, ll. 52-56.

37. RGAE, f. 8009, op. 2, d. 126, ll. 37-38

38. RGAE, f. 8009, op. 2, d. 126, ll. 37-38.

39. RGAE, f. 8009, op. 2, d. 126, ll. 39, 48, 49.

40. RGAE, f. 8009, op. 2, d. 127, ll. 90, 90 ob, 91, 94, 96, 96 ob.

41. RGAE, f. 8009, op. 2, d. 129, ll. 131,138, 139, 142.

42.Sigerist, *Medicine and Health in the Soviet Union*: 105.

43. Sergei Kolesnikov, Chairman of the Executive Committee of the Red Cross and Red Crescent society of the USSR, "American Medical Supplies in Soviet Hospitals," *Information Bulletin, Embassy of USSR* (August 14, 1943): 9, in NAUSA, File RG 489, Box 82, 10,300, BFDC, U. S. Dept. of Commerce. The slogan of the Society for Russian War Relief was "Russia's scorched earth calls to America's green fields." It raised six million dollars.

44. Gladkikh and Loktev, *Sluzhba zdorov'ia*: 168-169.

45.GARF, f. A482, op. 51, d. 42, ll. 9, 16, 17.

46.All information in above paragraph from GARF, f. A 482, op. 51, d. 42, ll. 15, 16, 17.

47. Kolesnikov, "American Medical Supplies in Soviet Hospitals," *Information Bulletin, Embassy of USSR*, NAUSA, ibid.

48.GARF, f. A482, op. 51, d. 42, l. 14.

49. Report no. 1251, from Moscow (Nov. 20, 1944): 2. Submitted by: M. D. Hall, Industrial Projects Unit, January 25, 1945 in NAUSA, RG 489, Box 82, 10,300, BFDC, U. S. Dept. of Commerce.

50. RGAE, f. 8009, op. 2, d. 130, ll. 1, 8, 9, 56-57, 69.

51. RGAE, f. 8009, op. 2, d. 130, ll. 1, 2, 15, 16, 53, 61 ob-65.

52. RGAE, f. 8009, op. 2, d. 130, ll. 65-66 ob..

53. Report No. 1251, from Moscow (Nov. 50, 1944): 2, submitted by: M. D. Hall, Industrial Projects Unit, January 25, 1945, NAUSA, RG 489, Box 82, 10,300. BFDC, U.S. Dept. of Commerce. Phenamin or Fenamin, in the Russian spelling,"was an energy-producing preparation claimed to be a product of research by Russian scientists," according to a news release in the U.S. National archives. This product was "said by the chairman of the Medical Council of the Red Army to give Red Army soldiers the strength to fight from 24 to 36 hours at a stretch if necessary (the British press states)." "Clipped from *Foreign Commerce Weekly*," (July 1, 1944), ibid.

54. A. Katkovski, "Output of Medicinal Produce in the Meat Industry," 3 pages, in "The Meat and Dairy Industry of the USSR," no. 1, 1945, *Economic Information* No. 341 (July 1945), NAUSA, RG 489, Box 82, 10,3000, BFDC, U. S. Dept. of Commerce.

55. "Drugs: Russia," *Chemical Trade Journal and Chemical Engineer* (July 27, 1945): 95, submitted by M. D. Hall, Industrial Projects Units (September 26, 1945), NAUSA, RG 489, Box 82, 10,3000, BFDC, U. S. Dept. of Commerce.

56 "The Extension of the Production of Vitamins," *Izvestiya* [sic] (July 19, 1944), "Joint Press Reading Service," in NAUSA, RG 489, Box 82, 10,300, BFDC, U. S. Dept. of Commerce. Kalinin was the pre-Soviet city of Tver', about two hours north of Moscow by train. Gorky was the pre-Soviet city of Nizhni-Novgorod', east of Moscow on the Volga River. Vologda was east of Leningrad and north of Moscow on the Neva River. Cheboksary was situated between Gorky and Kazan' in the Chuvash ASSR (Autonomous Republic).

57. RGAE, f. 8009, op. 2, d. 39, ll 40, 41, 43-45, 48, 49.

58. RGAE, f. 8009, op. 2, d. 39, ll.32-25, 55, 67, 68, 69, 73, 74.

59. RGAE, f. 8009, op. 2, d. 39, ll. 93-95.

60. RGAE, f. 8009, op. 2, d. 39, ll. 96, 97.

61. RGAE, f. 8009, op. 2, d. 39, ll. 73, 74.

62. RGAE, f. 8009, op. 2, d. 59, ll. 120-123. The woman head of Glavkhimfarmprom USSR is noted in "Nagrazhdenie meditsinskikh rabotnikov," *Farmatsiia*, vol. 8, no. 5 (1945): 48. Some of the information in this section on the pharmaceutical industry in "1945," in this chapter, first appeared in Mary Schaeffer Conroy, "The Soviet Pharmaceutical Industry and Dispensing, 1945-1953," *Europe-Asia Studies*, vol. 56, no. 7 (2004): 965-967.

63. "Economic News Bulletin" (July 27, 1945) from *Vechernaya Moskva* (July 23, 1945), in NAUSA, RG 489, Box 82, 10,300, BFDC, U. S. Dept. of Commerce.

64. "Drugs: Russia," *The Clinical Age* (September 8, 1945): 227, submitted by M. D. Hall, in NAUSA, RG 489, Box 82, 10,3000, BFDC, U. S. Dept. of Commerce.

65. "Drugs and Medicinals," *Vechernaya Moskva* (Nov. 21, 1944), *Sovetskoe Zdravookhranenie*, No. 10-11 (1945) in NAUSA, RG 489, box 82, 10,300, BFDC, U. S. Dept. of Commerce.

66. "Drugs and Medicinals," ibid.

67. Natradze, *Izvestiya* (November 15, 1945), NAUSA, RG 489, Box 82, 10,300, BFDC, U. S. Dept. of Commerce.

68. Katkovski, "Output of medicinal products in the meat industry," ibid.: 2.
69. RGAE, f. 8009, op. 2, d. 59, l. 13.
70. RGAE, f. 8009, op. 2, d. 59, l. 6.
71. RGAE, f. 8009, op. 2, d. 59, ll. 7, 47, 105.
72. RGAE, f. 8009, op. 2, d. 59, l. 18.
73. RGAE, f. 8009, op. 2, d. 59, l. 8.
74. RGAE, f. 8009, op. 2, d. 59, l. 138.
75. RGAE, f. 8009, op. 2, d. 59, l. 14.
76. RGAE, f. 8009, op. 2, d. 59, l. 9.
77. RGAE, f. 8009, op. 2, d. 59, ll. 10, 20.
78. RGAE, f. 8009, op. 2, d. 59, ll. 196-197.
79. RGAE, f. 8009, op. 2, d. 59, l. 20.
80. RGAE, f. 8009, op. 2, d. 59, ll. 23, 42, 44, 45, 48.
81. RGAE, f. 8009, op. 2, d. 59, ll. 38, 92.
82. RGAE, f. 8009, op. 2, d. 59, ll. 8, 70.
83. RGAE, f. 8009, op. 2, d. 59, l. 9, l. 138.
84. RGAE, f. 8009, op. 2, d. 59, l. 58.
85. RGAE, f. 8009, op. 2, d. 59, ll. 85, 90, 98, 120.
86. Christopher Burton, "Medical Welfare during Late Stalinism: A Study of Doctors and the Soviet Health System, 1945-1953," Ph. D. Dissertation (University of Chicago, 2000): 233-234.
87. RGAE, f. 8009, op. 2, d. 59, ll. 195, 196.
88. RGAE, f. 8009, op. 2, d. 59, ll, 224, 225, 260.
89. RGAE, f. 8009, op. 2, d. 59, ll. 83-85, 98-99.
90. RGAE, f. 8009, op. 2, d. 59, ll. 78, 79.
91. "Nagrazhdenie meditsinskikh rabotnikov," loc. cit.
92. RGAE, f. 8009, op. 2, d. 59, l. 218.
93. RGAE, f. 8009, op. 2, d. 59, ll. 42, 49.
94. RGAE, f. 8009, op. 2, d. 59, l. 147.
95. RGAE, f. 8009, op. 2, d. 59, ll. 144, 148.
96. RGAE, f. 8009, op. 2, d. 59, ll. 143, 187.
84. "U.S. S. R. Essential Oils," *The American Perfumer and Essential Oil Review*, vol. 47, no. 1 (January 1945): 44.
85. Dr. Ernest Guenther, Chief Chemist Fritzsche Bros., "Timely Survey of Ocimum Oils," *American Perfumer and Essential Oil Review*, vol. 47, no. 2 (February 1945): 50.
99. Kobrak, *National Cultures*: 74-75, 122-124 and passim.
100. "Lemongrass Plants to Russia," *American Perfumer and Essential Oil Review*, vol. 47, no. 2 (February 1945): 51.
101. "Packaging Portfolio," ibid.: 53.
102. "Russia Ships Coriander," *American Perfumer and Essential Oil Review*, vol. 47, no. 3 (March 1945): 44.
103. "Russian Essential Oils," *American Perfumer and Essential Oil Review*, vol. 47, no. 4 (April 1945): 46.

104. For a quick, photograph-studded survey of Grasse from the late nineteenth century to the Second World War , see Jean Michel Goux, *Grasse au temps des parfumeurs* (CLC et Plein Soleil, 2005) passim

105. Elena Zubkova, *Russia After the War* (Armonk: M. E. Sharpe, 1998): 40-43.

106. Conroy, *The Soviet Pharmaceutical Business*: 201-209, 246-249.

Chapter 8
At the *Apteka* during the Great Patriotic War

During the Great Patriotic War the civilian population of the Soviet Union, like Julius Caesar's Gaul, was divided into three parts. One contingent—in Belorussia and Ukraine—was trapped under enemy occupation. A second contingent was able to flee. But for many the trip on foot or in crowded, slow-moving trains was an agonizing experience. Eventually, the refugees reached their destinations in the deep rear (*tyl*)—often the Urals, the Central Asian republics, or Kazakhstan. While they were safe from the fighting, life frequently was difficult because the evacuees had limited income and, thus, could acquire few amenities. A third contingent of the Soviet population lived in the hinterlands or, although in Moscow, was safe from the war. The medical/pharmaceutical experiences of this last group provide a continuum with pre-war medicine and pharmacy. The second group was exposed to new diseases and many experienced hardships. Of course the lives of the first group were most precarious.

Civilians under Enemy Occupation

Belorussia—Belarus, as it is now called—was occupied by the Germans for some two and a half years. With the opening of the archives, more descriptions of life under the occupation have appeared and been published in English. For example, Uwe Gartenschläger's account of the citizens of Minsk and Hans-Heinrich Nolte's account of the Jewish Shtetl of Slonim paint a somber picture of those times. People dreaded working under the occupier and, in any case, "local manufacture of consumer goods all but ceased because of the devastation caused by the battle of Minsk and because the invaders had little interest in the local economy beyond what it could contribute to their military needs." Food was distributed at the workplace and through a ration system. People grew vegetables wherever they could find a plot of ground, procured necessities at the black markets and bartered. "Housing, health care and cultural needs . . . remained areas of tremendous difficulty [for the natives]." The Germans' mainly treated the natives disparagingly although some Germans sifted "through the Minsk archives . . . conducted social work with [local] youths," dabbled in archeology and wrote and directed plays. But "[P]rivate property was not respected."[1] As for the Jews, Belorussia had been part of the Pale of Settlement, where most Jews lived in Imperial Russia. The Shtetl of Slonim became part of Poland between 1921 and 1939, when it returned to Russia after the Red Army occupied Poland in September. Nolte notes that anti-Semitism was rife in Poland but stresses that the Soviet Union offered Jews social mobility. The "Communist Party did not bar Jews from membership, but on the contrary . . . Jews were overrepresented in the party" and in local government positions. Jews comprised only 8.2 percent of the population of Soviet Belorussia but occupied almost 50 percent of the republic's administrative posts. Some Jews in Belorussia joined the Partisans. Most Jews, however, were exterminated by the Nazis.[2]

Accounts about medical care in Belarus, in English, are rare. Tat'iana Petrishche, a historian and lecturer at the Medical Institute of Vitebsk has published numerous articles about medical and pharmaceutical care in Belarus during the Soviet period in the Russian language. Among her many articles is one which examines collaboration of medical workers in the Belorussian SSR with the enemy during the Great Patriotic War. In Soviet times it was asserted that the majority of medical personnel who remained in Belorussia during the war (139 doctors out of 508, 90 working in medical institutions) heroically refused to collaborate with the German occupiers. In President Lukashenko's Belarus this is still the contention. Tat'iana's article discusses the meaning of the term "collaboration," describes the medical system in Belorussia under the Germans, and analyzes the motives of health professionals who did "cooperate." She notes that local physicians and other health personnel were forced to work, at least overtly, for the occupiers, because they did not have enough physicians and health professionals in their own entourage.[3] Ironically, the same scenario had occurred when the Bolsheviks solidified their position in Belorussia in 1920. They attempted to outlaw private pharmacy and medical care. Regulations issued during the 1920s forced pharmacists and medical specialists in Belorussia, most of who had been in the private sector in Imperial Russia, to work for the government—in this case the Soviet government—and to tender medical/pharmaceutical assistance to the citizenry.[4]

During their occupation of Belorussia in the first three years of the Great Patriotic War, the Germans organized a health department (*otdel zdravookhraneniia*), a department of education, a railway and veterinary department, and a finance department. They allowed a modicum of health care because they feared epidemics. They paid the local physicians a low salary. As one would expect, the motives of physicians who cooperated varied. Some hoped to better the lives of their patients as well as to survive themselves and improve their own lot. Some not only treated patients but attempted to channel medical instruments and medicines to the Partisans waging guerrilla warfare against the Germans. Others, however, collaborated with the Germans because they hated Soviet power and even cooperated with the Nazis' grisly medical experiments.[5]

Information about the availability of pharmaceuticals in occupied Belorussia, in English, is virtually non-existent. Reminiscences of war survivors now living in Belarus give texture to the story of the German occupation and provide information on medical, pharmaceutical issues in particular. Tat'tiana Petrishche's mother and maternal grandparents, her father and paternal grandparents, her husband's maternal great-grandmother and great-grandfather, and her neighbor in the city of Vitebsk, all lived in the Belorussian SSR during the occupation. Tat'iana's relatives were Orthodox Christians and so, perhaps, was the neighbor woman. These respondents to our *anketa* wish to remain anonymous, perhaps because of the political situation now obtaining in Belarus.

Born in 1936, Tat'iana's mother lived "in the country in the territory of Shumilinskii *raion*, Vitebsk *oblast'*." She recalled that there were "practically no medicines before the war" as well as "during the war" and "[I]f during the war someone fell ill, then a miracle was hoped for. If such occurred the person recovered, if not, then not." During the war, new diseases flared up. "Many fell ill with typhus," although fortunately no one in her family did. There was soap, although Tat'iana's mother did not remember the quality or provenance of it. "Sometimes (very rarely) the Germans gave out soap. But this was the exception, not the rule." Indeed, one German named Hans, gave Tat'iana's maternal grandmother bread.[6] For these kindnesses, the lack of basic medicines before as well as during the war, and the harshness of the Soviet government, Tat'iana's mother and grandmother might well have been amongst those Soviet citizens who welcomed the Germans. For because of the swiftness of the German onslaught and because Tat'iana's grandfather lived in the countryside, he was not able to get to his Red Army post. Thus, he stayed with his wife in occupied Belarus. There were others in the same position. But, although Stalin was ultimately at fault for not adequately securing the Soviet border, because he refused to heed warnings about an impending German invasion, little people were made scapegoats. When the Red Army liberated Belorussia in 1944, Tat'iana maternal grandfather was punished by being put in a *shtrafbat* (punishment battalion). These troops were the first to storm the enemy's position and he was killed in February 1945 at Konigsberg.[7]

The family of Tat'iana's father also was trapped in occupied Belorussia but, although her paternal grandfather refused to join a collective farm and lived on his own farmstead during the war, the family supported the Partisans against the Germans. Lepel'skii *raion*, Vitebsk *oblast'*, where their farm was located, was a forested region where the partisans operated. Tat'iana's paternal grandmother baked bread for them. In the countryside in the Belorussian SSR of the 1930s, Tat'iana notes, pharmacies were located only in *raion* centers (analogous to a township seat in the United States) or in larger villages. Sometimes doctors and fel'dshers had medicines but they were difficult to reach and the arsenal of remedies was limited. For example, after the war a fel'dsher worked in the house of a former Polish nobleman, but it was a mile and a half from her father's village. Further, when a new fel'dsher came in 1957, more than a decade after the war, his only medicine was iodine. He applied it to every sickness. Thus before and during the war the family made their own medicines and their own soap.[8] Both procedures are described in the following chapter.

Tat'iana's neighbor was born in 1922 and so was an adult during the Great Patriotic War. Although she now lives in Vitebsk, before the war she lived in a village. Whereas an itinerant trader sold soap and other sundries in the 1920s and 1930s, during the war her father made soap which also will be described in the following chapter. Prior to the war the neighbor recalled, as noted in a previous chapter, "we had no medicines." During the war her access to medicines actually improved a little. She "worked as a '*sanitarka*' (nurse/cleaning woman) in a 'barrack-isolator' (isolation barrack) for typhus patients. She gave shots." These contained a "cardiac substance, of what kind she did not say," Tat'iana Petrishche notes parenthetically. The neighbor-woman paramedic also "cupped [with heated suction cups]." Still "there was practically no other medicine. If a typhus patient went through a crisis," the neighbor stated fatalistically, "it meant that he recovered."[9]

The great-grandmother of Tat'iana Petrishche's husband lived in the city of Vitebsk during the war. She averred that there was no medicine to be had during the occupation, thus corroborating Gatenschlager's chapter. However, in contrast to frequent portrayals of the Germans occupiers in Belorussia as bestial, she remembered that "[S]ometimes when someone had a serious illness" people "turned to the Germans" for medicine. "There were various kinds of Germans. Some of them gave medicines." Such was the case with the great-grandfather of Tat'iana's "husband, who suffered from tuberculosis of the lungs during the war."[10]

The Ukraine was occupied for approximately the same length of time as Belarus. Evgeniia Gorlova lived in Simferopol', in the Crimea, during the war. Her life and that of her mother, grandmother and female relatives was as dramatic as an adventure novel. Evgeniia's grandfather was a nobleman and Tsarist Army officer who became a Red Army officer. He was executed in Stalin's military purge of 1937. Evgeniia's mother was a trained operatic singer who could have been evacuated in the summer of 1941 with the rest of her theater collective—but without her daughter. So she stayed in Simferopol.' The family lived in one half of a large house with the female relative and her three-year old daughter, who turned four during the war. Evgeniia and her family were Orthodox Russian Christians—"although" they "did not practice"; the father of the little girl was Jewish. In 1941 and 1942 the German SS operatives occupied the other half of the house. In the fall and winter evenings of 1941/1942 they came to Evgeniia's side of the house and played the piano while her mother sang. On warm evenings the Germans sat in the garden, smoking, giving the little half-Jewess chocolate while she danced around—like the sprite in Mikhail Lermontov's story "Taman"—telling the occupiers how her father was fighting the Fascists. The Germans did nothing to harm the girl and her mother. They subsequently were saved from an extermination camp because their papers conveniently vanished. Needless to say, when the Germans were expelled, Evgeniia's mother's career was frozen because she had collaborated with the enemy. Although she won voice competitions to study in Moscow she was not allowed to go to the capital.[11] However, her fate might have been worse.

Insofar as medicines were concerned, for Evgeniia and her family they were nearly impossible to get, "except in military hospitals." Aspirin was available. However, there was no soap and as late as 1945, her father died in the hospital of a blood infection, because "there was no medicine to stop the process." People "treated themselves with *narodnaia meditsina* (popular medicine)." [12]

Evacuees

A second group of Soviet civilians consisted of those who evacuated or were evacuated during the Great Patriotic war. The mother-in-law of Tat'iana Petrishche and her mother were lucky enough to be properly dispatched from Belorussia due to the fact that the father of the family was a Captain in the Red Army. Mother and daughter lived in the Tatar Autonomous Republic during the war. Because they were in an officer's family they received packets containing liquid soap. Many personal packets like these had been ruined or disappeared from pharmaceutical factories, as related in Chapter 6. Thus the packets in question or many of the packets may have been available through lend lease. In any case, in addition to soap, other medicines were available. When Tat'iana's mother-in-law, who was about ten or eleven years old, came down with malaria, she was treated with quinine and Akrikhin.[13] Tat'iana's future mother-in law and her mother received these perquisites because they were affiliated with a Red Army officer. Most other evacuees did not have such a smooth transition.

Peter Gatrell's *A Whole Empire Walking* described the plight of those fleeing or deported from the western provinces of Imperial Russia during the First World War. But there were only from 3 to 7 and a half million refugees during that war since the Russian heartland was not invaded by Germans or Austro-Hungarians and the Ukraine was only over-run after the Peace of Brest-Litovsk, March 1918, established cessation of hostilities between Germany, on the one hand, and Soviet Russia and Independent Ukraine, on the other.[14] The epithet "A Whole Empire Walking"—or "On the Move"—more accurately applies to the Great Patriotic War. While some civilians were trapped near the front lines or stayed put to protect their apartments and possessions, like Samson Geltser's father who holed up in Moscow during the war to guard their communal apartment and possessions,[15] many Jews, Belorussians, Russians, and Ukrainians fled in panic from the German Blitzkrieg in the summer and fall of 1941. Some did so partly on foot. Others were packed into railway wagons heretofore used for transporting animals or other commodities. In the late summer and fall of 1941 some of the evacuees arrived at destinations in the hinterlands, far different from their places of origin

How did these people fare? Crowded quarters along evacuation routes, with inadequate toilet and bath facilities, allowed infectious diseases to flourish. The evacuees often went without adequate food and water for weeks or more, thus weakening them and making them more susceptible to disease. Some lived in inhospitable destinations, encountering unfamiliar diseases and medical conditions. With what sorts of medical problems and diseases did they grapple? What sorts of medical help were available to them en route and at their destinations?

Although Soviet accounts emphasize the lack of epidemics during the first year of the war, some civilians came down with serious diseases immediately, in the summer, fall and winter of 1941 and 1942. Others got sick and developed medical problems during the next two years of the war as they waited out their enforced exile before returning home in 1944 and 1945. Surprisingly, according to the recollections of the survivors, few evacuees died. However, they did suffer—some from lack of food and others from lack of pharmaceuticals, including medicines, vitamins, disinfectants, analgesics, anesthesia, and febrifuges. All reported shortages of soap and washing materials. In some cases these deficits were due to insufficient production before the war and insufficient stockpiles of pharmaceuticals for civilians on the eve of the war as well as insufficient output during it. Theft of pharmaceuticals and their sale on the black market sometimes rendered medicines that were available expensive and, thus out of the reach of ordinary civilians eking out an existence with makeshift, temporary jobs and meager pay. Inadequate pharmacy networks in and poor distribution to rural areas also made it difficult to obtain medicines and other medical items. The stories of the evacuees' travel to and life in their new places of residence present a mosaic of medical and personal situations.

Evacuees from blockaded Leningrad were brought by train via Yaroslavl' to Vologda in March 1942. Upon their arrival, however, they endured a lack of soap and basic pharmaceuticals. Some of the evacuees arrived sick. Those who were healthy were in danger of succumbing to typhoid, typhus, dysentery, and the like for an eyewitness report related that "There was a great deal of dirt and infestation by lice . . . there was no toilet block . . . no washing facilities and nowhere to wash." Changes of bed linen were insufficient. "There were no disinfection chambers. There was no regular supply of medicines and medical instruments, and no operating theater." There also were no ambulances. Patients were brought to various hospitals by bus. Fortunately, medical equipment and pharmaceuticals became more plentiful in the spring of 1942.[16] Many evacuees had a much harder time of it.

Peter Abramovich Geyman lived in the small town of Pervomaisk, near Odessa, before the war. He was ten years old in 1941. When the Germans bombed his village he, his family and "a thousand" others began walking eastward. It took six weeks for the group to make their way to Donetsk on foot. They camped at the railway station, sleeping on the floor until officials in the "Evacuation Commission" instructed them to board railway wagons for Oktiabrskaia Station in Kazakhstan. Although the refugees were able to buy food and there was a bath house at the railway station, lack of medicines, soap and disinfectants was dire. Peter vividly remembers the lice and dirt. He and his family reached the village of Martyk in Kazakhstan, their designated destination, at the end of August 1941. Here Peter was stricken with typhoid. There was a small hospital in the village. He "lay in the hospital a whole month." He does not know how he was treated, however, since "there were no medicines." He, like so many others who survived, must have had a strong constitution because he "succeeded in returning to the living."

Peter's problem was not lack of a hospital or lack of medical personnel but rather lack of medicine. He and his family did not use medicines. Partly this was because they were expensive. His mother washed other people's clothes and linen to obtain money. In 1943 Peter's father came from the Leningrad front to Kazakhstan. He worked as a bookkeeper and the family's fortunes improved. But, although White Streptotsid was sold at the market in 1943-1944, the price was very high. And some medicines were not available at any price. In 1944 Peter was stricken with malaria and "there was no quinine.[17]

Medicines may have been expensive because they were stolen from the factory or regular supply channels and sold on the black market, as Doctor David Genis noted was the case in Kazakhstan at the end of the war. He recalled that, in the city of Kzyl-Orda, in the southern part of Kazakhstan where his family lived (having evacuated from Khar'kov in September 1941), he, a lad of ten to fifteen years of age, first saw Red Streptotsid at the end of the war. It was very toxic. Thus White Streptotsid was used instead. But, it was possible "to buy" White Streptotsid "only at the bazaar from speculators." The same was true of Sul'fidin. This medicine also "appeared" in Kzyl-Orda "at the end of the war . . . it was not in pharmacies, it was sold in the bazaar by speculators, a once-only dose cost from 10-50 rubles. For comparison, a loaf of bread cost at the bazaar 100 rubles, the *zarplata* (pay) of a doctor was 500 rubles." Dr. Genis did not remember aspirin. He did remember that penicillin "appeared at the end of the war and cost a great deal at the bazaar." As for medical, surgical items, "[S]yringes were severely deficit . . . during the war it was very difficult to buy gauze, roller-bandages or cotton." But the reason for these shortages was that "[A]all these [items] went to the army and to military hospitals."[18]

Other evacuees and war survivors were given medicines for some diseases while they were given none for other diseases. In some cases, this was because, world-wide, pharmacologists had not devised remedies for the diseases, nor were vaccines effective against them. In other cases, however, remedies existed, but they were not available in the Soviet Union. Some Soviet citizens easily surmounted these problems. They were fortunate enough not to require medicines or medical help, experiencing only mild colds or medical problems from which they recovered on their own. Others, though, died from lack of treatment.

Raisa Kuskina's family lived in Belorussia before the war. Her father was killed while defending Mogilev at the outset of the war. Fleeing the German onslaught, she, her mother and her two sisters made their way to Tambov where they lived in the railway station four months. They then went by train to Voronezh and subsequently to western Kazakhstan. Raisa and her family lived in the village of Bogatsk, with about twenty other families. They worked on a *kolkhoz*, Raisa herself holding a cashier's position. Some aspects of their existence were fine. Raisa noted proudly that they lived "on the economy." They did not have to pay for lodging and food. Their home was good; indeed they had a bathhouse. They also had a kitchen garden, which afforded them an adequate diet. However, medical/pharmaceutical care was minimal. In the kolkhoz village "there was no doctor. There was a fel'dsher with a middle-school education. There was no *apteka*." Nevertheless, when Raisa came down with malaria she received "tablets of quinine" and for chesotka—the itch or impetigo—she was treated with ikhtiol salve.[19] This probably was Vishnevskii salve. Dr. David Genis explained that the salve, made from fish oil, is a "natural antibiotic."[20] On the other hand, when her mother was stricken with severe, prolonged diarrhea, there was no adequate remedy and the family had to turn to popular medicine (*narodnaia meditsina.*) The treatment will be described in the following chapter.[21]

Samson Geltser was fourteen years old when the war began. Life was not easy, even before the war, to some extent. He lived in Moscow, in a communal apartment. There were six rooms for six families, with one toilet and one bath with water heated by a stove. His family—mother, father, and nineteen-year-old sister—was loving and intellectual. His father was a bookkeeper, his elder sister studied at the Institute of Foreign Languages, he himself was a student and, after the war, his parents sent him to a technology institute where he became a specialist on repairing turbines. But his family was Jewish and suffered from anti-Semitism. As a result they had ill-paying jobs. Additionally, his father and mother were extremely anti-Soviet. They repudiated "Soviet propaganda" but did not talk to their son about their feelings until he was an adult, fearing repression. Samson's father stayed in Moscow during the war, as noted in a previous chapter. Samson, however, was evacuated to Riazan' with his school mates and teachers in July, when Moscow was subject to some bombardment. In October his mother and sister were evacuated to Kazakhstan. For the next two years his mother lived in a small village in Taldy-Kurgan; his sister studied in Alma-Ata where her Institute of Foreign Languages was relocated.

Influenced by the government's propaganda, Samson and his schoolmates believed the war would be over in a few weeks or a month at the most and they would be back in Moscow September 1 for the start of the new school year. Instead they endured a saga of hardships for the next two years. Their fifteen-, sixteen-day trip to the Urals was a nightmare. They were packed sixty to a railway wagon meant to hold twelve horses or thirty-six humans. The students were given straw mattresses for the floor or benches, girls sleeping on one side of the stove with the female teachers, boys on the other. Lack of water was a torment. The train "stood still more than it moved" but the teachers were afraid to let the students out at the stations to look for wells and water for fear they would be lost. Without water the students lost their appetite for the meager bread and sausage rations they received. A second scourge was lice. "For two months," Samson related, "the wagon had carried evacuated people from various places, then occupied by the Germans, but disinfecting, if it was done, was very bad." (One can only speculate on what a difference DDT would have made.) Oddly enough the students were given Akrikhin, the newly developed therapeutic, made by the factory of the same name near Moscow, to prevent malaria. The tablets were very bitter, he recalled. However, no one came down with malaria. Either the Akrikhin tablets were effective or there was no malaria in the area.

By the time the students reached Molotov (now Perm) one student had died and one was near death. But the rest revived after a visit to a cafeteria (*stolovaia*) and a good bath, their clothes being heated in a disinfecting chamber— for "children easily adapt."

The children continued their trip up the Kama River to the village of Maikor, far to the north. A collective farm was situated nearby. Here they bunked, fifteen to twenty to a room, in a two story wooden house that had once belonged to a rich pre-revolutionary merchant.

Samson lived in Maikor for two years from October 1941 to October 1943. During this time the main problem was lack of food. He recalled that the students never satisfied their hunger. And there were no vitamins to supplement the inadequate diet—another failing of the Soviet pharmaceutical industry. As a result Samson and the other students developed ulcerous sores on their faces, hands, and feet —he believes they had beri-beri. In the spring they were given boiled soup from nettles and the sores disappeared.

The postal service worked—"though irregularly and slowly." Samson begged his mother to let him leave and come to her in Kazakhstan. However, she disclosed that her life was bad and she had no money. At least he had food and a roof over his head.

He and other upper-class students were sent to work on a collective farm, which was eight kilometers away. They threshed grain and put it into silos and sacks to be sent to the government. The *kolkhozniki* (collective farmers) themselves lived abysmally—"like serfs." They worked as little as possible on the collective farm. "They received practically nothing for their work. The government took everything." Samson and his fellow students benefited, however. They got more bread (a pound a day in the autumn) than the unfortunates remaining in the boarding school and, in addition, they got milk (half a liter a day) and potatoes.

The only fatality was exogenous. The mother of one of the students came to the boarding school and died, probably from hunger. Samson helped bury her. Yet Samson and his fellow students hardly got sick. Hygiene was basic—the students went to the bathhouse every two weeks, where they washed with a piece of soap. The lice disappeared. This explains the lack of typhus. But as for why no other diseases occurred, it was subsequently theorized that the small food portions lowered the students' metabolism and made them resistant to disease. However, Samson's teeth hurt and he attributed this to poor diet. There was a polyclinic in the town and a dentist, which he visited for the dental problem. He received no anesthesia or analgesic when his teeth were removed, though. Further, he developed a hernia from carrying heavy sacks of grain. In 1943 he returned to Moscow. Knowing that products were scarce there, he carried crusts of bread and four liters of cranberries in a birch-bark sack. He wore bast shoes (*lapti*). His mother subsequently gave the latter to a neighbor in Moscow for theatrical performances. His sister and mother returned in 1944, reuniting the family.[22]

Other evacuees recounted that sulfa drugs, aspirin and some sort of soap were available. However, this was mostly the case for those evacuated to cities where there was a medical/pharmaceutical infrastructure in place. And there still were shortages of medicines and above of all shortages of soap, which is a major preventative of infectious diseases, including the common cold.

In Kzyl-Orda, in southern Kazakhstan, where Dr. David Genis and his family lived during the war, there was a "city hospital" with "a special children's polyclinic (*konsultatsiia)*" and "physicians came to" one's "home." "There was a First-Aid Station. All forms of medical care were free" (*besplatnye*). In the city were two large pharmacies." Nevertheless, his mother became ill with amoebic dysentery. His "father accidentally found . . . the medicine for this—*yatren*—in small city nearby. The medicine was not very effective" and his mother "was sick a long time," finally dying of complications to her liver some fifteen years later. The younger brother of Dr. Genis died shortly after the war, in 1948, at the age of twelve, from malaria. "He was not treated," Dr. Genis . . . said simply, indicating there was neither quinine nor Akrikhin or any other synthetic antimalarial available.[23]

Soap also was "greatly deficit" in Kzyl-Orda. "Linen was washed with *khozaistvennoe* soap. Dr. Genis recounted that "[t]his was a large black or dark-brown piece of soap, prepared in the local soap factory from refuse of the slaughterhouse; it contained a lot of alkali. This soap also could be purchased only at the bazaar and it was very expensive." As for "[T]oilet soap for hands and face," Dr. Genis remarked, "during the time of the war I . . . never saw any. We usually washed our hands simply with water."[24] The Genis family also made their own soap, as others did, by methods described in the following chapter.

Polina Savranskaya, who lived in the city of Dushambe, remembered the sulfa drugs, Streptotsid and Sul'fidin. But there was a severe deficit of aspirin.

Further, "there was a great problem with soap." During the war she "studied in a medical school and medical help became a little easier." [25]

Liudmila Ravvina lived in the city of Fergana, in Uzbekistan or the Uzbek SSR, during the war. Some medicine was available, probably because of her mother's connection to a nearby military hospital, but her family also relied on folk medicines which will be described in the following chapter. She remembered that "medicine was not sufficient." Nevertheless, during the war she became "ill with malaria and was given quinine." She also was "given aspirin for Rheumatic [fever]. Her brother came down with scarlatina and measles. She recalls that he was given some sort of medicine. [Since there was no medicine for measles, this might have been the scarlatina antitoxin.] Her "mother worked in a military hospital and, as a child" she "helped her carry medicine to the wounded." Among the medicines were "streptotsid and aspirin." Liudmila and her mother got soap (for bathing) with [ration] cards but they also resorted to home-made soap, described in the following chapter.[26] Sometimes, according to Anna Konetspolskaya, who spent her evacuation in Turkmenia in the city of Chardpsoa, Sul'fidin and aspirin were available. Her problems with asthma continued. Of course, for this there was no remedy available in the Soviet Union or in the United States. She and her family were supplied with *khozaiastvennoe mylo* (economy soap), receiving one piece per month by ration card. But the family also heavily relied on popular remedies, as described in the following chapter.[27] A mixed regimen was likewise the case for Mariiam Samoilovna Tartakovskaya in Tashkent, the capital of Uzbekistan, during the war. There was "green soap" in the *apteka.* There was aspirin. There was quinine for malaria. She recalls the availability of the heart preparation, Strofantan. Although derived from a botanical, this product was produced by pharmaceutical factories. Other medications were home made from botanicals familiar to her grandmother and will be discussed in the next chapter. [28] Maina Tsirkina had "difficulties with medicine during the war." She does not remember whether there were sulfa drugs and aspirin. As for soap, she used *khozaiastvennoe mylo* obtained with [ration] coupons. [29]

Yelena Kuznetskaya was nine years old, living in Zhiromir, in the Ukraine when the war began. Her father was called to the front, where he perished. She and her mother were evacuated "first to the North Caucasus, and when the German army got closer, evacuated [again] to Azerbaijan. They lived in the city of Sal'iany, near Baku. She became ill with scurvy. She was given some kind of medicine, but what, she does not know. In Azerbaijan" Yelena, like so many other evacuees, became ill with malaria. Hers was pernicious, because she was "seriously ill with malaria for two years . . . for two years she could not attend school. They gave her quinine, for free. But," Dr. David Genis interjects, for Yelena is now his wife and he is a specialist on malaria, "judging from the length of the disease, the quinine only weakly helped her." Yelena does not remember there being "other medicine."[30]

Fortunate were the civilians evacuated to the environs of Kuibyshev (in former Samara province), on the Volga, which was designated the "Second Capital" from 1941 to 1943, in case Moscow should fall. One such individual was Evgeniia Shteiman. Every member of her family was a musician or connected in some way with the Bol'shoi Theater. She recalled that, because her father worked at the Bol'shoi Theater in Moscow and Stalin highly regarded the theater, her family had all the medicines and soap they needed.[31] Yefim Kheyster was evacuated from a city in Belorussia to a village in Voronezh *oblast'* in July 1941. In November 1941 he was evacuated again to the village of Zagoskino in Kuibyshev *oblast'*. He lived there until July 1945. He seemingly had few medical problems during the war, noting that "during the war people were sick less than in peace time" and asserted that "the sick were guaranteed medicines."[32] Lidiia Rakhshmut was evacuated to the village of Isal'e, also in Kuibyshev *oblast'*. A loyal Soviet citizen, even though now in emigration, she notes that there were difficulties in obtaining medicines because "first in line for supplies were hospitals." But she remembers both White and Red Streptotsid being available, as well as Sul'fidin and aspirin. Moreover, she stoutly maintains that "all these could be replaced during the war with herbs, compresses . . . and so forth." While many kinds of soap were available before the war in her home city of Kiev, "during the war there was a major deficit of soap." However, there was "a large hospital and very competent doctors." But she does "not remember going there." "If the children got sick [Lidiia already was a mother] they were treated at home." The remedies are detailed in the following chapter.[33]

Nadezhda Elemelakh was three years old at the outset of the war. She, her mother, grandmother and siblings were fortunate to be in the last "echelon" (trainload) leaving Gomel, Belorussia. Her grandmother had a stroke by the time the train reached Kuibyshev. A Red Army commander insisted that she be taken from the station to a hospital but she died nonetheless. Life was hard for Nadezhda on the *kolkhoz* "Pobeda" (Victory), in Kuibyshev *oblast'*, where she lived with her mother and siblings during the war. There was not enough food. There was very little soap and no pharmacy or trained medical personnel. The only medicines were "popular . . . substances" like "herbs." A *znakhar'* treated Nadezhda for warts. She does not recall what this self-trained medical practitioner used. There also was little money. However, her resourceful mother made *valenki* (felt boots) and sewed clothes in order to "feed the children." Further, her administrative skills were recognized, resulting in some amount of upward mobility. Having "managed a *detskii sad* (kindergarten)" in Gomel, Nadezhda's mother was made an administrator on the collective farm.[34]

Soviet Civilians Out of Harm's Way

The third contingent of Soviet civilians stayed put or even went to Moscow. Tamara Nikolaevna Khazieva was one of those who remained in her natal town. Born in 1928, she was about thirteen years old when the war began. She was not evacuated but rather lived in her native city of Ufa, attending school during the first two years of the war and then working in a sewing factory there from 1943 to 1945. Ufa was about the size of Denver, Colorado, in the 1940s, and its ambience was similar. It was in the hinterlands but there was a Bacteriological Institute that produced vaccines and eight to ten pharmacies.[35] Nevertheless, Tamara and her family mainly used traditional, popular Russian medicines, as will be described in the following chapter. Still, they bought some of the ingredients for them from the pharmacy. They also purchased other products from pharmacies that were completely factory-made. One was Vishnevskii salve, used for boils. Other products purchased from the pharmacy were kerosene, turpentine oil for coughs, cupping glasses [which those living in the former Soviet Union and émigrés from the Soviet Union still use], and mustard. During the war, Tamara Nikolaevna's mother worked in a disinfecting station (*dezotstantsiia*). Tamara helped her mother disinfect houses against typhus, typhoid, and scarlatina. They used chlorine, which of course was a product of the chemical-pharmaceutical industry. Tamara emphasized, however, that the chlorine was not available to consumers but only to the disinfecting station. There were no epidemics but the disinfecting work was hard because people resisted the "disinfectors." [36]

Mariia Sergeevna Kuznetsova studied in a boarding school in Siberia during the first two years of the war. On the weekends she went home to her family who lived on the *sovkhoz* (state farm) "Partizan" in eastern Siberia. From 1943-45 she studied in Moscow. She hardly ever was sick during the war and "not once went to the polyclinic or to a doctor, since it was not necessary." She had only "minor colds and treated them with popular substances," described in the next chapter.[37]

An anomalous situation appears to have obtained in the Altai Krai, situated in the lower belly of Siberia, south of Novosibirsk and Kemerovo and north of Kazakhstan. Despite its remote area, V. A. Isupov cites statistics that show decline, between 1943 and 1945, in the mortality of infants under one year old, particularly from inflammation of the lungs, "toxic dyspepsia," and gastroenterocolitis." The author attributes this to "wide application of sulfanilamide therapy." [38]

Civilians in the Gulag

Finally, it should be mentioned that families of political exiles as well as prisoners in the Gulag itself lived in problematic medical conditions. Such was the fate, for example, of El'vira Yershova, who lived with her exiled grandparents and her mother in one room of a barrack at the Ural Aluminum Factory (UAZ) while her father fought at the front.[39] But El'vira does not seem to have experienced any major medical difficulties during the war, although she was found to be severely nearsighted and had heart problems afterward.

Variations in Pharmacies

It is evident from these reminiscences that medical care varied greatly during the war. Those lucky enough to live in cities far removed from the fighting had adequate or even good access to factory-prepared pharmaceuticals and medical care. There were deficits of sulfa drugs, aspirin and soap, however. But those in the thick of the fighting or evacuated to primitive regions in remote republics were bereft of many necessary items and qualified medical practitioners, although sometimes they were supplied with a modicum of soap for bathing and with quinine or the synthetic antimalarial, Akrikhin. Indeed, people's financial situation during the war impacted their access to medicines. Some evacuees totally "lived on the economy" in dwellings supplied by a collective farm and with food from their own garden. Other evacuees eked out an existence without adequate jobs and pay and could not afford medicines. They were hurt by the fact that medicines sometimes were misappropriated and sold at markets for high prices, thus making those that were produced in sufficiency unaffordable. While the war exacerbated these difficulties, many problems predated the war.

Certainly this was the case with the level of medical care and the availability of pharmaceuticals in the countryside. Rural medicine had been primitive in imperial times. It continued to be so in Soviet times. Peasants and rural dwellers—collective farmers (*kolkhozniki*), those working on state farms and "forestry workers"—who formed the vast majority of the population lived in unhygienic dwellings, devoid of plumbing. The network of pharmacies in rural areas continued to be skeletal in the interwar period. Pharmacies with the most basic stock were scarce as hens' teeth on collective farms in the late 1920s and 1930s.[40] Preventive measures, like inoculation and treatment of the local water supplies, did not compensate.[41]

More than sixty years later, Dr. David Genis, who practiced medicine in Kazakhstan in the post-war years, averred that "in the native villages (*v aulakh)* there were no pharmacies and medical institutions, with the exception of large medical and pharmacy points (*punkty*) and in some villages —district hospitals, where most often a *fel'dsher* (paramedic) and *akusherka* (midwife) worked. In the rural areas people frequently turned to *znakari* [he termed them witch-doctors] or *kostopravy* (bone-setters) since there were no medicines or physicians and for medicine it was necessary to go to the city, which was difficult in the absence of transportation."[42]

During the war, Soviet medical/ pharmaceutical personnel fully acknowledged the deficiencies of rural medicine. For example, in 1942 Ia. A. Frenkel' stated that "medical care in the village . . . before the war far from fully satisfied the needs of the rural population."[43] And in 1943, N. A. Baran, head of the Administration of Rural Treatment Institutions of the USSR Commissariat of Health admitted that "Before 1938 a large network of treatment-prophylactic facilities was not formally organized in the villages and only with the *postanovlenie* (resolution) of the USSR Sovnarkom of 23.IV.1938 about strengthening rural medical districts did building this network receive fully lawful structure."[44]

Pharmaceutical officials realized that improving rural medical/pharmaceutical facilities was imperative with the onset of the Great Patriotic War, because troops poured through the villages and city dwellers were being evacuated to the countryside,[45] thus escalating the spread of disease. A *Prikaz* of November 29, 1941, for example ordained "short seminars for all doctors, fel'dshers, sisters of mercy, and midwives without exception to acquaint them with measures to prevent typhus and also to guarantee mass-agitation antiepidemic work among the population."[46] Ia. A. Frenkel' described compliance with the directive in broad brush strokes averring that medical workers set to work to provide bathhouses, disinfecting chambers, and isolating the sick in hospitals.[47]

N. A. Baran praised attempts to improve rural medical care with the onset of the Great Patriotic War in more detail. But he also noted problems. Above all, the reforms were inconsistent. Rural treatment facilities increased across the Soviet Union 70 percent, expanding markedly in Georgia and Turkestan, despite medical personnel being called to the front. However, medical care did not improve evenly. Funds for in-patient care in the village continued and even increased in some republics. For example, in Kirov *oblast'* monies increased 10.7 percent; in the Komi ASSR, 10.4 percent; in Tambov *oblast'*, 5.8 percent; and in the Armenian SSR, 8.8 percent. Conditions thus were created for "introducing into the rural areas multi-faceted hospital-outpatient facilities and highly qualified medical care to the population with simple clinical-diagnostic methods of research and new treatment methods." But in-patient funds were cut in the Georgian Republic and the Tadzhik SSR and use of the funds was not always satisfactory. Dental facilities increased markedly but x-ray facilities "remained on the level of the pre-war time" [when, from archival accounts they were inadequate]. In some areas, Baran admitted, diagnostic laboratories were insufficient, for example, in Omsk *oblast'* where "of 64 laboratories in the villages 13 did not operate"; in Saratov *oblast'* where "of 50 [laboratories], 15 did not work"; and in Western Kazakhstan where "of 37, 11 did not work." He blamed local health-care managers, duly identifying them. Thus, while antiepidemic measures worked very well in some areas, for example in the Trostianskii rural medical district of Kuibyshev *oblast'* and other areas, which Baran identified with their health managers, in still other areas sanitary "work was not correctly organized." There "was no plan," "medical personnel . . . were not strengthened" and "the sanitary well being of the populace was not guaranteed." Baran named the inadequate medical districts and their managers.[48]

Of course medical/pharmaceutical care also deteriorated in some cities with destruction of housing, sewerage and the water supply. For example, Catherine Merridale relates that soldiers returning at the end of the war "might go 'home' to find their wives and children in a one-room flat, with no kitchen, no water, and a leaking roof. They might find everyone in an earth dugout, worse even than the ones they remembered from Stalingrad or the Crimea."[49] The inhabitants of cities also had to cope with shortages of pharmaceuticals and medical/surgical items.

As a result, many urban dwellers fell back on popular, traditional remedies, to compensate for lack of certain state-of-the-art, factory-prepared medicines. But evacuees consigned to rural areas, bereft of medical/pharmaceutical care, absolutely relied on popular, traditional therapies to survive, as we shall see.

To their credit, pharmacy professionals attempted to improve dispensing and the network of pharmacies in both cities and rural areas.

One of the most amazing characteristics of wartime pharmacy was how quickly pharmacies, production laboratories, and repair shops, albeit makeshift, were reestablished or newly established. Heroic pharmacists, working in the thick of battle and in less than acceptable evacuation conditions, as well as Stakhanovite producers, were duly applauded—and not in the least for husbanding state property. For example, by January 15, 1942, in the liberated *raions* of Orlov *oblast'* 8 pharmacies were operating. By March 1, 19 were operating in 15 *raions*; 6 were located in cities and 13 were situated in rural areas. "A whole range of pharmacy workers" were credited with "showing wisdom in saving and protecting state property" such as "Comrade Govorov, manager of Pharmacy No. 26 in Russkyi Brod, [who] in exceptionally difficult wartime conditions preserved the entire property and all the trade materials with a value of 1,078 rubles." Similarly, "Pharmacy No. 32 in the village of Varenoe was burned, but the manager . . . Zhilina preserved a significant part of the property and wares." Total destruction in Orel, was estimated at 546,000 rubles, including the ruin of five pharmacy buildings at 244,000 rubles, equipment and transport at 46,000 rubles, and wares and materials at 236,000 rubles.[50] Clearly, accounting was not to be dispensed with during the war.

In Riazan' *oblast'* special brigades were praised for taking inventories of remaining wares and evaluating pharmacy property. Despite destruction of pharmacy wares, cabinets, and weights the *oblast'* Pharmacy Department (*aptechnoe otdelenie*) hastily rebuilt facilities. By February 20, 1942, all pharmacies in Riazan' that had been freed from the enemy were said to be operating normally. Pharmacy workers risked their lives to save equipment. Comrade Dubinin, manager of one pharmacy, "aware that Germans planned to burn the pharmacy," organized nightly watch for a month. Another pharmacy worker in the city of Riazan', one Comrade Serkis, intercepted six incendiary bombs to save Pharmacy No. 1.[51] An honor roll cited factories (one a theater-furniture factory), artels, institutes, and individual pharmacists in Riazan' *oblast'* who produced crucial items, such as narcotic ether, Streptotsid, Urotropin, medicinal salts, glucose, and eyeglass materials. Some produced these items in temperatures below zero and with frozen water. One Gol'dberg, manager of a "drug store" supplied bandages to 100 wounded.[52]

In Moscow *oblast'*, "at the moment of the arrival of the German fascists into the territory of the USSR," there were 261 pharmacies, 60 "drug stores," 215 "pharmacy points," and 94 pharmacy stalls (*lar'ki*). By the second half of November 1941, "in conjunction with the full or partial occupation of 27 administrative *raions* and the proximity of the front, 86 pharmacies, 16 drug stores, 112 pharmacy points, and 17 pharmacy stalls closed. . . .During the period of military activity 24 pharmacies were fully destroyed and 12 partially ruined, so that they needed large-scale capital reconstruction, and about 30 pharmacies suffered small-scale damage, such as broken glass, ruined stoves, and stolen inventories." Losses amounted to 4,500,000 rubles, with buildings estimated at 2,000,000 rubles and wares at 2,500,000 rubles. Losses at the Central Pharmacy Warehouse amounted to 3,000,000 rubles. But a six-person brigade, headquartered in Volokolamsk began rebuilding at the end of January 1942. Other brigades began to join in and during February 1942 it was claimed that "normal medical help" was available to the population.[53]

In the city of Moscow, "in the first days of the war many pharmacy enterprises worked round the clock," particularly "Central Pharmaceutical Packaging in Pharmacy No. 1 [the former Ferrein pharmacy, the largest in the world in the early twentieth century], and Pharmacy No. 75." Pharmacy workers defused incendiary bombs, offered first aid to the injured, and frantically worked to supply "severely deficit medicines" and "strengthen" the local "production base," establishing a bandage workshop, a galenical laboratory producing Urotropin, calcium chloride, Adonilen, lemon-acid soda, optical glass, and so on.[54]

Pharmacy production and dispensing in Leningrad, of course, suffered greatly. Of 206 pharmacies, 20 not impacted by the blockade continued to function as did 40 behind the blockade, communicating with the pharmacy network by letter and telegraph. Only 40 pharmacies in Leningrad *oblast'* were functioning normally in 1942. In the city of Leningrad, of 96 pharmacies, including 3 homeopathic and one veterinary, 17 were temporarily closed, one because of destruction, one because of a fire, and "12 by agreement with the City Health Department because they were near other pharmacies." Many pharmacies, without light and heat, dispensed small amounts of medicines and gave succor to the wounded as bombs rained down. Attrition in the ranks of qualified pharmacists was severe. Of 1,100 pharmacy workers 615 left; 44 were mobilized, others died, got sick, were evacuated, or became invalids. One hundred thirty-six pharmacists, who graduated pharmacy school in 1941 but had not worked in pharmacies, and 15 from the pharmacy institute attempted to fill the vacancies.[55] At the end of 1941, 79 of the 96 pharmacies in Leningrad *oblast'* were operating. Only 18 pharmacies received medicines and supplies from the three pharmaceutical factories that functioned; 59 pharmacies prepared medicines on-site.[56] Undoubtedly the medicines prepared and dispensed were very basic, if not primitive.

By 1943, the number of pharmacies operating in the RSFSR had made a significant comeback as the table below illustrates:

Table 8.1 Rebuilding Pharmacies

	Urban Pharmacies	Rural Pharmacies
In January 1941	1922	2430
January 1, 1943	1621	1932
January 1, 1944	1760	2182

Sources: Chief Pharmacy Administration GARF, f. A482, op. 51, d. 42, ll. 4-5.

During 1943, 73 pharmacies opened in *raion* centers that had formerly not had pharmacies. Unfortunately, a handful of pharmacies were closed because their premises were unsuitable or because they were near other pharmacies. The number of "pharmacy points" decreased by 106, drug stores by 37, and stalls by 79 because of lack of medical workers and packaged goods. Four analytical laboratories and 11 analytical "tables," closed because of inadequate staff.[57]

Alongside stellar performance in some areas, however, the Chief Pharmacy Administration admitted that some cities and *oblasts* responded poorly and that illegal sales of medicines and bandages had occurred.[58] Indeed, lack of supplies and basic ingredients in the pharmacy was dire in 1943. The government sometimes responded favorably in one case but in another instance harassed pharmacists and pharmacy workers.

In most cases pharmacists and pharmacy workers probably were not responsible for deficits, given endemic shortages before the war and transport difficulties during the war. But to a government which habitually devolved blame for systemic problems on local officials and relied on exhortations and punishments to solve them, this was of no account. So in 1943, the government specifically applied the draconian law of August 7, 1932, "On Destruction of Socialist Property," that had more generally referred to collective farmers, to the pharmaceutical sector. Fines were levied on managers of pharmacies and pharmacy workers for "insufficient wares," the amount being ten times the amount of the insufficient item. For example, if an item sold for 20 rubles in the *preiskurant*, the fine was 250 rubles. Additionally, the manager of a pharmacy was held responsible for spoilage of wares if he had failed to create "normal conditions of operation." His responsibility was open to debate—but only "open to debate"—if "the issue was about waste which the manager of the pharmacy could not correct without resolution of the Pharmacy Administration or was connected with funded materials that the manager could not acquire."[59]

Pharmacists not punished because of shortages, were still faced with finding substitutes. In 1943, I. I. Levinshtein, who had regained his status in 1940, after purge attacks on him in 1937, averred that pharmacists should have been practiced in substituting because of prewar austerities: "already, in the past, the *apteka* received simple preparations from the center and few applied measures to prepare them in their labs. . . .When interruptions in fuel supplies prevented receiving distilled water in the *apteka* we advised workers to use glass equipment and electric burners." Some pharmacists refused to use substitute methods, however. "Pharmacists often refused to prepare medicines" when lacking ingredients that were stipulated in the pharmacopoeias, "although they had analogs of the absent ingredients . . . great was the surprise of pharmacists when they recognized that in the absence of salicylates it was not hopeless for them to treat rheumatism—they could use Pyramidon . . . chloride is the best disinfectant but there are cases in which it has been replaced with sulfates, iron and copper."[60]

In 1943, pharmacy journals contained many articles about compensating for items absent in the pharmacy. A method of cleaning ordinary ether to produce narcotic ether was suggested.[61] The Central Pharmaceutical Scientific Research Laboratory (TsANIL) worked out methods for using steam cooking in place of percolation; use of iodine products, including iodphenol in place of the deficit reagent dichlorphenolindophenol; and use of inert sugar in place of deficit glucose.[62] Meat-processing plants, unable to produce the protein-iron preparation, albumin, in special dryers, as before the war, resorted to producing the product without dryers. Pharmacists were given recipes to prepare hygroscopic cotton from ordinary grey cotton, neutralizing pollution from seeds, leaves, and other extraneous materials by bleaching.[63]

Archival materials emphasize that availability of medicines, basic substances, and equipment during 1943 was uneven. Certain items showed marked increases but there were still severe shortages of others. Hospitals received first priority and amounts of bismuth; the sulfa drugs, Streptotsid, Sul'fitsid; Urotropin, Liuminal, barium for x-rays, Novocain, cocaine, chloroform, syringes, needles, sterilizers, Bakha lamps, and other important items were said to "fully guarantee the hospital network."[64]

On the other hand, Dr. Genis' first-hand impressions, regarding shortages of medical surgical instruments and ongoing shortages of certain basic pharmaceuticals are verified by archival reports. They complain of lack of instruments for urology, such as catheters and certain types of syringes, instruments for eye, ear, nose and throat practice, and for neurosurgery. Obstetrical and gynecological instruments were limited. "Also there were interruptions" and limited availability of the disinfectant and antiseptic, Rivanol; Biokhinol, glucose, menthol, gypsum, cotton, and bandaging materials.[65] Despite concerted efforts, supplies of "standardized raw materials," such as agar-agar, pepton, sucrose, maltose, starch, and glycerin, supplies of certain items, including formalin were "still difficult." Tons of soap, dusting powder, glucose, and camphor; massive amounts of chloramine, Neopantotsid, and caffeine; 15,000 ampules of adrenalin, 3,800 syringes, 38,000 needles, 155,000 thermometers, were sent by the Antiepidemic Administration to needy localities. Nevertheless, disinfecting substances like Lysol, naftalizol, and chlorine were available only in "extremely limited amounts."[66] Glucose, Sul'fidin, aspirin, Urotropin, Vitamin D and Vitamin C, salicylic acid, pepsin, and caffeine were said to be funneled to children's institutions.[67]

Requirements for spirits had been realized only 88 percent; sugar, 61 percent; salt, 66 percent; and vegetable oils, 70 percent.[68] "The situation with guaranteeing eyeglasses to the population in 1943 was exceptionally difficult, since factories cut back their output of eyeglass lenses." Oddly enough, Leningrad began supplying Moscow with optical items in the fourth quarter of 1943, supplemented with products from Rybinsk.[69]

Deficits of certain crucial medicines and materials resulted from insufficient output, *brak* (spoilage) due to carelessness in the factory, theft, lack of packaging materials, inadequate numbers of pharmacies and pharmacists, and transportation difficulties. "Imports" or lend-lease helped "to supply treatment institutions and to satisfy the needs of the population" as the previous chapter has related.

Still, many Soviet citizens had little or no access to pharmacies, hospitals, polyclinics, and trained medical personnel. Thus, increased production, "imports," and the rebuilding of pharmacies did not benefit them. How they survived is told in the following chapter.

Notes

1. Uwe Gartenschläger, "Living and Surviving in Occupied Minsk," in Robert W. Thurston and Bernd Bonwetsch, eds., *The People's War: Responses to World War II in the Soviet Union* (Champaign: University of Illinois Press, 2000): 13-28, esp. : 18, 23.

2. Hans-Heinrich Nolte, "Destruction and Resistance: The Jewish Shtetl of Slonim, 1941-44," ibid.: 29-53, statistics on Jews prior to World War II: 30-31.

3. T. L. Latko and T. L. Petrishche, "Kollaboratsionizm meditsinskikh rabotnikov v period Velikoi Otechestvennoi Voiny," *Materialy 10-i Respublikanskoi konferentsii po istorii meditsiny i zdravookhraneniia*, Minsk, September 23, 2004 (Minsk: RNMB, 2004): 22-23.

4. T. L. Petrishche, "Motivatsionnye mekhanizmy upravleniia farmatsevticheskim personalom v usloviiakh novoi ekonomicheskoi politiki (1920-e gg.),"; "Legalizatsiia meditsinskoi i farmatsevticheskoi deiatel'nosti kak element gosudarstvennoi politiki v zdravookhranenii v period NEP," abstract from *Materialy IV s"ezda sotsial-gigienistov i organizatorov zdravookhraneniia Respubliki Belarus'*, November 30-December 1, 2000 g., (Minsk, 2000): 387-388.; "Nekotorye aspekty pravovogo regulirovaniia farmatsevticheskoi deiatel'nosti v period novoi ekonomicheskoi politiki," e-mailed me by the author, February , March 2006.

5. Latko and Petrishche, "Kollaboratsionizm meditsinskikh rabotnikov v period Velikoi Otechestvennoi Voiny," ibid.: 22-23.

6. Response to *anketa* from Tatiana Petrishche's mother, delivered via e-mail through Tat'iana Petrishche (Vitebsk, Belarus, September 25, 2006). Like the other respondents who currently live in Belarus, Tat'iana's mother wishes to remain anonymous. Undoubtedly this has to do with the political climate there at the present time.

7. Tat'iana Petrishche, e-mail communiqué (Vitebsk, Belarus, October 6, 2006).

8. Father of Tatiana Petrishche (anonymous), responses to *anketa* (Vitebsk, Belarus, September 25, 2006).

9. Anonymous neighbor of Tat'iana Petrishche, responses to *anketa* (Vitebsk, Belarus, September 25, 2006).

10. Tat'iana Petrishche, e-mail responses to *anketa* (Vitebsk, Belarus, September 25, 2006).

Professor Laurie Cohen of the University of Innsbruck, suggested that the Germans might have gotten the pharmaceuticals from Swiss Red Cross workers who, although they were ostensibly neutral, were sympathetic to the Germans. Conversation with Professor Laurie Cohen, Washington, D. C. (November 17, 2006).

11. Conversation with Evgeniia's daughter Masha, (Denver, CO, November 14, 2006).

12. Evgeniia Gorlova, responses to *anketa* (Denver, CO, September 2006).

13. Tat'iana Petrishche, e-mail responses to *anketa* (Vitebsk, Belarus, September 25, 2006).

14. Peter Gatrell, *A Whole Empire Walking* (Bloomington: Indiana University Press, 1999): 211-212.

15. Samson Geltser, e-mail communiqué, "Moia sem'ia vo vremia 1941-45 godov" (September 20, 2006) and phone conversation (Denver, CO., September 21, 2006).

16. Mikhail Frolov, "Evacuation from Leningrad to Kostroma in 1941-42," in Barber and Dzeniskevich, *Life and Death in Besieged Leningrad*: 75-79.

17. Peter Geyman, phone conversation (Denver CO, September 16, 2006) and responses to anketa (September 2006).

18. David Genis, responses to *anketa* (Denver, CO, August 20, 2006). Information about his evacuation, e-mail communiqué (Denver, CO, September 27, 2006).

19. Raisa Kuskina, responses to anketa (Denver, CO, August 28, 2006).

20. Interview with David Genis (Denver, CO, September 11, 2006).

21. Raisa Kuskina, responses to *anketa* (Denver, CO, August 28, 2006).

22. Samson Geltser, e-mail communiqué, "Moia sem'ia," (September 20, 2006) and telephone conversation (Denver, CO., September 21, 2006).

23. David Genis, responses to *anketa* (Denver, CO, August 20, 2006).

24. David Genis, responses to *anketa* (Denver, CO, August 20, 2006).

25. Polina Savranskaya, responses to *anketa* (Denver, CO, September 2, 2006).

26. Liudmila Ravvina, responses to *anketa* (Denver, CO, August 29, 2006).

27. Anna Konetspolskaya, responses to *anketa* (Denver CO, August 25, 2006).

28. Mariiam Samoilovna Tartakovskaya, responses to *anketa* (Denver, CO, September 2006).

29. Maina Tsirkina, responses to *anketa* (Denver, CO, August 28, 2006).

30. Yelena Kuznetskaya, response to *anketa* via e-mail communiqué from David Genis (Denver, CO, September 27, 2006).

31. Evgeniia Shteiman, responses to *anketa* (Denver, CO, September 2006).

32 Yefim Keyster, responses to *anketa* (Denver, CO, August 29, 2006).

33 Lidiia Rakhshmut, responses to *anketa* (Denver, CO, August 2006).

34. Nadezhda Elemelakh, responses to *anketa* (Denver, CO, October 12, 2006).

35. Conroy, *The Soviet Pharmaceutical Business During Its First Two Decades*: 149-157.

36. Tamara Nikolaevna Khazieva, e-mail communiqué (Ufa, Russia, June 15, 2006).

37. Mariia Sergeevna Kuznetsova, e-mail communiqué (Ufa, Russia, June 20, 2006).

38. V. A. Isupov, "Demograficheskoe 'chudo': sokrashchenie detskoi smertnosti v Sibri v 1943-1945 gg.," Elektronnyi zhurnal "Sibirskaia Zaimka", no. 7 (2002), www.zaimka.ru_2002/isupov_mortality ,Table 2. Accessed via an e-mail attachment sent by Rustem Khaziev, Ufa, Russia, sent June 15, 2006.

39. Yershova, "XX vek v sud'bakh rossiiskoi provintsial'noi sem'i,": 34-35 and conversations with the author.

40. Conroy, *The Soviet Pharmaceutical Business*: 139-148, 173-186. Page 181 depicts a "pharmacy on wheels" dreamt up to service several collective farms.

41. Conroy, ibid.: 149-172.

42. David Genis, responses to *anketa* (Denver, CO., August 20, 2006). The words "witch doctor" are Dr. Genis' own translation. Samuel C. Ramer credited *znakari* with having some medical efficacy bred from experience, at least in late Imperial Russia, in his chapter "Traditional Healers and Peasant Culture in Russia, 1861-1917," in Esther Kingston-Mann and Timothy Mixter, eds., *Peasant Economy, Culture, and Politics of European Russia, 1800-1921* (Princeton: Princeton University Press, 1991): 207-232.

43. Ia. A. Frenkel', "Zadachi sel'skikh vrachebnykh uchastkov v usloviiakh voennogo vremeni," *Fel'dsher i akusherka* (1942): 37.

44. N. A. Baran, "Mediko-Sanitarnoe obsluzhivanie sel'skogo naseleniia v voennoe vremia," *Sovetskoe zdravookhranenie*, [no volume number or edition number] (1943): 10-13.

45. Frenkel', "Zadachi": 36, 37.

46. Frenkel', "Zadachi": 37.

47. Frenkel', "Zadachi": 37-38.

48. Baran, "Mediko-Sanitarnoe obsluzhivanie sel'skogo naseleniia v voennoe vremia" : 10-14.

49. Catherine Merridale, *Ivan's War: Life and death in the Red Army, 1939-1945* (New York: Metropolitan Books, Henry Holt and Company, 2006): 361.

50. GARF, f. A482, op. 51, d. 34, ll. 12, 13.

51. GARF, f. A482, op. 51, d. 34, ll. 14, 16.

52. GARF, f. A482, op. 51, d. 34, ll. 21-24.

53. GARF, f. A482, op. 51, d. 34. Ll. 31-33.

54. GARF, f. A482, op. 51, d. 34, ll. 44-49.

55. GARF, f. A482, op. 51, d. 34, ll. 54-64.

56. GARF, f. A482, op. 51, d. 34, ll. 68-69.

57. GARF, f. A482, op. 51, d. 42, ll. 4-5.

58. G. Ia. Leibman, "Uporiadochit' aptechnoe khoziaistvo v evakogospitaliakh narkomzdrava Soiuza SSR," *Farmatsiia*, vol. 6, no. 1 (1943): 5.

59. I. Ia Bychkov, "O material'noi otvetstvennosti aptechnykh rabotnikov za ushcher prichinennyi uchrezhdeniiu. Iuridicheskaia konsul'tatsiia," *Farmatsiia*, vol. 8, no. 5 (1945): 41-43

60. I. I. Levinshtein, "O tekhminimume dlia aptechnykh rabotnikov," *Farmatsiia*, vol. 6, no. 2 (1943): 7.

61. Ia. A. Filakov, A. I. Kiprianov, L. M. Solts, "Otchet o rabote po polucheniiu efira dlia narkoza," *Farmatsiia*, vol. 6, no. 1 (1943): 14-17.

62.G. I. Smirnov, "Rabota tsentral'noi aptechnoi nauchno-issledovatelnoi laboratorii GAPU RSFSR (TsANIL)," *Farmatsiia*, vol. 6, no. 2 (1943): 9-11.

63. Ia. A. Filakov, V. A. Yezerskaia, "Uproshchenii metod pererabotki seroi vaty v beluiu gigroskopicheskuiu," *Farmatsiia*, vol. 6, no. 2 (1943): 14-16.

64. GARF, f. A482, op. 51, d. 42, ll. 8-9.

65. GARF, f. A482, op. 51, d. 42, ll. 8-9, 13-14.

66. GARF, f. A482, op. 51, d. 42, l. 10.

67. GARF, f. A482, op. 51, d. 42, l. 12.

68. GARF, f. A 482, op. 51, d. 42, ll. 13, 14.

69. GARF, f. A482, op. 51, d. 42, l. 18.

Chapter 9
Narodnaia Meditsina during The Great Patriotic War

Traditional remedies became a firm fixture of Soviet mainstream medicine during the Great Patriotic War along with the revival of traditions in other sectors. The Soviet military restored tsarist military insignia. Although Stalin had identified with Georgian poets and revolutionary leaders in his youth, from the early twentieth century he identified with "Great Russia" and in the 1930s, as he increasingly consolidated his power and imposed his cultural views on the Soviet Union, films, plays and books about Russian heroes rather than minority figures dominated.[1] During the war, hearkening back to Russia's historical greatness and the steadfastness of her citizenry in the face of earlier invasions was part of the psychological weaponry marshaled to achieve victory. In like vein, Stalin's speeches referred to Russia, to the Motherland and the Fatherland, rather than to the Communist Party. To mobilize popular support for the government, rather than as a real call for divine intervention, the *Vozhd* established close relations with the Orthodox Church. In medicine, time-honored, home-made remedies—*narodnaia meditsina*—became enshrined, both at the grass-roots level and among pharmacologists and physicians, but out of necessity rather than as a result of an orchestrated program.

Shortages of conventional and chemically synthesized pharmaceuticals and inadequacies of containers and delivery systems had propelled ordinary citizens to resurrect and pharmacologists to investigate botanical remedies and other indigenous, traditional therapies during the 1920s and 1930s. During the Great Patriotic War Soviet citizens relied heavily, in some cases almost exclusively, on botanical and other popular remedies that had been used for centuries. Some Soviet citizens—those that had access to military hospitals or those evacuated to favored and thriving centers like Kuibyshev on the Volga—had access to state-of-the-art pharmaceuticals. Most Soviet civilians, however, were left to fend for themselves. Bereft of pharmacies and factory-prepared pharmaceuticals, they retreated to the nineteenth century. They treated their wounds and illnesses with homemade therapies passed down for generations. They made soap at home to wash themselves, their dishes, their linen, and their clothes. Use of resources at hand, of course, occur in all societies during times of crisis and stress.

But Soviet pharmacologists also assiduously researched botanicals and popular remedies in order to establish their chemical properties and apply them on a scientific foundation. Some pharmacologists dredged up therapies used in Muscovite Russia in the sixteenth and seventeenth centuries. A few concocted therapies that were just plain bizarre—panicky responses to lack of authentic treatments. The notion that chemicals were "artificial" and that it was better to use and ingest "natural remedies" became a mantra not only for ordinary citizens but for doctors, nurses, pharmacists, fel'dshers, and health practitioners of all sorts. This concept remained a key aspect of Soviet medicine in the post-war period and even has resonance today.

Traditional Medicine at the Popular Level

Tamara Nikolaevna Khazieva, who still lives in the city of Ufa, hundreds of miles east of Moscow, presents us with a large and rich compilation of traditional remedies that her family used both before and during the Great Patriotic War. During the conflict Ufa was far from the fighting. It also boasted the Bacteriological Institute that produced vaccines and antitoxins since before World War I and eight or so pharmacies. Yet Tamara Nikolaevna stated that "[*M*]*edpomoshch*' (medical help) was very weak, practically no one went to the hospital, since no one was seriously ill, and there was very widespread popular treatment. . . .Medicines, sent from the pharmaceutical industry or ordered in the pharmacy, were practically not used." Instead people treated themselves with traditional remedies. Many of the ingredients for them were purchased from the pharmacy but others were compounded of plants and home-grown items.

She avers that most of the illnesses were in the nature of "colds"—she was not familiar with influenza (*gripp* in the Russian). Nevertheless, people did have fevers. There were no thermometers to take the temperature. But if people began "shivering strongly this was a signal that the temperature was raised. They were treated as of old with herbs (*po-starinke travami*). . . ." In the winter remedies included boiling the dry leaves of a plant called *dushitsa* or mint leaves. In the spring "in a teapot were boiled the fresh leaves of *dushitsa*, which were gathered in May. At night [the sick person] drank [a decoction of] dry raspberries, which we also gathered ourselves," she remembers, "in order to sweat profusely." Another remedy consisted of putting dry mustard into the nostrils at night" and steaming the feet. "If there was no mustard, then the feet were heated in hot water (the hot water was poured into a basin)."

"The Russian stove"—a large brick affair with a fire below the baking oven and room for people to sleep on top—"was liberally used to treat." The sick person lay on the top of the stove "in order to get thoroughly warmed." People also were "treated in the bathhouse, if they had no temperature." The Russian bathhouse, like the Finnish one, was a sauna. "This caused sweating." Tamara's own family did not have a bathhouse. Therefore, when they wanted to apply this remedy they "used their neighbors." In general, Tamara Nikolaevna counsels, the treatment was "a combination of herbs and the stove or the bath."

When there was "severe shivering [indicating a very high temperature] the body was rubbed with a solution prepared at home to lower the temperature. The solution was prepared thusly: into one liter of water was poured 100-150 grams of edible vinegar essence." There was a variation of this remedy. "On the head, for lowering fever, there were put rags or a small towel, saturated with the vinegar solution. By these means the temperature was brought down."

If the throat was sore, then into a glass of warm (boiled) water (200 grams) was stirred one teaspoon of salt." Chamomile also was boiled and gargled for sore throats. These solutions "were gargled every two to three hours." If the throat did not get better, it was "helped with a thin splinter spread with kerosene. The kerosene was very pure and helped [eliminate the pain]. For warming up the throat," Tamara continued, "we took ashes from the stove (from a warm corner), they were poured into a bag and affixed to the throat. These ashes could be taken only in the autumn, winter or early spring, when the stove was still warm," she notes. Therefore, "in the summertime, throats were treated with a steamed onion, which helped a great deal."

"For a cough, half a teaspoon of the juice of aloe leaves (the plant was grown in a tub or earthenware pot in the window) was drunk two to three times a day." A few items were procured at the pharmacy. "For a very strong cough, turpentine salve was bought at the *apteka* and rubbed on the chest, except in the region of the heart." Tamara's "grandmother also put cups on the spine," alternating these with mustard [plasters]. The cups and mustard "were bought in the pharmacy."

As noted in the previous chapter, Vishnevskii salve, a product made of fish oil, which had natural disinfecting properties and was purchased at the *apteka*, was used to prevent infections from cuts and wounds. But additionally "the leaves of the aloe plant or the leaves of plantain [a tropical fruit resembling a banana] were rubbed on the wound, but only in the summer."

During the war, Tamara's family "predominantly ate potatoes." But they also ate herbs and wild apples "to assuage our hunger." This caused "frequent diarrhea." The problem was countered with decoctions boiled from berries called "bird cherries" or "herbs such as horse sorrel." A weak solution of manganese also was used to treat stomach ailments. [2]

Ironically, those who were evacuated to Central Asia and Kazakhstan appeared to have more access to factory-prepared medicines than Tamara Nikolaevna, in her home town in the hinterlands. But the evacuees also used traditional medicines. And most had problems acquiring soap, many making their own or using substitutes,

Mariiam Samoilovna Tartakovskaya spent the war in Tashkent, Uzbekistan. Aspirin, green soap and quinine were available. One heart preparation, Strofantan, though derived from a botanical, was factory-produced. However people also used valerian, lily-of-the-valley (*landysh*) and *naperstianka* (foxglove, which includes digitalis). Miriiam noted that "people gathered and brought home medicinal botanicals, learning what parts of the plants were useful and how to prepare and use them, from their grandmothers."[3]

Anna Konetspolskaya, who spent the war in a city in Turkmenia, remembers Sul'fidin and aspirin sometimes being available, but people also used old fashioned remedies. They "drank warm milk" and "steamed the feet in hot water." They "lubricated wounds with salt," used [medicinal] mud and "used berries . . . various berries." "There was no toilet soap whatsoever." Her family washed their bodies, clothes, linen, and dishes with "economy soap," the dark soap made by the local soap factory or slaughter house.[4]

Raisa Kuskina's family had to make their own soap during the war, although they were lucky enough to have a bathhouse connected with their home, located on a collective farm in Kazakhstan. The soap was "was very soft and there was very little [of it]." In the bath house they "washed with alkaline." The family also ate well, due to their kitchen garden and Raisa was given quinine for malaria, as related in the previous chapter. However, when her mother became seriously ill with a long bout of diarrhea, she was treated "with the juice of wild tern." And because there was no pharmacy near (although there was a fel'dsher with a middle school education) people generally treated themselves with "cherries which they picked in the woods."[5]

Liudmila Ravvina, who lived in Fergana, Uzbekistan, during the war, had medicines due to the fact that her mother worked in a military hospital. However, although they got soap through ration cards, she remembers that "in order to wash clothes, soap often was replaced with ashes."[6]

Dr. David Genis, in Kzyl-Orda, Kazakhstan during the war, remarked that "soap was greatly deficit. . . .People used wood ash to wash dirty dishes. Linen was washed with 'economy' soap' . . . .This could be bought only at the bazaar and was very expensive." He "never saw toilet soap for hands and face during the war. We usually washed our hands simply with water."[7]

Polina Savranskaya's family had access to sulfa drugs in Dushambe where they spent their period of evacuation but "there was a great problem with soap." They used soda to wash clothes.

Even those in Moscow and Kuibyshev had problems with soap and medicines. The city of Kuibyshev was better supplied because it was designated as the Second Capital from 1941 to 1943 in case Moscow was taken by the enemy. Yefim Kheyster spent the war in the village of Zagoskino, in the Kuibyshev *oblast'*. Although outside the city itself, Kheyster had few problems with medicines. He emphasized that, in any case, he and many others were hardly ill. But, although his family received limited amounts of soap through ration cards, they "used ashes to wash their linen."[8] Lidiia Rakhshmut, also in Kuibyshev *oblast'*, although like Kheyster in a village, also experienced "a major deficit of soap." Further, she recalled that although there was a large hospital and experienced doctors, "if [her] children got sick we treated them at home . . . we heated their feet."[9]

Mariia Sergeevna Kuznetsova's fortunes improved during the war. Born in the mid-1920s, as related in a previous chapter, she grew up on a state farm in Siberia. During the first two years of the war she was in a boarding school some twenty kilometers or fifteen miles from her home, returning only on weekends. But from the autumn of 1943 through April of 1945 she studied at an institute in Moscow and then, until 1949, she studied at an institute in Odessa. Her odyssey reflects not only her own intelligence and achievements, but also illustrates how the war had abated by 1943 and how, while surely there were problems, people were rebuilding occupied cities in the Ukraine. Yet, although Mariia Sergeevna ultimately became urbanized, she still relied on old-time remedies.

For a cold she used the following traditional remedy: "When it was difficult to breathe through the nose or her throat was sore," she "boiled potatoes in their skins until they were soft, poured out the hot water and, covered with a thick quilt, breathed the steam from the hot potatoes." But in Moscow, and subsequently in Odessa, "she did not even suffer from a cold." Although her mother made soap in their village in Siberia before the war, in Moscow and in Odessa, "as a student she got soap with a ration card."[10]

Of course those living in Belarus during the war relied on home remedies. As before the war, the parents of medical lecturer, Tat'iana Petrishche, used honey as a therapeutic. During the war, the family of Tat'iana's father, who lived in the countryside, near a forest, used dried raspberries to treat colds. They used dried blackberries to treat stomach ailments. Both kinds of berries were gathered in the forest. They made their own soap from animals that had been killed. The family of Tat'iana's current neighbor, who lived in a village in Belarus during the war, bought soap from an itinerant trader at that time. But during the war the neighbor and her family "boiled soap ourselves from potash and horses and other animals that had been killed during the war. . . .The soap was boiled a long time."[11]

From a physician's perspective popular remedies were efficacious. Dr. David Genis remembers that in Kzyl-Orda, Kazakhstan, "people often used home-made medicines, for example, mustard plasters, cupping, infusions or decoctions, medicinal botanicals, which people either gathered themselves or bought in the bazaar or in the pharmacy." He opined that, "[T]hese popular substances had a good effect and helped restore health. For example, a dry or even strong cough was helped by milk, boiled with an onion. An infusion of dog-rose berries was a good source of Vitamin C. Some people [in Kazakhstan] were infected with tapeworm; for treatment they drank 50-100 grams of aircraft fuel."

During the war these popular remedies became a firm part of Soviet mainstream medicine.

Pharmacologists Promote Botanical and Popular Remedies

In 1943, repeating criticisms hurled at the industry in the late 1930s,[12] Ia. G. Ivenskii railed that the "insignificant degree of preparations based on botanicals introduced into the pharmacy network in 1939, 1940, and 1941 caused a strained situation in supplying the needs of the populace in evacuation hospitals and treatment clinics."[13] In other words, botanicals were not used enough.

Botanicals also played a role in the United States during World War II. Moldy fruit provided one source for penicillin.[14] Malaria was endemic and sometimes epidemic in the southeastern United States[15] and a grave danger to American forces fighting in the Pacific theater of the war. American soldiers were cool to Atabrine, a chemical synthetic of quinine, because the latter caused nausea, vomiting and headaches. The United States government began stockpiling quinine even before "Java fell to invading Japanese troops" in March 1942, closing off a major source of quinine. From April 1942, when the war Conservation Board rationed quinine until October 1942, since the active ingredients in quinine did not deteriorate over time, pharmacists and ordinary citizens were engaged in collecting quinine wherever and in whatever products they could find it—such as in tonic water, sun lotions, and hair preparations.[16]

It also ought to be noted that there were shortages of pharmaceuticals, chemicals and medicinal botanicals in the United States in 1942. Dennis Worthen, specialist on American pharmacy during the Second World War presents a table of about fifty six of these items in short supply in 1942, including four different kinds of alcohol, ascorbic acid, Belladonna, caffeine, chlorine, chloroform, formaldehyde, glycerin, guaiacol for cough syrups, lanolin, licorice [for expectorants, laxatives, and to coat pills, the best source of which was Russia], liver extract for anemia, menthol, various oils [including pine-needle oil, another Russian staple], potassium salts, sugar, theobromine, Vitamin A, and other botanical and animal products. Worthen further avers that "[B]y late 1942 glycerin, a common pharmaceutical solvent, was becoming increasingly difficult to obtain" and notes the shortage of tin, rubber goods and other items.[17]

The United States imported Belladonna, specifically, from ten countries, including the Soviet Union for a total of 83,251 pounds in 1938. Imports from the Soviet Union in that year amounted to well over one third and by far outnumbered those from other countries at 35,654 pounds. The cost for the United States was 2,844 dollars. The United States continued to import a smaller amount of Belladonna from the Soviet Union during the war.[18]

Despite the United States' dependence on foreign suppliers for medicinal botanicals as well as some other items, Worthen emphasizes that "[W]artime conditions did not create as many problems for drugstores as for other retailers. Drugstore owners experienced fewer merchandise shortages than other retailers and only a portion of their merchandise was subject to rationing." Indeed, some pharmacists believed that American pharmacies became more professional venues because they stopped selling sundries. Further, "[S]ales volume lost to these [merchandise] shortages was more than made up by increased sales of health items." [19]

The pharmaceuticals' situation in the United States, in sum, was not dire. And, although, from the current author's memory, people used home-made remedies like mustard plasters and inhaled steam for respiratory problems, factory-produced medicines, salves and the like were readily available at drug stores.

In the Soviet Union, on the contrary, medicinal botanicals played a much larger role than in the United States and so did traditional, home-made remedies of all sorts. Botanicals and popular remedies were needed to fill major gaps in conventional therapies. Moreover, some had real promise. As for botanicals specifically, cultivating and collecting them boosted the psyche of ordinary citizens who participated in the process.

Until 1942, the All-Union Medicinal Plant Trust (Lekrastrest) housed in the USSR Commissariat of Health was in charge of collecting botanicals and producing medicines from them. Because Lekrastrest was short of staff, it outsourced production through other organizations—Tsentrosoiuz, pharmacy administrations, and pharmacies. The USSR dealt with the entire territory of the Soviet Union. Thus, to improve collection and preparation of medicinal botanicals in the Russian Republic specifically, in 1942 the government of the RSFSR instituted a special department, Roslekraskontora, in the republic's Chief Pharmaceutical Administration. This office was mandated to collect and prepare medicinal plants grown exclusively on the territory of the Russian republic and then to supply these raw materials to the enterprises of the Russian Medical/Pharmaceutical Industry, Glavmedfarmprom, the Chief Pharmaceutical Administration and the pharmacies of the RSFSR.[20]

Pharmacy workers bore the brunt of collecting. Additionally, as during World War I, the populace, including schoolchildren and Komsomol youth, were pressed into service.[21]

Although the respondents above explained that they learned to gather medicinal botanicals from their grandmothers, unfortunately, some pharmacy workers, not to mention school children, were not familiar with the plants they were to collect.[22] So, also reminiscent of World War I, when the Russian Society for Assisting Development of the Chemical Industry hastily published handbooks for newly recruited collectors, [23] in 1942 a "Commission on Collecting Useful Plants" published fourteen brochures, averaging 150 pages each, in editions of 200,000, and distributed them free of charge to quickly educate collectors.[24] Some of the publications were more useful than others. *Dikorastushchie lekarstvennye rastenye Bashkirskoi ASSR* (Wild Medicinal Botanicals of the Baskir ASSR), a 155-page, free handbook edited by Biologist M. I. Kotov and Dr. of Pharmacy Ia. A. Fialkov, which described fifty-seven plants from five zones of the Bashkir area and methods of preserving them, was given high marks.[25] Other brochures were problematical. For example a short handbook on plant collecting, targeting schoolchildren and costing 35 kopeks, entitled *Lekarstvennye rasteniia na sluzhbu frontu: Posobie dlia shkolnikov* (Medicinal Botanicals in the Service of the Front: Handbook for Schoolchildren), complied by S. E. Zemlinskii and Ia. G. Ivenskii, was attacked for not describing some important plants like chamomile (romashka), foxglove, mint, and chereda trekh-razdel'naia or zolototushnaia trava (*Bidens tripartite L.*)—the last used against scrofula or tuberculosis of the lymph glands; for not clarifying the useful parts of plants that were identified; and for not warning children to wash their hands after picking poisonous plants![26] Additionally, guidebooks frequently arrived too late, in part because of lack of paper, but when the optimum date for picking the plants had passed.[27]

In 1942 some 1,000 tons of 108 forms of plants were collected as compared with lesser amounts of only 27 forms in 1941.[28] Still, as during World War I, acquiring the most crucial plants foundered. The reasons varied. In the case of valerian root, not enough diggers were available; in the spring and fall, school children were, of course, in the classroom and, more importantly, digging required strength that schoolchildren did not have.[29] Amateurs made mistakes in preserving the plants. [30] Sometimes needed plants were available only in limited amounts or only in inferior, less efficacious species. For example, there was not enough lime-blossom in the Bashkir ASSR. The best variety of chamomile grew only in the Ukraine, which of course, was occupied territory. Thus, useless green chamomile was collected in the RSFSR.[31] In some cases the collection plan arrived too late—in June—when the optimum collection date had passed.[32] Foot dragging also occurred. Some regions hurled themselves into action. Located mainly in the region from the Volga River through the Ural Mountains, they were: Gorky *oblast'*, on the middle Volga; the Tatar ASSR and Kuibyshev *oblast'*, both to the south, along the east side of the Volga; Kirov *oblast'* (east of Gorky) and Molotov *oblast'* (east of Kirov) moving toward the Ural Mountains on the Trans-Siberian Railway; Sverdlovsk and Cheliabinsk *oblasts,* in the Ural Mountains; the Bashkir ASSR, with its capital Ufa, on the southwestern edge of the Urals; and Novosibirsk, in the southern part of western Siberia. Other regions, however, were lambasted for their feeble participation, particularly the Buriat Mongol ASSR, near Lake Baikal in eastern Siberia, and the Mari ASSR wedged between Gorky *oblast'* and the Tatar ASSR, where quotas were filled only 7.7 percent and 9 percent, respectively.[33]

In 1942, the plan called for 1,400 tons of medicinal plants and 575 tons of technical plants. During 1942 only 1,012.3 tons of medicinal plants had been prepared and 322.3 tons of technical plants. The amount of technical plants prepared declined in 1943; only 238.1 tons or 40.5 percent of the plan was fulfilled. On the other hand, 1,198 tons of medicinal plants were prepared, amounting to 85.7 percent of the plan.[34]

Despite shortfall of botanical plants in general in 1942 the Soviet Union exported 6,809 pounds of Belladonna to the United States at a price of 3,135 dollars. In 1943, the Soviet Union shipped 10,521 pounds of Belladonna to the United States at a cost of 4,431 dollars. "There were no imports in 1944," the American report notes.[35] Whether this was a partial exchange for the vast amounts of lend-lease pharmaceuticals and medical equipment the United States had sent to the Soviet Union since 1941 or whether the exports shorted civilians in the Soviet Union, is difficult to tell.

In any case, pharmacologists assiduously examined many traditional remedies derived from medicinal botanicals.[36] In 1942 sweetbriar (*shipovnik*) was recommended for the "struggle against scurvy" because it contained Vitamin C. Botanists proposed that powders be made from the fruit and liquid extracts from other parts of the plant. Additionally they advised that conifer needles could supply Vitamin C.[37] In fact conifer needles had supplied Vitamin C in the 1930s for the young construction workers of Komsomol'sk who were suffering from scurvy, according to Esfir' Falkovkich, a war survivor now living in Denver,[38] as noted in a previous chapter. The infusions made from these plants were to be sent to treatment institutions, children's institutions of "the closed type," cafeterias (*stolovye*), public buffets, and dining halls (*pishchevye bloki*) of treatment institutions. Order No. 6036 issued in May 1942 by the USSR Government (Sovnarkom) directed the Commissariat of Food "to organize in 50 existing food production enterprises production of Vitamin C" from sweetbriar according to a technological scheme." More primitive production was developed by the "All-Union Hygiene and Sanitation Institute (VGSI)" which "sent instructions to the hinterlands about the collection, preservation and usage of conifer needles in simple conditions and instructions about the use of preparing . . . solutions and dry concentrations of Vitamin C." [39]

A 1943 article in the journal, *Fel'dsher*, emphasized that medicinal botanicals had been important in Russia from the eleventh century. The author provided a laundry list of valuable botanicals used against heart diseases, to lower blood pressure, against bronchial asthma, against stomach remedies, as sources of vitamins, as cathartics, and so on. The author noted where the botanicals were cultivated or gathered most successfully—on the shores of the Black Sea, in the Caucasus, in Central Asia, in Western Siberia, in the Far East and made an impassioned plea for more collection, cultivation and research to aid the motherland during the Great Patriotic War.[40]

An unidentified English-language newspaper announced that according to the Russian Information Bureau, "Eight thousand tons of herbs were gathered in 1944" by the "All-Union Medicinal Trust" [sic] and, in early 1945 "Russia" had "100,000 Acres" on 10,000 collective farms . . . planted to medicinal herbs, and in the near future thirty new stations of the All-Union Medicinal Trust [sic] will begin gathering wild herbs and assisting in their cultivation . . . as well as in their processing. Particularly important were thermopsis and a botanical from the Turkmenian desert. A vast amount of thermopsis was discovered in the "Tien-Shan mountains. The seeds of this botanical were used "in the production of medicines for treatment of ailments of the respiratory tract." The botanical from Turkmenia produced Salsolin, which was used to lower blood pressure.[41]

Biologicals

Pre-Soviet Russian pharmacologists had made a reputation in researching and producing biologicals, such as spermine.[42] During the Great Patriotic War a great deal of faith was placed in items produced from animal substances. English-language reports from the Soviet Union noted that "[O]rganic preparations," such as adrenalin and insulin, "were produced before the war only in the enterprises" of People's commissariats "for Public Health in Moscow, Khar'kov, Kiev and Odessa. They treated endocrine substances obtained from the meat treating [sic] factories . . . In view of the special importance of this medicinal" production "the government passed a decision on September 4, 1942 instructing the P.C. [People's Commissariats] for the Meat and Dairy Industry to organize the production of medicaments in the meat treating enterprises." Factories organized shops and trained workers; five special factories and ninety-four shops "were built" during 1943. Workers received special bonuses "which greatly increased the quantity of materials collected." Since the "meat industry did not have the special equipment . . . [W]ithout waiting for imported equipment to arrive" the endocrine products were produced with equipment at hand. In 1942 only four endocrine products were produced. By 1944 forty "medicines" were put out.[43]

By late 1944 commitment to biolgicals had expanded. "Production . . . of sinestrol, a synthetic follicular (follikulin) preparation which plays a large role in the treatment of gynecological ailments" had "been partly organized. In zootechnics sinestrol may be used for milk barrenness." By 1945 it was being produced in Factory No. 9 of "Glavmedfarmprom of the Commissariat of Public Health of the USSR and in the Ukraine Institute of Endocrinology." It was planned to increase metilkofein [sic] from uric acid.[44]

In 1945 there were plans to "produce pholliculin [sic] from the urea of stallions and mares with foal, collecting it in the factory stables." Additionally, public reports noted that "[W]e must study methods of taking blood from sheep and goats for the production of dry hematogen as the amount of blood which we produce is insufficient to meet the purposes of health protection." Further, it was stated that "[P]lacenta has not yet been used for medical purposes" although "the latest scientific researches show that it can produce substances similar to prolan, so our scientific organizations must find ways of using this raw material." But this would take added resources. So, continuing in the subjunctive, it was noted, more soberly, that the "Moscow factory of endocrine produce must train 260 foremen for the various producing shops and the meat factory schools must train workmen in the various skilled professions connected with the production of this produce." Bonuses, not yet in place, must be organized and, very important, standards of the biologicals must be raised. Additionally, the proposed production required more ampules and glass.[45]

Dubious Remedies

The desperation evidenced by concentration on botanicals and endocrine products, although admittedly important, resulted in the development of more questionable remedies. One involved the use of smoke on wounds of the soft tissue. This was a popular remedy, dating from the sixteenth, seventeenth centuries and contained in old manuscripts. It was based on a belief that curative chemicals were released in the smoke. V. V. Soinikov first used the treatment in 1936, through a device consisting of two tubes. A. A. Kozlovskii used smoke to treat firearm injuries of the soft tissue in the autumn of 1941 in Leningrad. He invented an apparatus called an *odymitel*—a gas generator—to produce the smoke. Groups of patients at a time breathed smoke from large "*odymitely*" with six smoke holes. Portable ones were used to spray injuries.[46] One cannot but wonder what effect the carcinogens emitted had on the patients.

The "Anti-reticular cytotoxic serum" developed by Academician Alexander Alexandrovich Bogomolets strained incredulity even further. In 1932 Bogomolets was a fresh-faced professor of Pathological Physiology at the Second Moscow University.[47] In the decade following he received fame for his theories on longevity. By 1944, when interviewed by the American Naval attaché in Moscow, Academician Bogomolets was "a small, thin, wiry individual" of "about 76 years of age." "Although his face" was "lined and wrinkled," the American observer found him "enthusiastic," "cordial," and "responsive," with "a magnetic type of personality." Bogomolets asked voluminous questions about American medicine—he was familiar with Professor A. Baird Hastings in the United States—and to the interviewer, he exhibited "no evidence of mental senility." But Bogomolets' use of anti-reticular cytotoxic serum was strange indeed. The serum was produced by injecting human reticulo-endothelial elements, from the spleen and bone marrow of persons who had just died from accidents or gunshot wounds—but not from infectious diseases—into horses for six months. The antigens which developed were then re-injected into humans to "stimulate the physiology of supportive tissue and the repair of supportive tissue." Bogomolets claimed that he had records of "several hundred thousand cases" of successful regeneration of fibrous tissue in wounds or fractures where other treatment had failed. Bogomolets claimed that his serum also had successfully treated "the metastasis of cancer after the primary malignancy had been removed," particularly "metastasis of the lymph nodes." Bogomolets admitted that his serum was "contra-indicated in conditions of excessive formation of fibrous tissue as for example cirrhosis of the liver, arterio-sclerotic kidneys or certain forms of arthritis," but he believed it was "of value" in treating typhus, since this was "a disease in which rickettsiae invade the living cells lining the reticulo endo-thelial system." Although dire shortages of other therapies existed, Bogomolets claimed that production of anti-reticular cytotoxic serum had "reached such a stage in Russia that it could now be provided for all of the allies" and offered to "furnish it in any quantities desired by the medical services of the British, American and other allied commands involved, *if and when the second front ever did open up on the continent of Europe.*" [Italics mine] [48]

In August, 1943, one Dr. Alex Hrdlicka of the National Museum reported on Bogomolets' serum, although he did not specifically identify it, and called it "one of the most significant discoveries in the field of biological medicine," claiming that it could be used to increase human life expectancy. Hrdlicka also reported on Soviet tetanus cures and a solution of calcium phosphate to treat "nervous breakdown in the short space of fifteen minutes."[49]

Results

These therapies might have been harmful as well as merely useless. They began a trend toward charlatan-like treatments which, along with valuable alternative remedies like phages, are still in vogue in post-Soviet Russia and amongst émigrés from the Soviet Union in the United States.[50] But even the most promising alternative therapies could not entirely compensate for shortages of basic pharmaceuticals like aspirin, glucose, iodine preparations, the antimalarial Akrikhin and shortages of sulfa drugs, anesthesia, and medical and surgical instruments. Foreign assistance helped to a certain extent. Some people were well taken care of during the war. But the vast majority of Soviet civilians appear to have relied on their own resources.

Notes

1. Many books have been written about Stalin but the first two books of Robert C. Tucker's trilogy remain among the best. See Robert C. Tucker, *Stalin As Revolutionary, 1879-1929* (New York: W. W. Norton and Company, 1974) and *Stalin in Power: The Revolution from Above, 1928-1941* (New York: W. W. Norton and Company, 1990).

2. Tamara Nikolaevna Khazieva, e-mail communiqué, Ufa (Russia, June 15, 2006).

3. Miriiam Samoilovna Tartakovskaya, responses to *anketa* (Denver, CO, September 2006).

4. Anna Konetspolskaya, responses to *anketa* (Denver, CO, August 25, 2006).

5. Raisa Kuskina, responses to *anketa* (Denver, CO, August 28, 2006).

6. Liudmila Ravvina, responses to *anketa* (Denver, Co, August 2006).

7. David Genis, responses to *anketa* (Denver, CO, August 20, 2006).

8. Yefim Kheyster, responses to *anketa* (Denver, CO, August 29, 2006).

9. Lidiia Rakhshmut, responses to *anketa* (Denver, CO, August 2006).

10. Mariia Sergeevna Kuznetsova, e-mail communiqué (Ufa, Russia, June 20, 2006).

11. Information channeled through an e-mail communiqué from Tat'iana Petrishche (Vitebsk, Belarus, September 25, 2006).

12. "Voprosy tret'ei piatiletki: o planirovanii farmatsevticheskoi nauki: sovremennyi problemy sovetskoi farmatsii," *Farmatsiia i farmakologiia* , no. 2 (1937): 27; repeated in N. L'vov, "V nauchnykh organizatsiiakh: v Academiia nauk SSSR," ibid., no. 3 (1937): 39; also "Pervaia vsesoiuznaia konferentsiia farmakologov i toksikologov (1-5 iiunia 1937)," *Farmakologiia*, vol. 1, no. 1 (1938): 84.

13. Ia. G. Ivenskii, "Sbor i zagotovka lekarstvenno-tekhnicheskogo syr'ia v RSFSR v 1942 godu," *Farmatsiia*, vol. 6, no. 3 (1943): 8. (Total article: 8-16)

14. Scoutaris, "'Moldy Mary' and the Illinois Fruit and Vegetable Company," *Pharmacy In History*, vol. 38, no. 4 (1996): 175-177.

15. Grob, *The Deadly Truth*: 185-186.

16. Worthen, "The Quinine Pool," *Pharmacy in World War II*: 84-90; quote: 84.

17. Worthen , *Pharmacy in World War II*: 76-99; charts: 80 and 97. Before the war the United States aimed to store 200,000 pounds of Belladonna, including 60,000 pounds of leaves and roots. (Chart: 80)

18. "Belladonna Leaves and Roots," Chemicals, Drugs and Pharmaceuticals," Industrial Reference Service, U. S. Department of Agriculture, vol. 3, part 2, no. 53 (December, 1945): 3 in NAUSA, RG 489, Box 82, 10,300, BFDC, U. S. Dept. of Commerce.

19. Worthen, *Pharmacy in World War II*: 99.

20. Ivenskii, "Sbor i zagotovka," *Farmatsiia*, vol. 6, no. 3 (1943): 8.

21. E. Iu. Shass, "Iz opyta RSFSR zagotovki lekarstvennykh rastenii v 1942 g.," *Farmatsiia*, vol. 6, no. 2 (1943): 42. For the "the medicaments crisis" in Russia during World War I, see Conroy, *In Health and In Sickness*, chapter 16: 320-348; on plant collecting see : 335-339.

22. Shass, "Iz opyta RSFSR zagotovki lekarstvennykh rastenii v 1942 g.," *Farmatsiia*, vol. 6, no. 2 (1943): 42.

23. Conroy, *In Health and In Sickness*: 336-339.

24. Ivenskii, "Sbor i zagotovka," *Farmatsiia*, vol. 6, no. 3 (1943): 11.

25. "Bibliografiia," *Farmatsiia*, vol. 6, no. 2, 1943, pp. 44-45; E. Shass was the reviewer.

26. Ibid.: 45-46. E. Shass also was the reviewer. For discussion of chereda or *Bidens tripartita L.* to treat scrofula and as a possible abortifacient before the war see Z. I. Ivantova, "K farmakologii keredy," *Farmakologiia*, vol. 1, no. 1 (1938): 64-65; for uses in the Soviet Union in recent times see A. D. Turova and E. N. Sapozhnikova," *Lekarstvennye rasteniia i ikh premenenie* (Moscow, 1984): 234-235. In recent times chereda was still used to treat scrofula and also for respiratory diseases, toothaches, and other problems.

27. Shass "Iz opyta RSFSR zagotovki lekarstvennykh rastenii v 1942": 42; Ivenskii, "Sbor i zagotovka lekarstvenno-tekhnicheskogo syr'ia v RSFSR v 1942 g.": 11.

28. Ivenskii, "Sbor i zagotovka" : 8-9.

29. Ivenskii, "Sbor i zagotovka,": 9. On schooling during the war see John Dunstan, *Soviet Schooling in the Second World War* (Basingstoke: Macmillan Press, Ltd. and New York: St. Martin's Press, Inc., 1997): 74-203.

30. Shass, "Iz opyta": 42.

31. Ivenskii, "Sbor i zagotovka": 9-10.

32. Shass, "Iz opyta": 42.

33. Shass, ibid.: 42-43; Ivenskii, "Sbor i zagotovka": 10.

34. GARF, f. A482, op. 51, d. 42, l. 19.

35. "Belladonna Leaves and Roots," Part 2, Chemicals, Drugs and Pharmaceuticals, U. S. Department of Commerce: 3.

36. *Farmakologiia i toksikologiia,* vol. 6 (1943): passim. For example, M. D. Mashkovskii, "Farmakologicheskoe issledovanie alkaloidov iz rasteniia cocculus laurifolius," (Research had begun in 1893), *Farmakologiia i toksikologiia,* vol. 6, no. 2 (1943): 36-44;

37. V. S. Chetverikov, "Sanitarnoe delo v SSSR vo vremia pervykh dvukh let voiny," *Gigiena i sanitariia*, vol. 9, no. 4 (1944): 22.

38. Interview with Esfir' Falkovich, Denver, CO, May 21, 2004, cited in Conroy, *The Soviet Pharmaceutical Business During Its First Two Decades*, p. 261, note 8.

39. Chetverikov, "Sanitarnoe delo v SSSR vo vremia pervykh dvukh let voiny": 22.

40. D. M. Rossiiskii, "Lekarstvennye sokrovisshcha SSSR," *Fel'dsher* (1943): 34-37.

41. Clipping entitled "Grows Healing Herbs," stamped with the date (March 11, 1945) in NAUSA, RG 489, Box 82, 10,300, BFDC, U. S. Dept. of Commerce.

42. Conroy, *In Health and In Sickness* : 142-143.

43. A. Katkovski, "Output of Medicinal Produce in the Meat Industry," The Meat and Dairy Industry of the USSR, No. 1 (1945) *Economic Information*, No. 341(July 1945) in NAUSA, RG 489, Box 82, BFDC, U. S. Dept. of Commerce.

44. A. G. Natradze, statement in *Izvestiya* (News) (November 15, 1945) translated version in the *Economic News Bulletin* (November 15, 1945) in NAUSA, RG 489, Box 82, 10,300, BFDC, U. S. Dept. of Commerce. These biological preparations were underlined in the original report in the archives.

45. Katkovski, "Output of Medicinal Produce in the Meat Industry," ibid.

46. Smirnov, ed., *Opyt sovetskoi meditsiny,* vol. 14 : 269-274.

47. "Physik und Medizin," *Sowjet-Medizin: Sonderbeilage zum "Berliner Tageblatt"* (December 6, 1932): 11, NAUSA, RG 489, Box 82, 10,300, BDFC, US Dept. of Commerce.

48. Assistant Naval Attaché, Moscow, Interview with Academician Bogomolets (April 29, 1944): 1-4 in NAUSA, File RG 489, Box 82, 10,300, BFDC, US Dept. of Commerce.

49. "Hrdlicka Extols New Soviet Serum" *The New York Times*? (August 26, 1943) in NAUSA File RG 489, Box 82, 10,300, BFDC, U. S. Dept. of Commerce. The newspaper is unidentified.

50. For example, Barbara Plampin of Chesterton, Indiana, notified me (December 2001) of a treatment for asthma, described to her by Russian friends, in which patients inhale salt in a salt chamber. Friends from the Soviet Union now American citizens and living in Denver have apprised me of many unusual home-made remedies.

Chapter 10
Reforming the Pharmaceutical Sector: Ideas from Below and Their Fate

During the war, as before it, Soviet officials thought in the subjunctive or present perfect, adumbrating wish-lists that would be fulfilled in the future. In 1941/1942 the RSFSR Chief Pharmacy Administration (GAPU) was confident that in the post-war period pharmaceutical factories would be built in the Altai region, Molotov, Krasnoiarsk, and Chalovsk; assortment would be wide, and so on.[1] Additionally, the Chief Pharmacy Administration praised Stalin's "wise leadership."[2]

Nevertheless, reports from the RSFSR Chief Pharmacy Administration unabashedly pointed out negative features in the Soviet planned, administrative economy that hampered purchasing for pharmacies and ultimately affected consumers. Particularly criticized were over-centralization, the planning process itself, and the cleavage between the supply side and the consumer end, that is, the separation of the pharmaceutical industry and ancillary industries from local pharmacy administrations and pharmacies.

The RSFSR Chief Pharmacy Administration accused the core pharmaceutical industry, Glavkhimfarmprom, of "first and foremost guaranteeing the needs of its own factories" and "not properly addressing the interests of the pharmacy administrations."[3] The glass industry—and economic planners—came under fire for shortages of pharmacy vessels. Although it was admitted that transportation difficulties and increased breakage contributed to the shortages, the glass industry was blamed for not producing the proper mix of petri dishes, laboratory vessels, and ampules; lack of the latter, in particular, sometimes prevented pharmacy administrations from dispensing vaccines and serums.[4]

Due to the exigencies of the war, more responsibilities were heaped on local pharmacy administrations. In October 1941 nine *oblasts* in the RSFSR, including Iaroslavl', Ivanov, Vologda, Gorky, Kuibyshev, Saratov, and Stalingrad, were ordered to establish workshops for repair of syringes and surgical instruments. At first seven areas—Kirov, Molotov, Penza, Voronezh, Kursk, Moscow, and the Udmurt Autonomous Republic (ASSR) and then two other areas—the Altai Krai and the Tatar ASSR—were ordered to establish galenical and packaging laboratories.[5]

As in the pre-war period, in 1942 local pharmacy administrations were to shoulder funding. In view of the policy "all for the front," local areas were warned that "in the future" they could "not count on" government funds and that "final resolution of the pharmacy vessel problem must be done immediately through departments in the localities by means of building some small glass factories."[6] Centralized planning was not to be dispensed with entirely, however. The Chief Pharmacy Administration was to help with instruction, some monies, and necessary materials.[7]

Implementing a policy of decentralization in 1942 was difficult, though, for a decade and more of centralized control had enervated pharmacists. The Chief Pharmacy Administration lamented that by the spring of 1942 a number of localities—including Altai, Novosibirsk, Gorky, Penza, Mordova, Astrakhan, Riazan', and the Tatar ASSR—had not shown "any initiative" in responding to the administrative directives to produce medicines and disinfectants that relied on local raw materials, but "continued to work as before and assumed they would receive the stated substances only on central funds and from state enterprises."[8] Directors of local pharmacy administrations were accused of dereliction of duty. "In place of organizing new production . . . they sent telegrams to Narkomzdrav (the People's Commissariat of Health) and GAPU and waited for the wares to come." The laggards were warned that they would "be judged not by words but by deeds."[9]

In Molotov, Ivanov, and Saratov, on the other hand, production did develop due to the energy of pharmacy administration directors, and assistance from party and Soviet officials.[10] Some pharmacy departments "vigorously collected used pharmacy vessels." Pharmacy glass was successfully produced in the Urals.[11]

Financing, of course, was crucial to the post-war robustness of pharmacies. At the outset of the Russian-German war it appeared that there was to be some tinkering with financing to enable local pharmacy administrations to function more efficiently. In 1941, the RSFSR Chief Pharmacy Administration complained about lack of adequate funds, as before the war, and decried lack of correlation between retail and wholesale prices. It was admitted that "in 1940 the financial position of the entire pharmacy system was very precarious and urgent requests for loans and late payments" were common. Retail prices did not adequately cover local pharmacy departments' expenditures. In 1941, thus, the Chief Pharmacy Administration attempted to put the local pharmacy departments on a sounder financial footing, by "again" petitioning Narkomzdrav "to abolish the existing *Apteka* Tax (the price list for medicines) and establish a correct relationship between retail prices for medicaments and medical equipment and distribution prices for the products of Narkomzdrav industries" that local pharmacy administrations had to pay. The Chief Pharmacy Administration also requested Gosbank to introduce "privileged credit terms for commodity circulation" with a view toward increasing the local departments' share from 25 percent of their own means to 30 percent.[12]

By 1943, as the tide of war changed, it was obvious that the idiosyncratic financial system that was the hallmark of the planned economy was not to be done away with. A full-fledged market system was not going to be allowed to determine efficiencies in the pharmaceutical sector. Cost accounting was not to be fully recognized. Supply and demand were not going to dictate prices; prices were not going to signal effective use of resources. Foreign competition was not going to spur innovation. Local pharmacy departments were not to be allowed to fully manage sourcing and their own income, finance their own production facilities, or decide staffing. The government was still to be a controlling parent and the Chief Pharmacy Administration its chief steward. While local pharmacy administrations were asked to do a great deal to restore the pharmaceutical sector they were sternly reminded that their duty was to obey higher authorities.

Through 1941, local pharmacy administrations continued to be categorized according to their turnover income.[13] In 1943 the RSFSR Chief Pharmacy Administration claimed that its financial situation was "firm." Some local pharmacy administrations, however, were experiencing "financial difficulties" for various reasons. Banks had imposed sanctions on them because, lacking qualified bookkeepers, their accounting records had not been prepared in time. Their turnover revenue was insufficient because of shortages of wares and expenditures that were higher than those provided for in the Plan.[14] A latter-day Soviet historian of pharmacy assessed the behavior of the local pharmacy administrations more harshly, commenting that "[A]t the end of 1943 negative tendencies appeared in the pharmaceutical sector, connected with the violation of the principles of 'self financing' (*khoziaistvennoe raschet*). Many local departments began to systematically lower purchasing."[15]

To resolve the problems, the RSFSR Chief Pharmacy Administration, first redistributed monies to balance indigent local departments with those more prosperous.[16] The administration also worked out an elaborate budget for 1944, emphasizing that while local departments were to play a major role in rebuilding the pharmacy sector, central authorities would control financing.[17] Finally, "analysis of trade-production activity" having "brought to light the causes of the negative trends in the pharmaceutical economy," Sovnarkom issued a new price list for medicines and pharmaceutical items in June 1944, raising some prices, lowering others, and leaving others the same.[18]

Thus it appeared that at the local level, at the retail end, not much was to change. However, in the immediate aftermath of the war, some high health officials as well as those at the bottom rung, who interacted with the populace on a day-to-day basis and had to bear the brunt for shortages, forthrightly criticized the prevailing pharmaceutical system and even audaciously indicted the macroeconomic system, suggesting radical changes in some instances. These recommendations can only be summarized here since they already have been published in the author's article in a recent edition of *Europe-Asia Studies*.

For example, Assistant Commissar for Health A. G. Natradze criticized the lack of affinity between the pharmaceutical industry and ancillary industries due to the severe vertical organization of the Soviet economy. Some pharmacy specialists blamed worker incompetence for the great losses due to breakage and spoilage. Some railed at poor distribution urging the need for more decentralization. Some recommended differential salaries to punish slackers and reward the efficient. But others blamed the whole chain of command citing niggardly government funds, the need for streamlining, lax management of *aptekoupravlenie* warehouses and pharmacies, where products sometimes lay unused, and called for more central control.[19]

The Soviet pharmaceutical system limped throughout the 1980s. During this decade many books on medicinal botanicals for medical personnel and home consumption were published in the Soviet Union. Several were printed in the Ukraine, which historically had played a major role in supplying medicinal botanicals. Some of these books dealt with fairly simple, if irritating medical problems. But one focused on medical botanicals and cancer.[20] After the Soviet Union fell apart in 1991 the handbooks on botanicals, replete with drawings and photos of different parts of the plants, continued to be sold in bookstores and used by Russians, making up medicaments at home.[21]

Somewhat ironically, the use of medicinal botanicals also expanded in the United States during this period. However, there was no shortage of factory-made pharmaceuticals in the United States, whereas there continued to be in post-Soviet Russia, where one could witness individuals selling medicines of domestic and foreign provenance on the street.

In the early 1990s, when the planned, centrally directed macroeconomic system was dismantled, things began to change in the Soviet Union. Although consumers now had to worry about affordability, pharmaceuticals at least became more abundant. Imported pharmaceuticals appeared in *apteki.* More importantly, pharmaceuticals began to be produced domestically in greater numbers. They also were of higher quality.

Some emerged from pharmaceutical companies that rose like phoenixes from old enterprises which had been retooled. Some of these, in turn, reverted back to their pre-Soviet names. The Karpov factory in Moscow once again became the Ferrein Factory as did its flagship Apteka No. 1 near the Kremlin—albeit with Ferein as the spelling, in deference to the representatives of the Ferrein and Wagner families living in Europe and the United States. Both the Ferein factory and pharmacy were spruced up. Under the management of Vladimir Bryntsalov, who ran for the post of President of the Russian Federation in 1996, along with Boris Yel'tsin, the Ferein Factory issued glossy brochures of its pharmaceutical products.[22] The Akrikhin Factory, still located in the village of Staraia Kupavna, about an hour's drive from Moscow by automobile, appeared to be a success story in 2003, although the management and staff admitted that the remodeling of the enterprise was not complete. Outfitted with state-of-the-art Italian equipment, it began to produce and advertise some well regarded vitamins and other pharmaceuticals.[23] The Farmakon Factory in St. Petersburg, proudly noting its 1907 founding, was overhauled and advertised twenty-eight "Chemical and Pharmaceutical Raw and Useful Materials"—various acids, ethers, hydroxide, caffeine, spirits, and so forth, with their Russian names, their chemical formulae, and corresponding English names.[24] The Ufa Vitamin Factory gained cachet and touted its products on the Internet.[25] And many other Russian pharmaceutical firms did so as well. Many capitalized on the fact that their ingredients were "natural."[26]

Other cutting-edge products came from new start-ups. Biokhimik, for example, was founded in 1998.[27] Whether venerable or greenfield, initially many post-Soviet companies benefited from joint ventures with foreign firms.[28] For example, Akrikhin was outfitted with Italian equipment, Biokhimik with German. A British company, Novolytics Limited, has formed a joint venture with the Eliava Institute in Georgia to produce phages that may counter antibiotic-resistant bacteria.[29]

By the summer of 2000 one wholesaler, Protek, advertised that it distributed products from one hundred fifty-nine Russian pharmaceutical companies. [30] Anthony Rimmington lists some seventy post-Soviet pharmaceutical companies and conglomerates with multiple subsidiaries on his recently established website, Biopharm Analytica.[31] These post-Soviet enterprises are producing world-class biological and chemically synthesized medicaments. Most of the entities on his list were started after 1991, although a few subsumed Soviet-era factories. The managers and boards of directors of the post-Soviet companies and conglomerates are young physicians, biochemists, accountants and bankers, advertising and computer specialists, and so on, such as the founders of Otechestvennye lekarstva (Native Medicines). This holding company was established in the post-Soviet era of 1997. It subsumed three Soviet pharmaceutical companies: the Shelekovskii Vitamin Factory, located near Moscow and Novosibkhimfarm, located in Novosibirsk and Krasfarma, located in Krasnoiarsk, Siberia. The company now supplies 15 percent of Russian pharmaceuticals. Its sales in 2006 amounted to about 3 billion rubles. It has "daughter" companies in Ukraine, Kazakhstan, and Vietnam. It produces about 200 tablets, capsules, ampules, bandages, and plasters, including Amoxicillin, Streptomycin, and other antibiotics; sulfa drugs; cardio preparations; Novocain; glucose; vitamins; a protective toothpaste for pregnant women; and so forth. Its newest four products include Zorex, a preparation that "protects the kidneys" and Phenotropil, a products that enhances memory, brain activity, and concentration. Each year the holding company sponsors a competition with a large cash prize for a pharmaceutical "Golden Idea."[32] Viferon, founded in 1998, produces interferon (for Hepatitis-C sufferers) and products for those suffering from immune system disorders.[33] Sotex, founded in 1999, puts out Angiozel, for heart disease, a hemostatic substance, and Tsereton, a choline substance.[34] Veropharm, established in 1997 produces medical plasters and oncology items. One of the factories that comprises it, located in Voronezh, was established in 1934.[35] Pharmacy Chain 36.6 (named for the optimum Centigrade temperature of a healthy individual) was started in 1991. According to its website it now is a "leading Russian health and beauty retailer offering to its patrons high quality, affordable health and beauty goods." Consolidated sales in 2006 were about 525 million dollars. It is a publicly held company whose shares now range at about 80 dollars on the Russian Stock Exchange.[36] Farmstandart, founded in 2003, is yet another innovative company.[37]

The websites of the new and retooled post-Soviet Russian companies are professional, with snappy photos of the management, factories, product line, and so on. The provide information about the history of the company or conglomerate, its management, products—including in some cases chemical formulae, the company's compliance with Russian laws, comparisons between the company products and foreign ones, and so forth—in English as well as in Russian.

With its shackles removed the pharmaceutical industry in the FSU—the former Soviet Union—is approaching the standards of the industry in developed countries. In the 2007 introduction to Biopharm Analytica, Anthony Rimmington avers "In Russia . . . it is evident, that globally significant capabilities are being established in key areas of pharmaceutical development including drug discovery, pre-clinical and clinical trials, and industrial production facilities are rapidly adopting international GMP standards." He quotes from an article in *The Times*, November 2006, that "'[L]ast year the Russian pharmaceutical market was worth 8.4 billion dollars, a 32 percent increase from 2004, making it the fastest growing one in the world. . . . This brisk expansion,'" the article continues "'is driven by a flourishing economy. . . .'"[38] The author of *The Times* piece cites the robust Russian oil and gas industry as the spur to the growth of the post-Soviet Russian economy and in turn a boost to the pharmaceutical industry. However, the elimination of government ownership and central planning (even if the plans were not followed) obviously were contributing factors to the growth and health of the post-Soviet industry as the links to the companies on Rimmington's website and the websites and literature of separate companies make clear. For companies were now free to source; determine their product lines; hire research, financial and sales' talent; determine prices; and drum up investment for overhauling outmoded factories and establishing brand-new ones.

The pre-Soviet, Soviet and post-Soviet pharmaceutical sector bears mute testimony to the benefits of autonomous, decentralized production and distribution of health products, with government oversight over the quality of the products but sans micromanagement, and to the benefits of competition and market principles. Some Americans are under the impression that the American pharmaceutical industry should be recast in the image of the Soviet one. Hopefully, the lackluster performance of the Soviet industry, before World War II and during it, despite a plethora of talented scientists, dedicated physicians, and many committed pharmaceutical factory managers and workers, should dissuade them.

Notes

1.GARF, f. A 482, op. 51, d. 34, l. 9.
2.GARF, f. A482, op. 51, d. 34, l. 26.
3.GARF, f. A482, op. 51, d. 34, l. 8.
4.GARF, f. A482, op. 51, d. 34, ll. 6, 7.
5.GARF, f. A482, op. 51, d. 24, l. 3.
6.GARF, f. A482, op. 51, d. 34, l. 9.
7.GARF, f. A482, op. 51, d. 34, l. 10.
8.GARF, f. A482, op. 51, d. 24, l. 5.
9.GARF, f. A482, op. 51, d. 34, l. 4.
10.GARF, f. A482, op. 51, d. 34, l. 4.
11.GARF, f. A482, op. 51, d. 34, ll. 6, 7.
12.GARF, f. A482, op. 51, d. 22, ll. 8, 10.
13.GARF, f. A482, op. 52. D. 21, ll. 2, 7.
14.GARF. F. A482, op. 51, d. 42, l. 31.
15.V. M. Salo, "Iz istorii farmatsevticheskoi sluzhby v gody velikoi otechestvennoi voiny," *Farmatsiia*, vol. 34, no. 2 (1985): 9.
16.GARF, f. A482, op. 51, d. 42, ll. 31-32.
17.GARF, f. A482, op. 51, d. 42, ll. 32-100.
18.Salo, "Iz istorii": 9.
19. Conroy, "The Soviet Pharmaceutical Industry and Dispensing, 1945-1953," *Europe-Asia Studies*, vol. 56, no. 7 (2004): 981-985.
20. K. P. Balitskii, *Lekarstvennye rasteniia i rak* (Kiev: "Naukova dymka," 1982)
21. For example, M. M. Zhadan, *Apteka v lesu* (Simferopol': Izdatel'stvo "Tavriia," 1979); D. S. Ivashin et al, *Spravochnik po zagotovkam lekarstvennykh rastenii* (Kiev: "Urozhai," 1983); A. D. Turova and E. N. Sapozhnikova, *Lekarstvennye rasteniia SSSR i ikh premenenie* (Moscow: "Meditsina," 1984).
22. The author visited Apteka No. 1 many times and visited the Ferrein Factory in Moscow in the summer of 1993, speaking briefly with Bryntsalov. Brochures from the factory, advertising insulin, antibiotics, such as Amoxicilin; antihistamine preparations; analgesic substances, including Anal'gin; cardiac preparations and others, with Russian names, trade names, and ingredients are in the author's possession. Information about the Ferrein family in part is from the author's correspondence with Wencelaus Wagner, the grandson of Vladimir Karlovich Ferrein. Wagner, an international lawyer left Russia as a baby in 1919.
23. Visit by the author (July 4, 2003).
24. History and Products of OAO Farmakon, http://www.farmacon.ru/ rus/ contact. http://www.farmacon.ru/rus/history.htm(twopages);http://www.farmacon.ru/rus/sirye.htm (three pages). Accessed 6/8/2002.
25. Ufavita: Ufimskii vitaminskii zavod. http://www.ufaviota.ru, copyright 2000. The advertisement on the Internet included a flower, the slogan "Energiia Prirody v nashikh vitaminakh!" ("The Energy of Nature in Our Vitamins!," photos of the vitamin bottles and a menu of choices: "O prepariiatii, Novosti, Produktsiia, Prais-list, Firmennye apteki, Informatsiia, and Obratnaia sviaz. ("About the Preparations," "News," Production," Price-list" Firm pharmacies," Information," and "Return connections"). An e-mail address was provided. Accessed 6/8/2002.

26. "Evalar," www.evalar.ru. The advertisement emphasized that this was "A pharmaceutical enterprise producing natural medicinal preparations." There was a display of bottles, the slogan "Sovremennoe zdorov'e v garmonii s prirody!" (Contemporary health in Harmony With Nature!) and a menue of choices "O sebe," Novosti," "Katalog," Tseny," Apteka," Zakaz," and "Gazeta" ("About ourselves," "News," "Catalogue," Prices," Pharmacy," Orders, and Newspaper.") This firm was part of the Russian Medical Banner network. Accessed 6/8/2002.

The very name "Organica JSC" in Novokuznetsk, Kemerovo oblast', emphasized the theme of its Russian-language advertisement: "contemporary, high-quality preparations" sold albeit at low prices. Photographs displayed the factory, the pills and gelatin capsules, and machinery of the company. http://www.organica.kemerovo.su/ organica/ Accessed 6/8/2002.

27. ABOLmed Ltd announced that it "was founded on the 1st of April, 1998 in town [sic] of Vidnoye, located close to Moscow. On September 29th, 1998, the Company obtained the Federal License for production, storage and selling of medicaments and on 11th of November has produced the first vial of cefasolin sodium." ABOLmed's website stated that its manufacturing equipment was "supplied by Bausch+Stroebel—one of the leading manufacturers and suppliers of the equipment for the manufacturers of pharmaceutical products." The company produces first to third generation sephalosporin antibiotics. In one summer month in 2002 the company "increased the production volume from 150,000 to 2,000,000 vials per month." Simultaneously, "the Company specialists prepared the technical documentation and insured commercial introduction of Cefamandole, Cefotaxime and Ceftriaxone." Other antibiotics were on line in 2002. The company prided itself on the high quality of its antibiotics. There had been no claims against the company for the two years of its existence. The company offered "100 percent quality guarantee," "flexible discounts," and "favorable ready delivery conditions." In 2002 the company began constructing another plant in Novosibirsk. http://www.abolmed.ru/english/pages/company-engl.htm. Accessed 6/8/2002.

28. For example, Biokhimik boasted that for forty years it had been one of the largest producers of medical substances. It had a wide assortment, qualified personnel, high quality, many years of experience of working with our partners. . . .Today OAO makes more than sixty named medicinal preparations among them: antibiotics, antitumor substances, plasma replacement solutions…diuretic substances, preparations for anesthesia, and blood preservation . . . anti-inflammatory substances, sulfanilamide preparations, ointments. . . .The firm had won awards. These included the "Golden Globes" award in the United States. www.moris.ru/homepage/ pages/ Biohimik/ History.html. This website included a History of the Company, Price-list, Wares Distributed, and Orders. Accessed 6/8/2002.

29. Clair Murphy,"Red Army" virus to combat MRSA," BBC News, http://newsvote.bbc.co.uk/mpapps/pagetools/print/news.bbc.co.uk/2/hi/health/6943779.stm. Sent via e-mail by Dan Goldberg 8/14/2007.

30. http://www.protek.ru/en/suppliers.shtml, pp. 1-2. Accessed 9/6/2007.

31. http://www. Biopharmanalytica.com/index.asp. Accessed 9/6/2007.

32. "Onlain press-tsentr Kholinga otechestvennye lekarstva": http://www.hotlek.ru/about_comp.pjp;http://www.hotlek.ru/19042007.php; http://www.hotlek.ru/ management.php;http://www.hotlek.ru/about_plants.php; http://www.hotlek.ru/medlist.php; http://www.hotlek.ru/press.php; http://www.hotlek.ru/faq_zorex.php (In the Russian Zorex is spelled Zoreks); http://www.hotlek.ru/faq_phen.php; http://www.hotlek.ru/goldenidea.

php. All accessed 9/6/2007.

33. http://www.viferon.com/company.htm. Accessed 9/6/2007.

34. http://www.sotex.ru/ (Sotex is Soteks in the Russian). Accessed 9/6/2007.

35. http://www.veropharm.ru/articles/about.shtml. http://www.pharmacychain366.com/company/veropharm. Accessed 9/6/2007.

36.http://www.pharmacychain366.com/company/history;http://pharmacychain366.com/
company. Accessed 9/6/2007. Veropharm and pharmacychain36.6 appear to be affiliated.

37. http://www.pharstd.ru/ Accessed 9/6/2007.

38. http://www.biopharmanalytica.com/index/asp: 1. Accessed 9/6/2007.

Bibliography

Primary Sources

Archival Sources

Central State Historical Archive, Ufa, Republic of Bashkortostan (TsGIA, RB)

R. Fond 1203, opis 1, delo 17
R. Fond 1203, opis 1, delo 35
R. Fond 1203, opis 1, delo 33
R. Fond 1203, opis 1, delo 43
R. Fond, 1203, opis 2, delo 12
R. Fond 1203, opis 2, delo 14
R. Fond 1203, opis 2, delo 17

Russian State Archive of the Economy, Moscow (RGAE)

The Pharmaceutical Industry

Fond 8009, opis 2, delo 3 (1938).
Fond 8009, opis 2, delo 5
Fond 8009, opis 2, delo 7
Fond 8009, opis 2, delo 11
Fond 8009, opis 2, delo 13
Fond 8009, opis 2, delo 22.
Fond 8009, opis 2, delo 25.
Fond 8009, opis 2, delo 33
Fond 8009, opis 2, delo 34
Fond 8009, opis 2, delo 36
Fond 8009, opis 2, delo 38
Fond 8009, opis 2, delo 59
Fond 8009, opis 2, delo 126
Fond 8009, opis 2, delo 127
Fond 8009, opis 2, delo 129
Fond 8009, opis 2, delo 130
Fond 8009, opis 20, delo 176
Fond 8009, opis 20, delo 211

Soap Industry TEZhE

Fond 8551, opis 1, delo 5
Fond 8551, opis 1, delo 4

State Archive of the Russian Federation, Moscow (GARF):
Chief Pharmacy Administration

Fond A 482, opis 51, delo 34
Fond A 482, opis 51, delo 15
Fond A 482, op. 51, delo 42

United States of America, National Archives (NAUSA)
Bureau of Foreign and Domestic Commerce, U. S. Department of Commerce

RG 489, Box 82, 10,300
RG 489, Box 82, 10,700
RG 489, Box 82, 11,100
RG 151, 231, Box 1004

Books

Borodin, George. Red Surgeon (London: Museum Press, Limited, 1945).

Bradley, Ernestine. *The Way Home: A German Childhood, an American Life* (New York: Pantheon Books, 2005).

Genis, David E. *Meditsinskaia parazitologiia*, edition 2, rewritten and enlarged (Moscow: Meditsina, 1979).

Sigerist, Henry. *Medicine and Health in the Soviet Union* (New York: The Citadel Press, 1947).

———. *Socialized Medicine in the Soviet Union* (New York: W. W. Norton, 1937)

Tucker, Robert C. and Cohen. Stephen F., eds. *The Great Purge Trial* (New York: Grosset and Dunlap, 1965).

Reference Works

Khimicheskoe Delo v Rossii (Odessa: Tipografiia "Poriadok," 1913),

Smirnov, E. I., gen. ed., *Opyt sovetskoi meditsiny v Velikoi Otechestvannoi Voine, 1941-1945* (Moscow: Medgiz, 1950-1955) 35 volumes with publication dates between 1950 and 1955.

Brochures

Narkomzdrav SSSR, Glavnoe upravlenie khimiko-farmatsevticheskoi promyshlennosti: Zavod Akrikhin, *Bulletin' po obmenu opytom na pravakh rukopisi*, 1-2 (1940).

Narkomzdrav RSFSR, Upravlenie medico-farmatsevtich. Promyshlennosti "Medfarm-prom," *Informatsionnyi bulleten'*, no. 2 (1940).

Selected Journal Articles

(Most articles about the uses of medicinal botanicals and animal products are listed in Chapters 5 and 9 but are not repeated here.)

Anon. "Chto takoe antivirus voobshche i v chastnosti protivogrippoznyi antivirus," *Farmatsiia*, vol. 3, no. 9-10 (1940): 30-31.

Anon. "Death for 19 Asked at Russian Trial," *The New York Times* (Sunday, March 12, 1938).

Anon. From Our U.S. Correspondent. "War Medicine and Pharmacology in Russia," *The Australian Journal of Pharmacy*, vol. 24, March 30 (1943): 150.

Anon. "K istorii otkrytiia otechestvennogo penitsillina," *Antibiotiki i khimoterapiia*, vol. 39, no. 1 (1994): 13-32.

Anon. "Lemongrass Plants to Russia," *American Perfumer and Essential Oil Review*, vol. 47, no. 2 (February 1945): 51.

Anon. "Phage v. Staph," *Time*, vol. 37, no. 19 (May 12, 1941): 43.

Anon. "Russia Ships Coriander," *American Perfumer and Essential Oil Review*," vol. 47, no. 3 (March 1945): 44.

Anon. "Russian Essential Oils," *American Perfumer and Essential Oil Review*," vol. 47, no. 4 (April 1945): 46.

Anon. "65,000 Reich troops Move Into Austria," *The New York Times* (March 13, 1938): 1.

Anon. "Soviet War-Time Surgery," *Nature*, vol. 152 (December 25, 1943): 756.

Anon. "USSR Toilet Goods," *The American Perfumer and Essential Oil Review*, vol. 34, no. 2 (February, 1937): 72.

Anon. "U.S.S.R. Essential Oils," *The American Perfumer and Essential Oil Review*, vol. 47, no. 1 (January 1945): 44.

Astrakhantsev, P. I. "Pomoshch' VNIKhFI farmatsevticheskoi promyshlennosti v god otechestvennoi voiny," *Farmatsiia*, vol. 8, no. 4 (1945): 12-16.

Astrakhantsev, P. I. and Vasil'ev, S. M. "Molekuliarnoe soedinenie belogo streptotsida i urotopina (Strepturin)," *Farmatsiia*, vol. 3, no. 9-10 (1940): 24-28.

Babich, L. E. "Aptechnoe delo v zaparnykh oblastiakh Ukrainy," *Farmatsiia*, vol. 3, no. 11 (1940): 13-14.

Balezina, T. I. "K istorii polucheniia Z. V. Yermol'evoi penitsillina," *Antibiotiki i khimoterapiia*, vol. 43, no. 5 (1998): 7-9.

Baran, N. A. Mediko-Sanitarnoe obsluzhivanie sel'skogo naselenie v voennogo vremeni," *Sovetskoe zdravookhranenie* [no volume or edition number] (1943): 10-13.

Bauer, O. E. and Velik, M. A. "Nabliudeniia nad deistviem sukhogo dizenteriinogo bakteriofaga," *Voenno-sanitarnoe delo*, no. 9 (1941): 35.

Bergol'ts, M. Kh. "Galenovye preparaty v novykh izdaniiakh farmakopei (XII) i natsional'nogo formuliara (VII) SShA," *Farmatsiia*, vol. 8, no. 6 (1945): 36-39.

Borodkina, L. V. "Opyt primeniia preparata '805' v klinke legochnogo tuberkululeza," *Farmakologiia i toksikologiia*, vol. 6, no. 3 (1943): 15-17.

Bychkov, I. Ia. "O material'noi otvetstvennosti aptechnykh rabotnikov za konsul'tatsiia, *Farmatsiia*, vol. 8 (1945): 41-43.

Carling, E. Rock. "Medical and Surgical Achievement in the U.S.S.R. during the War," *Nature*, vol. 133, no. 3884 (April 8, 1944): 419-424.

Carling, Sir Ernest Rock. "Medical Mission to Moscow," *Inter-Allied Conferences of War Medicine: Unclassified Subjects,* Convened by the Royal Society of Medicine, (n. d.): 404-405.

Chetverikov, V. S. "Sanitarnoe delo v SSSR vo vremia period pervykh dvukh let voiny," *Gigiena i sanitariia*, vol. 8, no. 10 (1943): 31-38.

———. "Sarnitarnoe delo v SSSR vo vremia period pervykh dvukh let voiny," *Gigiena i sanitaria*, vol. 9. no. 4 (1944): 20-25.

Clouston, H. R. "Puerperal Fever or Scarlet Fever," *The Canadian Medical Association Journal* (1930): 705-707.

"Deistvitel'nost' sektsii farmakologii i toksikologii moskovskogo obshchestva fiziologov, farmakologov i biokhimikov po 21 dek. 1936 g. po 28 sent. 1938 g.," *Farmakologiia*, vol. 1, no. 2-3 (1938): 159-160.

Dmitriev, G. "Vse dlia nuzhd leningradskogo fronta," *Farmatsiia*, vol. 6, no. 1 (1943): 41-42.

Frenkel', Ia. A. "Zadachi sel'skikh vrachebnykh uchastkov v usloviiakh voennogo vremeni," *Fel'dsher i akusherka*, [no vol., no. no.] (1942): 36-38.

Gordon-Taylor, Gordon. "The Anglo-American-Canadian Surgical Mission to Russia, July, 1943," *The British Journal of Surgery*, vol. 31, no. 123 (January 1944): 205-207.

Graschenkov, Rrof. N. "Soviet Medicine in War-time," *South African Medical Journal*, vol. 17 (June 26, 1943): 185-187.

Halpern, Daniel, "Russian Medicine in Wartime," *Quarterly of the Chicago Medical School*, vol. 3 (1942-1943): 7-8 and 36-37.

Ivanova, V. "Analiz Sul'fidin No. 32," *Farmatsiia*, vol. 3, no. 9-10 (1940): 28-29.

Ivenskii, Ia. G. "Sbor i zagotovka lekarstvenno-tekhnicheskogo syr'ia v RSFSR v 1942 godu," *Farmatsiia*, vol. 6, no. 3 (1943): 8.

Iz otcheta farmakologicheskogo komiteta uchenogo meditsinskogo siveta NKZrava o rabote za 1943 g.," *Farmakologiia i toksikologiia*, vol. 7, no. 3 (1944): 3-11.

Kaganovich, Iu. Ia. "Medikamentoznoe snabzhenie v dni otechestvennoi voiny v Leningrade," *Farmatsiia*, vol. 8, no. 6 (1945): 14-16.

Kirsenko, V. K. "O techenie dizenterii u vaktsinirovannykh protivnee po Bezredka," *Voenno-sanitarnoe delo*, no. 8 (1940): 75-77.

Koifman, S. I. "Opyt lecheniia batsilliarnoi dizenterii bakteriofagom," *Voenno-Sanitarnoe delo*, no. 8 (1940): 72-73.

Kolesnikov, S. A. "Sovetskoe zdravookhranenie v dni otechestvennoi voiny," *Sovetskaia meditsina*, vol. 7, no. 7-8 (1943): 1-8.

Koten, Bernard. "Soviet Medicine in Wartime," *Hygeia* (American Medical Association), vol. 21 (1943): 268-270 and 280.

Lavrentiev, Professor. "Experimental Medicine in Russia in the War," *Journal of the American Medical Association* (Chicago), vol. 121 (February 6, 1943): 436-437.

Levinshtein, I. I. "O tekhminimume dlia aptechnykh rabotnikov," *Farmatsiia*, vol. 6, no. 2 (1943): 7-8.

Liebman, G. Ia. Uporiadochit' aptechnoe khoziastvo v evakogospitaliakh narkomzdrava Soiuza SSR, *Farmatsiia*, vol. 6, no. 1 (1943): 4-6.

Natradze, A. G. in "K istorii otkrytiia otechestvennogo penitsillina," *Antibiotiki i khimoterapiia*, vol. 39, no. 1 (1994): 21-22.

———. " O dal'neishem razvitii meditsinskoi promyshlennosti," *Farmatsiia*, vol. 8, no. 6 (1945): 1-7.

———. Zadachi khimiko-farmatsevticheskoi promyshlennosti v 1945 g.," *Farmatsiia*, vol. 8, no. 1 (1945):12-13.

Penfield, Wilder. "The British-American-Canadian Surgical Mission to the U.S.S.R.," *The Canadian Medical Association Journal*, vol. 49, no. 6, Toronto (December 1943): 455-461.

"Pervaia vsesoiuznaia konferentsiia farmakologov i toksikologov, 1-5 iunia 1937 g.," *Farmakologiia*, vol. 1, no. 1 (1938): 84-85.

Popov, G. "Osnovnye printsipy organizatsii mediko-sanitarnoi sluzhby naslennykh punktov i zadachi aptek i apteknykh predpriatii," *Farmatsiia i farmakologiia*, no. 1 (1938): 30-35.

Portugalov, S. O. "Opyt primeneniia penitsillina pri tiazhelykh formakh gnoino-septicheskoi infektsii," *Voenno- meditsinskii zhurnal* (1945): 29-37.

Ravikovich E. M. and Mayerman, O. E. "Materialy po epidemiologii difterii i skarlatiny v gody otechestvennoi voiny," *Zhurnal mikrobiologii, epidemiologii, i immunobiologii* (1945): 15-21.

Rossiiski, D. M. "Lekarstvennye sokrovisahcha SSSR," *Fel'dsher* (1943): 34-37.

Samokhin, G. I. Lechenie batsilliarmoi dizinterii sul'fidinom," *Voennaia meditsina Glubnogo Tyla*, Tashkent (1943) 567-571.

Sapezhinskaia, N. V. "K farmakolgii narodnolekarstvennykh rastenii," *Farmakologiia i toksikologiia*, vol. 4, no. 1 (1941): 5-9.

Scadding, J. G. "Comparative Effects of Sulphonamide Drugs in Mild Bacillary Dysentery," *The Lancet* (June 14, 1944): 784-786.

Shass, E. Iu. "Iz opyta RSFSR zagotovki lekarstvennykh rastenii v 1942 g.," *Farmatsiia*, vol. 6, no. 2 (1943): 42-43.

Siroko, A. L. "Novoe v bor'be s dizenteriei," *Voenno-sanitarnoe delo*, no. 10 (1940): 100-101.

Skvortsov, V. "Bor'ba s batsilliarnoi dizinteriei (Gemokolitami) v vesenne-letnii period," *Voenno-sanitarnoe delo*, no. 4 (1940): 22-24.

Smirnov, G. I. "Rabota tsentral'noi aptechnoi nauchno-issledovatel'skoi laboratorii GAPU RSFSR (TsANIL), *Farmatsiia*, vol. 6, no. 2 (1943): 9-14.

"Soobshchenie o rabote plenuma v vsesoiuznogo vitaminogo komiteta prokhodivshego v moskve s 11 X po 13 XII 1940," *Farmakologiia i toksikologiia*, vol. 4, no. 2 (1941): 79-80.

Sorokin, A. I. "Puty razvitiia farmatsevticheskoi promyshlennosti," *Farmatsiia*, vol. 3, no. 7-8 (1940): 9-10.

———. Zadachi aptechnogo khozaistva v 1943 godu," *Farmatsiia*, vol. 6, no. 1, (1943): 1-4.

Stolkin, I. G. "O rabote mestnoi farmatsevticheskoi promyshlennosti," *Farmatsiia* , vol. 1, no. 3 (1938): 35-37.

Travin, A. I. "Sinticheskii vitamin B1 (Tiamin)," *Farmakologiia i toksikologiia*, vol. 4, no. 1 (1940): 79-81.

Troitskii, "Predokhranitel'naia vaktsinatsiia protiv dizinterii," *Dostizheniia sovetskogo meditsiny*, no. 1 (1943): 84-96.

Vsesoiuznaia konferentsiia farmakologov i toksikologov, 1-5 iunia 1937 g.: Po dokladu ot VILAR: Sovremennnoe sostoianie i perspektivy osnoveniia lekarstvennogo syr'ia SSSR," *Farmakologiia*, vol. 1, no. 2-3 (1938): 173.

Yefimov, N. I. "K farmakologii preparata sul'fanilamidmetilpirimidina, ego natrievoi soli, '063'," *Farmakologiia i toksikologiia*, vol. 6, no. 1 (1943): 61-64.

Selected Interviews, 2006-2007

Binevich, Vladimir. Denver, CO.
Geltser, Samson. Denver, CO.
Genis, Dr. David. Denver, CO.
Geyman, Peter Abramovich. Denver, CO.
Khazieva, Tamara Nikolaevna. Ufa, Russia.
Kuznetsova, Maria Sergeevna. Ufa. Russia.

Secondary Sources

Books

Afanas'ev, V. K. et al. *Zhivi, "Akrikhin"!* (Staraia Kupavna, 1996).

Ascher, Abraham. *P. A. Stolypin: The Search for Stability in Late Imperial Russia* (Stanford: Stanford University Press, 2001).

Ascherson, Neal. *The Struggles for Poland* (New York : Random House, 1987).

Balitskii, K. P. *Lekarstevnnye rasteniia i rak* (Kiev: "Naukova dymka," 1982).

Ball, Alan M. *Russia's Last Capitalists: The NEPmen, 1921-1929* (Berkeley: University of California Press, 1987).

Barber, John and Dzeniskevich, Andrei, eds. *Life and Death in Besieged Leningrad, 1941-1944* (Palgrave Macmillan, 2005).

Broekmeyer, Marius. *Stalin, The Russians, and Their War* (Madison: University of Wisconsin Press, 2005).

Chandler, Alfred D. *Shaping the Industrial Century: The Remarkable Story of the Evolution of the Modern Chemical and Pharmaceutical Industries* (Cambridge, MA: Harvard university Press, 2005).

Conroy, Mary Schaeffer. *Emerging Democracy in Late Imperial Russia* (Boulder: University Press of Colorado, 1998).

———. *In Health and In Sickness: Pharmacy, Pharmacists and the Pharmaceutical Industry in Late Imperial, Early Soviet Russia* (East European Monographs, 1994).

———. *Peter Arkad'evich Stolypin: Practical Politics in Late Tsarist Russia* (Boulder: Westview Press, 1976).

———. *The Soviet Pharmaceutical Business During Its First Two Decades, 1917-1937* (Peter Lang, 2006).

Conquest, Robert. *Harvest of Sorrow: Soviet Collectivization and the Terror Famine* (New York: Oxford University Press, 1986).

Cottam, Kazimiera J. *Women in War and Resistance: Selected Biographies of Soviet Women Soldiers* (Nepean, Canada: New Military Publishing, 1998).

Dallin, David J. *Soviet Russia and the Far East* (New Haven: Yale University Press, 1948; reprint, Archon Books, 1971).

Dunstan, John. *Soviet Schooling in the Second World War* (Basingstoke: Macmillan Press, Ltd. And New York: St. Martin's Press).

Evans, Richard J. *The Third Reich in Power* (New York: The Penguin Press, 2005).

Esakov, V. D. and Levina, E. S. *Delo KR* (Moscow: Institute rossiiskoi istorii, 2001)

Fedorov, Boris G. *Petr Arkad'evich Stolypin* (Moscow: Rosspen, 2002).
Fitzpatrick, Sheila. *Stalin's Peasants: Resistance and Survival in the Russian Village After Collectivization* (new York: Oxford University Press, 1994).
Gatrell, Peter. *A Whole Empire Walking* (Bloomington: University of Indiana Press, 1999).
Getty, J. Arch and Manning, Roberta T., eds. *Stalinist Terror: New Perspectives* (Cambridge: Cambridge University Press, 1993).
Gladkikh, P. F. and Loktev, A. E. *Sluzba zdorov'ia v Velikoi Otechestvennoi Voine, 1954-1945* (St. Petersburg: Dmitrii Bulanin, 2005).
Glantz, David M. *Colossus Reborn: The Red Army at War, 1941-1943* (University Press of Kansas, 2005).
Glantz, David M. and House, Jonathan M. *The Battle of Kursk* (Lawrence: University Press of Kansas, 1999).
Gregory, Paul R. *Before Command: An Economic History of Russia from Emancipation to the First Five-Year Plan* (Princeton: Princeton University Press, 1994).
Grob, Gerald N. *The Deadly Truth: A History of Disease in America* (Cambridge, MA: Harvard University press, 2002).
Haller, John. *Medical Protestants: The Eclectics in American Medicine, 1825-1939* (Carbondale: Southern Illinois University Press, 1994).
Harrison, Mark. *Accounting for War: Soviet production, employment and the defense burden, 1940-1945* (Cambridge: Cambridge University press, 1996).
Harcave, Sidney. *Count Witte and the Twilight of Imperial Russia: A Biography* (Armonk: M. E. Sharpe, 2004).
Hessler, Julie. *A Social History of Soviet Trade* (Princeton: Princeton University Press, 2004).
Holloway, David. *Stalin and the Bomb* (New Haven: Yale University Press, 1994).
Ivanova, Galina Mikhailovna. *Labor Camp Socialism*. Raleigh, Donald J., ed; Flath, Carol, trans. (Armonk, N. Y.: M. E. Sharpe, 2000).
Ivashin, D. S. et al. *Spravochnik po zagotovkam lekarstvennykh rastenii* (Kiev: "Urozhai," 1983).
Kaser, Michael. *Health Care in the Soviet Union* (London: Croom Helm, 1979).
Khaziev, Rustem A., ed. *Bubliki dlia respubliki* (Ufa: Bashkir State University, 2005).
Kingston-Mann, Ester and Mixter, Timothy, eds. *Peasant Economy, Culture, and Politics of European Russia, 1800-1921* (Princeton: Princeton University press, 1991).
Klevniuk, Oleg V. *The History of the Gulag: From Collectivization to the Great Terror* (New Haven: Yale University Press, 2004).
Kobrak, Christopher. *National Cultures and International Competition: The Experience of Schering AG, 1851-1950* (Cambridge: Cambridge University Press, 2002).
Krementsov, Nikolai. *The Cure* (Chicago: Chicago University Press, 2002).
Lesch, John E. *The First Miracle Drugs: How the Sulfa Drugs Transformed Medicine* (Oxford University Press, 2007).
Levin, Moishe. *Russian Peasants and Soviet Power: A Study of Collectivization* (New York: W.W. Norton and Company, 1968).
Madison, James H. *Eli Lilly: A Life, 1885-1977* (Indianapolis: Indiana Historical Society, 1989).
Merridale, Catherine. *Ivan's war: Life and Death in the Red Army, 1939-1945* (New York: Metropolitan Books, Henry Holt and Company, 2006).
McCauley, Martin. *The Soviet Union Since 1917* (London: Longman, 1983)

Michaels, Paula. *Curative Powers: Medicine and Empire in Stalin's Central Asia* (Pittsburgh: University of Pittsburgh Press, 2003).

Misiunas, Romuald and Taagpera, Rein. *The Baltic States: Years of Dependence, 1940-1990* (Los Angeles and Berkeley: University of California Press, 1993).

Murphy, David E. *What Stalin Knew: The Enigma of Barbarossa* (New Haven: Yale University Press, 2005).

Natradze, A. G. *Ocherk razvitiia khmiko-farmatsevticheskoi promyshlennosti SSSR* (Moscow: Izdatel'stvo "Meditsina," 1979).

P. A. Stolypin: Grani talanta politika (Moscow: Rosspen, 2006).

Reuben, Bryan G. and Wittcoff, *Harold A. Pharmaceutical Chemicals in Perspective* (New York: John Wiley and Sons, 1989).

Rodengen, Jeffrey L. *The Legend of Pfizer* (Fort Lauderdale, Fl: Write Stuff Syndicate, Inc., 1998).

Shabad, Steven; Viola, Lynne; Danilov, V. P. ; Ivnitskii, A. eds. *The War Against the Peasantry, 1927-1930: The Tragedy of the Soviet Countryside*, Vol. 1 (New Haven: Yale University Press, 2005).

Siatinia, M. Ia. *Istoriia farmatsii* (L'viv, 2002).

Solomon, Peter H. *Soviet Criminal Justice Under Stalin* (Cambridge University Press, 1996).

Solomon, Susan Gross, ed., *Doing Medicine Together: Germany and Russia between the Wars* (Toronto: University of Toronto Press, 2006).

Stone, David R. *Hammer and Rifle: The Militarization of the Soviet Union 1926-1933* (Lawrence: University press of Kansas, 2000).

Thurston, Robert W. and Bonwetsch, Bernd, eds. *The People's War: Responses to World War II in the Soviet Union* (Champaign: University of Illinois Press, 2000).

Tucker, Robert C. *Stalin As a Revolutionary, 1879-1929* (New York: W. W. Norton, 1974).

———. *Stalin In Power* (New York: W. W. Norton, 1990).

Turova, A. D. and Sapozhnikova, E. N. *Lekarstvennye rasteniia SSSR i ikh primenenie* (Moscow: Izdatel'stvo "Meditsina," 1984).

Viola, Lynne. *Peasant Rebels Under Stalin: Collectivization and the Culture of Peasant Resistance* (New York: Oxford University Press, 1999).

Vishnevskii, Anatoli. *Demograficheskaia modernizatsiia Rossii, 1900-2000* (Novoe izdatel'stvo, 2006).

Williams, Stephen F. *Liberal Reform in an Illiberal Regime: The Creation of Private Property in Russia, 1906-1915* (Stanford: Hoover Institution Press, 2006).

Worthen, Dennis B. *Pharmacy in World War II* (Binghamton: Haworth Press, 2004).

Zgadan, M. M. *Apteka v lesu* (Simferopol': Izdatel'stvo "Tavriia," 1979).

Zubkova, Elena. *Russia After the War* (Armonk, NY: M. E. Sharpe, 1998).

Chapters

Abelshauser, Werner. "Germany: guns, butter, and economic miracles," in Harrison, Mark, ed. *The Economics of World War II: Six great powers in international comparison* (Cambridge: Cambridge University Press, 1998): 122-176.

Cherepenina, Nadezhda. "The Demographic Situation and Healthcare on the Eve of War," in Barber and Dzeniskevich, eds. *Life and Death in Besieged Leningrad, 1941-1944*: 13-27.

Eckart, Wolfgang. "'Creating Confidence': Heinz Zeiss as a Traveler in the Soviet Union, 1921-1932," in Solomon, ed., *Doing Medicine Together: Germany and Russia Between the Wars*: 199-239.

Frolov, Mikhail. "Evacuation from Leningrad to Kostroma in 1941-42," In Barber and Dzeniskevich, eds. *Life and Death in Besieged Leningrad, 1941-1944*: 71-85.

Gartenschläger, Uwe. "Living and Surviving in Occupied Minsk," in Thurston, Robert W. and Bonwetsch, Bernd, eds. *The People's War*: 13-28.

Lesch, John E. "The Discovery of M&B 693 (Sulfapyridine)," in Higby, Gregory and Stroud, Elaine C., eds. *The Inside Story of Medicines* (Madison, WI: American Institute for the History of Pharmacy, 1997): 101-114.

Manning, Roberta T. "The Soviet Economic Crisis of 1936-1940 and the Great Purges," in Getty, Arch and Manning Roberta T., eds., *Stalinist Terror: New Perspectives* (Cambridge University Press, 1993): 113-141.

Nolte, Hans-Heinrich. "Destruction and Resistance: The Jewish Shtetl of Slonim, 1941-44," in Thurston, Robert W. and Bonwetsch, Bernd, eds. *The People's War*: 29-53.

Porter, Thomas and Gleason, William. The Zemstvo and The Transformation of Russian Society," in Conroy, Mary Schaeffer, ed. *Emerging Democracy in Late Imperial Russia* : 60-87.

Ramer, Samuel C. "Traditional Healers and Peasant Culture in Russia, 1861-1917," in Kingston-Mann, Esther and Mixter, Timothy, eds. *Peasant Economy, Culture, and Politics in European Russia, 1800-1921* : 207-232.

Reidl, Renate A. "A Brief History of the Pharmaceutical Industry in Basel," in Libenau, Jonathan; Higby, Gregory; and Stroud, Elaine C. eds., *Pill Peddlers: Essays on the History of the Phamaceutical Industry* (Madison, WI: American Institute of the History of Pharmacy, 1990): 49-72.

Rimmington, Anthony. "The Soviet Union's Offensive Program," in Wright, Susan, ed. *Biological Warfare and Disarmament: New Problems/New Perspectives* (Lanham: Rowman & Littlefield, 2002): 103-148.

Journal Articles, Printed

Adams, David P. "Wartime Bureaucracy and Penicillin Allocation: The Committee on Chemotherapeutic and Other Agents," *Journal of the History of Medicine and Allied Sciences*, vol. 44 (1989): 196-217.

Conroy, Mary Schaeffer. "Malaria in Late Tsarist Russia," *Bulletin of the History of Medicine*, vol. 56, no.1 (1982): 41-55.

———. "Pharmacy in Soviet Russia before the Great Patriotic War (1941-1945)," *Pharmacy in History*, vol. 40, no. 1 (1998): 3-24.

———. "The Soviet Pharmaceutical Industry and Dispensing, 1945-1953," *Europe-Asia Studies*, vol. 56, no. 7 (2004): 963-991.

Dixon, Bernard. "Sulfa's True Significance," *Microbe*, vol. 1, no. 11, 2006, pp. 500-501.

Harrison, Mark. "Counting Soviet Deaths in the Great Patriotic War: Comment," *Europe-Asia Studies*, vol. 55, no. 6 (2003): 939-944.

Haynes, Michael. "Clarifying Excess Deaths and Actual War Deaths in the Soviet Union During World War II: A Reply," *Europe-Asia Studies*, vol. 55, no. 6 (2003): 945-947.

———. "Counting Soviet War Deaths in the Great Patriotic War: A Note," *Europe-Asia Studies*, vol. 55, no. 2 (2003): 303-309.

Latko, T. L. and Petrishche, T[at'iana] L. [Medical Institute of Vitebsk] "Kollaboratsionizm meditsinskhikh rabotnikov v period velikoi otechestvennoi voiny," Materialy 10-i Respiblikanskoi konferentsii po istorii meditsiny i zdravookhraneniia, Minsk, September 23, 2004 (Minsk:RNMB, 2004): 22-23.

Neushul, Peter. "Science, Government, and the Mass-Production of Penicillin," *The Journal of the History of Medicine and Allied Sciences, Inc.*, vol. 48 (1993): 371-395.

Parascandola, John. "John Mahoney and the Introduction of Penicillin to Treat Syphilis," *Pharmacy in History*, vol. 43, no. 1 (2001): 3-13.

Petrishche, Tat'iana. [Medical Institute, Vitebsk, Belarus] "Belmedtorg i lekarstvennoe obespechenie naseleniia BSSR v 1920-e gody," *Vitebsk gosudarstvennyi meditsinskii universitet.* (E-mailed to me by the author, October 13, 2006).

———. "Motivatsionnye mekhanizmy upravleniia farmatsevticheskim personalom v usloviiakh novoi ekonomicheskom politiki (1920-e gg.)," "Legalizatsiia meditsinskoi i farmatsevticheskoi deiatel'nosti kak element gosudarstvennoi politiki v zdravookhranenii v period NEP," abstract from *Materialy IV s"ezda sotsial-gigienistov i organizatorov zdravookhraneniia Respibliki Belarus'*, November 30-December 1, 2000 g. (Minsk, 2000): 387-388.

———. "Nekotorye aspekty pravovogo regulirovaniia farmatsevticheskoi deiatel'nosti v period novoi ekonomicheskoi politiki," (no. journal listed; e-mailed to me by the author February, March , 2006)

Salo, Viktor Matveevich. "Deiatel'nost'aptechnykh upravlenii v predvoinyi period (1936-1940 gg.)," *Farmatsiia*, vol. 28 (1979): 17.

———. "Iz istorii farmatsevtiocheskoi sluzhbu v gody velikoi otechestvennoi voiny," *Farmatsiia*, vol. 34, no. 2 (1985): 9.

Scoutaris, Milton. "'Moldy Mary' and the Illinois Fruit and Vegetable Company," *Pharmacy in History*, vol. 38, no. 4 (1996): 175-177.

Worthen, Dennis B."Selective Service and the Pharmacist: Necessary Men in WWII," vol. 43, no. 4 (2001): 124-133.

———. "The National Quinine Pool: When Quinine Went to War," *Pharmacy in History*, vol. 38, no. 3 (1996): 143-147.

Yershova, El'vira, "Sem'ia v vospominaniiakh rodnykh," from "XX vek v sud'bakh rossiiskoi provintsial'noi sem'i," in *INFOR, "Veter Vremeni": Materialy k pokolennym rospisiam rossiiskikh rodov Ural*, No. 1, June 2005): 7-37.

Electronic Articles (On the Internet)

ABOL. http:// www.abolmed.ru/english/pages/company-engl.htm.

(About Dick, George and Gladys). http:// www. Bookrags.com/Scarlet fever: 1-11.

Anon., "American Biogenic Sciences Negotiates L. Anthrax and Smallpox Vaccine Agreement," November 26, 2001, MABA Recent Stock News: Investing MSN Money.

Anon., "2/3 of Russia's Pharmaceutical enterprises Not in Line With Global Demands," *Kommersant*, March 23, 2007, www.kommersant.com.
Answers.com: Pneumonia: 1-33
Biokhimik. http://www.moris.ru/homepage/pages/Biohimik/Hitosy.html.
Edlow, Jonathan A. et al. "Tick-borne Disease, Tularemia," http://www.emedicine.com/emerg/topic591/
"Evalar." www.evalar.ru.
Farmakon OAO, History and Products of, http://www.farmacon.ru/rus/history.htm; contact, ibid., sirye, ibid.
Gaufberg, Dr. Slava V. "Emergency Medicine in Russia" http://www.emedicine/emerg/topic727.html.
Hagen. Steven. "New Approach Could Lower antibiotic requirements by 50 times," SCI Press Office, Chemistry and Industry, http://chemind.org
"Illinois Department of Public Health: Health Beat," http://www.idph.state.il.us/public/hb/ybtulare.htm.
Istoriia sanitarnykh avtomobilei Rossii I SSSR 1941-1945, http://ambulences.ru/history_rus_41.shtml.
Isupov, V. A. "Demograficheskoe 'chudo': sokrashchenie detskoi smertnosti v Sibiri v 1943-1945 g.g.," Elektronnyi zhurnal Sibirskaia zaimka, no. 7, 2002, www.zaimka.ru_2002/isupov_mortality.
Kiefer, David M. "Miracle Medicines," *Chemical Chronicles*, vol. 10, no. 6 (2001): 59-60. http://pubs.acs.org/subscribe/jounrals/tcaw/10/i06/html/06chemch.html.
Organica JSC. http://www.organica.kemerovo.su/organica/
Pediatric Advisor 2006.2: Pneumonia Admission information and Discharge Instructions, http://www.med.umich.edu/1libr/pa/pa_dpneumon_hhg.htm.
http://www.protek.ru/en/suppliers.shtml : 1-2.
Roberts, Michelle. "What caused Gwyneth's Spots," BBC News Online Health Staff, 2 pages.
Ufavita: Ufimskii vitaminskii zavod. http://www.ufaviota.ru (copyright 2000).
"What are Lytic Bacteriophages?" in Phage Biotech, Ltd., "Phage Therapy," http://www.phage-biotech.com/links.html.
"What is Cupping Therapy," http://www.chinajnbook.com/cupping/into.htm, 2 pages.

Dissertations and Manuscripts

Burton, Christopher. Medical Welfare during Late Stalinism: A Study of Doctors and the Soviet health System, 1845-1953 (University of Chicago: Ph. D. Dissertation, 2000).
Geltser, Samson. "Moia sem'ia vo vremia 1941-45 godov," sent in an e-mail communiqué to the author (September 20, 2006).

Index

"About Responsibility for Putting Out Poor-Quality Products" (1940), 62
Academy of Sciences, 96
Acetyl sulfapyridine, 129
Acetylcholine, 98
Aconite root, 119
Aconitine, 93, 94
Aconitum Anthora L., 95
Aconitum Tianschanicum F., 95
Actinomycin, 55, 71n58
Adalin, 78
Adonilen, 191
Adova, Anna Nikolaevna, 164
Adrenalin, 65, 117, 122, 124, 208; production of, 161
Advertisements, 71n50, 78, 79, 217
A. E. Mullen American Perfume Laboratories, 28
Agaev, 30, 36n69
Akrikhin, 18, 59, 60, 61, 63, 82, 83, 126, 135, 217; development of, 143n117; losses of, 134; production of, 73n105, 164; shortage of, 184, 210; using, 117, 179, 183, 188
Akrikhin Factory, 18, 19, 25, 58-59, 60, 62, 65, 153, 167; *brak* at, 134; contamination of, 63; evacuation of, 121; losses at, 134; prizes for, 166; problems at, 124, 145n166; production at, 121, 122, 123, 124, 127, 133; report by, 63; Shop No. 1, 129; success for, 216; war and, 119, 121
Alexander Leaves, 97
Alimentary dystrophy, 117
Alkaloid Factory, 19, 21, 24, 59, 62, 92, 126, 142n117, 145n166; accident at, 123; evacuation of, 120-121; prizes for, 166; production at, 126, 133; war and, 119, 121
Alkaloid of opium, 61, 78, 96, 124
All-Russian Institute of Plant Production, lobelia and, 94
All-Russian Office of the Union of Medicinal Plants, 97
All-Union Food Institute, 54
All-Union Hygiene and Sanitation Institute (VGSI), 207
All-Union Institute for Experimental Medicine, 54, 132, 161
All-Union Institute of Medicinal and Aromatic Botanicals (VILAR), 20, 30, 94, 120
All-Union Medicinal Plant Trust (Lekrastrest), 165, 205, 207
All-Union Ministry of Health, 78
All-Union Scientific-Research Chemical-Pharmaceutical Institute (VNIKhFI), 30, 54, 56, 91, 95, 96, 142-143n117; Soviet Aconitine and,94; war and, 119-120
All-Union Vitamin Committee, 52
All-Union Vitamin Institute, 54

Allakhverdibekov, G. D., 95-96
Allied Products Plant, 28
Allopathic practitioners, 89, 93
Aloe, 97, 201
Alternative medicine, 9, 10, 210
Ambrin, 137
Ambulances, 6, 40-41
American Perfumer and Essential Oil Review, The: on essential oil, 168; on lemongrass oil, 168; on perfume production, 167; on soap production, 25; on Zemchuzhina, 28
American Red Cross, Russian War Relief and, 158
Ammargen, 78
Ammonia, 124
Amoxicillin, 217
Amtorg Trading Company, 28, 90
Amur Adonis, 96
Anabasis, 92, 102n15
Anabazin, 60
Analgesics, 19, 180, 184
Analgin, 54, 58
Ancistrodon Blomhofii ussuriensis s Emelianoff, venom from, 97
Anemia, combating, 129
Anestezin, 24, 60
Anesthetics, 2, 3, 18, 19, 110, 124, 137, 148, 184; research on, 92; shortage of, 147, 152, 180, 210
Angiozel, 217
Anopheles mosquito, malaria and, 113, 116
Anthrax, vaccine for, 115
Antibiotics, vii, 14n29, 100, 132, 217, 220n27; resistance to, 11; using, 10
Antidysentery serum, 19
Antiepidemic Administration, 194
Antigen, 148
Antimalarials, 2, 21, 90, 188
Antipyrine, 63, 143n124, 170n27; development of, 143n117; medical/technical, 64; shortage of, 153
Anti-reticular cytotoxic serum, 169n3, 209, 210
Anti-Semitism, 7, 17, 176
Antiseptics, 2, 18, 56, 116, 125; availability of, 193; production of, 19, 24; shortage of, 21, 148
Antitoxins, 1, 3, 49-53, 115, 118; availability of, 152; production of, viii, 5, 6, 19, 45, 115, 200; research on, 90; shortage of, 2, 6, 47, 49, 85
Antivenereals, 118
Apteka, 29, 78, 79, 182, 185, 193, 201
Apteka No. 1, 216, 219n22
Apteka Tax, 214
Aptekarskie magaziny, 75, 77
Aptekoupravleniia, 14n14, 19, 20, 21, 136
Aremkuz factory, 40
Arrowsmith (Lewis), 100
Arsenoxide, 118
Arsphenamine, 118
Asafetida, 97
Ascetylcholine, 92
Ascorbic acid, 122, 123, 143n117, 204
Asparagines, 100
Aspirin, vii, 23, 60, 61, 66, 125, 127, 152, 194; availability of, 186, 202; colds and, 82; lack of, 179; production of, 164; shortage of, 68, 185, 188, 210; using, 184, 185
Asthma, vii, 2, 78, 88n46, 185; treatment for, 212n50
Atabrine, 90, 142n115, 164, 204
Atofan, 78
Atropine, 92, 98, 117
Australian Journal of Pharmacy, The, 150, 151
Autoclaves, 51, 81, 157
Azerbaijan Medical Institute, 95

Bacteria, viii, 48, 53, 151
Bactericides, 100, 101, 132
Bacteriophages, 3, 14n29, 47, 49-53, 69n21, 115, 150; dysentery and, 46, 99; faith in, 99; infections and, 100; lytic, 98;

production of, viii, 19, 50; research on, 56; shortage of, 6, 49, 50; using, viii, 10, 11
Bagdasarov, Professor, 147
Bakteriotsid, 54
Balezina, T. I., 130
Bandages, 42, 164, 193
Bandaging factories, problems for, 155
Bandaging Materials Factory, *brak* at, 134
Baran, N. A., 189
Barium, 81, 112, 193
Bashnarkomzdrav, 50
Bathhouses, 182, 189; problems with, 116, 180; using, 116, 184, 201, 202
Bausch+Stroebl, 220n27
Bayer, 53, 76
Bekdamirov, 30, 36n69
Belladonna, 90, 93, 117, 119, 206, 207; shortage of, 204, 211n17
Belmedtorg, 20, 164
Benzal'degid, 56
Benzoic soda, 21, 58
Benzosul'fo chloride, 64, 73nn110, 111
Benzyldenzoate, 117
Berezicheskii Glass Factory, shortages at, 165
Bezrodnyi, Director, 57
Binevich, Vladimir, 32n4
Biokhimik, 217, 220n28
Biokhinol, 60, 153, 170n27, 193
Biological weapons, 5, 32n10, 45, 53, 68n3, 112, 113, 139n24; production of, 18
Biologicals, 161, 208-209
Biomedicine, 9
Biopharm Analytica, 217, 218
Bismuth, 124, 164, 170n27; production of, 24; shortage of, 193
Bisulfate, 23, 33n31
Black market, 14n14, 176, 180, 181
Blood plasma, freezing, 149, 150
Blood transfusions, 40, 150, 158; blood for, 148, 151; organization of, 147; shock after, 149; Soviet system of, 149
Bogomolets, Alexander Alexandrovich, 147, 148, 210; anti-reticular cytotoxic serum by, 169n3, 209
Boichuk, Director, 50, 51
Bol'shoi Theater, 137, 186
Botanicals: availability of, 202; cancer and, 216; colds and, 82; collection of, 91, 97, 205, 206; concentration on, 209; foreign suppliers of, 204; plan for, 206; promotion of, 204-208; researching, 200; shortage of, 204, 206-207; using, 82, 89, 90-92, 185, 199, 216
Botkin's disease, 84
Bradley, Ernestine, 11-12, 152
Brak, 70n26, 127, 160, 216; criticism of, 213; fines for, 167; problems with, 24, 61-62, 63, 66, 134, 135, 157, 166, 194
Braz, G. I., 142n117
British-American-Canadian Surgical Mission, 147
Brodsky, M. G., 167
Bromine, 24, 117
Bromural, 61, 153, 170n27
Bryntsalov, Vladimir, 216, 219n22
Budagov, G. S., 166
Bukharin, Nikolai, 17, 67
Bukin, Professor: penicillin and, 133

Cabot, Hugh, 151
Caffeine, 56, 60, 124, 127, 128, 159, 193, 194; shortage of, 81, 204
Caffeine Factory, 30, 120
Calcium chloride, 78, 118, 124, 170n27, 191
Camphor, 58, 72n74, 93, 124, 167, 193; synthetic, 168
Cancer, 100-101, 209, 216
Cardio preparations, 217
Carling, Ernest Rock: on surgery, 149
Carter, Professor, 158
Castor oil, 29, 82

Cathartics, 207
Central Archive (Ministry of Defense), 125, 155, 158
Central Committee (Ukrainian Communist Party [Bolshevik]), 22
Central Credit Bank, 135-136
Central Institute of Experimental Medicine, 99, 148
Central Pharmaceutical Packaging, 191
Central Pharmaceutical Scientific Research Laboratory (TsANIL), 193
Central Pharmacy Warehouse, 191
Centralization, 30, 65, 213, 214, 216, 218
Chagall, Marc, 84
Chamomile, 82, 97, 201, 206
Chandler, Alfred D.: on pharmaceutical companies, 5
Chapochnikova, Ludmilla, 28
Charles Pfizer and Co., Inc., 129, 130, 144n136
Chemical Pharmaceutical Institute, Sul'fidin and, 66
Chemical-Pharmaceutical Trading industry, 30
Chemical warfare, 52, 70n40
Chemotherapy, 10, 13n6, 53; replacing, 89; shortage of, 150
Chereda, 93, 206, 211n26
Chesotka, 182
Chetverikov, V. S., 48, 111, 114
Chief Chemical Trading industry, 30
Chief Pharmaceutical Administration, 42, 164, 192, 205; decentralization and, 214; reports of, 158
Chimkent Dzerzhinskii Factory, 60, 123, 128
Chloral hydrate, 117, 170n27
Chloramine, 24, 33n32, 116, 141n79, 193
Chlorethyl, 42, 124, 137
Chloretin, 61, 127
Chloride, 116, 193
Chlorine, 47, 187, 194, 204
Chloroform, 60, 61, 70n40, 137; shortage of, 193, 204
Cholera, 19, 45, 149; epidemic of, 131; protecting against, 150; vaccine for, 115
Churchill, Winston, 129
Cinchona, 93, 97
Clouston, H. R.: scarlatina antitoxin and, 87n25
Cocaine, shortage of, 81, 193
Codeine, 124, 126, 164
Coghill, Roger: penicillin and, 142n115
Collectivization, 8, 67, 88nn47, 48
Colloid infusine, 148
Colon blockages, treating, 82
Commercial Bank, 59
Commission on Collecting Useful Plants, brochures by, 205
Committee on Evacuation, 120
Common colds, 82, 131, 182, 184
Communist Party, Jews and, 176
Conservation Board, 204
Constitution of 1936, 67
Construction Trust, 58
Coriander, 168
Cosmetics, 25, 27, 28, 29
Costs, 67, 215
Cotton, availability of, 193
Council of Labor and Defense (STO), 59
Cupping, 82, 89, 101n2, 187
Currie, James, 129, 144n136
Cytisin, 92, 93

Dallin, David J., 32n8, 39
Darmin, 126
Daucua carota, 96
DDT, vii, 117, 129, 140n67, 183; approval of, 116, 140n57
Dead Souls (Gogol), 29
Deadly Truth, The (Grob), 2
Deaths, 110, 151, 138n6; childhood, 13n6; wartime, 1, 46. *See also* Mortality
Decentralization, 12, 136, 216, 218
Demerol, 54

Denikin, Anton, 67
Dental facilities, 154, 155, 184, 189
Dermatitis, 114
Detergents, 7, 46
Deutsche Rotawerk, 54
Diarrhea, 45, 137, 182
Dichloramin, 62, 64
Dichloritan, 64, 143n124
Dick, George and Gladys: antitoxin by, 80
Diet: inadequate, 183, 184; starvation, 48
Diethilamine, 126, 134
Digaleneo, 60
Digitalis, 82, 202
Dikain, 110
Dikhlorakridin, 126, 134
Dikkerman, Director: criticism of, 66
Dikorastushchie lekarstvennye rastenye Bashkirskoi ASSR (Kotov and Fialkov), 205
Diphenilamine, 116
Diphtheria, 6, 19, 116; antitoxin for, 49, 50, 52, 115; decline in, 4, 52; outbreak of, 47; serum for, 69-70n22
Diseases: deaths from, 138n6; susceptibility to, 180; wartime, 110-115, 153, 175, 177
Disinfectants, 2, 3, 5, 7, 22, 29, 48, 89, 116, 125, 187, availability of, 193; pre-packaged, 76; production of, 6, 19; shortage of, 4, 21, 47, 100, 113, 147, 148, 181; using, 115
Disinfecting chambers, 115, 116, 157, 180, 183, 189
Disinfecting stations, 116, 187
Disinfectors, 40, 187
Distribution, 30, 45, 66, 153, 163, 166; improving, 11; problems with, 4, 19, 22, 23, 40, 57, 81, 216, 217
Disul'fan, 129
Diuretin, 61, 137, 164
Divaccine, 49, 69n21; losses of, 70n26; production of, 19
Dizulon, 129
Dmitrieva, Lida, 122
Dnepropetrovsk Pharmaceutical Institute, 96
Dochez, Alphonse: antitoxin by, 80
Domagk, Gerhard, 48, 53
Donovan, Charles: leishmaniasis and, 140n67
Dorogomilovskii Chemical-Pharmaceutical Factory, 18
Dovers Powders, 137
Drug stores, 191, 192; medicines at, 205; per capita, 76; problems with, 75, 77, 78, 79; wartime, 204
Dubnin, Comrade, 190
Duquesnel, aconitine and, 94
Dushitsa, 200
Dysentery, 5, 6, 55, 113; amoebic, 45-46; antitoxin for, 19; bacillary, 98, 99; bacteriophages and, 46, 99, 117; combating, 33n32, 47, 116, 117, 129, 150; deaths from, 110; incidence of, 46, 111, 180; outbreak of, 21, 22, 24, 46; sulfa drugs and, 98-99, 117, 118; vaccine for, 50, 69n21, 70n22, 115; winter-spring, 47
Dzerzhinsk Railway, 154
Dzerzhinskii Factory, 19-20, 60, 120-121, 126, 128, 161, 165; materials at, 124; production at, 123; war and, 119

Eau de cologne, 25, 28
Economic system, criticism of, 11, 216
Eczema, 94, 114, 118
Eighteenth Party Congress, 31
Elemelakh, Nadezhda: recollections of, 186
Eli Lilly, 55
Eliava Institute, 217
Encephalitis, 131
Endocrine and Vitamin Factory, 165,

166-167; boiler system for, 153; losses at, 135; production at, 65, 126, 127; war and, 119, 121-122
Endocrine Factory, 19, 21, 30, 59, 62; penicillin from, 131
Endocrine products, 131, 208, 209
Enteritis, treating, 137
Enterocolitis, treating, 137
Ephedrine, 126
Epidemics, 6, 8, 176, 180; preventing, 128
Erell, Dr.: bacteriophages/dysentery and, 99
Ergot of rye, 119
Essential oils, production of, 167, 168
Ether, 27, 81, 92; narcotic, 24, 123; vinyl, 150
Ethnomedicine, 9
Europe-Asia Studies, 216
Evacuation, 186; problems with, 121, 122; routes/diseases on, 180
Evacuation Commission, 181
Evacuation hospitals, 158; botanicals/popular remedies at, 204
Evacuees, 175, 179-186; traditional medicines and, 201-202
Evans, Richard J., 53
Eyeglasses, 157, 160, 191, 194

Factory No. 1: 66
Factory No. 3: 19, 167
Factory No. 4: 19, 157
Factory No. 8: 40
Factory No. 9: 208
Factory No. 13, penicillin from, 131
Factory No. 17: 167
Factory No. 35: 121, 122, 165; production from, 133-134
Factory No. 36: 121, 122, 165; prizes for, 166
Factory No. 37: 121, 122, 123, 127, 136, 167; prizes for, 166; production at, 134, 135; transformer for, 153
Factory No. 38: 121, 122, 143n124; prizes for, 166; production at, 123
Factory No. 39: 121, 127; losses at, 135; materials/equipment for, 122; production at, 135
Factory No. 40: 142-143nn117; penicillin from, 131; prizes for, 166
Factory of Artificial Teeth, 20; relocation of, 121; war and, 120
Factory of Medical Preparations, 66
Factory of the Fourteenth Anniversary of October, 154, 155
Fal'kovich, Doctor, 55
Falkovich, Esfir', 82, 92, 207
Famine, 3, 22
Farmakologiia i toksikologiia, 31, 52, 92, 96
Farmakon Factory, 19, 59, 61, 67, 165; advertising by, 217; boiler system for, 153; problems for, 57, 58; production by, 121; war and, 119
Farmatsiia, 54; advertisements in, 79; on awards, 166-167; Sorokin in, 80; on Stalin, 30-31, 67
Farmatsiia i farmakologiia, 18, 54
Farmkhimprom Georgia, 60
Farmkhimprom Narkomzdrava Gruzinskoi SSR, 59
Farmstandart, 218
Farmzavod, 20
Febrifuges, 2, 19, 180
Fel'dman, I. Kh.: Akrikhin and, 143n117
Fel'dshers, 82-83, 178, 182, 188, 200, 202, 207; seminars for, 189
Fenamin, 54, 170n53
Fenetidin, 126
Fenotiazin, 60
Feoktistov, A. E.: venom and, 97
Ferrein, Vladimir Karlovich, 219n22
Ferrein Factory, 19, 30, 97, 104n47, 131, 219n22; brochures by, 216
Ferrein pharmacy, 76, 191
Ferroaskorbin, 129
Ferro-Hematogen, 55

Fialkov, Ia. A., 205
Fillopos'iants, T. T., 30
Finances, problems with, 67-68, 134-136, 163, 167, 215
Finnish War, 46, 150
First-Aid Station, 184
First All-Union Congress of Pharmacologists and Toxicologists, 22, 91
First Miracle Drugs: How the Sulfa Drugs Transformed Medicine (Lesch), 2
Fizostizmin, 92
Flatworms, 98
Fleming, Alexander: penicillin and, 129, 130
Florey, Howard W.: penicillin and, 129, 131
Folia sennae, 97
Folinerin, 94, 96
Folk medicine. *See* Popular medicine
Follicular (follikulin), production of, 65, 208
Folliculine, 95
Food supplements, 3, 19; production of, 6-7; shortage of, 58
Foot-and-mouth disease, 45
Foreign aid, 157-159
Formaldehyde, 124, 204
Formalin, 117, 193
Foxglove, 202, 206
Francisella tularensis, 112
Frenkel', Ia. A.: on typhus prevention, 116; on village medical care, 188-189
Friedland, Professor, 148
Frostbite, 117, 150

Galen, 76
Galenicals, 20, 29, 45, 214
Galostochin, 96
Gandrofil'naia, 137
Gangrene, 53, 55, 137, 149; combating, 151, 152
GAPU. *See* RSFSR Chief Pharmacy Administration
Garmin, 92
Gastroenterocolitis, 187
Gastrointestinal diseases, 46
Gartenschläger, Uwe: recollections of, 175, 178
Gatrell, Peter, 179
Geksenal, 110, 117, 127
Gel'perin (Helperin), N. I.: penicillin and, 131
Gel'tser, Samson, 179; recollections of, 8, 9, 182-184
Genis, David, 3, 11, 182, 188, 196n42; on acquiring pharmaceuticals, 81; on bathhouses, 116; on black market, 181; on criminals/shortages, 81; dysentery and, 116; on herbal products, 10; malaria and, 113-114, 184, 185; on medical instruments/ shortage, 193; military wounds and, 152; on pharmacy administration, 79-80; popular remedies and, 203; questionnaire by, 7; recollections of, 8, 184; Red Streptotsid and, 128; sanitary *propusk* and, 155; scarlatina and, 80, 86n24; soap and, 184, 202; typhus and, 111; on worker theft, 135; on worms, 114, 117
Geyman, Peter Abramovich: recollections of, 8, 181
Giardia, 46
Gidroksal, 137
Gladkikh, P. F., 112, 113
Glantz, David: on medical care/Red Army, 153
Glass factories, 21, 120, 163; criticism of, 213
Glaucium fimbrilligerum, 96
Glavk Administration, 25, 124, 155
Glavkhimfarmprom, 41, 54, 57, 58, 59, 60, 91, 121, 163-164; criticism of, 213; Glavmedfarmprom and, 120; production of, 119

Glavmedfarmprom, 59, 121, 142n117, 167, 205, 208; Glavkhimfarmprom and, 120
Glavmedinstrumentprom, 41, 154
Glavparfiumer, 25
Glavpromsnabsbyt, 59
Glavrezinprom, 158
Glucose, 124, 148, 153, 191, 194, 217; availability of, 193; losses of, 135; production of, 133, 164; shortage of, 210; storing, 42
Glycerin, 167, 193, 204
Gogol, Nikolai, 29
Golovchinska, E. S., 142n117
Gonorrhea, 72n64, 129
Gonovaccine, 51
Gorbovitskii, I. E., 143n117
Gordon-Taylor, Gordon, 147
Gorky Auto Plant, ambulances from, 40
Gorky Institute of Experimental Medicine, 98
Gorlova, Evgeniia: recollections of, 178-179
Gosbank (State Bank), 14n14, 121; finances and, 167; RSFSR Chief Pharmacy Administration and, 215
Govorov, Comrade, 190
Gramitsidin, 118, 129, 132
Grashchenkov, N. I., 130, 150
Grigorovskii, A. M., 142-143n117
Grinkevich, Chief Doctor, 52
Grishakova, A. P., 164
Grob, Gerald, 2
Guaiacol, 164, 204
Gulag, civilians in, 187-188
Gvishiani, G. S., 95

Hahn, Otto, 53
Haller, John, 90
Halpern, Daniel, 149-150, 151
Hamamelis virginianis, 93
Harrison, Mark, 1, 126
Hastings, A. Baird, 209
Haynes, Michael: on war deaths, 1
Health care, 10; government decisions about, 12; preventive, 1; quality of, vii; shortages and, 101; wartime, 12
Health of Labor Factory, 124, 128; *brak* at, 135
Health of Workers Factory, relocation of, 121
Hemocolitis, 45, 137
Hemostatics, 2, 149
Henbane leaves, 119
Hepatitis, 110, 217
Herba bidentis, 93
Herbs, 77, 93; gathering, 207; using, 10, 200, 201
Hippocrates, 76
Hitler, Adolf, 17, 18, 71n47, 159; folk medicine and, 10, 89; Jews and, 8; pharmaceutical sector and, 53, 89; scientific research and, 53
Hoechst, 53
Holistic approach, viii, 11
Home-made remedies, viii, 83, 84, 212n50; using, 199, 200, 203, 205
Hörlein, Heinrich, 53
Hormones, 90, 91, 93
House of Imperial Russe, 168
Hrdlicka, Alex, 210
Hydrokhinon, 24, 64
Hygiene, 1, 13n6, 184; problems with, 22, 46, 113

Iakolev Factory, 58, 120
Iaschenko, Dr., 99
I. G. Farben, 11, 53, 152; government interference at, 89; sulfa drugs from, 10; Uliron and, 151
Immune system disorders, 217
Imports, 157-159, 159 (table), 194
Infant formula, 2, 48
Infant mortality, 21, 22, 187
Infectious diseases, 40, 47; increase in, 52; responding to, 48; as weapon, 115
Influenza, 131, 200
Insecticides, 3, 7, 22, 102n15, 116; production of, 6; shortage of,

21
Institute of Biochemistry, penicillin and, 130
Institute of Endocrinology (Khar'kov), relocation of, 121
Institute of Endocrinology (Kiev), relocation of, 121
Institute of Experimental Medicine, 92, 130
Institute of Foreign Languages, 182
Institute of Hygiene of Labor and Professional Diseases, 36n72
Institute of Microbiology, 99
Insulin, 122, 126, 208; production of, 161, 164
Interferon, 217
Iodine, 29, 47, 116, 123, 165, 170n27, 178; improvement of, 153; obtaining, 148; production of, 20, 24, 33n16, 164, 169n4; shortage of, 46, 162, 210
Iodine-Bromine Bureau, 30
Iodine factories, 30, 120
Iodoform, production of, 127
Irbit factory, 122-123
Isupov, V. A.: infant mortality and, 187
Ivanov, F., 74n135
Ivanovna, Galina, 31n4
Ivenskii, Ia. G., 204, 206

Jews: flight of, 7, 8-9, 53; social mobility of, 176
Journal of the American Medical Association, 150

K- (anti-parasite) soap, 110, 125
Kagan, A. A., 166
Kalinskaia, Technician, 137
Kal'tseks, 137
Kaluga perfume, 28
Karpov Factory, 19, 21, 25, 59, 60, 104n47, 153, 216; Benzal'degid and, 56; *brak* at, 24; evacuation of, 121, 122; penicillin from, 131; prizes for, 166; production at, 24, 123, 125-126, 127, 133; training at, 124; war and, 119, 121; workers' skills at, 166
Karpovisskaia, Olga, 28
Kazakh Commissariat of Health, 94
Kazan' Experimental Factory, 154
Keler Factory, 19, 26
Kemerovo Factory, 128
Kerosene, 187, 201
Khar'kov Medical Institute, 94, 99
Khar'kov Production Artel "Sanhygiene", 66
Khaziev, Rustem, 43n14
Khazieva, Tamara Nikolaevna, 116; on bathhouses, 201; recollections of, 186-187; traditional remedies and, 200
Kheyster, Yefim, 82, 186; recollections of, 202
Khimfarmprom, 19, 21, 24, 54, 58, 94, 167; *Upravlenie* of, 30, 35n69
Khimfarmsnab, 30, 59
Khimfarmtorg, 30, 59, 78
Khinolin, 55
Khlevniuk, Oleg V.: on purges, 31n4
Khloratsid, 57
Khloretil, 153, 170n27
Khlorsuktsinimid, 128
Khodorkov, F.: open letter by, 66
Khrushchev, Nikita Sergeevich, 11, 32n4
Kiev Factory of Dental Equipment, evacuation of, 154
Kirov, Sergei M., 92
Kirov Meat-Processing Plant, 55
Kirsenko, V. K., 47
Klave, 45
Klinsk Glass Factory, 163, 165
Kliueva, Nina, 100
Kniss-Plotnikov, Director, 51
Kobrak, Christopher, 11, 22, 53, 152
Kogan, R. I., 30, 35n69, 131, 166-167
Kolesnikov, Sergei, 157-158
Kolkhoz, 182, 183, 186, 188, 192; and *obshchina* compared, 85
Kollargol, 57, 58, 170n27
Kommersant, 10

Konetspolskaya, Anna, 83, 84;
recollections of, 185, 202
Kononenko, Oleg: biological weapons and, 18
Konstantinovskii Factory, 64
Koten, Bernard: wartime medicine and, 149
Kotenerin, 94
Kotov, M. I., 205
Kozlovskii, A. A., 209
"K-R" cancer cure, 100-101
Krause, V., 151
Kravkov, N. P., 92
Krechetovich, L. M., 104n49
Krezanol, 54
Kritskin, Director: report by, 50
Krontovskaia, M. K., 110
Krovokhlebka, 137
Kruts, De Kosta: on bacteriophages, 99
Kudryashev, Dr.: Thrombin and, 151
Kursanov, L. I.: *Penicillium crustosum* and, 130, 131
Kuskina, Raisa, 81; recollections of, 182, 202
Kuznetskaya, Yelena: recollections of, 185
Kuznetsov, Anatolii Vasil'evich, 151-152
Kuznetsova, Mariia Sergeevna, 83; recollections of, 151-152, 187, 203

Labeling, 76
Laboratory of Biochemical Microbes, penicillin and, 130
Labzin, V. P., 167
Lancet, The, 98
Lanolin, 159, 204
Laocoon, 45
Lavender oil, 168
Lavrov, A. V., 54
Lebedenko, Professor, 148
Lebetina L., venom from, 98
Leishmania brasiliensis, 114
Leishmania donovani, 114
Leishmania tropica, 114
Leishmaniasis, 117, 140n67
Lekarstvennye rasteniia na sluzhbu frontu: Posobie dlia shkolnikov (Zemlinskii and Ivenskii), 206
Lekrastrest. *See* All-Union Medicinal Plant Trust
Lemon-acid soda, 137, 191
Lemongrass oil, 168
Lenin, V. I., 31, 67
Lenin Factory, 155; syringes/needles from, 157, 160
Leningrad Food Kombinat, 163
Leningrad Health Department, 46
Leningrad Scientific Research Pharmaceutical Institute, 56, 96, 137
Leprosy, 45
Lermontov, Michael, 179
Lesch, John E., 11, 53, 152; on folk medicine, 10; sulfa drugs and, 2, 55
Levinshtein, Izrail Ionasovich, 67, 74n135; pharmacy education and, 18; shortages and, 193
Lewis, Sinclair, 100
Lice, problems with, 157, 183, 184
Licorice, shortage of, 204
Liebau, Robert, 54
Life expectancy, statistics on, 22
Lilly, Joshua K., 55
Lily-of-the-valley, 82, 96, 202
Linen, washing, 83, 202, 203
Liubushin, A. A., 94
Liuminal, 61, 117, 127; production of, 126, 164; shortage of, 81, 193
Lobelia, cultivated/wild, 93-94, 102n22
Lobelin, 24, 124
Loktev, A. E., 112, 113
Lomonosov Factory, 20; *brak* at, 24; relocation of, 121; war and, 119
Lukashenko, President, 176
LVEN, 30, 120
Lysenko, Trofim: biological theories of, 113

Lysol, 116, 194

M&B 693, development of, 129
MacNeal, Ward J.: on bacteriophages, 100
Maevskii, Dr., 110
Magidson, Professor, 142n117
Magnesia Pergidrop, 21
Magnolamin, 94
Magnolia, 94, 97
Magnolin, 94
Maiorov, I. A., 30, 35n69
Malaria, 3, 55, 82, 93, 134, 139n30, 182, 184; danger of, 181; deaths from, 110; incidence of, 4, 21, 122; outbreak of, 113-114, 116; preventing, 116, 117, 183; problems with, 204; treating, 2, 21, 90, 179, 185, 188
Malforsen, 118
Malnutrition, diseases from, 21
Manchenko, I. I., 167
March 8 Bandaging Factory, 58, 128; problems for, 155; transfer of, 121; war and, 120, 122
Marfanil, using, 152
Marie, Grand Duchess, 28
Mariupolskii Machine Building Factory, 154
Materials, imported, 158 (table)
Maternity Home (Kirov), 51, 52
May and Baker, remedies by, 79, 129
Mayerman, O. E., 47
Measles, 4, 21, 152, 185
Mechnikov Institute, 55
Medapparatura, 167
Medfarmprom, 29, 56, 66
Medical autobuses, production of, 40-41
Medical care: civilians and, 153; deterioration of, 190; emergency, 10, 149; free, 9, 82, 184; quality of, 3, 188, 189; Red Army, 152, 153; rural, 189; under occupation, 176; village, 188-189; wartime, 1, 109
Medical Council of the Red Army, 171n53
Medical Institute (Vitebsk), 84, 176
Medical instruments: Glavk budget of, 155; inadequate, 10; for Partisans, 177; performance of, 153; production of, 154, 155, 156 (table), 160, 161; shortage of, 42, 190, 193, 210
Medical instruments industry, 154-157; finances of, 163; growth of, 41; performance of, 159-160; plan for, 160
Medical mud, 84
Medical points, 83, 188
Medical Protestants, 90
Medical schools: special courses at, 48; surgeons from, 39-40
Medical supplies, 79, 133; availability of, 7; production of, 153; shortage of, 6, 12n2, 40
Medicinal and Pharmaceutical Institute, 96
Medicinal plants. *See* Botanicals
Medicinal salts, 190-191
Medicine, 29, 168, 211n21; acquiring, 81-82, 85; alternative, 9, 10; availability of, 75, 79, 179, 185; chemically synthesized, 11, 89, 90, 91; factory-prepared, 10, 190, 201; from Germans, 178; military, 7, 152; packaged, 76, 77; pre-war, 175, 177; problems with, 202; production of, 208; shortage of, 7, 8, 9, 159, 177, 178, 179, 180; wartime, 149, 185
Medics, 10, 40, 115
Medinstrumentprom, 41
Mednikian, G. A.: venom and, 97-98
Medsisters (medical sisters), 152
Meerson, E. A., 167
Mel'nik, Dr., 99
Menchikov Institute, bacteriophages/dysentery and, 99
Meningitis, 45, 131

Men'shikov, S. P., 92
Menthol, 164, 170n27, 193
Merck, 76, 130
Merkulov, L. G., 92
Merridale, Catherine, 190
Methadone, 54
Methyl Anabasine, 92
Methyl-caffeine, 128, 145n166, 161, 164; production of, 164
Methylcytisin, 92, 93
Methylsalicylate, 127
Metizol, 56
Miazdrikova, A. A., 95
Mice, shortage of, 53
Michaels, Paula: on biomedicine, 9
Midwives, 82-83, 188, 189
Mikhailov, Dr., 99
Military Medical Academy, 95
Military-Veterinary Academy, 104n49
Ministry of Defense, Central Archive of, 125, 155, 158
Ministry of Food, penicillin and, 133
Ministry of Health, penicillin and, 133
Mint, 168, 200, 206
Miterev, G. A.: decrees by, 114
Mittner, Lise: nuclear fission and, 53
Molds, experimentation with, 144n136
Molotov Institute, 137
Morbidity, 140n64; pharmaceutical shortage and, 2; wartime, 110
Morphia, 42, 124, 151
Morphine, 24, 96, 117
Mortality, 150-151; infant, 21, 22, 187; pharmaceutical shortage and, 2; wartime, 110. *See also* Deaths
Moscow Bacteriological Institute, 47
Moscow Bandaging Factory, 165
Moscow Chemical-Technological Institute, 25
Moscow Institute of Experimental Medicine, 70n40
Moscow Medical Institute, 95
Moscow Organo-Therapeutic Drugs factory, 161
Moscow Pharmacy Institute, 164
Moscow Pharmacy School, 25
Moscow Scientific-Pharmaceutical Association, 74n135
Mosfil'm, 40
Moyer, Andrew, 144n136
MSTO Factory, 155
Murov, Maxim Pavlovich, 122
Murphy, David E.: on German intelligence/locals, 43n3
Mustard, 82, 187, 200, 201, 205

Naftalan, 117
Naganin, 60
Narkolan, production of, 21
Narodnaia meditsina, 9, 199; scientific foundation of, 98; using, 10, 11, 82-85, 89, 179, 182
National Formulary, 119
National Pharmacopoeia, 119
Nationalization, 13n14, 19, 23, 76
Natradze, Alexander Grigorevich, 164, 166; criticism by, 68; criticism of, 216; on investment, 60; new processes and, 127; penicillin and, 131, 132; on pharmacies, 4
Needles, 158, 194; quality control over, 160; shortage of, 193
Neftechalinsksii Factory, 20, 36n69
Neopantotsid, 116, 193
Neosalvarsan, production of, 61
NEP. *See* New Economic Policy
Neriofolen, 96
Nerium Oleander, 96
Nerve gas, 54
New Economic Policy (NEP), 77, 87n45, 123, 154
New York State Medical Society, 100
Nicholas II, 84
Nicotine acid, 54, 128, 137
Nicotine therapy, 150
Nikitskii Botanical Garden, 92
Nikolaev, V. V., 74n135
Nitric acid, 70n40, 127
Nizhni-Tagil Factory, 154
Nolte, Hans Heinrich, 175
Norsuifazol, 142n117, 161

Novarsenol, 56, 153, 163; production of, 24, 61; shortage of, 68
Novocain, 117, 125, 145n166, 148, 170n27, 217; acquiring, 83; improvement of, 153; production of, 24, 61, 126; shortage of, 81, 193
Novodevichii Convent, 18
Novolytics Limited, 217
Novosibkhimfarm, 217
Novosil'tsev, Chemist, 137
Nulevich, Mark, 152
Nutritional dystrophy, infectious morbidity in, 140n64

OAO, medicinal preparations from, 220n28
Obshchina, 84-85
Occupation, civilians under, 175-179
Odessa Auto-body Factory, 154
Odessa Medical Institute, 96
Office of Medicinal Plants, 120
Office of Production Research and Developments, penicillin and, 130
Oleadrin, 94
Oleander, 94, 96
Olisko, Dr., 99
"On the Destruction of Socialist Property" (1932), 192
Ophthalmology, 149
Opium, 96, 104n49; alkaloid of, 61, 78, 96, 124
Opyt sovetskoi meditsiny v Velikoi Otechestvennoi Voine, 1941-1945 (Smirnov), 110, 146n179, 157; DDT and, 116; frostbite and, 117; iodine and, 116; malaria and, 113; skin diseases and, 114; sulfa drugs and, 118
Orbant, Dr., 99
Orekhov, A. P., 93, 94, 95
Orekhov, M., 66, 92
Osteomyelitis, 100
Ovarin, production of, 65

Packaging, 20, 25, 192; plants, 30, 120, 214; problems with, 163, 164; shortage of, 119, 194
Pale of Settlement, 176
Pantopon, 117, 124
Pantosept, 116
Pantotsid, 21, 63, 116, 145n166
Paranitrotoluol, 133, 145n166
Paratyphoid, 19, 45, 115
Paratyphus, 45
Parin, V. V., 130
Party-Economic *Aktiv,* 57
Pasteur Institute, bacteriophages/dysentery and, 99
Pats, President, 70n37
Peace of Brest-Litovsk (1918), 179
Peace of Moscow (1940), 45
Pellagra, 54
Pel'ts, Semen Isakovich: arrest of, 17
Penal battalions, 8
Penfield, Wilder, 147, 148-149
Penicillin, vii, 80, 161, 204; mass-produced, 2, 101n4, 130, 144n136; production of, 90, 129-130, 131, 132, 133, 142n115, 142-143n117, 164; research and development on, 131; Soviet, 128, 130, 131; using, 10, 55, 118, 132
Penicillium strains, 129, 131, 144n136; testing, 130
Peppermint oil, 90
Pepsin, 24, 161, 194
Pepton, 24, 193
Peptone, 161
Perfume, 25, 27, 28, 29; essential oils and, 167; production of, 168
Periplotsin, 96
Perm Gypsum Factory, investigation of, 66
Pesticides, 5, 116
Petrishche, Tat'iana, 84, 85, 179, 195n6, 203; recollections of, 176, 177-178
Petrov, B. A., 35n69, 151
Phages, 89, 98-100, 118; dysentery and, 117; supply of, 49; using,

11
Pharmaceutical Chemicals in Perspective (Reuben and Wittcoff), 2
Pharmaceutical companies: in eastern Poland, 45; increase in, 216; websites of, 28
Pharmaceutical factories: changes for, 29; creativity/heroism of, 128; evacuation of, 120, 121, 122; postwar, 213; problems at, 81, 123; rationalizing work in, 166; restoration of, 160; second-/third-tier, 66, 136-138, 141n82; wartime, 115; women directors of, 164
Pharmaceutical industry, vii, 101, 160-163; American, 90; core, 4, 13n14, 118-124; criticism of, 45, 68, 79; decentralization of, 218; German, 8, 53, 89; improvements for, 4, 11; market forces/entrepreneurship in, vii; organization of, 7; performance of, vii-viii, 163-164; problems for, 5, 11, 31, 47, 89, 136, 168-169; production by, 118, 119, 125, 133-134, 153, 162 (table); property destruction and, 192; reorganization of, 29-30; reports by, 161; research and development in, 90; restructuring, 120, 215; success for, 159; support for, 68; wartime, 109-110
Pharmaceuticals: acquiring, 81; availability of, 1, 7, 49, 188; distribution of, 11; importing, 216; production of, 1, 6, 7, 11, 42, 52, 153, 165, 188, 189; in rural areas, 29; shortage of, viii, 2, 3, 4, 5, 8, 10, 12n2, 29, 58, 80, 138, 153, 180, 190, 199, 204; storing, 42; supplemented, 66
Pharmacies: factory, 17; monitoring, 76-77; number of, 4, 192; per capita, 76, 78; Polish, 75, 76; problems with, 76, 78, 80-81; in *raion* centers, 177-178; rebuilding, 192 (table); rural/urban, 77; variations in, 188-194; wartime, 190
Pharmacists, 200; harassment of, 192; Jewish, 76; shortages and, 192, 193; trained, 78; Ukrainian, 76
Pharmacological Committee, 127
Pharmacopoeia, 76, 90-91, 119, 193
Pharmacy Administrations, 77, 79-80, 136, 192, 215; funding and, 214
Pharmacy Chain 36.6: 218
Pharmacy Committee of Scholars, DDT and, 116
Pharmacy Institute, 17, 191
Pharmacy journals, 158, 193
Pharmacy managers, criticism of, 79
Pharmacy No. 1: 76, 190, 191
Pharmacy No. 26: 190
Pharmacy No. 32: 190
Pharmacy No. 75: 191
Pharmacy owners, profits for, 75
Pharmacy points, 77, 188, 191, 192
Pharmacy stalls, 191
Pharmacy workers, 45; collecting by, 205; harassment of, 192; shortages and, 192; statistics on, 191; theft by, 81
Phenacetin, 24, 61, 133, 170n27; production of, 164; shortage of, 153
Phenol, 23, 33n31, 116
Phenolphthalein, 61
Phenotropil, 217
Phytin, 127
Pirazolon, 57, 64
Pirogov, Nikolay Ivanovich, 149
Pituikrin, 65
Placenta, 208
Plague, 45, 115
Plampin, Barbara, 212n50
Plans: criticism of, 213; fulfillment of, 133; underfulfillment of, 160. *See also* Central planning

Plasmochin (Plasmoquine), 117
Plasmodium falciparum, 3, 55, 113
Platyfyllin, 95
Plazmotsid, 117; losses of, 134; production of, 164
Pneumonia, vii, 6, 55, 114; causes of, 48; etiology of, 48; infant, 46; outbreak of, 46; sulfa drugs and, 48; treating, 48, 129
Pobeda furniture factory, 122
Pokrovskii, G. N., 94
Poliakov-Stanevich, N. G., 92, 95
Polio, 2
Popov, G., 18
Popular medicine, 9, 10, 53, 89, 185, 199; promotion of, 204-208; researching, 200, 203
Postovskii, I. Ia., 142n117
Praktikanty, problems with, 78
Preiskurant, 192
Preparation 063, development of, 129
Preparation 805, development of, 128
Preparation K, 46
Preparation No. 19, 129
Prevention, 115-118
Prikaz No. 104 of March 12, 1941, 49
Process, development of, 127-128
Production, 30, 153, 163, 191, 209; improving, 11, 156; new methods of, 127-128; percent of plan fulfilled, 125 (table); problems with, 6, 22, 23, 57-62, 133, 163; Stakhanovite Movement and, 34n34; in thousands of units/tons, 125 (table); wartime, 6, 68, 124-126, 128-129
Profilaktikum, 56
Prontosil, 53, 152
Proskurnina, Professor, 94, 95
Protargol, 57, 170n27
Protek, 217
Punishment battalion, 177
Purges, 17, 23, 31n4, 113, 178
Pyramidon, 54, 57, 58, 60, 61, 63, 64, 66, 128, 143n124, 170n27; development of, 143n117; losses of, 62; production of, 126, 164; shortage of, 153; technical difficulties with, 145n166; using, 193
Pyridine, 56, 143n124

Quality, concerns about, 162-163
Quarantine quarters, 51
Quinine, 82, 90, 93; acquiring, 142n115; availability of, 202; factory-prepared, 10; shortage of, 181, 184; sources of, 119; stocking, 204; tablets of, 182; using, 179, 185, 188

Rabinovich, E. M., 30, 35n69, 47
Raddae BTTG, 98
Raion centers, 83; pharmacies in, 177-178
Rakhshmut, Lidiia, 81, 186; recollections of, 203
Ralle and Broker, soap production by, 25
Ramaninskii factory, 20, 36n69
Ravikovich, E. M., 47
Ravvina, Liudmila, 152; on medical care, 83-84; recollections of, 185, 202
Raw materials, 214; delivery of, 23, 157; needed/supplied, 34n33; shortage of, 23 (fig.), 33n31, 57, 66, 81, 119, 133, 136
Reagents, 4, 19
Red Army, 30, 92; casualties for, 147; death rates for, 46, 110; emigres and, 7; Far East battles for, 39; illnesses in, 110, 111; panic for, 109; penicillin for, 132; pharmaceuticals for, viii, 19, 52, 133 ; vitamins for, 52
Red Guard Medical Instruments Factory, 154, 155, 157, 166
Red Navy: penicillin for, 132; pharmaceuticals for, 19
Red Star Factory, 20, 21, 24, 25, 54, 58; conditions at, 63-64;

production at, 61-62; report by, 64, 65; war and, 119
Red Streptotsid, 42, 63, 82, 126; availability of, 186; *brak* with, 127; buying, 181; losses of, 134; toxicity of, 3, 128
Refugees, 175, 179
Reiter method, 64
Reklamatsiia, 62, 162-163
Remedies, 181-182; dubious, 209-210; home-made, viii, 83, 84, 199, 200, 203, 205, 212n50; natural, 11, 89, 200; popular, 185, 203, 204; traditional, 200; types of, 115-118
Renadae ursini Christ, 98
Research and development, 5, 13n14, 30, 90, 92-97; impressiveness of, 21; penicillin, 131; Soviet versus German, 52-57; wartime, 126
Reuben, Brian G., 2, 3
Rheumatic fever, 185
Rheumatism, 193
Ribbentrop-Molotov Pact (1939), 39
Rickets, 78
Rimmington, Anthony, 5, 18, 45, 113; on pharmaceutical development, 217, 218
Rivanol, 116, 117, 135, 141n79, 145n166; availability of, 193
Roche, 124
Roosevelt, Eleanor and Franklin D.: penicillin and, 132
Rose oil, 168
Rosfarmtrest. *See* Russian Pharmaceutical Trust
Roskin, Grigory, 100
Roslekraskontora, 205
Rosvitaminprom, 161
RSFSR Chief Pharmacy Administration (GAPU), 81, 213, 214, 215
RSFSR Commissariat of Health, 20, 51, 66
RSFSR Council of People's Commissars, 20
Rubel Ice Plant, 130
Rubrakol, 161, 164
Ruchko, Dr., 99
Ruchkovskii, Dr., 99
Russian Chemical Industry, 25
Russian Information Bureau, 207
Russian Medical Banner network, 220n26
Russian Pharmaceutical Trust (Rosfarmtrest), 29
Russian Society for Assisting Development of the Chemical Industry, 205
Russian Stock Exchange, 218
Russian stove, 200-201
Russian War Relief, 158, 170n43

Sacco and Vanzetti Dental Equipment plant, 154, 155, 157
Salicylate, 23, 33n31, 123, 162, 164, 193
Salicylate Factory, 19, 21, 23, 30, 59, 65, 127, 145n166, 167; evacuation of, 121; losses at, 135; plan and, 133; prizes for, 166; technological troubles at, 122, 124; war and, 119, 121
Salicylic acid, 164, 194
Salipirin, 63
Salmonella, 19
Salol, 23, 164
Salsola, 95
Sal'solidin, 95
Sal'solin, 95, 208
Sal'varsan, 118
Salves, 20, 124, 182, 187, 201; ikhtiol, 182; sulfuric, 117; zinc, 29
Samokhin, G. I.: sulfa drugs and, 47
Sanal'bin, 137
Sangailo, A. K., 92
Sanitary doctors, 49
Sanitary inspectors, 49, 114, 115
Sanitary Institute, 128
Sanitary stores, 77, 79
Sanitary trains, 111-112

Sanitary work, 49, 114
Sanitation, 1, 47; problems with, 21, 22
Santonin, 60, 61, 119, 126; production of, 20
Saratov Regional Pharmacy Administration, 57
Sarin, 54
Saunas, 201
Savranskaya, Polina, 83, 202; recollections of, 184-185
Scabies, 114, 117
Scadding, J. G., 98, 104n58, 118
Scarlatina, 4-5, 6, 19, 116, 152; antitoxin for, 49, 50, 51, 69n22, 80, 86n24, 87n25, 115, 150, 185; decline in, 21, 52; outbreak of, 47, 113; preventing, 187; problems with, 80, 111
Scarlet fever. *See* Scarlatina
Schering Factory, 22, 24, 53, 56; ammonia from, 124; Atophan from, 78; camphor from, 168; government interference at, 89; nationalization of, 19; production from, 154
Scientific Chemical-Pharmaceutical Research Institute (VNIKhFI), 24, 25, 56, 95, 121, 127, 129; relocation of, 121
Scientific-Research Chemical-Pharmaceutical Institute of the Georgian SSR, 91
Sclerosis, 150
Scrofula, 93, 206, 211n26
Scurvy, 92, 185, 207
Second Five-Year plan, medicinal plants and, 91
Secondary factories, 66; production from, 136-138, 141n82
Semashko Factory, 19, 55, 59, 60, 122, 123, 127, 136, 145n166; evacuation of, 121; materials at, 124; prizes for, 166; production at, 26, 126, 134; war and, 119, 121
Seneca, 95
Septicemia, 131
Septurit, 56
Sergozin, 24
Serkis, Comrade: Pharmacy No. 1 and, 190
Serums, 3, 5, 22, 115, 118, 148; availability of, 152; production of, viii, 6, 19, 42, 45; replacing, 89; research on, 90; shortage of, 46, 49, 85
Sevast'ianov, G. T., 96
Shass, E., 95, 104n49
Shcherbakov factory, 97
Shelekovskii Vitamin Factory, 217
Sheveleva, Kh. M., 164
Shiga infections, 99
Shortages, 124, 126, 134, 136, 162, 177; criticism of, 213; impact of, 101, 133; implied, 151; problems with, 147, 148-149, 150, 153, 159, 180, 181, 184, 192, 193, 199, 202, 204, 205, 210, 215; reasons for, 13n2; severe, 193
Shteiman, Evgeniia: recollections of, 186
Shtetl of Slonim, 175, 176
Shuvalov, Ivan Gregor'evich, 18, 62
Siatinia, M. Ia.: on pharmacy sector, 4
Sigerist, Henry, 68, 157
Sila, V. I., 94
Sinestrol, production of, 208
Sisters of mercy, 189
Skin diseases, 94, 114
Skvortsov, V., 47
Slutskii, G. A., 167
Sluzhba zdorov'ia v Velikoi Otechestvennoi Voine (Gladkikh and Loktev), 110, 111, 155; dysentery/phages and, 117; evacuation and, 120; malaria and, 113; production and, 124; tularemia and, 117
Smallpox, 19, 50; decline in, 4, 21;

vaccine for, 51
Smirnov, E. I., 12n1, 39
Smirnov volumes. See *Opyt sovetskoi meditsiny v Velikoi Otechestvenoi Voine, 1941-1945*
Snakes, studying, 97-98
Soap, 2, 5, 7, 48, 177; anti-parasite, 110, 125; availability of, 85, 179, 184, 201, 202; economy, 185, 202; factory-made, 26, 83; green, 185, 202; home-made, 185, 200; medical, 25; pre-packaged, 76; problems with, 185, 202; production of, 6, 25, 26-27, 28, 116, 203; selling, 178; shortage of, 9, 25, 26, 27, 46, 47, 83, 100, 113, 179, 180, 181, 184, 185, 186, 188, 202, 203; toilet, 25, 26, 27, 28, 184; using, 184, 188
Soap and Toiletries Trust (TEZhE), 7, 25, 26, 27, 116
Socrates, 76
Sodium chloride, 116, 127, 135
Soinikov, V. V., 209
Sokolova, V. N., 142n117
Solnechnogorsk Glass Factory, 135, 165
Sorokin, A. M., 66
Sorokin, A. N.: on pharmacies, 80-81
Sotex, 217
South African Medical Journal, The: on medical advances, 150
Sovetskaia farmatsiia, 17
Soviet Penicillin, development of, 128, 130, 131
Soviet Pharmacopoeia, 90-91
Soviet Red Cross and Red Crescent Society, 157-158, 159
Sovkain, 54, 110, 117
Sovkhoz, 83, 85, 91, 187, 188
Sovnarkom, 19, 59, 120; order by, 20, 189, 207; price list by, 215
Soyuzoborudovanie, 41
Soyuzvitaminprom, 161
Speiss and Company, 45
Spermine, 65, 208
Squibb, penicillin and, 130
Stakhanovite Movement, 24, 27, 190; worker productivity and, 34n34
Stalin, Joseph, 28, 177, 186; infectious diseases and, 115; leadership of, 27, 213; pharmaceutical sector and, 67, 89; purges by, 113, 178; speeches by, 30-31, 199
Stalingradskaia Pravda, report by, 66
Staphylococcus, 55, 100, 131
State Archives of the Russian Federation, 158
State Budget, 135, 136
State Factory of Disinfecting and Sanitary Equipment, 154
Statutory Fund, 28
Sterilizers, 157, 158; shortage of, 76, 160, 193
STO. *See* Council of Labor and Defense
Stolypin, P. A., 83, 84, 88n47
Stolypin Agrarian Reforms, 84
Strelkov, P. G.: penicillin and, 131
Streptocide, 148, 151
Streptococci, 55, 56, 148
Streptomycin, 55, 117, 217
Streptotsid, 42, 55, 56, 61, 63, 72n64, 128, 144n166, 152, 170n27, 190; losses of, 62; production of, 24, 64, 123, 126, 127, 142n117, 143n124, 162, 164; shortage of, 68, 193; using, 184
Strepturin, 56
Strofantin, 93, 137, 185
Strophantin, 95, 159
Sukharanskii Factory, representatives from, 36n69
Suknev, Dr., 99
Suksunskii Sanitary Equipment Factory, 154
Sulfa drugs, 3, 5, 6, 101, 125, 126, 132, 151, 217; availability of, 202; development of, 56, 90, 129, 153; distribution of, 66; dysentery and, 98, 99, 117, 118; fatalities and, 110; importance of, 2; ingredients for, 56; pneumonia

and, 48; production of, 10, 18, 54, 64, 123, 164, 167; shortage of, 11, 21, 47, 48, 58, 61, 62, 63, 85, 100, 152, 188, 193, 210; using, 10, 46, 47, 55, 98, 118, 152, 184
Sulfadine, 151
Sulfanilamide, 48, 56, 72n64, 142n117, 151, 159; development of, 128; using, 187
Sulfapyridine, 119, 150, 159
Sulfathiazole, 119, 150
Sul'fatsil, 129
Sul'fazol, 56, 126, 145n166, 151; production of, 123
Sul'fidin, 42, 54, 56, 63, 82, 99, 161, 170n27, 194; availability of, 186; buying, 181; distribution of, 66; losses of, 134; production of, 122, 123, 126, 127, 142n117, 143n124, 164; using, 47, 118, 184, 185, 202
Sul'fitsid, 193
Sul'fochloride, 126, 145n166
Sulfonamide, 148-149, 167
Sulfuric acid, 23, 33n31, 135
Sulfuric barium, production of, 164
Sulphaguanidine, 104n58, 118
Sulphapyridine, 104n58, 118
Sulphathiazole, 104n58, 118
Sulphonamides, 150
Suphanilamide, 118
Surakhanskii factory, 20
Surgical instruments, 56; availability of, 7; import of, 158; inadequate, 10; performance of, 153; plan for, 160; production of, 7, 153, 154, 155, 156 (table), 161; quality of, 157; repairing, 213-214; shortage of, 6, 12n2, 40, 42, 147, 149, 190, 210
Surgical Workshop, 57
Svetsova, E. V., 167
Svoboda Factory, theft at, 166
Swiss Red Cross, 8, 195n10
Syphilis, combating, 131, 142n115
Syringes, 181, 194; production of, 157; quality control over, 160; repairing, 213; shortage of, 193

Tagiev, 30, 36n69
Talyzin, F. F.: venom and, 98
Tannidgen, 129
Tapeworms, 114, 117, 203
Tartakovskaya, Mariiam Samoilovna, 83, 185; recollections of, 202
Tbilisi Caffeine Factory, 56
Tbilisi Chemical-Pharmaceutical Factory No. 1, 56
Tbilisi Medical Institute, 99
Tchaikovsky, Peter, 120
Technical plants, plan for, 206
Terent'ev, Chairman, 30, 35n69
Tetanus, 45; combating, 151; Soviet cures for, 210; vaccine for, 115, 119, 151
TEZhE. *See* Soap and Toiletries Trust
Theft, problems with, 134, 135, 166
Theobromine, 137, 204
Thermopsis alterniflora, 93
Thermopsis lanceolata, 93, 96
Thiocol, production of, 164
Third Five-Year Plan, medicinal plants and, 91
Third-level factories, production from, 136-138, 141n82
Thompson, Samuel, 93, 102n22
Thrombin, development of, 151
Thymol, 167
Time, on bacteriophages, 99, 100
Times, The: on Russian pharmaceutical market, 218
Tiokain, 21, 24, 61
Tiumen Factory No. 14: 154
Toilets, inadequate, 180
Tomsk Factory, 128
Toothpaste, 25, 28, 217
Toxic dyspepsia, 187
Toxicologists, defense of, 31
Trachoma, 21
Traditional medicine, 83, 89, 101n2;

mainstream medicine and, 199; at popular level, 200-203; using, 92
Transportation, problems with, 157, 188, 213
Trans-Siberian Railway, 206
Treatment institutions, 160; botanicals/popular remedies at, 204; deaths in, 138n6
Trichanosis, 114
Trivalent antimony, 117, 140n67
Troitskii soap factory, 28
Trotsky, Leon, 67
TsANIL. *See* Central Pharmaceutical Scientific Research Laboratory
Tsentrosoiuz, 205
Tsereton, 217
Tsirkina, Maina, 82, 185
Tsobkallo, G. I.: venom and, 98
Tuberculosis, 54, 55, 78, 93, 128, 131, 178, 206
Tuberculosis Institute, 54
Tularemia, 45, 68n3; combating, 113, 117; outbreaks of, 112, 113; vaccine for, 115
Turnover monies, 136
Typhoid, 6, 19, 45, 46, 55, 113; danger of, 180, 181; decline in, 4, 21; divaccine for, 49, 50, 51; incidence of, 111; outbreak of, 22, 24, 46; preventing, 33n32, 116, 187; vaccine for, 115; wartime, 110
Typhus, 4, 8, 19, 21, 45, 46, 113, 116, 149, 177; combating, 115, 129, 150; danger of, 180; deaths from, 110; increase in, 111; outbreak of, 22, 46, 111; preventing, 110, 116, 157, 184, 187, 189; problems with, 111; treating, 178, 209; vaccine for, 51, 115, 150

UAZ. *See* Ural Aluminum Factory
Ufa Bacteriological Institute, 51, 52, 87n24; Annual Report of, 50; departments of, 49; problems at, 49, 50; production at, 19, 49, 50, 200; scarlatina antitoxin from, 80; vaccines from, 187
Ufa Vitamin Factory, Internet and, 217
Ukraine Institute of Endocrinology, 208
Ukrainian Experimental Culinary Institute, 95
Ukrainian Institute of Experimental Medicine, 95
Ukrainian Institute of Experimental Pharmacy, 94
Ukrainian Research Chemical-Pharmaceutical Institute, 137
Ukrmedfarmprom Narkomzdrava U[kr]SSR, 59
Ulcers, 84, 85
Uliron, 151, 152
Undulant fever, 55
Union of Medicine Plants, 97
USSR Academy of Sciences, 99
USSR Commissariat for the Meat and Dairy Industry, 208
USSR Commissariat of Education, 18
USSR Commissariat of Enlightenment, 154
USSR Commissariat of Food, 207; soap production and, 27; Vitamin Trust and, 161
USSR Commissariat of Health (Narkomzdrav), 18, 19, 20, 25, 41, 51, 54, 62, 116, 149, 161, 166, 189, 205, 214; collecting by, 97; core pharmaceutical industry and, 119; *prikaz* of, 48, 59; research by, 128
USSR Commissariat of Heavy Industry, 59, 62
USSR Commissariat of Public Health, 114, 208
USSR Institute of Food, 54
United Nations, 159
U.S. Department of Agriculture, 101n4, 129; Currie and, 144n136; penicillin and, 130, 133

U.S. Office of Scientific Research and Development, 130
U.S. Pharmacopoeia, 90-91
University of Chicago, fission experiment at, 134
Ural Aluminum Factory (UAZ), 187
Urotropin, 24, 56, 127, 170n27, 190, 191, 194; shortage of, 193
Utkin, L. M., 142-143n117
Utrotropin, 124

Vaccines, 1, 3, 22, 47, 49-52, 118; availability of, 152; effective, 181; production of, viii, 5, 6, 19, 42, 45, 115, 187, 200; research on, 90; shortage of, 2, 6, 10, 46, 47, 49, 85
Valerian, 202, 206
Validol, 60
Varlakov, Dr., 137
Vechernaya Moskva, 164
Venereal diseases, 56, 61, 118
Venom, using, 97-98
Veronal, 61
Veropharm, 217-218
Viferon, 217
VILAR. *See* All-Union Institute of Medicinal and Aromatic Botanicals
Vinegar anhydride, 72n75, 133, 145n166
Vinegar essence, 201
Vinnitsiia Spirit Trust, 67
Viruses, 48, 98
Vishnevski, Alexander, 150
Vishnevskii, Anatoli, 4, 22
Vishnevskii salve, 124, 182, 187, 201
Vissarionova, Zinaida: penicillin and, 133
Vitamin A, 65, 150, 204
Vitamin B1, 54, 71n54, 117, 150, 161
Vitamin C, 21, 54, 150, 161, 194, 207; production of, 65
Vitamin Factory, 59, 62
Vitamin Trust, establishment of, 161
Vitaminol, production of, 65
Vitamins, 2, 3, 19, 52, 54, 55, 91, 93, 117, 161, 183, 207, 217; development of, 90; liquid, 47; production of, 6; shortage of, 21, 92, 180
Vitebsk Eyeglass Factory, evacuation of, 154
VNIKhFI. *See* All-Union Scientific-Research Chemical-Pharmaceutical Institute
Vokhimfarm, 19, 28
Volokolamsk, 191
Volova, Docent, 137
Volynkin, N. I., 137
Vorob'ev, M. A., 167
Voronezh Medical Institute, 94
Voronezh *Sovkhoz* for Medicinal Plants, 94
Voroshilovgrad Meat-Processing Plant, 55
Vozhd, 199

Wagner, Wencelaus, 219n22
Waksman, Abraham, 55
Waksman, Selman, 55
War Food Administration, lemongrass plants and, 168
War Production Board, penicillin and, 130
Warehouses, 124, 191
Washing powders, 25
Wehner, A.: *penicillium* and, 130
White-Finn War, battlefield medicine and, 39
White Streptotsid, 42, 56, 63, 72n64, 82, 126; availability of, 186; buying, 181; losses of, 134; production of, 18, 122, 123, 135; sales of, 181; using, 118
Whole Empire Walking, A (Gatrell), 179
Whooping cough, 4, 21, 51
Winter War, 39, 45, 47, 48, 57
Witch-doctors, 188, 196n42
Wittcoff, Harold A., 2, 3
Witte, Sergei, 88n47

Worms, 98, 114, 116, 117, 203
Worthen, Dennis, 11, 119, 126, 204
Wounds: causes of, 150; dealing with, 152, 200; deaths from, 138n6, 151

X-ray machines, 81, 148, 158, 189

Yel'tsin, Boris, 216
Yemlianinov, S. I., 167
Yermol'eva, Zinaida Vissarionovna, 143n117; penicillin and, 130, 131, 132
Yershova, El'vira, 32n4; recollections of, 187-188
Yohimbine, 95
Yudin, Professor, 147, 149

Zakaliapin, Boris, 109
Zemchuzhina, Paulina, 28
Zemlinskii, S. E., 206
Zhilina, 190
Zinc ointment, 164
Znaeva, K. I., 142n117
Znakari, 188, 196n42
Znakhar', 186
Zorex, 217

About the Author

Mary Schaeffer Conroy received her B. A. from St. Mary's College, Notre Dame, IN, in 1959 and her Ph. D. from Indiana University in 1964. She taught at Kansas State University and the University of Illinois, Chicago Circle, and currently is Professor Emerita, Russian History, University of Colorado at Denver. She has published articles, chapters and books about politics in late Imperial Russia, including *Peter Arkad'evich Stolypin: Practical Politics in Late Tsarist Russia* (1977) and *Emerging Democracy in Late Imperial Russia* (1998), as well as articles, chapters and books on health care and, more particularly, pharmacy and the pharmaceutical industry in Imperial Russia and the Soviet Union, including *In Health and In Sickness: Pharmacy, Pharmacists and the Pharmaceutical Industry in Late Imperial, Early Soviet Russia* (1994) for which she received the George Urdang Medal in 1997, and *The Soviet Pharmaceutical Business During Its First Two Decades, 1917-1937* (2006).